D1234422

TRANSACTIONS OF THE
ROYAL HISTORICAL SOCIETY

FIFTH SERIES

VOLUME 31

LONDON

OFFICES OF THE ROYAL HISTORICAL SOCIETY

UNIVERSITY COLLEGE LONDON, GOWER ST., WC1E 6BT

1981

ISBN 0 901050 73 3

Made and printed in Great Britain by Butler & Tanner Ltd., Frome and London

DA
20
.R88

196843

CONTENTS

TRANSACTIONS OF THE

ROYAL HISTORICAL SOCIETY

EIGHTEENTH-CENTURY ENGLISH RADICALISM BEFORE WILKES

By Linda Colley, M.A., Ph.D.

READ I FEBRUARY 1980

ADDRESSING a Society consecrated to the advance of historical studies is bound to be an awesome experience: it is a particularly sobering one for me because the central argument of this paper would have been familiar to British historians writing in the early nineteenth century. In his *Constitutional History of England*, published in 1827, Hallam asserted, seemingly without fear of contradiction, that

'it must be evident to every person who is at all conversant with the publications of George II's reign, with the poems, the novels, the essays, and almost all the literature of the time, that what are called the popular or liberal doctrines of government were decidedly prevalent. The supporters themselves of the Walpole and Pelham administrations ... made complaints, both in parliament and in pamphlets, of the democratical spirit, the insubordination to authority, the tendency to republican sentiments, which they alleged to have gained ground among the people.'[1]

It is easy enough to document Hallam's reference to contemporary complaints. When the Commons discussed the publication of debates in 1738, one of the major arguments against this concession was that the extra-parliamentary nation was already dangerously politicized: 'The People of Great Britain are governed by a power that never was heard of as a supreme authority in any age or country before ... It is the government of the press.' However much dissident M.P.s might criticize the growth of the executive, Viscount Perceval warned five years later, 'the popular interest' and 'the Republican Spirit' had been 'for many Years invisibly increasing in a far greater Proportion'.[2]

More recent accounts of the eighteenth century would compel us to

---

[1] H. Hallam, *The Constitutional History of England, from the Accession of Henry VII to the Death of George II* (4 vols., London, 1827), II, p. 653.

[2] [John Perceval], *Faction detected by the Evidence of Facts* (2nd edn., London, 1743), p. 134; printed in G. Midgley, *The Life of Orator Henley* (Oxford, 1973), p. 216.

dismiss these complaints as unrealistic or deliberately alarmist. On the first page of his well-known survey, Basil Williams summed up the distinctive tone of early Hanoverian Britain: 'an oasis of tranquillity between two agitated epochs'. Few historians have chosen to bask in this oasis; those who have, tend only to reaffirm its static quality. Under Walpolian statecraft we are told, the rage of party gave way to an integrated ruling élite. Such high political dissidents as remained confined themselves to the Country tradition of protest, advocating shorter parliaments, the abolition of placemen, and controls on electoral corruption. If implemented, such measures would certainly have modified the Walpolian state, but, argues John Brewer, their proponents were concerned only to purify the existing mode of government, not to make government a more open process.[3] This, John Pocock tells us, is the crucial divergence in mid-eighteenth-century Anglophone dissidence: while American radicals increasingly stress the need for autonomous civic action to secure redress, the English are content with superficial reformism.[4]

If we turn from formal political activity to what Edward Thompson has termed the 'self activating' plebeian crowd, we are again confronted with a sporadically turbulent force totally lacking in dynamism. Thompson's crowd prefers the safety of anonymous and traditional riot to the risks involved in more organized protest. It prefers most of all to abstain from riot completely and appeal for redress to the established local hierarchies. The mid-eighteenth-century pleb is concerned not with acquiring new rights, but with preserving his time-honoured perks: 'the larger outlines of power, station in life, political authority, appear [to him] as inevitable and irreversible as the earth and the sky'.[5]

Given this high political and grass-roots scenario, it is scarcely surprising that historians seeking the genesis of eighteenth-century English radicalism have exuded a certain desperation. Maccoby, in the first of his books on the subject, simply dodged the issue and started the story in 1762. Other historians, working on the assumption that protest was likely to have originated amongst the politically and socially disadvantaged, have looked to the dissenters. Their premise is, it seems to me, correct, but it was not in fact the nonconformists

[3] B. Williams, *The Whig Supremacy 1714–60* (2nd edn., Oxford, 1962), p. 1; J. Brewer, *Party Ideology and Popular Politics at the Accession of George III* (Cambridge, 1976), pp. 19–20.

[4] J. G. A. Pocock, 'Virtue and Commerce in the Eighteenth Century', *Journal of Interdisciplinary History*, iii (1972), 122–4.

[5] E. P. Thompson, 'Patrician Society, Plebeian Culture', *Journal of Social History*, vii (1974), 388; and see his 'Eighteenth-Century English Society: class struggle without class?', *Social History*, iii (1978), 133–65.

who suffered most from political discrimination in the early Georgian era.[6]

Most dissenters were pro-government until the 1760s. Indeed, non-conformist polemicists tended to lay great stress on their movement's loyalty and social respectability, and these emphases were only accentuated by the growth of Methodism, which was tory in inspiration and deliberately plebeian in its appeal. After the Jacobite scare of 1744-5 even the Methodists tended to succumb to whig politics: John Wesley being terrified lest his movement's high tory origins invite government persecution.[7] And the nonconformists' political compliance did not go unrewarded. The repeal of the Occasional Conformity Act in 1719 and the Indemnity Acts passed thereafter allowed affluent dissenters with flexible consciences to penetrate the highest reaches of central and local office. Dissenting plaintiffs usually found that the whig judiciary was sympathetic. In one of the classic cases of the eighteenth century, the London dissenter, Allan Evans, was able to challenge the provisions of the Test Act and have his right to do so confirmed by the Court of Judges Delegate and by Lord Mansfield in the House of Lords. 'From that day', wrote Sir Anthony Lincoln, 'no Dissenter spoke ill of Lord Mansfield', but neither after 1760 did the bulk of dissenters speak ill of the Lord Chief Justice's *bête noir*, John Wilkes.[8] In the late eighteenth century the parliamentary reform movement won extensive and committed nonconformist support. Before 1760, however, it is more common to encounter boroughs like Taunton where the local dissenters formed a club to extract higher electoral bribes, than it is to find a bona fide example of dissenting resistance to establishment politics as one does, to a limited degree, in Tiverton. And even in Tiverton, where from 1722 to 1754 dissenting artisans campaigned for a wider borough franchise, their remarkable cohesion owed more to nascent trade unionism than to their religious persuasion. Before the 1754 election, wrote Tiverton's historian,

'the principal members of the said societies, wool-combers, weavers,

[6] S. Maccoby, *English Radicalism 1762-1785. The Origins* (London, 1955). For a discussion of the often tenuous connection between eighteenth-century Dissent and political independence, see J. E. Bradley, 'Whigs and Nonconformists: "Slumbering Radicalism" in English politics, 1739-1789', *Eighteenth Century Studies*, ix (1975-6), 1-27. Note the implicit assumption that political dissidence was whig-bound.

[7] Philip Doddridge complained of Old Dissent's increasing stress on social respectability in *Free Thoughts on the Most Probable Means of Reviving the Dissenting Interest* (London, 1730), pp. 11-16. The limitations of such nonconformist political protest as existed in the mid-eighteenth century emerge from N. C. Hunt, *Two Early Political Associations: the Quakers and the Dissenting Deputies in the Age of Sir Robert Walpole* (Oxford, 1961). See John Wesley's 'Word to a Freeholder', printed in *The Works of the Rev. John Wesley* (14 vols., London, 1872), XI, pp. 196-8.

[8] Sir Anthony Lincoln, *Some Political and Social Ideas of English Dissent, 1763-1800* (Cambridge, 1938), p. 46.

scribblers, etc. assembled daily at their club-houses, to consult upon the best means of promoting their end and design; and at night frequently beat brass pans, as signals for meeting together in larger bodies, to strike terror into the minds of the members of the corporation, or any other persons that might attempt to oppose their claim of electing the members of parliament'.[9]

(A description which must, I think, raise questions about the sufficiency of Thompson's presentation of the mid-eighteenth-century *canaille*'s social and political conservatism.)

If, before 1760, most dissenters did not feel so alienated from the state as to be compelled into political protest, who did? Again, the answer was clear enough to our nineteenth-century forbears. In his essay on Chatham, Lord Macaulay remarked on the curious 'transformation which, during the reign of George the First, befell the two English parties ... the Tory rose up erect the zealot of freedom, and the Whig crawled and licked the dust at the feet of power ... the successors of the Old Cavaliers had turned demagogues'. Macaulay, like Hallam, was merely superimposing rhetoric on informed eighteenth-century opinion. In order to extricate themselves from proscription, Viscount Perceval argued in 1743, the tories would 'bait the People by the Project of an Encrease of Popular Power, by proposing Alterations in the Constitution, the Effects of which ... the common sort are by no means able to understand'.[10]

What I wish to suggest in this paper is that what can be called the whig interpretation of English radicalism is misleading. Political protest did not materialize after 1760 merely because the socio-economic strains of increasing industrialization, urbanization, literacy and population growth had reached combustion point. Rather, throughout the eighteenth century, miscellaneous popular grievances were lent coherent political expression by way of the opportunistic sorties into extra-parliamentary politics made by a succession of high-level dissidents. John Wilkes was a gentleman politician outlawed after 1763 into street agitation. In the same way the tories—outlawed from the political centre from 1714 to 1760—were tempted into contact with the socially and politically excluded. By succumbing to this temptation they rehearsed much of the extra-parliamentary organization and many of the political arguments which characterized the more familiar radicalism of the later eighteenth century.

[9] Martin Dunsford, *Historical Memoirs of the Town and Parish of Tiverton, in the County of Devon* (Exeter, 1790), p. 239. For Taunton, see Bradley, 'Whigs and Nonconformists', 19-20.

[10] [Perceval], *Faction Detected*, p. 51; Lord Macaulay, *Critical and Historical Essays contributed to the Edinburgh Review*, ed. F. C. Montague, (3 vols., London, 1903), III, pp. 398-9.

I

Before I develop my argument let me make two qualifications to it. Firstly, unlike Thompson and Isaac Kramnick, I am not convinced that tory rapport with the excluded was based on the embattled squirearchy's superior social concern. In this context and company I have no intention of venturing an opinion on the eighteenth-century English land market. I will only say that there is no proof that such landowners as were declining in this period were predominantly tory, and little evidence that tory gentry were more socially sympathetic than were their whig equivalents.[11] To cast the tories as forlorn paternalists is in fact invidious because it breaks the continuity of eighteenth-century protest. John Wilkes may be allowed (by some) to have initiated the alternative politics of the traditionally excluded, but tory popularists have to be consigned to the historical attic as nostalgic revanchists. And to describe the tories as bucolic economic losers is to presuppose their isolation from those urban, professional and commercial classes who were also excluded from the full benefits of Georgian society. Thompson is forced to condemn the mid-eighteenth-century middle classes to complacent perdition (they were, he asserts, 'consenting adults in their own corruption') because his own erroneous description of the tories' socio-economic base robs the bourgeoisie of high-political auxiliaries. Yet if one looks at the centres of mid-eighteenth-century extra-parliamentary dissidence (London, Westminster, Norwich, Coventry, Newcastle and Bristol) and at the more politicized unrepresented towns (Manchester, Birmingham and Leeds), their activists are usually of bourgeois type and the professed politics of these activists is usually tory.[12]

Secondly, it would be wrong to attribute tory popularism entirely to the party's proscription. Many of the more attractive components of the tory platform had their origins in the seventeenth century. Tory-royalists had hated excises ever since Parliament had employed this tax to finance the New Model Army. Consequently tory M.P.s opposed excises in the 1690s, in 1711, in 1723, in 1733 and in 1756; in 1731 and 1733 the tories also introduced bills to cut turnpike charges which again they regarded as a form of socially regressive indirect

---

[11] See I. Kramnick, *Bolingbroke and his Circle: the politics of nostalgia in the age of Walpole* (London, 1968). I have discussed the sociology of eighteenth-century toryism and the extent to which tory-plebeian rapport was or was not based on a common economic dispossession in chapters 1 and 6 of *In Defiance of Oligarchy: the Tory Party 1714-60*, to be published by Cambridge University Press in 1982.

[12] Cf. Hume's argument that toryism flourished most within England's middle classes (D. Forbes, *Hume's Philosophical Politics* (Cambridge, 1975), p. 94; Thompson, 'Eighteenth-Century English Society', 142-3).

taxation.[13] The popular resonance of this tory stance can be gauged from the fact that between 1715 and 1760 some 72 per cent of England's tax revenue was derived from indirect taxation, and contemporary commentators like John Shebbeare, Joseph Massie and Josiah Tucker were convinced that a disproportionate weight of this taxation burden was borne by the labouring and manufacturing classes.[14] Another pre-1715 tory development was the party's increasing success in open constituencies and its consequent vested interest in championing wide franchises. In the 1690s it was Thomas Langham, the tory Deputy Alderman for Bishopsgate, who led an abortive campaign to extend London's franchise. Tories went on to champion a wider franchise in Norwich in 1722, in London in 1725, and in Bristol in 1734.[15] In 1731—again, for sound partisan reasons—the party introduced a bill to have Manchester's Work House Guardians chosen by popular vote; and during this campaign, tory apologists employed arguments which ran counter to any association of the franchise with a certain level of property:

'We look upon ourselves [as] embarked in THE GOOD SHIP MANCHESTER, and whenever we apprehend her in the least danger, are ready to work as hard as if we were never so considerable sharers in her cargo.'[16]

As the tories became increasingly dependent upon open constituencies—in 1741 more than two-thirds of the party in the Commons sat for county seats or for boroughs with over 500 voters—so they were compelled into a more subtly accommodating relationship with their

[13] For the longstanding tory aversion to excises, see E. Hughes, *Studies in Administration and Finance 1558-1825* (Manchester, 1934), pp. 119-91. See also J. H. Plumb, *The Growth of Political Stability in England 1675-1725* (London, 1967), pp. 149 and 155; *Commons Journals*, XX, p. 319; Lord Ilchester, *Henry Fox, First Lord Holland, his Family and Relations* (London, 1920), I, p. 309. For tory parliamentary agitation over turnpikes, see *Commons Journals*, XXI, pp. 823, 836 and 867; *ibid.*, XXII, pp. 39 and 84.

[14] P. Mathias and P. O'Brien, 'Taxation in Britain and France, 1715-1810. A comparison of the social and economic incidence of taxes collected by the central government', *Journal of European Economic History*, v (1976), 606. For contemporary opinion, see [John Shebbeare], *A Third Letter to the People of England* (3rd edn., London, 1756), pp. 46-7; William Kennedy, *English Taxation 1640-1799: an essay on policy and opinion* (1964 reprint), p. 107n; and R. L. Schuyler, *Josiah Tucker: a selection from his economic and political writings* (New York, 1931).

[15] G. Stuart de Krey, 'Trade, religion and politics in London in the reign of William III', Princeton University, Ph.D. thesis, 1975, pp. 260-9 and 310. For tory agitation over Norwich and London, see D. G. D. Isaac, 'A study of popular disturbances in Britain 1714-54', Edinburgh University, Ph.D. thesis, 1953, pp. 211-13; for Bristol, see 'A necessary CAUTION', in *The Poll Book ... to which is prefix'd the controversy on both sides* (Bristol, 1739).

[16] The tory campaign over Manchester's work-house can be traced in 'The private journal and literary remains of John Byrom', I, Part II, ed. R. Parkinson, Chetham Society, xxxiv (1855), 440-90.

enfranchised and unenfranchised constituents. And this is where the growth of literacy and popular political awareness in the eighteenth century does, perhaps, become important. Many of the techniques used by the tories to engage support—local clubs, processions, and the promotion of voting rights—would have been familiar to the first whigs of the 1670s; in mid-eighteenth-century conditions and as employed by the tories, these manipulative devices had to make some genuine concessions to popular opinion and participation.

In the early 1740s the tory-jacobite antiquarian, Thomas Carte, drew up a scheme 'for the setting up in all Market towns or larger Parishes, clubs of Independent Electors'. Such a network of societies, Carte argued, would be able to monitor the parliamentary conduct of M.P.s and synchronize popular resistance to electoral oligarchy, by, for instance, 'an agreement among the United Societies in the County not to lay out any money with Tradesmen that vote for corruption'. Professor Greaves printed Carte's scheme as long ago as 1933: what is seldom realized is that it was only tory actuality formalized and writ large.[17] Whether by way of the Charter Club in Colchester, the Half-Moon Club in Cheapside, London, the Bean Club in Birmingham, or the Independent Electors society in Coventry, the tories sought media for socio-political contact with their grass-roots supporters.[18] These societies not only mobilized the tory vote, they were also used by the voters for dialogue with and to put pressure upon the responsible M.P. In Bristol in 1737 the tory Merchant Venturers founded the Steadfast Society as a constituency pressure group, and went on to promote a chain of independent societies in every Bristol parish. This system widened the scope of tory electoral activity—essential with an electorate of 5000—and it also introduced men of very modest means to the local political process. At every contested Bristol election the parish clubs were expected to subscribe to the tory campaign fund; in return they were given at least the illusion of political responsibility. Tory candidates were required to visit each parish society to explain their policy attitudes, and whenever leading Bristol tories dispatched Instructions and petitions to Westminster, these documents were similarly ratified at parish society level.[19]

[17] One version of Carte's scheme is printed in R. W. Greaves, 'A Scheme for the Counties', *Eng. Hist. Rev.*, xlviii (1933), 630–8.

[18] For a detailed discussion of these societies see my *In Defiance of Oligarchy*, chapters 5 and 6. See also I. G. Doolittle, 'The Half Moon Tavern, Cheapside, and City Politics', *Transactions of the London and Middlesex Archaeological Society*, xxviii (1977); and A. F. J. Brown, *Colchester in the Eighteenth Century* (Colchester, 1969), pp. 12–20.

[19] See chapter 5 of my *In Defiance of Oligarchy*, and Thomas Carte's rather inflated assessment of the Steadfast Society in *The History of Parliament: The House of Commons 1715–54*, ed. R. Sedgwick (London, 1970), I, p. 245.

The tory association with the Independent Electors of Westminster is an even more extensive illustration of how electoral self-interest could merge the party with low-level political activity. The Independents were not a tory creation. A group of middling tradesmen, lawyers and some artisans had assembled in 1741 to support the Westminster candidature of the opposition whigs, Viscount Perceval and Admiral Vernon. When Perceval went over to the Ministry in 1742, many of the Independents disowned him and, as he later noted, a sub-group, 'mostly of ye lowest ranks', persisted in meeting on a monthly basis at the Crown and Anchor Tavern. It was the vociferous extremism of this plebeian rump which helped to forge the anti-democratic emphasis of Perceval's brilliant pamphlet *Faction detected by the Evidence of Facts*, and it was this same group which the tories sought to annex.[20] It is indeed arguable that the high-political crisis of 1742 whereby Pulteney and his friends joined the Old Corps in government and left their tory allies in the lurch was a crucial stage in tory radicalization. Deserted by many of its Westminster allies, the party looked without and became, predictably, much more aware of the need for fundamental reform. 'We must so act', a tory spokesman is supposed to have told a party meeting, 'as every Individual, if possible, may feel himself interested in our Endeavours, and actually become a Gainer by the Event.' So it is that tory pamphlets in 1742 and 1743 bristle with demands for the repeal of the Black and Riot Acts, for reform of the representative system, and for a broader base in local government.[21]

As the tories moved—if I may employ an anachronism—leftwards, so the extra-parliamentary nation became potentially more volatile. In the 1740s both the population and the price of basic food-stuffs began to rise after some eighty years of relative stability. While these demographic and economic factors threatened low-level quiescence, the more politicized sectors of English society gave way to disillusionment and, occasionally, to anger, as the national revival, so long anticipated from Walpole's fall, turned out in practice to be just another whig re-shuffle. G. A. Cranfield noted long ago how local newspapers reflected the mood of their post-1742 readership by adopt-

---

[20] For the Independent Electors, see Perceval's draft history in B.L., Add. MS. 47159, and N. Rogers, 'Aristocratic Clientage, Trade and Independency: popular politics in pre-radical Westminster', *Past & Present*, 61 (1973), 70–106. I think Dr. Rogers has understated the society's tory connections, for which see Lord Egmont (the former Perceval) to Frederick, Prince of Wales, 17 November 1749 'Leicester House Politics, 1750-60', ed. A. N. Newman, *Camden Miscellany XXIII* (R. Hist. Soc., 1969), p. 188.

[21] *A Key to the Present Session ... Certain Important Hints deliver'd to an Assembly of Independents* (London, 1742), p. 35; A. S. Foord, *His Majesty's Opposition 1714-1830* (Oxford, 1964), pp. 234-5.

ing an increasingly cynical stance on national politics.[22] In the capital at least, this popular alienation often sought republican expression: the figure of Oliver Cromwell appears again and again in London political prints, stigmatizing the corruption and oligarchy of English government.[23] The Independent Electors of Westminster undoubtedly attracted republican members—the society features in contemporary caricatures as the Calves Head club—and tory politicians tolerated this ideological bias for the sake of the grass-roots support the Independents could give them. The society canvassed potential tory and opposition voters at election time, issued propaganda, and seems to have raised electoral subscriptions. In return it demanded a say in the selection of opposition candidates for Westminster and was also consulted on the Middlesex tory candidature in 1747. The society had organizational links with the tories' London headquarters, the Cocoa Tree, and schemes were devised there for a reform in Westminster ward government, for a reduction in duties on coal sold in the city, and for improvements in its street lighting.[24]

The Independents' effective existence as a constituency society and as a pressure group was very limited, but this does not much matter. What is significant is the tories' deviation from customary electoral practice. Faced with a constituency which was over-shadowed by the Court and permeated with whig aristocratic commercial patronage, the tories responded with a broader electoral strategy and with a civic rather than an individual appeal.

The 1740s also witnessed an increase in tory appeals to the represented to assert themselves autonomously against electoral control and corruption. This tory rhetoric was of course self-interested and often disingenuous. Tory parliamentary candidates were frequently guilty of bribery and coercion. But this did not detract from the socially provocative effect of their appeals to voter solidarity. At every general election tory local newspapers abound with reports of tory voter rectitude. Thus in 1754, Abingdon's voters were praised for accepting whig bribes only to reject them before voting: 'They had received 20, 30 and 50 pounds, not by them taken as the Price of their Votes, but that they might become Instruments of exemplary Punishment to those who dared to seduce them ... This conduct it seems was the effect of an uniform resolution taken among them.' Popular resistance was not only lauded, it was also incited and

[22] See P. Mathias, *The Transformation of England: essays in the economic and social history of England in the eighteenth century* (London, 1979), p. 118; G. A. Cranfield, *The Development of the Provincial Newspaper 1700–60* (Oxford, 1962), pp. 133–7.

[23] See F. G. Stephens, *Catalogue of Prints and Drawings in the British Museum* (London, 1877), III, part II, print nos. 3340 and 3508.

[24] *Ibid.*, print nos. 805, 2142–4, 2494 and 2856.

sponsored. Just as Wilkes was to champion Bedford's resistance to its duke and electoral patron in 1768, so, twenty years earlier, a group of tory M.P.s lent money and support to Derby's burgesses when they revolted against the electoral stranglehold of the Stanhope and Cavendish families.[25]

And in their publicity tory politicians and country gentlemen often presented themselves not only as the auxiliaries of the excluded, but also as the co-victims of whig aristocratic and executive persecution. In 1748 the Staffordshire tories set up a race-meeting at Lichfield which attracted widespread party support, and which was intended to rival the races held locally by Lord Gower, the tory peer who had defected in 1745, and who was used in the tory race advertisements as the personification of all that was wasteful and predatory in the whig state.

> 'To all Placemen, Pensioners, Officers of the Excise, Post-Masters, Window Peepers etc etc etc
> There are two races advertised for Lichfield the one in August, the other in September: To prevent mistakes, 'tis proper to address you with the following Caution. The former [the tory races] will probably be crowded with Country Squires, Freeholders, Yeomen, Mechanicks, and such like ... by the sweat of their Brows ye are enabled to live like Gentlemen.'

In contrast to this carefully selected and clearly virtuous social amalgam, the actual and aspiring drones of society were invited to take themselves off to the September races, where 'Your new Patron [Gower] exhibits himself ... if any officer, Military or Ecclesiastical, wants an Advance, let him attend and his Fortune is made.'[26]

In the 1750s tory politicians were to find a more durable *cause célèbre*, replete with libertarian and republican overtones, in the Richmond Park affair. Thompson has cited this dispute as exemplifying popular concern for customary rights: the bounds beyond which the average untutored Englishman would not be pushed. 'When', he writes, 'in the quiet 1750s [notice 'quiet'], Princess Amelia tried to close all access to Richmond New Park, she was opposed by a vigorous horizontal consciousness which stretched from John Lewis, a wealthy local brewer, to Grub Street pamphleteers, and which embraced the whole local "populace".' It would be more accurate to say that the Richmond Park affair demonstrates how a protracted popular grievance could only acquire coherent and vigorous expression by way of spon-

---

[25] The Derby revolt and its sponsors were reported in *The Worcester Journal*, 29 December 1748; see also the poll book for this by-election at the Institute of Historical Research. For Abingdon, see *Jackson's Oxford Journal*, 20 April 1754.

[26] Tory advertisement printed in *The Worcester Journal*, 11 August 1748.

sorship from above. The Richmond villagers had had their customary rights of access to the Park eroded since the 1720s; it was not until a group of tory lawyer M.P.s took their case to the Courts in 1754, 1755 and, successfully, in 1758, that the villagers' misfortunes found publicity and ultimate redress.[27]

In the 1754 Richmond trial, counsel for the villagers included the tory M.P.s for Hereford, Abingdon, Hull, Wigan and Preston, and, most significantly, the Steadfast Society's two nominees for the Bristol election of that year, Sir John Philipps and Richard Beckford. Richard was the younger brother of William Beckford, the plutocratic tory M.P. for London, and both men sponsored the radical newspaper, *The Monitor*. In the 1760s William Beckford was to work for parliamentary reform in close if uneven collaboration with John Wilkes; in the 1750s he acquired experience in extra-parliamentary agitation by masterminding the tories' exploitation of the Richmond Park affair. And in much of the propaganda spawned by the Richmond episode, one can see the central Wilkite tactic—the dramatization of a petty and specific dilemma into an event of nationwide and general significance—being rehearsed with considerable effect. So John Lewis, a tory middle class brewer who lived in Richmond, argued in 1756 that

'whenever you shall discover any flagrant attempt upon the rights of one single Briton; you [should] make his cause the cause of the nation ... Nor can you do this better, than by backing [him] ... with Addresses or petitions in his behalf ... from every county, every city, and every corporation in the Kingdom; and likewise by aiding him in his Suits depending in the Courts of Justice, by Voluntary Subscriptions.'

Not surprisingly, Lewis went on in the 1760s to be associated with the Society for the Supporters of the Bill of Rights which organized petitions and subscriptions on Wilkes' behalf.[28]

II

So far I have tried to indicate—in what has necessarily been a rather hectic and compressed fashion—some of the ways in which the tories sought extra-parliamentary support and catered to the extra-parlia-

[27] Thompson, 'Patrician Society', 397. This and the next paragraph are based on a paper 'Richmond Park, radical toryism, and republicanism in the mid-eighteenth century', recently delivered to the Cambridge Historical Society. I hope to publish an extended version in the near future.

[28] [John Lewis], *The Sequel of Advice to Posterity, concerning a Point of Last Importance* (London, 1756), p. 69. And see his comments on the Law and England's lower orders in his *Advice to Posterity* (London, 1755), pp. 8–9.

mentary nation's sense of its own political weight in so doing. But were these miscellaneous tory endeavours given any continuity and focus by a campaign for parliamentary reform? The short answer is no, but this is not a sufficient answer: During the mid-eighteenth century the tory party always stressed an M.P.'s political responsibility to the represented. It is not clear when constituency pledges were first attempted in England, but they certainly antedated the Wilkite era. In 1722 several constituencies demanded undertakings from their tory candidates that, once elected, they would work to restore triennial parliaments.[29] The Bristol Steadfast Society seems to have demanded more detailed pledges from its candidates well into the century: if one bears this in mind and then thinks of Edmund Burke's rebuke to his Bristol constituents in 1774 after they had attempted to instruct him, the dangers of any straightforwardly crescendo interpretation of eighteenth-century radical activism are made apparent.[30]

Constituency Instructions also implied an M.P.'s accountability to his electors and, after 1733, tory politicians were far more sympathetic to these devices than were dissident whigs. William Pulteney, Viscount Perceval, and, indeed, the Rockingham whigs of the later eighteenth century, repeatedly expressed their hostility to the constitutional and social implications of Instructions. Thus Perceval rejected Westminster's Instructions in 1742, telling his voters that 'When I differ from your Sentiments I shall do it with the greatest reluctance, and then only when your true Interest must extort it from me.' The extra-parliamentary classes, in other words, could not know their own interests best.[31]

The proclaimed tory attitude was quite different. For the tory M.P. for Minehead, speaking in 1745, M.P.s were the peoples' attorneys; for Velters Cornewall in 1756

'no more than their trustees pro tempore ... if they should, ex mero motu, instruct us, and we grow restive, and scorn their advice, we shall be then no longer good and faithful stewards, but be turned adrift, and richly deserve it, at the next general election.'[32]

[29] For pledges in the 1722 election see *The Freeholder's Journal*, 21 March 1722, and John Barlow to Sir John Pakington, 22 February 1721 (Worcestershire R.O., Acc. 4657, vol. 3). For the distinction between electoral pledges and Instructions, see Betty Kemp, 'Patriotism, Pledges and the People', *Century of Conflict*, ed. M. Gilbert (London, 1966), pp. 40-3, and Lucy S. Sutherland, 'Edmund Burke and the Relations between Members of Parliament and their Constituents', *Studies in Burke and his Time*, x (1968).
[30] See *Edmund Burke on Government, Politics and Society*, ed. B. W. Hill (London, 1975), pp. 156-8; cf. Brewer, *Party Ideology and Popular Politics*, pp. 236-7.
[31] 'Lord Perceval's answer to a deputation of the Independent Inhabitants of Westminster' (West Sussex Record Office, Goodwood MS. 109, fo. 890), quoted by courtesy of the Trustees of the Goodwood Estate Company Ltd.
[32] *The Gentleman's Magazine*, xxvii (1757), 344.

All this popularist rhetoric should not obscure the fact that most tory Instructions were synthetic: formulated by the M.P.s themselves or at an assizes meeting of a county's tory gentry. The dubious origins of many Instructions did not, however, cancel out their popular impact, especially when they were reprinted in the London and provincial press. Particularly splenetic or controversial Instructions were invariably printed in pamphlet form. The anti-Walpolian Instructions of 1740-42—the great bulk of them tory inspired—appeared as *Great Britain's Memorial.* The 1756 Addresses and Instructions for an inquiry into Britain's loss of Minorca appeared—significantly—as *The Voice of the People* and could be purchased for twelve pence.[33] And because many tory M.P.s represented large and volatile electorates, they were often compelled to obey their constituents' real or ostensible demands. When the tory M.P. for Exeter ignored his city's Instructions and voted for the Jew Bill in 1753, he lost his seat at the general election of the following year.[34]

Contemporaries were fully aware of the wider significance of Instructions. The protests over the Jew Bill were, argued one pamphleteer, 'A Proof that the Sense of the Nation may differ from the Sense of Parliament; and that therefore the Voice of Parliament is not the only Evidence of the Sense of the Nation'. From this it was but a short step to suggesting that the representative system be adjusted so that Parliament did represent the National Will. Pamphleteers also pointed the logic of the tories' criticism of indirect taxation. When the predominantly tory Common Council of London instructed against Walpole's Convention treaty with Spain in 1739, one writer vindicated the participation in this protest of the so-called 'meaner sort'. 'Where are these mean people' he inquired,

'is there a Man in England who does not either drink beer, wear shoes, or now and then smoak a pipe of tobacco? Can he do any of these without contributing to the support of the Government? ... All who support a thing, have a natural interest in the thing they support ... it follows that even the meanest Man in the Kingdom has an interest in the Publick ... Amongst a free People, who has a right to controul the Majority?'[35]

---

[33] *Great Britain's Memorial* (London, 1741) and *The Second Part of Great Britain's Memorial* (London, 1742); *The Voice of the People* (London, 1756). For the manipulation of Instructions see P. Langford, *The Excise Crisis* (Oxford, 1975), pp. 47-61. This was the only mid-century petitioning campaign in which dissident whigs were well represented, though still easily outnumbered by their tory counterparts.

[34] H.M.C., *Report on the Records of the City of Exeter*, pp. 245-6.

[35] *The Livery-Man: or plain thoughts on publick affairs* (London, 1740), pp. 7 and 56; *Considerations on the Addresses lately presented to His Majesty on Occasion of the Loss of Minorca* (London, 1756), p. 11.

Here, twenty-five years before the Stamp Act crisis and fifty years before Thomas Paine, we have the argument for universal manhood suffrage.

Tory M.P.s came nowhere near to advocating this concession in the mid-eighteenth century. Like the radical whigs of the 1670s—and for the same self-interested electoral reasons—they did support a re-distribution of parliamentary seats in favour of the counties and larger boroughs. They also supported the enfranchisement of the new towns: Birmingham, Manchester, Leeds, Halifax and Sheffield. In July 1734 Lord Bolingbroke submitted an essay to *The Craftsman*, lauding the superior rationality of the Instrument of Government's allocation of seats in 1653 and urging that distribution should reflect each county's taxation burden.[36] At every subsequent election year these limited reform polemics were a standard component of tory and opposition whig propaganda—so when John Almon's reform manifesto appeared in *The Political Register* before the general election of 1768, it marked not the inception of the reform campaign, but a continuation of an Opposition tradition.[37] What distinguished the tory contribution to the mid-century reform debate was, first, the party's insistence on the need for public agitation—Parliament could not be expected voluntarily to reform itself—and, secondly, tory journalists' enthusiasm for parliamentary reform even in non-election years. The abolition of rotten boroughs and the enfranchisement of the new towns was a constant theme of William Beckford's *Monitor* in the 1750s, while in 1759, the high tory *Jopson's Coventry Mercury* demanded a re-distribution of seats as well as the payment of M.P.s.[38]

Why, when large electorates were so conductive to tory electorate success, did the party not commit itself to extensive parliamentary reform? There are three main reasons, all of which impinge on one of the central arguments of this paper: namely, that radical in effect as they indubitably were, mid-century tories were never disinterested reformers.

It has sometimes been suggested that the tories hesitated to advance parliamentary reform lest it strengthen the manufacturing and commercial classes. But this is to postulate an antagonism between the party and these interest groups which the tories' urban experience in the mid-eighteenth century hardly corroborates. The party had good reason to be confident of its electoral prospects were the unrepresented

---

[36] See *The Gentleman's Magazine*, iv (1734), 381.

[37] For some of the reform arguments published before the 1747 election, see *The Gentleman's Magazine*, xvii (1747), 329-31. On Almon, see J. Cannon, *Parliamentary Reform 1640-1832* (Cambridge, 1973), pp. 54-5.

[38] See Marie Peters, 'The "Monitor" on the Constitution, 1755-65: new light on the ideological origins of English radicalism', *Eng. Hist. Rev.*, lxxxvi (1971), 706-27; *Jopson's Coventry Mercury*, 26 March and 23 April 1759.

towns to be enfranchised; it had no way of knowing how its electoral base in the counties, reliant as it was on traditional tory landlord influence, would be affected by a dilution of the freeholder franchise. The second obstacle to tory support for an extended franchise was Dissent. In some of the great cities where toryism was electorally entrenched—Exeter is an example—many of the poorer inhabitants were nonconformist: a wider franchise in these constituencies would have redounded to the whigs' advantage.[39] Finally, since neither George I nor George II was invariably opposed to tory promotions, and since therefore whig supremacy rarely appeared irreversible, the tory parliamentary party was bound to be distracted from an extensive and possibly subversive assault on the established order by the prospect of political recovery by means of high-level and orthodox manœuvre.

Hence of course the tories' supersession by John Wilkes after 1760. For the tories the accession of George III meant re-admission to the promised land of state employment. In contrast Wilkes after 1763 had to rebel against conventional politics if he was not to relapse into oblivion. And in this rebellion Wilkes could draw, without fear of loss, on nonconformist auxiliaries. Both in its personnel and in its platform, the Wilkite movement also drew on the tory radical experience of the mid-eighteenth century. Wilkes had contacts at the highest level of the tory party: Lord Lichfield, Norborne Berkeley, and more significant if less bonhomous allies in William Beckford, Sir Robert Ladbroke, William Dowdeswell, Sir Watkin Lewes, Robert Jones, and the secretary of the S.S.B.R., Robert Morris—all tory M.P.s or men of tory background.[40] In 1768 the St. James Chronicle remarked how the voters in the eastern division of Middlesex, who had given Wilkes his best support, had also rallied to George Cooke, the tory M.P. returned for that county in 1750 who 'greatly availed himself of this numerous body of little freeholders'.[41] As an early exercise in psephology this claim was only partially correct; it is none the less significant that the comparison between tory and Wilkite electoral support was made. In Bristol, Newcastle, Coventry, Norwich, Colchester and, most of all, in

---

[39] A. A. Brockett, 'The Political and Social Influence of the Exeter Dissenters and Some Notable Families', *Report and Transactions of the Devonshire Association*, xciii (1961), 184–5. For estimates of English nonconformist voters in 1715, see E. D. Bebb, *Nonconformity and Social and Economic Life 1660–1800* (London, 1935), pp. 182–3.

[40] For tory–Wilkite links in terms of personnel, symbolism and constituencies, see chapter 6 of my *In Defiance of Oligarchy*. The Welsh Wilkite–tory nexus is noted in J. P. Jenkins, 'Jacobites and Freemasons in Eighteenth-century Wales', *Welsh History Review*, ix (1979), 399–401.

[41] N. Rogers, 'London politics from Walpole to Pitt: Patriotism and independency in an era of commercial imperialism, 1738–63', Toronto University, D.Phil. thesis, 1974, pp. 480–2.

the metropolis, there was indubitably some concordance between former tory and subsequent radical allegiance. In London the tory Half-Moon Club and the Independent Electors of Westminster were both associated with the new movement. Since the latter society had already absorbed the number '45' into its internal organization, and since the Independent Elector, Alexander Murray, had been paraded through the city to shouts of 'Murray and Liberty' in 1751, this transition must have been a comfortable one, made even more consonant perhaps by the Wilkite employment of blue ribbons and songs of an emotive and indicative ancestry like 'True Blue will never stain'.[42]

III

If the tory experience in the mid-eighteenth century dictated some of the content of the Wilkite movement, it also indicates its crucial weakness. John Brewer has argued that the debate on America, the parliamentary reform movement, and what one contemporary styled the 'Wilkomania' of the 1760s, marked the emergence of focussed radicalism in Britain.[43] This seems to me to be debatable. As we have seen, much of the parliamentary reform argument had been rehearsed before Wilkes, and the connexion between taxation and representation had become a polemical commonplace long before the Stamp Act crisis. For the great mass of British people the only novel and emotive focus of the 1760s was John Wilkes himself. But while Wilkes' publicity style and individual *élan* were inimitable, his long-term political impact was minimal. Few plebeian Wilkites translated their support for the man into an abstract and durable commitment to political or social change. Wilkes' real achievement was rather to make thousands of illiterate and semi-literate men and women identify with and become absorbed in events outside their own immediate experience. And even here, could it not be argued that John Wesley's phenomenal peregrinations through Britain had an analogous impact on the popular imagination, and that he affected many more people over a much longer period of time?

A major weakness of both the Wilkite and the Wyville movements was their lack of reliable intra-parliamentary support. In 1770 the Rockingham whigs were only eighty M.P.s strong and, as befitted a faction led by a borough patron and a *dévot* of the Pelhamite tradition, were equivocal and divided in their attitude to parliamentary reform. And while the Rockinghams have sometimes been portrayed as the

[42] J. Brewer, 'Political argument and propaganda in England, 1760-70', Cambridge University, Ph.D. thesis, 1973, pp. 21 and 156.
[43] Brewer, *Party Ideology and Popular Politics*, pp. 17-22.

Bolsheviks of the whig party, their principled aloofness from the political centre was not comparable either in duration or degree with the tories' experience of exclusion. The tories were, after all, the anomalies of what C. B. Macpherson has called England's 'Opportunity State'.[44] As contemporary foreign observers were never tired of noting, and as historians have rarely failed to repeat, eighteenth-century English society was relatively open. Its aristocracy was not endogamous but tolerated *nouveaux riches* heiresses. The heiresses' fathers could usually win admission to polite society and, possibly, a parliamentary seat. As Drs. McCahill and Money have shown, landed peers and M.P.s were responsive to industrial and commercial lobbies from the unrepresented towns, not least because the pattern of their own investments made them sympathetic to entrepreneurial ventures.[45] Such a flexible society, it is often contended, was able to neutralize and absorb potentially disruptive socio-political tensions. Yet for forty-five years this otherwise flexible society discriminated against tories in central and local government, in polite London society, and in the professions, and by so doing created an unprecedented rift in England's landed élite. The so-called 'fragmentation of the political élite' in the 1760s, which Brewer has cited as a crucial pre-condition of radical success, never jeopardized political and social stability to remotely the same degree.[46]

Let me take just one example of the potentially subversive effects of tory proscription: the Law. Between 1714 and 1723 every English County Commission was purged one or more times to ensure a whig majority of J.P.s. In most counties this process was not reversed until after 1760. What impact this had on mid-century county justice has yet to be ascertained: in some counties class unity on the Bench does appear to have been compromised. In 1726 a Wiltshire tory landowner was reported to have aided local weavers in their riots against the county's clothiers, because 'he is left out of the Commission of the Peace which he was formerly in'.[47] Some of the prime victims in the purges of tory J.P.s had been the Anglican clergy. At the death of George II these most ubiquitous and effective agents of social control made up only 11 per cent of all J.P.s. In the reign of George III this percentage doubled, and, as Dr. McClatchey has shown, in late eighteenth-century Oxfordshire at least, it was the

[44] C. B. Macpherson, *The Political Theory of Possessive Individualism* (Oxford, 1962), pp. 160-93.

[45] M. W. McCahill, 'Peers, Patronage, and the Industrial Revolution, 1760-1800', *Journal of British Studies*, xvi (1976), 84-107; J. Money, *Experience and Identity: Birmingham and the West Midlands 1760-1800* (Manchester, 1977), *passim*.

[46] Brewer, *Party Ideology and Popular Politics*, p. 18.

[47] Printed in the appendix of Isaac, 'A study of popular disturbances', pp. 27-8.

clerical J.P.s who were the most zealous in undertaking criminal prosecutions.[48]

It was not just the legal process in the counties which tory proscription threatened. While there were many tory lawyers and attorneys, the top legal posts and honours were almost always closed to them, as were those political offices for which a legal education was desirable. As a result, in the mid-eighteenth century many tory gentlemen seem to have abandoned the legal profession. Graduates of Oxford University had made up 64 per cent of Lincoln's Inn admissions in the 1710s and Cambridge graduates only 31 per cent. By the 1750s the predominantly tory Oxonians made up only 38 per cent of Lincoln's Inn admissions, while the whiggish Cambridge contingent had risen to 48 per cent. This partial tory defection helped to make the reign of George II what Paul Lucas has described as 'an era of unprecedented opportunity for the relatively lower orders' in the Law. In 1758 William Blackstone was to devote his inaugural lecture at Oxford to warning his audience of the radical repercussions of social dilution in Britain's legal profession.[49]

Blackstone need not have worried. George III's reign saw the end of tory proscription and, as a result, a remarkable rise in the number of bright and landed tory gentry entering the Inns of court. Tory re-entry into high professional and political life was surely a crucial component of what Norman Ravitch has called the 'aristocratic resurgence' of late eighteenth-century England. After 1760 England's landed élite increased its hold on political office, on the law, on the respectable professions, and on the economy.[50] In the long run this aristocratic resurgence must have lent the lower classes of society a sharper sense of their dispossession and their distinct identity; in the short term it intensified social control and political stability.

IV

The proscription of the tory landowning classes after 1714 and their consequent temptation to political and social irresponsibility sowed the vital seeds of eighteenth-century extra-parliamentary organiza-

---

[48] D. McClatchey, *Oxfordshire Clergy, 1777–1869: a study of the Established Church and the role of the clergy in local society* (Oxford, 1960), pp. 178–201. E. J. Evans, 'Some Reasons for the Growth of English Rural Anti-Clericalism c. 1750–c. 1830', *Past & Present*, 66 (1975), 101.

[49] P. Lucas, 'A Collective Biography of Students and Barristers of Lincoln's Inn, 1680–1804: a study in the "Aristocratic Resurgence" in the eighteenth century', *Journal of Modern History*, xlvi (1974), 227–61; see also his 'Blackstone and the Reform of the Legal Profession', *Eng. Hist. Rev.*, lxxvii (1962), 456–7.

[50] N. Ravitch, 'The Social Origins of French and English Bishops in the Eighteenth Century', *Historical Journal*, viii (1965), 319.

tion and protest. I would like to suggest that one of the reasons why radicalism made such limited progress later in the century, was that Britain's landed élite was not only consolidating its economic supremacy via the Industrial Revolution, but had also been restored to collective attachment to the *status quo* by the end of tory proscription, and by the abrogation at the centre of politics of clear-cut party distinctions.

GREGORY THE GREAT'S EUROPE

By Professor R. A. Markus, M.A., Ph.D., F.R.Hist.S.

READ 21 MARCH 1980

GREGORY became pope in the summer of 590, to succeed his predecessor who had been carried away by the plague. Nearly fifty years had passed since the first outbreak of the plague in the time of Justinian. Let the plague serve as our signpost to a period of upheaval across Europe. If the 530s were the 'age of hope'[1] a disastrous reversal began in the 540s. The succeeding half-century was a time of collapsing hopes and darkening horizons: the prospect of imperial reconquest and peace receding after 540, never to be more than ephemerally and precariously realized; the dreams of spiritual and political unification revealed as illusory; war, plague and the obscure workings of 'demographic forces' combined to turn the Italy of Boethius into that of Gregory the Great in the course of some sixty years. The contours of the societies of late Antiquity were becoming displaced to produce a new social landscape. Some of this transformation has left visible traces in our evidence and has been extensively studied; much of it has been concealed from us, either through lack of evidence or through failure to ask the right questions. It is only in recent years, to take one example, that the subtle shifts in Byzantine religiosity and political ideology discernible in the later sixth century have begun to cohere into something like a unified picture of a 'new integration'[2] of culture and society in the towns of the Eastern Empire. How far the world of Western Europe was exposed to analogous changes may be a question impossible to answer; in any case, it needs approaching piecemeal and with the necessary discrimination of time and place.

The question I am asking in this paper forms part of such an enquiry, but a very modest part: how did Gregory the Great, a particularly sensitive and intelligent Westerner, moreover a Westerner who had lived in Constantinople and remained in touch with the capital as well as with several other great ecclesiastical centres of the Eastern Mediterranean, see his Europe? What were the horizons that defined the centre and the edges of his world? Erich Caspar's magisterial account of his pontificate[3] has accustomed us to seeing it in

---

[1] T. Honoré, *Tribonian* (London, 1978), pp. 17–20.

[2] A. Cameron, 'Images of Authority: elites and icons in late sixth-century Byzantium', *Past & Present*, 84 (1979), 3–35, which gives a conspectus of her recent work in this field and references to other studies.

[3] *Geschichte des Papsttums*, II (Tübingen, 1933), esp. p. 408.

terms of two spheres: that of the Empire, distinguished sharply—perhaps too sharply—from that of Germanic Western Europe. In Gregory's Italy, the two worlds of Germanic Europe and of the Empire overlap; but Gregory was one of the great *Grenzgestalten* of European history in more important senses than this, historical cartographical, respect. How, then, were these two worlds related in Gregory's own imagination?

The Empire—the Empire of Justinian and his immediate successors—was both the major sphere of the pope's activities and the permanent backdrop to all his awareness. Justinian was the watershed which divided the papacy of Gregory I from that of Gelasius a century before him. Gelasius had been able to drive a wedge between the sacred authority of the clergy and the power of secular rulers; but there was no room for such a division in Gregory's world. The Church had become a public institution of the Empire and the Empire itself was deeply and thoroughly 'ecclesiastified', if I may be permitted the barbarism. Gregory's church was Justinian's *Reichskirche*: the English phrase 'imperial church' fails to convey the radical integration of church and secular society, the impossibility of thinking of them in dualistic terms. There is no need for us to survey the evidence—there is plenty of it and its bearings are clear and generally agreed—which shows how unambiguously Gregory accepted the ecclesiastical dispensation of Justinian's imperial establishment.[4] Even an occasional protest against what he considered ungodly exercise of imperial authority in religious matters is stated in a key very different from that adopted by Gelasius a century before: it displays Gregory's refusal, perhaps inability, to place such questions on the level of a conflict between spiritual and secular powers. I suspect that careful study would reveal that Gregory's political language is more at home in the comparatively homogeneous and more thoroughly integrated society of Byzantine Christendom than in the societies of Western Europe where those tensions which were to be endemic in the Middle Ages, between sacred and secular, were already latent.[5] But this is a study which has not yet been undertaken and, anyway, it would take us too far afield. So I shall confine myself to the more specific question: how far did Gregory liberate himself from the forms of the post-Justinianic Empire in his dealings with Frankish, Gothic and, especially, English

---

[4] See Caspar, *Geschichte*, II, p. 465 seq.; F. H. Dudden, *Gregory the Great* (London, 1905), II, pp. 248-67, esp. p. 249. For a full survey of his relation with the emperors and attitudes to the imperial office, see E. H. Fischer, 'Gregor der Grosse und Byzanz: ein Beitrag zur Geschichte der päpstlichen Politik', *Zeitschrift der Savigny-Stiftung für Rechsgeschichte, Kanonistische Abteilung*, 36 (1950), 15-144.

[5] For a suggestive recent discussion, see J. L. Nelson, 'Symbols in Context: rulers' inauguration rituals in Byzantium and the West in the early Middle Ages', *Studies in Church History [SCH]*, ed. D. Baker, 13 (1976), pp. 97-119.

barbarians? How far was his vision of Germanic Europe shaped by the concepts of imperial ideology?

The polite conventions of formal correspondence are not always to be trusted as expressions of real attitudes, but they can give useful clues. In his letters Gregory always uses the standard language of imperial protocol: the emperor is addressed as his *christianissimus*, *piissimus* or *serenissimus dominus*, and, along with the formulae, we find there the appropriate attitudes of deference. But we are in the presence here of more than personal or even institutional attitudes: these are linked with a cluster of instinctive assumptions which form a part of Gregory's mind. His political imagery saw the Empire as grounded in the hierarchical order of the world, an integral part of the cosmic hierarchy.[6] This is the old image of a world dominated by Rome, whose universal Empire was part of the fixed order of things. Even some of the less savoury commonplaces associated with Roman imperialism flowed quite easily from Gregory's pen: it is the duty of the clergy, for example, to pray for the emperors 'that almighty God may subject the barbarian nations beneath their feet, grant them a long and felicitous reign so that faith in Christ may rule throughout the Christian Empire'.[7] It is the age-old justification, in a Christian version, of Roman imperialism, the natural subordination of barbarians to Romans, as of slaves to free men, and it turns up dismayingly often in Gregory's letters.[8] His use of the old *topoi* is all the more revealing because of the contrast with his attitudes to the barbarian nations of Western Europe and their rulers, as revealed in his actual dealings with them. His readiness to treat the barbarian nations as fully autonomous in their own right, possessing their own national churches and their own Christian destinies, might incline us to view his readiness to lapse into the vocabulary of Roman chauvinism as no more than reasonable flattery on appropriate occasions. Taking this view we might then think that his tact, sensitivity and flexible pastoral imagination put the concepts of Roman imperialism in their right place. Such a view, however, would do much less than justice either to the complexity and coherence of Gregory's mind, or to the deep hold that these concepts had on it.

[6] A particularly striking statement: *Ep.* V. 59, i. 371 (Gregory's letters are throughout referred to in the edition of the *Registrum* by P. Ewald and L. M. Hartmann, *Monumenta Germanie Historica* [*MGH.*], *Epistolae* [*Epp.*] i and ii, followed by page and line references where appropriate).

[7] *Ep.* VII, 5, i. 448. 30–32. See also VII. 7, i. 451. 21; VII. 24, i. 470. 3–4.

[8] *Ep.* XI. 4, ii. 263. 9–11; XIII. 4, ii. 397. 21–23. The classic statement is in Aristotle's *Politics* I. 1252b4, 1255a1–b10. On the whole theme, see J. Vogt, 'Kulturwelt und Barbaren: zum Menschenbild der spätantiken Gesellschaft', *Akademie der Wissenschaften und der Literatur, Abhandlungen der Geistes- und Sozialwissenschaftlichen Klasse*, 1 (Mainz, 1967).

His ideas on the conduct of Christian missions are a particularly revealing example which allows us both to appreciate the power of ancient commonplaces over his mind, and the growth in it, or the sudden dawning, of a consciousness that the old formulae are no longer adequate, the course of action implied by them no longer what the situation demands. Missionary activity was one of the pre-occupations which formed a continuous thread throughout Gregory's pontificate, and may even, according to legend, have ante-dated his accession to the papacy.[9] At any rate, there is firm evidence of continued missionary interests from the first months of his pontificate. Only the Easter preceding Gregory's accession in September 590 the Lombard king had prohibited Catholic baptism for his subjects, per-haps in an attempt to rally his people, at a moment of crisis in its national cohesion, to the Arian faith.[10] This gave the impulse to Gregory's first missionary project, and from this time on, for the next ten years, his correspondence bears ample witness to his concern for the conversion of pagans and heretics. In all the far-ranging enterprise of these years there is a striking uniformity about the means to be adopted envisaged by Gregory. The method is always the same: the preaching of the Gospel is to be supported by the coercive authority of the powers that be: by a praetor in Sicily, by local landowners, officials, military commanders, minor chieftains or kings, as well as the personnel in charge of administering the Church's estates. The pattern is constant and never questioned during these ten years. Neither, however, is it ever discussed—it is simply assumed as the natural and obvious way of making Christians.

The assumption is entirely in line with the commonplaces about secular authority and its responsibilities which crop up repeatedly in the formulae of the pope's official correspondence. Thus, for instance, we find an outstanding soldier, the exarch of Africa Gennadius, praised in a series of letters in which the preliminary courtesies include a reference to the many wars he had fought 'not for desire of shedding blood, but for the good of the *res publica* in which we see God being served, in so much as the name of Christ is spread abroad among the conquered peoples by the preaching of the faith'.[11] There is no thought-out missionary strategy here. What both the commonplaces which preface official correspondence and the instinctive assumptions

[9] On what follows, see my paper 'Gregory the Great and a Papal Missionary Strategy', *SCH*, 6 (1970), pp. 29–38, where details and references are to be found.

[10] According to G. P. Bognetti, *L'età longobarda*, I (Milano, 1966), p. 197, and II, p. 155. This view of Lombard Arianism may, however, require some qualification: see P. M. Conti, 'Aquileian, Eastern and Roman Missions in the Lombard Kingdom', *Miscellanea Historiae Ecclesiasticae*, 3 (Louvain, 1970), pp. 62–70.

[11] *Ep.* I. 73, i. 93. 16–18; see also *Ep.* I. 59 and 72, and, for the emperor as guardian of orthodoxy, the references above at note 6 and below at note 12.

about missionary strategy reveal are not so much the results of reflection as part of the stock of *idées reçues* which formed Gregory's inherited
mental furniture. As late as February 601 they still held unquestioned
sway over his mind: he was still thinking of coercive power at the
service of the Gospel and of imperial authority as charged with en-
forcing Christian orthodoxy.[12] It was only to be expected that when
Gregory sent off his mission to the heathen English in 596, the same
ideas should be active in his mind. That they were is clearly indicated
by his first reactions to the reports that reached him in 601, when
some of the first party of missionaries returned to Rome for reinforcements. Evidently the pope was somewhat disappointed by the part
played by the English king. His expectation had been that those who
had the power to coerce would, if fired with Christian zeal, coerce
their subjects. But king Aethelberct evidently had not exerted himself
as much as could be wished; so he was now admonished 'to hasten the
spread of the Christian faith among the peoples subject [to him], to
increase [his] righteous zeal for their conversion, to repress the worship
of idols, to destroy the shrines', and so forth.[13] It is the same model as
had underlain all the pope's missionary enterprise so far; but a noteworthy addition here reveals its background and context: the example
was held up to the English king of 'the most pious emperor Constantine, who had subjected the Roman Empire along with himself to
almighty God and Jesus Christ'. As the invocation of this model shows,
Gregory's ideas on the conduct of Christian missions belong to a larger
deposit of political commonplaces, again instinctively adopted, which
formed part of the conglomerate of his half-conscious assumptions.
The marriage of Christian orthodoxy and the imperial establishment
in the Christian Empire inaugurated in the fourth century is the model
which Gregory—like so many others[14]—instinctively adopts and,
along with it, its implication of Catholic orthodoxy as the official and
publicly enforced religion.

[12] *Ep.* XI. 28, ii. 298. 15-20. This is also a normal, set formula: see *Ep.* IX. 135, ii.
133. 33-134. 3, and the praise heaped by Gregory on king Reccared (*Ep.* IX. 228, ii.
222. 1-13).

[13] *Ep.* XI. 37, ii. 308. 25-309. 6, for the whole passage.

[14] See Avitus's letter to Clovis (*Ep.* XXXVI (*Alcimi Ecdici Aviti Opera*, ed. R. Peiper,
MGH. Auctores Antiquissimi, VI/2), p. 76). On the model of Constantine, see E. Ewig,
'Das Bild Constantin des Grossen in den ersten Jahrhunderten des abendländischen
Mittelalters', *Historisches Jahrbuch*, 75 (1956), 1-46. On the 'conversion' of Germanic
kings and the consequent expectations, F. Graus, *Volk, Herrscher und Heiliger im Reich der
Merowinger* (Prague, 1966), pp. 148-9. The idea of evangelization current in late Roman
Christianity has been fully surveyed by W. H. Fritze, 'Universalis gentium confessio.
Formeln, Träger und Wege universalmissionarischen Denkens im 7. Jahrundert',
Frühmittelalterliche Studien, 3 (1969), 78-130, esp. 123-130. On coercion, see H. D. Kahl,
'Die ersten Jahrhunderte des missionsgeschichtlichen Mittelalters', *Die Kirche des früheren
Mittelalters*, ed. K. Schäferdiek (*Kirchengeschichte als Missionsgeschichte*, II/1, Munich,
1978), pp. 11-76, esp. pp. 55, 64-7.

The example of the English mission shows the power of such instinctively held ideas to mould the forms of action. But Gregory's mind was not so dominated by its inherited assumptions that he could not shake himself free of their spell. It is a tribute to a remarkable flexibility of mind that in the course of less than four weeks in June and July 601 he was able to discard these assumptions, when their inappropriateness to the situation in England was brought home to him. He had just received the first-hand reports of the returning missionaries and sent them back, with reinforcements, to England. As he considered their reports, which no doubt enabled him to appreciate the tenacity of popular paganism against which the Christian court could achieve little, and that only slowly, he came to see the situation more clearly. His second thoughts are contained in the famous letter which he despatched post-haste after abbot Mellitus, already in Gaul, on his way back. It shows a wholly new approach, effectively countermanding the orders he had given only a few weeks before. Deep-rooted assumptions suddenly give way under the pressure of a new situation. His pastoral imagination and realism could discard the settled habits of years. We can observe here an important ingredient of the theology of the Christian Empire suddenly yielding to the pressures of the moment.

The example of the strategy for the conduct of English mission reveals both the power and the fragility of old political commonplaces. It is not at all clear how far they are to be seen at work in the original despatching of the mission. A distinguished tradition of English historiography from Edward Gibbon to Sir Frank Stenton[15] has represented the mission as a kind of imperial enterprise, a latter-day ecclesiastical *renovatio* of Roman sovereignty. The evidence here must be confessed to be ambiguous. On the one hand, as we have seen, at the time of Augustine's sending Gregory's mind was firmly within the grip of universalistic imperial concepts and, as we shall see,[16] Gregory was in general inclined to take a view of Western Germanic kingdoms as still in some way within the Empire. Moreover, he may well have thought, as it was possible to think in sixth-century Byzantium, that the English were subject to the Frankish kings,[17] and envisaged their

---

[15] *Decline and Fall of the Roman Empire*, ch. 45; F. M. Stenton, *Anglo-Saxon England* (2nd edn., Oxford 1947), where Stenton, though not doubting Gregory's 'simple desire for the conversion of [Britain's] heathen inhabitants', thought that 'Gregory was in the succession of ancient Roman statesmen, and could not have been indifferent to the political advantages that would follow from the reunion of a lost province of the Empire to the church of the capital' (pp. 103-4). The tenacity of this tradition since Stenton could easily be illustrated by more recent examples.

[16] Below, pp. 28-9.

[17] Procopius, *Wars*, VIII. xx. 10. See the remarks of J. M. Wallace-Hadrill, 'Rome and the Early English Church: some questions of transmission', *Settimane di studio del*

christianization within the setting of his plans for the revitalization of the Frankish Church. Such considerations might incline us to interpret the despatch of the mission itself as an exercise within the *imperium christianum*. On the other hand, a formidable array of texts can be found in Gregory's writings even before he became pope which suggest that the idea of the Church's universal mission, in no way bound to the political and social structures of the Empire, had matured in his mind—perhaps under the inspiration of St. Augustine of Hippo—long before he had the opportunity of sending one.[18] I am not sure that this ambiguity can be resolved. A pastorally conceived mission and one conceived in terms of an imperial ideology are not, however, mutually exclusive, and it could well be that both notions were at work in Gregory's mind. Their practical implications—a mission must be sent—were, after all, identical, and did not force Gregory to discriminate between alternative grounds for his Christian duty. If forced to discriminate, there can be little doubt where Gregory's choice would have fallen. In his *Dialogues*[19] he tells us among the many 'delightful miracles' ('iocunda miracula') a truly delightful story about abbot Equitius, whom his excessively clerical critics had denounced for travelling about the countryside of Valeria preaching the Gospel, despite his being only a layman and not even possessed of a papal licence. He was duly summoned to appear at Rome to explain himself and learn proper ecclesiastical discipline; but he was miraculously vindicated before he could be brought to Rome. The pope who could relish the story of the triumphant vindication of abbot Equitius's charismatic, though unlicensed, missionary zeal was not the man to look at missionary enterprise in legalistic or political terms.

There can be no doubt that pastoral concern for the good of souls was the bedrock of Gregory's missionary enterprise, in England as elsewhere, as it was the driving force of his reforming efforts in the Frankish Church. In this respect Gregory's missionary initiatives, and especially their crowning example, the English mission, have rightly been seen as revolutionary. For the first time a Roman bishop took to heart the command to go and teach all nations. The assumption which had held almost unquestioned sway in the minds of churchmen for more than two centuries was that Christianity and the Roman Empire were co-extensive. Even St. Augustine came to reject it only after a long intellectual struggle, and his almost solitary protest was

---

Centro italiano sull'alto Medioevo [*Settimane*], 7 (Spoleto, 1960), pp. 519–48, esp. pp. 521–6.

[18] See Fritze, 'Universalis confessio', 109–13. I have not been able to consult P. Benkart, *Die Missionsidee Gregors des Grossen in Theorie und Praxis* (Phil. Diss., Leipzig, 1946).

[19] I.4 (ed. U. Moricca, Rome, 1924, pp. 31–7); for 'iocunda miracula', see III.22 (p. 191, l. 16).

ignored even by his own disciple, Orosius.[20] This goes far to explain the lack of missionary activity beyond the imperial frontiers[21] and the frequency with which missions within Roman territory were represented as securing law and *concordia* within the Christian Empire.[22] These were not the notions which determined Gregory's ideas of Christian missions. With them he transcended, as a German scholar has recently put it, 'the concept of mission as held in the tradition of the *Reichskirche*'.[23] But if Gregory's missionary ideas sprang from different roots, it does not follow that he discarded the whole political ideology from which the previous tradition sprang.

There are, in fact, many hints that Gregory saw the Western German kings in a decidedly Byzantine perspective. While, in practice, quite ready to deal with them as the rulers of autonomous peoples, the modes of address employed by the papal writing office reflect the official protocol of the civil administration.[24] The practice of the

[20] See my *Saeculum: History and Society in the Theology of Saint Augustine* (Cambridge, 1970), esp. pp. 39-40 and 161-3.

[21] E. A. Thompson, 'Christianity and the Northern Barbarians', *The Conflict between Paganism and Christianity in the Fourth Century*, ed. A. Momigliano (Oxford, 1963) pp. 56-78; originally in *Nottingham Medieval Studies*, i (1957) 3-21. See also E. Molland, 'L'antiquité chrétienne a-t-elle eu un programme et des méthodes missionaires?', *Miscellanea historiae ecclesiasticae*, 3 (Louvain, 1970), pp. 53-61; O. Bertolini, 'I papi e le missioni fino all metà del secolo VIII', *Settimane*, 14 (1967), pp. 327-63, mainly on Italy. On the ἐν τοῖς βαρβαρικοῖς ἔθνεσι τοῦ θεοῦ ἐκκλησια[ι] of I Constantinople c. 2 and [οἱ] ἐν τοῖς βαρβαρικῆς ἐπισκοπο[ι] of Chalcedon c. 28, see H. G. Beck, 'Christ-liche Mission und politische Propaganda im Byzantinischen Reich', *Settimane* 14 (1967), pp. 649-74, and G. Dagron, *Naissance d'une capitale: Constantinople et ses institutions de 330 à 451* (Paris, 1974), pp. 483-7.

[22] E.g. Vigilius of Trent, *Ep.* I. 1 (*PL.*, 13. 550); Paulinus of Nola, *Carmen* 17. 205-64 (*PL.*, 61. 487); Jerome, *Ep.* 60. 4 (*PL.*, 22. 591-2).

[23] K. Schäferdiek, 'Die Grundlegung der angelsächischen Kirche im Spannungsfeld insular-keltischen und kontinetal-römischen Christentums', *Die Kirche*, ed. Schäferdiek, pp. 149-91, at p. 152.

[24] There has been no systematic study of the titulature used in Gregory's correspondence and its background. My conclusion is based on a general survey. The usage is not absolutely consistent: barbarian rulers as well as top-ranking imperial officials and persons of patrician rank are regularly addressed as *excellentia* etc.; some of them, however, are also, on occasion, *gloriosi*. The equation of barbarian rulers with the highest class of official is, however, generally clear throughout. (See 'Index rerum, verborum, grammaticae', *MGH.*, *Epp.* ii, pp. 543, 550.) In this respect Gregory's usage follows the style of the papal *scrinium* already established before his time (see Pelagius I's letters in *Epistolae Arelatenses* 48, 51, 52, 54 (ed. W. Gundlach, *MGH.*, *Epp.* iii; ed. P. M. Gassó and C. M. Battle (Montserrat, 1956), nos. 9, 12, 13, 7). *Filius* is included in the address as a specifically ecclesiastical ingredient, expressing the relation between a bishop and a layman. It is, significantly, omitted by Gregory when writing to the Arian king Agilulf (*Ep.* IX. 66, ii. 86) and included—though only in the third person, in a letter not addressed to him—in a phrase referring to the emperor, 'piissimus dominus filius noster' (*Ep.* VII. 24, i. 469. 19). This, too, is clearly a matter of established usage; see, for example, Auspicius of Toul addressing Arbogast as 'fili' (*Ep. Austrasiacae* 23,

scrinium during Gregory's pontificate followed the precedents established under his predecessors. There is little doubt that the procedures
of the papal *scrinium* derived, ultimately, from those of the *scrinia* of
the imperial administration. There is not enough more or less contemporary material surviving to allow us to construct a detailed and
systematic correspondence, but what there is suggests that papal protocol still followed imperial protocol quite closely. It is worth laying
some stress on this apparently trivial continuity of administrative
routine, for it is the key to the contrasting modes of address accorded
to the emperor and to barbarian kings by the papal writing office.
Whereas the emperor is always addressed as the pope's 'most serene
Lord', or something of the kind, barbarian rulers, kings, dukes and so
forth, are his 'most excellent' or 'glorious sons'. Far from indicating[25]
that this contrast reveals the pope's assertion of his *principatus* over
Western barbarian rulers, it shows nothing more clearly than his
readiness to adhere to established administrative procedures, even
with the somewhat anachronistic imperial perspective on barbarian
kingdoms implied by the traditional formulae of the official titulature.
Gregory's own dealings with their rulers, to be sure, were certainly
not confined within such limits; but that is a large subject, and one on
which more evidence would have to be marshalled than is possible
here. Whatever his practice, he continued to write to barbarian rulers
as if they were, and as the imperial writing-office long continued to
pretend they were, occupying a place officially assigned to them in
the Empire's administrative hierarchy.

Gregory's 'Europe' fell much more easily into the mould of the
traditional Byzantine representation of barbarian nations as subjected
under divine providence to the universal Empire of his earthly representative, the most Christian emperor, than it does into that of a kind
of anticipation of a later, Western, Latin *imperium christianum* under
the *principatus* of the Roman see. In his seminal book, *The Growth of
Papal Government in the Middle Ages*, Walter Ullmann has represented
Gregory's pontificate as a step in the emancipation of the papacy from
its 'Byzantine captivity'. By withdrawing from the *Reichskirche* of the
Empire and creating a new orbit for the exercise of its authority
among the Germanic nations in the West, it embarked on the creation
'of that body politic which received its cementing bond from the

---

MGH., *Epp.* iii. 136. 37) and has no political implications. In general, see H. Wolfram,
Intitulatio, I: *Lateinische Königs- und Fürstentitel bis zum Ende des 8. Jahrhunderts* (Vienna,
1967), and J. F. O'Donnell, *The Vocabulary of the Letters of Saint Gregory the Great*
(Washington, D.C. 1934), Part IV.

[25] As suggested by W. Ullmann, *The Growth of Papal Government in the Middle Ages* (2nd
edn., London, 1962), p. 37.

Christian faith as expounded by the Roman Church'.[26] It is, in fact, the mission to the English which furnishes the main basis for this interpretation of Gregory's view of the Western kingdoms in relation to the Empire on the one hand, to the papacy on the other. The obverse to this dramatic extension of the papal sphere in the West, Ullmann thought, was the repudiation by Gregory of the papacy's 'Byzantine captivity' in his protest against the epithet *oikoumenikos* used by the patriarch of Constantinople. This protest, as Ullmann emphasized, came at the very moment that the English mission was being prepared: in June 595, 'barely three months before the advance party left for the Frankish kingdom to prepare the way for the English mission'.[27] 'The mission to England', writes Ullmann, 'occasioned Gregory's protest. What the title meant was that the patriarch claimed universal jurisdictional power, the same claim that was enshrined in the *principatus* of the Roman Church. The envisaged extension of Christianity and the consequential exercise of the *principatus* of the Roman Church necessitated a sharp remonstration against the title claimed by the patriarch. In order to safeguard the claim of the Roman *principatus* towards the West, Gregory I was bound to protest vigorously to the East.'[28]

It is a powerful argument, which rests on the twin premises that the issue at stake in this conflict was a claim to jurisdiction; and that the pope's rejection of the patriarch's claim was chronologically closely related to the planning of the mission. Neither premise, however, can be sustained. To take the chronological link first: the title 'ecumenical patriarch' had, of course, a long history before this time and had been in regular use for more than seventy years before Gregory's pontificate.[29] Since the time of Justinian it had been a recognized part of the patriarch's official style, and the usage had been long known to Gregory, who was no stranger to the Eastern capital. This would, of course, give Ullmann's argument all the more force if in fact the pope

[26] Ullmann, *Growth*, p. 106. The description refers to Carolingian Christendom. For a similar view, see Bognetti, *L'età longobarda*, II, p. 230: 'un altro passo per la scissione della Chiesa di Dio della Chiesa di stato'.

[27] This seems to assume that the appointment of Candidus as *rector* of the Roman Church's patrimony in Gaul is to be interpreted as a preparation of the mission. This is possible, but it was probably primarily a part of the general patrimonial reorganization.

[28] Ullmann, *Growth*, p. 37. For the whole argument, see pp. 36-7.

[29] For a survey of the history of and controversy over the title, see S. Vailhé, 'Le titre de Patriarche Oecouménique avant saint Grégoire le Grand', and 'Saint Grégoire le Grand et le titre de Patriarche oecouménique', *Echos d'Orient*, 11 (1908), 65-9 and 161-71. On its meaning, see A. Tuilier, 'Le sens de l'adjectif oikoumenikos dans la tradition patristique et dans la tradition byzantine', *Studia Patristica* 7 (*Texte und Untersuchungen*, 92, Berlin, 1966), pp. 413-24, and F. Dvornik, *Byzance et la primauté romaine* (Paris, 1964), pp. 70-2.

had failed to make a protest until June 595. But in a letter written in
July 595 Gregory rehearsed the whole history of the controversy: his
predecessor Pelagius II had quashed the *acta* of a synod held at
Constantinople in 587 or 588,[30] on account of the 'unspeakable word
of pride', and had forbidden his representative in Constantinople to
communicate with the patriarch, John.[31] On succeeding Pelagius
Gregory protested, he tells us, verbally, not in writing, both on previous occasions through his representatives, and now through his
apocrisiarius, Sabinianus, who had been instructed to refrain from
communicating with John if the pope's protest went unheeded, and
already, in the preceding months, Gregory had been rebuked by
the emperor for his intransigence in this matter.[32] In other words,
Gregory's protest, far from coming out of the blue in June 595, was
one of an unbroken series, maintained throughout his pontificate and
continuing from his predecessor's. Gregory's Register contains only
two previous letters to the patriarch (if we leave aside the formal
synodical letter, I. 24, addressed to all the patriarchs, where pursuit of
a special dispute with one of their number would have been entirely
out of place). The first (I. 4) announces his election to the see of Rome,
and the absence of any remonstration here scarcely calls for comment.
The other (III. 52), written in July 593, concerned an Eastern priest
and a monk whose cause the pope considered not to have been satis-
factorily dealt with by the patriarch. The patriarch is bidden, with
some asperity, to obey the canons; but there is no mention, as there
might have been, of the offending title. This, however, is the only
occasion on which we might have expected mention of this affair in

[30] The date (3 July 595) is given by *Ep.* V. 41, i. 332: 'ante hos ... annos octo'. I am
not convinced that this refers to the council reported by Evagrius (*Historia ecclesiastica*,
VI. 7), though this is possible. See Caspar, *Geschichte*, II, p. 366, n. 4.

[31] *Ep.* V. 44, i. 339. 5-10; see also V. 41, i. 332. 3-11, and John the Deacon, *Vita
Gregorii*, III. 51.

[32] *Ep.* V. 44, i. 339. 10-14. For the emperor's rebuke, see *Ep.* V. 37, i. 323. 5, 18 seq.;
V. 39, i. 327. 8; and V. 45, i. 344. 17-20. Gregory's own account of the previous course
of the controversy is considered by Ullmann (*Growth*, p. 37, n. 3) and interpreted as
retrospective self-justification. There is no independent evidence to confirm Gregory's
own statements. It is clear, however, that the emperor's rebuke had reached Gregory
before 1 June 595 and that Gregory's protest must therefore ante-date the present
exchange of letters. Certainty beyond this is impossible, but I can see no grounds for
dismissing Gregory's assertion that Sabinianus's predecessors (though the plural may
be discounted) in the office of *apocrisiarius* in Constantinople had received instructions
from the pope on this matter (*Ep.* V. 44, i. 339. 11). Sabinianus took up office in July
593 (*Ep.* III. 51, i. 208. 1; III. 52, i. 210. 4). His commission included dealing with the
difficulties which had provoked *Ep.* III. 52 (see below), which he was taking with him.
There would be nothing unusual in his mandate including verbal supplementation of
the written documents he was charged to deliver. It seems to me highly likely that his
instructions included some remonstrations against the title, and it is not impossible that
verbal protests were delivered before this date.

any of the surviving correspondence; and even here, if Gregory, anxious to secure the patriarch's compliance on another specific matter, and from tact, not wishing to overstrain an old friendship, and perhaps in the hope of amendment on the matter in hand, preferred to keep his protest on a less formal verbal level, nothing could be more in keeping with his character. The conflict flared up in the next exchange of letters, the one we have been considering, of June and July 595, and, significantly, it had originated in exactly the same matter: Gregory had at last received the patriarch's long overdue report on the case on which he had been pressing him for satisfaction repeatedly over some years.[33] Now that the report was at last to hand, 'almost every paragraph',[34] as the pope complained, bristled with the offensive title. This was too much; Gregory's patience was fully stretched already; the much-resented reprimand from the emperor, which seemed so unjust to Gregory, the 'threat of barbarian swords',[35] the breakdown of his plans for peace with the Lombards (V. 36), the rapaciousness of officials, their tolerance of pagans and their oppression of the poor (V. 38), the malice of the exarch towards him (V. 40) and imperial connivance at a scandalously uncanonical episcopal election (V. 39)—all this, on top of his illness (V. 42, 43): why, it was all just too much, and Gregory's cup was overflowing. He had no time even for reading the Scriptures, among his many cares of the moment (V. 46). This was clearly no time for playing down the apocalyptic conflict with evil, for compromise and for tactful connivance with wickedness. He may have given up all hope of John's repentance; at any rate, his patience broke. I hardly think we need to invoke ripening plans for the English mission to explain why this moment should see his verbal protest harden into pained and formal written form.

The tension flared into crisis in the early summer of 595, and it may, indeed, be the case that the English mission was conceived in the apocalyptic mood of these months. But it is evident that Gregory's objection to the title was of long standing and not elicited by the project of the mission. In any case, however, his implacable detestation of the 'proud and pestiferous title' had nothing to do with the *principatus* of the Roman Church, and can therefore have no bearing on its westward extension. Whatever he thought the title meant, it was something that could not be claimed for the Roman Church any more than it could be claimed for Constantinople. Gregory tells us this in

---

[33] *Ep.* III. 52, i. 208. 13. The letters alluded to (which have not survived) evidently contained no protest against the title, though they may well have been accompanied by verbal protest (see above, n. 32).

[34] *Ep.* V. 45, i. 344. 14–16.

[35] *Ep.* V. 44, i. 343. 32–3; V. 42, i. 336. 13 seq.

the explanation he repeatedly gives of the grounds of his objection, most emphatically in a reply to a letter from the patriarch of Alexandria. He had been an old friend and supporter of Gregory's in his conflict with John the Faster, and had received the pope's recent request for support. In his reply he had called the pope, of all things, 'ecumenical patriarch'.[36] Evidently he had been anxious to please Gregory and to give him moral support, while, perhaps, less than painstaking in his efforts to understand what the dispute was about. Perhaps he thought the title was a meaningless honorific, or took it to involve some claim to jurisdiction; we cannot tell. At any rate, he was willing to oblige the pope by denying it to the patriarch of Constantinople, and—with supreme indifference to the pope's abhorrence— to apply it to the pope himself. His well-meant *faux pas* gave Gregory the occasion for his clearest exposition of the reason for his detestation of the title. The claim to universal bishophood implied in it undermines the proper standing of each and every bishop in his own church. What the Constantinopolitan claim injures is not, in the first place, Rome's *principatus*, but the status of each individual bishop—and that would be equally injured if Rome were to claim the offending title. Whatever it was that the patriarch was claiming for Constantinople, or rather, whatever it was Gregory took him to be claiming, it was something that Gregory rejected on behalf of Rome. What he was defending in this controversy, based as it was on ancient misunderstanding and a certain inflation of trivialities,[37] was the honour and the rightful status of each and every bishop, not the Roman *principatus*. That, too, had been a theme close to Gregory's heart throughout his pontificate.

There is no reason, therefore, for reading either the conflict with Constantinople over the title of 'ecumenical patriarch' or the sending of the mission to the English, linked or separately, in terms of a desire to 'emancipate' the papacy from its 'Byzantine captivity'. The vision of a Western Christian society subject to the *principatus* of the Roman Church and unrestricted by its subjection to the ecclesiastical establishment of the Byzantine Empire was not Gregory's vision. When he was requesting a Lombard queen to encourage her husband not to reject the *societas rei publicae christianae*, he was not inviting the Lombards to enter the orbit of a Western Christian society over which the Roman Church exercised its *principatus* unimpeded by its subjection to the Empire—an idea which Professor Ullmann has rightly charac-

---

[36] *Ep.* VIII. 29, ii. 31 seq. See also V. 41, i. 332. 25 seq.; V. 37, esp. at i, 322. 9 seq.; and IX. 156, ii. 157-8. A classic statement of the same principle is to be found in a totally different context as early as 592 in *Ep.* II. 52, i. 156. 36-41.

[37] It is evident that the matter also seemed trivial to Anastasius, patriarch of Antioch (*Ep.* VII. 24, i. 469. 18-20).

terized as 'the prophetic vision of medieval Europe'.[38] Gregory, however, was not dreaming prophetic dreams, but merely using standard
diplomatic terminology and urging the Lombards to keep a treaty
with the Empire. The *res publica christiana* meant for him, as for all his
contemporaries, the Christian Roman Empire ruled by the emperor
at Constantinople.[39] Gregory certainly had his differences with the
government over the policies to be adopted towards the Lombards.
Greater realism, or deeper pessimism, prevented him from sharing the
last vestiges of the hope of re-conquest which still lingered at the court
of the emperor Maurice, and he was prepared to envisage a permanent
Lombard settlement in Italy as a pastoral opportunity, not as an
ingredient in a Western Christian society alternative to the unity of
the Empire.

Roman Christians liked to think of Gregory as the foremost Roman
in a heavenly replica of their city: as *consul Dei*, in the words of the
epitaph they gave him. Gregory stood at the end of a process which
had transformed, over something like two hundred years, the traditions of Roman aristocratic self-consciousness into Christian terms.
The city had become a Christian Rome, and with its Senate gone, its
bishop now stood at its head, in earth as in heaven. But the *Europa* of
which Charlemagne came to be seen as the father two hundred years
later had not yet come into being; not even in Gregory's imagination.
When he, or his contemporaries, spoke of 'Europe', the word still bore
its ancient and geographically somewhat loose sense.[40] The development which was, by the end of the eighth century, to lead to a more
narrowly defined 'Europe'[41] still lay in a distant future. It is certainly
true that a very considerable part of Gregory's activity fell outside the
limits of the imperial Church, but nothing in his career suggests that

[38] Ullmann, *Growth*, p. 37, on *Ep.* IX. 67, ii. 88. 5–6.

[39] *Societas* here bears its well-established sense of peaceful association, secured by treaty.
See Eugippius, *Vita Severini* (31. 6), for an earlier, and Paul the Deacon, *Historia
Langobardorum* (IV. 27) (ed. L. Bethmann and G. Waitz, *MGH., Scriptores rerum lango-
bardicarum*, 125. 15), for a later example. The *res publica christiana* (or, sometimes, *sancta*)
is, as always, the Empire: see, for example, *Ep.* I. 73, i. 94. 2; VI. 61, i. 436. 24–5. The
usage is normal and identical with that of the submission of the Istrian bishops to the
emperor (*Ep.* I. 16a, i, 18. 5–7 and.29; i. 20. 1–2 and 17; i. 21. 4), and also the exarch's
letter (*Ep. Austras.* 40 (*MGH., Epp.* iii. 147. 4–5)). The phrase must clearly be translated
as 'treaty [or 'peace'] with the Empire'.

[40] *Ep.* V. 37, i. 322. 13 seq.; compare Columbanus, *Ep.* 1.1 and 5.1 (ed. W. Gundlach,
MGH., Epp. iii. 156, 170; ed. G. S. M. Walker, *Scriptores latini Hiberniae*, 2 (Dublin,
1957), pp. 2, 36).

[41] See R. Buchner, 'Kulturelle and politische Zusammengehörigkeitsgefühle im euro-
päischen Frühmittelalter', *Historische Zeitschrift*, 207 (1969), 562–83; H. Gollwitzer,
'Zur Wortgeschichte und Sinndeutung von "Europa"' *Saeculum*, 2 (1951), 161–72;
C. Erdmann, *Forschungen zur politischen Ideenwelt des Frühmittelalters* (Berlin, 1951), pp. 1–31;
H. Löwe, 'Von Theoderich dem Grossen zu Karl dem Grossen', *Deutsches Archiv*, 9
(1952), 353–401, repr. in *Von Cassiodor zu Dante* (Berlin, 1973), pp. 33–74.

he ever questioned either the ideological foundations or the daily realities of its institutional framework. On the contrary: as we have seen, missionary ideas derived from the political traditions of the Christian Empire had so powerful a grip on his mind that they were abandoned only after they had come into collision with newly dis-covered needs. In this respect Gregory's pontificate was no premature anomaly in the unquestionably imperial orientation of the papacy until well into the eighth century. Only then did anti-Greek feeling and a sense of alienation from the Empire gather momentum in Italy. Before that time there certainly was hostility to the government, though it never was more than sporadic, and stemmed from resent-ment of maladministration, fiscal exaction and, on occasion, of doc-trinal error; but it co-existed, paradoxically, with a strong conscious-ness of the continuance of a universal Empire as part of the established order of the world.[42] The sense of alienation from *the* Empire co-existing with the felt need for *an* empire, springing from the images deeply embedded in the way men saw their world ordered, produced a tension eventually resolved in the political ideology of the Donation of Constantine and the creation of Charlemagne's Empire. Of its significance for the papacy and its links with the Empire and with Western kingdoms no one has given us a finer account than Walter Ullmann: 'Charlemagne's coronation was, so to speak, the final and solemn and public act by which the papacy emancipated itself from the constitutional framework of the Eastern empire.'[43] The temptation to trace the process of this emancipation back to Gregory I should, however, be resisted. The parochialism of the Carolingian age, the readiness to see 'Europe' narrowed to the community of Western nations united under Roman *principatus* in a Christendom cast in Latin moulds—that was the creation of a later age. Papal perspectives were, indeed, to remain strikingly ecumenical for generations while horizons were contracting, in both East and West; and Gregory's 'Europe' had very far from split into two distinct spheres, whether they be charac-terized as imperial and papal, as Eastern and Western, or as Greek and Latin.

We have been looking at Gregory the Great's 'Europe': not, to be sure, at the Continent of Europe as it was in his day, but rather at the perspective in which he saw it. Gregory's 'Europe', like anybody else's,

---

[42] See D. H. Miller, 'The Roman Revolution of the Eighth Century: a study of the ideological background of the papal separation from Byzantium and alliance with the Franks', *Medieval Studies*, 36 (1974), 79-133; T. S. Brown, *Social Structure and the Hierarchy of Officialdom in Byzantine Italy, 554-800* (Ph.D. thesis, Nottingham, 1975; forthcoming), and the same author's 'The Church of Ravenna and the Imperial Administration in the Seventh Century', *Eng. Hist. Rev.* xciv (1979), 1-28.

[43] Ullmann, *Growth*, p. 99.

is a construct: the product of an experience refracted through the inevitably distorting medium of habitual assumptions. But a construct is not a private world. The real, public world is, to use the sociologists' phrase, a social construction, and we must think of Gregory's 'Europe' as one point on an arc whose radii converge towards a centre. *The 'Europe' of his time is an elusive and problematic entity, related in a variety of ways to the overlaps, the points of contact, the gaps between the perspectives in which his contemporaries saw their world.* Historians have only very recently begun to explore the changing perspectives of the later sixth century. The studies of Professor Averil Cameron,[44] to take only one example, are pointing towards a Europe undergoing profound shifts in its culture and spirtuality in the later sixth century. But significantly, her work has also shown something of the extent to which Western Europe was touched by the same tremors which were shaking the surface of Byzantine religiosity at this time. Much more work of this kind will be needed before we can take the measure of the extent to which Gregory and his contemporaries were still inhabiting the same world, as well as of the rifts that had opened or were beginning to open in it. Only then shall we be able to see Gregory's 'Europe' in its proper context; and I would dare to predict that it will turn out to be in every way closer to the Europe of Justinian that to that of Charlemagne.[45]

[44] See above, n. 2.
[45] It will be evident that I cannot claim Professor Ullman's support for my argument in this paper. I wish, however, to place on record my gratitude for his friendly and generous criticism which has helped me to avoid several pitfalls.

THE PARLIAMENTARY DIMENSION OF
THE CRIMEAN WAR[1]

By Professor J. R. Vincent, M.A.

READ 25 APRIL 1980

THE central issue in most wars is how to win. The central issue in the Crimean War was whether there should be a war. Throughout most of the war, the question of peace or war remained an open one, dependent on military prospects, diplomatic vicissitudes, and the shuttlecock of parliamentary faction. That British public opinion was hotly for war was interpreted by players of the parliamentary game only as meaning that it might become pacific with equal volatility.[2] The supposed political invincibility of Palmerston in 1855-6 had some reality outside Parliament, but little inside Parliament where it mattered. If events in Parliament varied in line with the war, it was also true that parliamentary prospects could affect the war.

The highly precarious and ambiguous nature of Palmerston's parliamentary regime in 1855 throws light on a number of other issues. Among these were what difference Palmerston made as a war leader; why he failed to convince the generals of his views on strategy and personnel; whether he envisaged a revolutionary war to reconstruct the map of Europe; and why there was no Crimean general election. Palmerston's attempt to dismantle Russia was certainly, as A. J. P. Taylor remarks, the most successful of its kind, but it was from first to last subject to the constraints of parliamentary manœuvre.

Palmerston's war was a success. It reduced Russia to exhaustion and achieved a humiliating peace. Its achievements were lasting. When Russia next attacked Turkey, she had to do it the hard way, by land, and not by means of naval supremacy in the Black Sea. Turkey has never again been in danger of becoming a Russian satellite. The Crimean War was a rare example of a war which achieved what it set

---

[1] I wish to thank the Broadlands Archives Trust and the Royal Commmission on Historical Manuscripts for permission to consult and quote from the Palmerston (Broadlands) Papers. I am indebted to Lord Clarendon for permission to quote from the Clarendon MSS. at the Bodleian Library, and to the Hon. Jacob Rothschild for permission to quote from the correspondence of Disraeli to Mrs. Brydges Willyams in his possession.

[2] Sir George Lewis, Palmerston's Chancellor of the Exchequer, thought not long before the fall of Sebastopol that the public 'before long will begin to tire of the war' (21 Aug. 1855) (*The Greville Memoirs*, ed. G. Lytton Strachey and R. Fulford, 8 vols., London, 1938, VIII, p. 153).

out to achieve. Yet historians, concentrating on the horrors of the first Crimean winter, have passed lightly over the more auspicious period under Palmerston.

Palmerston's distinctive contributions were few. He was no Churchill or Chatham. There was no 'blood, sweat, and tears', no Don Pacifico speech. He was neither a warlord, nor a resonant leader of opinion in wartime. He hardly spoke out of doors.[3] He was not an agitator for war, any more than Cobden and Bright were for peace. He was a parliamentarian and diplomatist concerned with managing undercurrents in the limited milieu in which he had spent his life. He resembled Churchill in sincere private aggressiveness and in not having a party at his back. Before entering into details, let us announce three themes: that his control of military operations was slight; that his dominance in Parliament was imperfect; and that his handling of diplomacy was excellent.

Palmerston was not expected by other politicians to stay the course. The reasons given were physical. He was seen not only as older than everybody else, but as much decayed. His teeth hindered his speaking; he appeared to maunder. This view of him was not only a political miscalculation, but was clinically wrong. Palmerston's diary for January 1855 dispels any doubts as to his vigour.[4] It shows him as leading a vigorous outdoor life in hard weather, hunting, shooting, and improving his estates. Far from being an old man huddled by his fireside, Palmerston's difficulty was to find outlets for his energy.

This problem remained during his prime ministership. During the session of 1855, Palmerston had nothing worse than 'a Touch of Gout in the Little Finger'. In spring and autumn he took on the work of the Colonial Office during vacancies. He also had an architect and builders at work on Broadlands during the summer of 1855. He took no holiday at the end of the session; kept a colt in training; looked after his business interests in Welsh slate; proposed to reform the Irish judiciary;[5] tried to set up a great Turner Gallery, to raise messengers' salaries, to rearrange the paths in London parks,[6] to save Smithfield

---

[3] Even his two outdoor speeches at Melbourne and Romsey, made to celebrate the fall of Sebastopol, were very minor affairs. At Romsey he did not even alight from his cab.

[4] National Register of Archives, Broadlands MSS. D/16 (diary for 1855). No diary for 1856 survives in this collection. The entries for the period of the ministerial crisis of 23 Jan.–7 Feb. 1855 have been printed in *W. E. Gladstone. III: Autobiographical Memoranda 1845–1866*, ed. J. Brooke and Mary Sorensen (H.M.C., *The Prime Ministers' Papers Series*, London, 1978), pp. 274–7.

[5] Palmerston to Carlisle, 29 May 1855 (B.L., Palmerston Letter Books). Palmerston argued that senile Irish judges must be made to retire, things being 'too scandalous to be allowed to continue'. '... If I mistake not, there are at least four wholly incapable.'

[6] Palmerston to Molesworth, 8 July 1855 (B.L., Palmerston Letter Books); Palmerston to Sir Benjamin Hall, 25 Sept. 1855 (*loc. cit.*), on redesigning paths in the interests of pedestrians.

market from redevelopment, to preserve the rights of landlords in Prince Edward Island,[7] and to secure promotion for a Dublin clergyman who preached common sense.

Though ably supported socially by Lady Palmerston, and continually present in the House of Commons, Palmerston for the first time in his career found himself without an executive or departmental function. The signs of underemployment are to be found in his relations with the service departments. Palmerston, who as Home Secretary under Aberdeen had been allowed to intervene in questions of defence, now found that an interfering prime minister commanded less respect than a pushing Home Secretary with a letter of resignation in his pocket. The Admiralty and the War Office effectively kept him out of the war. Only Clarendon wanted to be guided, and so Palmerston's role as premier came to lie very largely in guiding Clarendon. The more Palmerston applied his restive mind to sidelines, the clearer it became that he was not to control military operations.

Palmerston's impact in executive matters was mainly in matters like manpower, health, naval rearmament, and technical improvements. (He illicitly ordered a submarine on his own initiative, in defiance of the Admiralty.) He increased available manpower by a factor of nearly ten, doubled the navy, converted it to an emphasis on steam, gunboats, and mortar vessels, and got the death rate from illness down to peacetime levels. In such ways he usefully aided a recovery which was already under way when he took office. But, even with popular opinion behind him, he was unable to find a commander who was more than the least unsatisfactory; and he had to continue a strategy of which he disapproved. Palmerston, with a layman's belief in intelligence, did not believe in the assault on Sebastopol, and would have preferred to attack the Russians in an undefended position in the open field. He, Napoleon, and Prince Albert put their strategic heads together, but to no avail, their intentions being overruled by the men on the spot. Palmerston ended as the parliamentary manager of Pélissier's war of attrition.[8]

Palmerston would have liked to be, and would have excelled at being, a great prime minister winning a great war by means of 'new thinking', high technology, worldwide recruitment of troops, and an aggressive grand strategy culminating in a Waterloo somewhere on the Crimean steppes, and a Trafalgar which would have reduced Cronstadt to rubble. But, though this was not to be (even if it was in prospect late in 1855), there is a case for considering Palmerston

[7] Palmerston to Molesworth, 30 Aug. 1855 (*loc. cit.*); Palmerston to Labouchere, 19 Dec. 1855 (*loc. cit.*).
[8] For Pélissier, see B. D. Gooch, *The New Bonapartist Generals in the Crimean War. Distrust and Decision-making in the Anglo-French Alliance* (The Hague, 1959).

chiefly as a durable leader of the House of Commons. The war could not be won there, but it could have been lost there. Palmerston's feat was to mollify a disorganized House without giving status or position to the unofficial war party on the one hand, and without giving openings for a peace opposition on the other. In Parliament Palmerston had to put aside his normal executive personality, and invent a parliamentary identity which was flexible and capaciously open rather than energetic and committed. However much Palmerston in private might play the Harrovian bully who, from a deep geopolitical russophobia, sought to give 'the naughty Govt of Russia'[9] a 'good drubbing'[10] and 'as much Chastisement as he absolutely requires',[11] in the belief that the 'next Campaign will not be advantageous to the Ruskys',[12] in Parliament he faced attacks from all quarters and on all grounds, and had perpetually to modify his position accordingly.

In the spring of 1855, when the British forces might still have been driven into the sea, Palmerston at least left room for peace if necessary, by offering places to known peace men like Pakington, Stanley, Lewis, Laing, Carlisle, and the Peelites. Palmerston's cabinets were not put together on any basis of principle about the war; they were merely put together. Using the Vienna negotiations to dampen all issues and gain time, Palmerston's main danger in the spring came from a 'peace' combination by his rivals if the war did not improve. Faced with a 'peace' threat, he was peaceable, yet used his diplomacy to avert a peace which would have so affronted the war party as to bring his ministry to an end. In the spring, then, the only safe line was either to have no line, or rather to have two opposite lines at once. In May military confidence returned, the Derbyites changed their tune, and came out for a strong war line. Palmerston was thus enabled, and also forced, to come out in strongly warlike colours himself. This in turn, combined with military stagnation after the failure of the first attack on Sebastopol on 18 June, caused his challengers to drift back towards peace in the late summer. Russell is a case in point. Strongly bellicose in 1854, he would have played the great war leader in February 1855, but was denied the chance, and instead used the Vienna negotiations to establish himself as a man of peace. He again became warlike in the early summer, only to move towards peace in July and August, retreating to a more Palmerstonian position after Sebastopol. That victory was a Pyrrhic one for Palmerston. It forced him to modify his tone to meet possible opposition combinations, and to accept that if

[9] Palmerston to Clarendon, 5 June 1855 (Bodleian Library, Clarendon MSS.).
[10] Palmerston to Sir William Temple, 24 Dec. 1855 (Broadlands MSS.).
[11] Same to same, 7 Nov. 1855 (*loc. cit.*).
[12] Same to same, 24 Dec. 1855 (*loc. cit.*).

Russia wished to make peace on British terms she would have to be allowed to do so.

When Palmerston came to power, both supporters and enemies expected him soon to be overthrown.[13] His survival is perhaps the main fact of 1855 and 1856. The question is why the opposition made no united attack on the issues of peace in 1855 (and why it did not attack at all in 1856). Both questions are linked to the absence of that wartime general election which Palmerston had looked forward to on taking office. The cabinet considered dissolution seriously after Sebastopol, but thought it too high a card to play and so kept it in reserve.[14] Palmerston's renunciation of electoral glory in autumn 1855 suggested an intention to hold a plebiscite in 1856 on continuing the war, an intention which by its mere possibility dismantled any opposition ideas of a peace combination. Before the dictatorship of 1856 was reached, Palmerston had to surmount a whole series of hurdles which stretched from May to August 1855.

Palmerston took office as the avowed upholder of the foreign policy of Lord Aberdeen. He also inherited Aberdeen's coalition, and a war which might get worse as the campaigning season returned. Palmerston lay low throughout the spring, hedging both against military failure and against Russian acceptance of peace, both of which would have brought him down. The Vienna Conference occupied Russell, placated the Peelites, and isolated the Derbyites. Russell's re-appearance in Parliament on 30 April marked the beginning of a month of acute warfare.

The debates of May were the most important of the war. The fact that there was a strong war feeling in the country had as little to do with the parliamentary outcome as the fact that the war was getting nowhere. Palmerston, the Derbyites, and the Peelites all entered the debates with their positions undefined. Palmerston may claim credit for outwitting his assailants and for ending up in a position privately congenial to him.

Ellenborough's resolutions (14 May) were defeated 181–71, a sign of general Derbyite support for Palmerston in the Lords. The features of the debate were Ellenborough's bid[15] for one radical section by

---

[13] Gladstone told Palmerston that if he formed a ministry, 'he would certainly start it amidst immense clapping of hands, yet he could not have any reasonable prospect of stable parliamentary support ... He argued only rather faintly the other way, and seemed rather to come round to my way of thinking' (H. C. F. Bell, *Lord Palmerston*, 2 vols., London, 1936, II, p. 111).

[14] See Sir George Lewis to Palmerston, 18 Sept. 1855 (Broadlands MSS.), arguing that 'by dissolving now, we deprive ourselves of a great card which may be played next session, if the House proves intractable'. On 12 Nov. 1855 Sir George Grey wrote to Palmerston, 'Ellice too writes strongly for dissolution, but I think our decision upon that was right' (*loc. cit.*).

[15] *Parl. Deb.*, 3, cxxxviii, cols. 466–83 (14 May 1855).

attacking favouritism and mediocrity, and for the peace men by
denouncing the very idea of invading the Crimea as a strategic mistake
(a genuine quirk with him, although he was the shadow war minister[16]). Derby kept his options open by attacking the Aberdeen ministry, and no more, while ministers in reply avoided the question of
the war. By mid-May neither government nor opposition had shown
their hand.

Palmerston, speaking on 19 May, hovered between 'peace with
honour' and 'war with victory', waiting for others to commit themselves first. Whatever his private views, he was not publicly Palmerstonian. On 21 May, with a peace motion from Gibson pending,
S. Herbert asked after government policy. Palmerston said a compromise peace was still possible. The Peelites professed themselves
satisfied at having secured Palmerston for peace, and, anxious to avoid
connection with the Manchester men, they disbanded their attack.

Palmerston's apparent wobble towards peace paid good dividends.
It took in Disraeli, who leapt into the trap laid for him. With Palmerston open to attack as an appeaser, Disraeli had the field before
him as the champion of victory. Disraeli, scenting an ignominious
peace, therefore committed the Derbyites to a war policy, urging that
the time for negotiations was past. This suited Palmerston well. It
served to separate Peelites from Derbyites, to link the unpopular
Peelites with the more unpopular Manchester men, and to discourage
Russell from making a bolt for 'peace' by denying him numbers. The
war flag once nailed to the Derbyite mast, Palmerston had only to
slip back into a warlike posture to ensure temporary immunity from
Derbyite attack. Thus Palmerston's 'peace' hints of 19 and 21 May
allowed him, within the week, to become a red-blooded Palmerstonian.

Disraeli's views were as capacious as those of Palmerston. He was
not against the Vienna terms, had recommended an armistice, and
thought 'there really is no point to fight about. It is now a mere
question of military honour.'[17] Even while preaching war, he continued to seek peace votes by condemning the invasion of Russia as
a great error. But his speech of 24 May took the Derbyites beyond the
point where they could become the focus of a peace opposition. Co-

[16] Ellenborough had written a memorandum, dated 8 Aug. 1854, opposing the
invasion of the Crimea on strategic grounds. This document was given to Granville at
the close of the 1854 session by Ellenborough, with a request that it should be circulated
to the cabinet. This was not done, though Newcastle sent it to some military men.
Argyll retrieved it from Newcastle some time in 1855, with a view to using it to discredit
Ellenborough (Broadlands MSS.).

[17] W. F. Monypenny and G. E. Buckle, *The Life of Benjamin Disraeli, Earl of Beaconsfield*
(6 vols., London, 1910–20), IV, p. 3; Disraeli to Mrs. Brydges Willyams, 13 Apr. 1855
(New Court MSS.).

inciding as it did with a temporary military improvement, Palmerston was able to forget peace from late May to early July.[18]

The debates before Whitsun showed 'that the House did not wish to bring in Lord Derby'.[19] They also showed that the House supported war provided the war was going well. They did not show that a successful combination against Palmerston was unlikely, or that the House would patiently endure a fruitless war. Palmerston's majority on Disraeli's motion of 319–219 was impressive not as a vindication of a war policy for which he offered no rationale but banter, not as a sign that he had a majority party or a stable body of opinion at his back, but simply as testimony to his power to divide the opposition.[20] The Derbyite failure to lead a peace offensive while the war was still in the doldrums in the early summer was caused by the enticing mirage of a weak Palmerston which Palmerston perhaps deliberately held out to them.

The debate of 24 May was also important for the announcement by Gladstone, an enthusiastic supporter of the Crimean invasion the previous autumn, that the continuation of the war was against God's will.[21] The question then became whether Gladstone was the right man to put together a body of peace opinion, and, when it emerged he could not, whether he would find allies outside the Peelites. A second debate in the Lords, on 28 May, on a motion by Lord Grey, saw Derby come off the fence and commit himself strongly to a war of aggression, while his intimate, Malmesbury, attacked Gladstone violently. Palmerston had nothing to fear from Peelite–Derbyite rapprochement for the moment. As Cobden said, 'The language of ministers was one continual see-saw'; the see-saw, and not commitment or leadership, had created an invincible Palmerston who ruled without party and to some extent without colleagues. The final debate of early summer, that on Baring's motion (4 June), showed a sudden idealization of the war in resistance to the unpopularity of the Peelite 'auxiliaries of the Czar', while for the war radicals, Roebuck, not known for his flattery, praised Palmerston's steady purpose.

The government's strength was founded on the logic of faction, and that logic changed, not only in response to, but even in anticipation of, military events. In the short term, the opposition had to look for

---

[18] On 19 June 1855, the day after the failure of the first assault on Sebastopol, Palmerston wrote to his brother, Sir William Temple: 'I hope to hear before long that we have driven the Russians out of the Crimea' (Broadlands MSS.).

[19] Lewis to Sir Edmund Head, 10 June 1855 (*Letters of the Right Hon. Sir George Cornewall Lewis, Bart., to Various Friends*, ed. Sir Gilbert Frankland Lewis, London, 1870, p. 296).

[20] In debate ministers tended to evade the question of peace or war by pushing forward the merits of aristocratic government as a safe diversionary issue.

[21] *Parl. Deb.*, 3, cxxxviii, cols. 1036–75 (24 May 1855).

a side wind which might make criticism respectable. They found it in Administrative Reform. On Layard's (15 June) and Scully's motions (10 July), the government won by 359-46 and 140-125, but on both occasions Gladstone and Disraeli found themselves speaking on the same side. This was the beginning of the 'Gladstone–Dizzy coalition' of 1855. The debates on Administrative Reform did little to rock the Palmerstonian boat. They showed a recognition on the part of the opposition that, having failed to unite on peace in May, they must try to unite on something else. They showed parliamentary reluctance to become involved with middle-class agitation. They also showed that Palmerston's strength lay in large part in his resisting the spirit of the age. There were more votes in red tapes and routine, than in attacks upon them. A senior minister spoke rightly of having 'snubbed the Administrative Reformers ...'[22]

On 18 June, the first allied assault on Sebastopol failed disastrously. On 28 June, Lord Raglan died. Despondency was 'the greater because we had become so accustomed to success ...' July and August were months of gloom about the war for both government and opposition. Both Palmerston and Louis Napoleon were against the strategy of direct attack, but were overruled by their generals, Palmerston's own war minister conspiring to outwit him. This despondency seemed unlikely to take parliamentary form: 'people had made up their minds that the Session should close, and were going out of town very fast'.[23] Then Russell resigned.

The truth about Russell's motives is unlikely to come to light. His contemporaries thought his tactical ineptness could not be overrated, but that it went with a remarkable grasp of strategy. The normal view of the Russell affair is that, faced with malicious revelations from Vienna about his diplomacy in the spring, and in reply to an awkward question in the House, he blurted out an embarrassing truth. Sceptical Whigs saw things differently. One saw Gibson's awkward question as planted by Russell himself; two senior ministers thought the damning truths about Russell's commitment to peace were not truths at all, but concoctions; and Shaftesbury saw it as an attempt to lay claim to the leadership of the nascent peace party, calculating 'on a growing unpopularity of the war'.[24] The manner of Russell's going was painful—but it nearly destroyed the government; and in succeeding months, if one listens to what people were saying, one is told of a statesman ruined beyond repair, while if one looks at actions, one sees both opposition and government trying to draw closer to Russell.

[22] Sir Charles Wood to the third Earl Grey, 16 July 1855 (Grey MSS., Department of Palaeography, University of Durham).

[23] *Loc. cit.*

[24] Shaftesbury's diary, 5 July 1855 (Broadlands MSS.).

Rabid ambition, tactical ineptness, and an instinct for centrality went hand in hand in his conduct.

Russell left office free to take up either a 'war' or 'peace' line, having good credentials in both respects. Strategically cautious, as Disraeli and Gladstone were not, he stayed close to the centre of the political chessboard. He knew, everyone knew, that his departure had strengthened the Derbyites, shown the Palmerston government to be built on sand, and that he might step forward as the leader of the reversionary interest on any military failure. In August 1855 it looked as though Sebastopol might not fall. The Duke of Newcastle, on the spot, declared it invincible; Clarendon, Palmerston's closest ally, was in despair; Disraeli, Gladstone, and Russell saw no risk of success. A near defeat in a vote on the Turkish loan was only one sign of increasing loss of control. The guarantee, essential if Turkey were to stay in the war, was attacked by Gladstone, Disraeli, and Cobden, and passed by only 135–132 (20 July).

Roebuck's attack on the record of the Aberdeen ministry (17 July) also showed Palmerston's weakness. His evasion of the challenge by the device of putting the previous question (carried 289–192) was seen more as humouring than controlling the House. A feature of the debate was support of Russell by Bright, implying that if Russell were to form a 'peace' opposition, support would not be lacking.

Further indications that Russell's resignation had been a good investment for him came with Laing's peace motion of 3 August. Gladstone, negotiating in public, looked to Russell as a man of peace, and took a boldly defeatist view of the 'serious military reverse' of 18 June. Sniffing defeat in the air, he wanted Russell to sniff it too, and was in effect resigning the leadership of the peace party to him. Whatever Russell's real objects were is comparatively unimportant compared with those with which his fellow malcontents supplied him.

Faced with a possible combination of Disraeli, Gladstone, and Russell, Palmerston reacted in his usual way. While he benefited from having Gladstone as an opponent, he wished to eliminate the risk from the other two: Russell he treated in friendly manner, avoiding any sign of public rupture, and the Duke of Bedford, Russell's paymaster, was brought in to repair injured feelings.[25] With Disraeli Palmerston was more original. Just after Russell's defection, he proposed sending Disraeli to take over from Stratford in Constantinople; and he again touched on the idea just before the fall of Sebastopol.[26]

---

[25] *The Greville Memoirs*, VII, pp. 155–6, 160–3.
[26] Palmerston to Clarendon, 20 July 1855: '... if you wanted for Vienna or Constantinople a man of ability and not belonging to the present diplomatic Body, there is Disraeli ready to your Hand; and barring any little objection to the wife, I take it you could not have a better agent' (Clarendon MSS.). See also the same to same, 3 Sept.

On 7 August, Russell at last emerged.[27] He made gloomy military predictions, with an implied call for a compromise peace. (On 17 July he had left the question of an early peace open.) Russell, with transparent mischief, raised an issue which divided France from Britain, and both from Austria, and on which Gladstone had well-known views: the Papal States. Gladstone had bid for Russell on 4 August; now Russell was bidding for Gladstone, on a topic which no good protestant could oppose. Russell thus came to the end of the session with his options nicely balanced. If Sebastopol did not fall, he was poised to take over the movement for a compromise peace from Gladstone and Disraeli, who could not succeed on their own. If Sebastopol fell, then Russell would not have gone so far along the 'peace' road as to find himself in opposition to national euphoria. When Sebastopol fell, Russell readily found himself uttering Palmerstonian words.

When the session closed, Palmerston had not established himself. His support fluctuated from vote to vote. Russell retained a kind of mystic leadership of the Whig and Liberal party which seemed to survive all reverses. The opposition were biding their time, and thought their chances good, while Palmerston's supporters gave their adherence subject to conditions. As the Chancellor of the Exchequer put it at the end of the session: 'As long as our army remains in the trenches before Sebastopol, no Government can have any stability. Our domestic politics are entirely dependent on the events of the siege, as they occur from day to day.'[28] Or as Derby predicted at the time of the Russell crisis: 'I think the present state of things cannot go on. Palmerston may be able to save himself for a time by throwing Johnny overboard, but it will only be for a time.'[29] The government was a war government without victories; it had all the disadvantages of being a purely Whig concern, without the advantage of being a Whig party government based on secure and disciplined loyalties; and its leader's status was based largely on popular opinion, which parliamentary

---

1855: 'The only radical Remedy for this State of Things would be to bring Stratford away and send a better Man, Hamilton Seymour, or Disraeli or any other' (loc. cit.). The Russell revelations of early July 1855 removed the arguments for keeping Stratford at Constantinople in order to silence him. See Palmerston to Clarendon, 2 June 1855, arguing that if Stratford 'came home angry as he would do, he would furnish his friend and leader, Derby, with materials for attacking our Vienna policy, the concessions made by Lord John Russell, and one might find him as inconvenient at home as he is at Constantinople' (Clarendon MSS.).

[27] Parl. Deb., 3, cxxxix, cols. 1930–8 (7 Aug. 1855).

[28] Sir George Lewis to Sir Edmund Head, 17 Aug. 1855 (Lewis, Letters, pp. 297–8).

[29] Monypenny and Buckle, Disraeli, IV, p. 11, citing Derby to Disraeli, 11 (?12) July 1855.

logic made it necessary for him to resist rather than to mobilize. Back-benchers on the government side had a natural alternative leader in Russell; and cabinet ministers, while deploring his conduct, took pains to remain on good terms with this king over the water.

Derbyites and Peelites alike justified their weakness in hindsight by citing Palmerston's titanic stature and its firm base in the current mood.[30] They did not believe in either the stature or the mood at the time. Disraeli, for instance, was ready in late July to take office with a 'strong Government which will astonish the world. The men who are now at the helm cannot wield it any longer. It will not be necessary to upset them: they will fall by themselves.'[31] In late August he saw nothing but an 'ignominious peace in the offing'.[32] Even in early September, six days before the fall of Sebastopol, Disraeli could say, 'I see little prospect of anything happening.'[33] If Palmerston as a war prime minister resorted to every sort of transparent expedient in debate—to deliberate flippancy and banter, to patriotic rodomontade, to coarse personal abuse (suggesting Cobden should be put in an asylum)—it was not because he was a genial old humbug without views, but because in an uncertain military situation there was really very little he could say with safety at a serious level.

The fall of Sebastopol on 8 September was very necessary to Palmerston, but it led to his having to accept that he could stay in power only by accepting the policies of the opposition. Sebastopol was no Waterloo; half of Sebastopol remained, indeed, in Russian hands; and Palmerston's bright hopes of giving the Crimea to Sardinia or Turkey were soon dashed. Palmerston's eagerness for a further campaign in 1856 was soon, and rightly, either suspected or leaked. This produced, or was thought by Palmerston and Clarendon to have produced, 'a Treaty of Alliance between Dizzy and Co. and Gladstone and Co. ... The Coalition is to be founded on the Peace Principle.'[34] It was little consolation that the Derbyites were split, and that Russell was friendly, for Palmerston assumed the Derbyites would sooner or later vote on party lines *nolens volens*, and Russell's skill in defecting at the last moment from a position of friendliness could hardly be denied.

[30] I owe this argument to A. B. Hawkins, 'British Parliamentary Politics, 1855 to 1859' (University of London Ph.D., 1980)—an important study.

[31] Monypenny and Buckle, *Disraeli*, IV, p. 16, referring to July 1855.

[32] Disraeli to Lord Henry Lennox, 21 Aug. 1855 (*ibid.*, IV, p. 17).

[33] Disraeli to Mrs. Brydges Willyams, 2 Sept. 1855: 'There is a great pause in public events, and I see little prospect of anything happening' (New Court MSS.).

[34] Palmerston to Clarendon, 15 Sept. 1855 (Clarendon MSS.). See also Palmerston to Sir George Lewis, 16 Sept. 1855: 'I am told that Dizzy and Gladstone have concluded a compact upon the Peace Principle, and that this has produced a schism among the Conservatives, many of whom don't chuse to follow the devious footsteps of Dizzy, and it is said that neither Derby nor Stanley are with him' (B.L., Palmerston Letter Books).

Whether the 'Dizzy–Gladstone coalition' had even a prospective reality matters much less than that Palmerston, in the aftermath of Sebastopol, chose to behave as though he attached great importance to it. Sebastopol fell on 8 September; Palmerston announced the coalition on 15 September; on 16 September he declined an overture from France for continuing the war on Polish grounds.[35] Laying down his policy on Poland for the first time, Palmerston refused to provide France with a new and glamorous ideal which might have kept her in the war. France was war weary, Britain the reverse, yet it was Palmerston who in the aftermath of Sebastopol decided, as it now appears, that Russia should escape lightly. There were many vicissitudes between October 1855 and March 1856, and Palmerston, eager for war as he probably was, and certainly appeared to be, did not consent to peace readily. But, of all the chances open to him for keeping France in the war, there was never another so promising as the Polish card for maintaining French ardour. There were many reasons for this, some military, some diplomatic. One was certainly parliamentary. In September and October 1855, Palmerston, like other senior politicians, had his eyes fixed on a hypothetical peace amendment to the Address which all sections of the opposition, and probably many ministerialists would support. The impact of Sebastopol was that it made it possible to say without being unpatriotic that the war was over, and that Palmerston's evident wish to prolong it called for his parliamentary isolation.

If the peace coalition of the early autumn had continued until Parliament met in the New Year, Palmerston might well have been tempted to risk defeat and to take the issue to the country, where he would probably have been successful. Derby, however, perceived that if the opposition pursued an open interest in 'peace', this might give Palmerston the chance of launching a 'war' platform which he really wanted. On 25 October 1855, Derby forbade Disraeli's project for a 'peace' combination.[36] Disraeli, ever resilient, turned in November to 'Administrative Reform' as a substitute *cheval de bataille* for the coming session, with the evident intention of offering a programme which would unite Peelites, progressive Liberals, Russell, and the Derbyites.[37]

When Parliament met, neither Derby nor Palmerston gave a lead on the question of peace or war. Palmerston had neutralized the opposition, but at the price of adopting their policy and jettisoning

---

[35] Palmerston to Clarendon, 16 Sept. 1855 (Clarendon MSS.). This was the first time since becoming premier that Palmerston had discussed Poland with Clarendon or other senior ministers.

[36] Derby to Disraeli, 25 Oct. 1855 (Monypenny and Buckle, *Disraeli*, IV, pp. 21–2).

[37] *Ibid.*, IV, pp. 34–41.

his own. The circumstances created by the fall of Sebastopol had drawn the sting from both sides. Russell had continued to be tactically friendly, reminding Palmerston that he could take no risks with a rival who stayed too close to Palmerston's own position ever to be attacked by him, but whose mere existence exerted a kind of blackmail. When Russell toured the schools and hospital at Cheltenham, it was a reminder that Palmerston was weak about 'progress'.[38] When Russell addressed the Y.M.C.A.,[39] it was a reminder that he, and not Palmerston, embodied the Liberal tradition of civil and religious liberty. When Russell piously hoped that Britain and the U.S.A. 'would unite' in spirit, he pointed out a suitable ground for broadly based attack on Palmerston's adventurism. Even in a religious address, Russell's references to 'uninterrupted progress towards a far better social organization than any we have yet enjoyed' reminded the world that Palmerston was not likely to remain for long the normal leader of a Liberal party. It was a tribute to Russell that Palmerston's only social visit in 1855 was a well-publicized visit to Woburn a month before the session.

Palmerston's war of 1856 was one of the best wars that never took place. His war of 1855 was waged within unpredictable parliamentary constraints which were full of danger. His inability to get his hands on military operations, and the uncertainty of the French alliance, meant that his successes lay in linking an apparently aggressive private diplomacy to a mainly defensive parliamentary strategy. It is tempting, in retrospect, to see the aggressive diplomatic line (the price that 'opinion in the country' required) as real, and the parliamentary defences as mere cover. In fact both were real; he could not make an unpopular peace, and he had to survive in the parliamentary jungle in a war where both success and failure were dangerous. The Czar's best protection in 1855-6 was the unlimited fluidity of British parliamentary politics.

[38] *The Times*, 3 Dec. 1855.
[39] *Ibid.*, 14 Nov. 1855.

MILITANCY AND LOCALISM:
WARWICKSHIRE POLITICS AND
WESTMINSTER POLITICS, 1643–1647

The Alexander Prize Essay

By Ann Hughes, B.A., Ph.D.

READ 30 MAY 1980

I

MOST discussions of political divisions in the counties controlled by
parliament during the civil war have taken place within a very clear
framework. Following the work of Professor Everitt on the 'county
community', the main conflict is judged to have been between gentry
who sought to defend the integrity of the local community and those
who were prepared to sacrifice local autonomy to the needs of the
national struggle. Within this polarity, moderate or neutralist gentry
were the champions of localism while the more 'extreme' parliamentarians were nationally minded. Thus Mr. Pennington described how
'Localism, compromise and social conservatism opposed centralism,
militancy and Revolutionary Puritanism', while in *The Revolt of the
Provinces*, Dr. Morrill coupled 'conservatism and localism'. In one of
the most recent formulations, Professor Underdown wrote of 'the now
familiar conflict between nationally minded militants and locally
minded moderates [which] can be found in all the parliamentarian
counties'. Only Professor Holmes has challenged this consensus.[1]

It has been recognized that political conflicts in Warwickshire do
not fit this 'familiar' pattern. In 1643–44 a militant county committee
was apparently the upholder of localism, blocking all the efforts of
the Earl of Denbigh, the moderate commander in chief of the West

---

[1] A. M. Everitt, *The Local Community and the Great Rebellion* (Historical Association
Pamphlet, G. 70, London, 1969); D. H. Pennington, 'The County Community at War',
The English Revolution 1600–1660, ed. E. W. Ives (London, 1968), p. 73; J. S. Morrill,
The Revolt of the Provinces: Conservatives and Radicals in the English Civil War 1630–1650
(London, 1976), *e.g.* p. 120; D. Underdown, ' "Honest" Radicals in the Counties 1642–
1649', *Puritans and Revolutionaries: Essays in Seventeenth Century History presented to Christopher
Hill*, ed. D. Pennington and K. Thomas (Oxford, 1978), p. 191. C. Holmes (*The Eastern
Association in the English Civil War* (Cambridge, 1974), and 'Colonel King and Lincoln-
shire Politics 1642–1646', *Historical Journal*, 16 (1973), 451–84) emphasizes the inter-
relationships between local and national politics.

Midlands Association, to raise an effective army that could contribute to the wider war effort. The interpretations of this paradox are either that the committee's localism limited or contradicted its militancy, or else that its obstruction of Denbigh was merely a stratagem to defeat a political rival.[2]

I hope, however, that a detailed examination of the conflict between Denbigh and the committee will show that neither of these interpretations is correct: the committee's localism was a necessary part of its militancy rather than a contradiction of it. A further aim of this paper is to suggest that it is misleading to see divisions in Warwickshire simply as conflicts between localists and those who were nationally minded. Neither Denbigh's problems, nor the later moderate attacks on the county committee, can be explained in terms of a dichotomy between local and national concerns; rather, they reveal a more complex picture of a constant inter-relationship between local and national politics.

II

Basil Feilding, second Earl of Denbigh, became commander in chief of the associated counties of Warwickshire, Staffordshire, Worcestershire and Shropshire in June 1643,[3] in succession to Lord Brooke who had been killed at Lichfield in March. In contrast to Brooke, who had been a radical opponent of Charles I from his youth, Denbigh was an unlikely parliamentarian. As the nephew of the Duke of Buckingham, he had spent all his adult life in court service. His father had recently been killed at Birmingham, riding in Prince Rupert's troop of horse, while his mother remained the intimate friend of Henrietta Maria, a circumstance that was to cause her son some embarrassment. In the national politics of the 1640s, Denbigh followed a shifting course, although he usually contrived to end up, reluctantly and with qualifications, on the winning side. Widely regarded in the early 1640s as little better than a crypto-royalist, Denbigh nevertheless sided with the army and the more militant wing of parliament in the summer of 1647. Despite his part in the last-minute attempts to save Charles I in 1648, he sat on the Council of State until 1650 and was named to local committees throughout the Interregnum. The earl was one of the unashamed survivors of the mid-century upheaval, reappearing in 1661 to petition Charles II for repayment of debts he and his father had incurred in royal service before 1640, and asking the king to put

[2] R. Ashton, *The English Civil War: Conservatism and Revolution 1603-1649* (London, 1978), pp. 221-2, is one example.
[3] *C.J.*, III, pp. 121, 127.

a 'faire construction' on 'intermediate accidents and Revolutions of affaires'.[4]

In Warwickshire, however, Denbigh more consistently supported the view—shared by the leading non-royalist gentry—that the civil war should not be allowed to undermine the social hierarchy. He was reported as saying of committees, 'they are not borne to it', and in sharp contrast to the county committee he recruited many of his senior officers from the leading gentry. He tried to limit the extent to which political divisions undermined the solidarity of the county élite, intervening to secure lenient treatment for royalist neighbours like Viscount Conway and Sir Thomas Leigh.[5]

Denbigh had little in common with the men who formed the Warwickshire county committee. In 1642 the parliamentarians under Lord Brooke had taken control of the county despite the royalism or neutralism of most of the senior gentry. Brooke had relied on lesser gentry who shared his own radical religious and political views, and had gained significant support from the ranks below the gentry. After his death, Brooke's allies controlled Warwickshire through the county committee. From 1643 until the eve of the Restoration the dominant political figure in Warwickshire was William Purefoy, M.P. for Warwick, aptly described by the royalists as 'that old firebrand of those parts'. As a pre-war J.P., although never of the quorum, Purefoy was at least on the fringe of the county élite, unlike any other committeeman.[6] In a county where the dominant role in administration before the civil war had been played by gentry from southern Warwickshire, the membership of the county committee comprised minor northern gentry like William Colemore of Birmingham and Thomas Willoughby of Sutton Coldfield; Coventry merchants like John Barker and Thomas Basnet, and complete strangers. Indeed, two of the active committeemen, from a regular membership of about ten, were

---

[4] *D.N.B.*, VI, pp. 1151-3. For doubts about Denbigh's loyalty, see below, and P.R.O., SP. 18/3/103-04, accusations of 1644 but presented again by William Purefoy in 1649; for 1647, see *L.J.*, IX, pp. 351-74; for 1648-49, see Ashton, *English Civil War*, pp. 344-5; for attendance at the Council of State, see *Calendar of State Papers Domestic, 1649-1650*, p. lxxv; for nomination to local committees, see *Acts and Ordinances of the Interregnum*, ed. C. H. Firth and R. S. Rait (3 volumes, London, 1911), II, *passim*; for the petition to Charles II, see H.M.C., *Seventh Report*, Appendix, pp. 223b-24b.

[5] P.R.O., SP. 18/3/103; H.M.C., *Denbigh*, pp. 78-9 (Denbigh Civil War Letters (microfilm at Warwick County Record Office), vol. 1/96 (Conway)); B.L., Egerton MS. 785, fo. 58v; 787, fo. 80r (Denbigh to Sir Samuel Luke who farmed Leigh's Bedfordshire estates).

[6] For Brooke's seizure of power in 1642, see Ann Hughes, 'Politics, Society and Civil War in Warwickshire 1620-1650' (Liverpool University Ph.D. thesis, 1980), pp. 250-87; for William Purefoy, see *Mercurius Aulicus*, 2-9 December 1643, and *Quarter Sessions Order Book, Easter 1625 to Trinity 1637*, ed. S. C. Ratcliff and H. C. Johnson (Warwick County Records, vol. I, Warwick, 1935), p. xxiii.

Yorkshiremen: George Abbott, Purefoy's stepson, and Godfrey Bosvile, Brooke's stepbrother, who was Purefoy's fellow M.P. at Warwick.[7] The committee itself sat not in Warwick, the county town, but
at Coventry, a city that had traditionally kept aloof from the general
life of Warwickshire. Most of the committeemen active in 1643 served
parliament throughout the civil war. Warwickshire was not a county
where militants of lesser rank gradually pushed out moderate, established gentry; here such men dominated from the first, and the moderate challenges came later.

When Denbigh was appointed, the committee was busy repairing
the chaotic military and financial situation left to them on Brooke's
death. Brooke's association army had disintegrated after Lichfield
while the unpaid Warwickshire forces were mutinous and rapidly
deserting.[8] In the summer of 1643 the committee established a financial and military organization based on Warwickshire alone. By the
end of the year some 2,000 foot and 600 horse had been raised,
organized into three regiments commanded by the committeemen
William Purefoy, as Colonel of horse, and Barker and Bosvile as
Colonels of foot.[9] The forces were paid from the weekly tax imposed
by parliament in February 1643. The proceeds of this tax did not go
to the committee's treasurer; instead a system was developed whereby every captain of foot and every corporal of horse was assigned
a small group of parishes which provided pay for him and his
men.[10]

In many ways this organization was remarkably effective. As the
soldiers were collecting their own pay, and resorted to distraint if they
did not receive it, the proportion of tax collected was often as high as
90% and the arrears of Warwickshire soldiers were usually a matter
of weeks rather than months for service between 1644 and 1646.[11] The
good pay of the county's forces was envied by other commanders.
In April 1645 Edward Massey complained that 'our troupes daily
leave mee & now they see the Warwicke troupes soe well cloathed,
horsed and armed & soe well payed, I feare I shall not keepe one
quarter part of those I have'.[12] Warwickshire did not experience the

[7] Hughes, 'Politics, Society and Civil War', pp. 298-306.
[8] For the situation in spring 1643, see P.R.O., SP. 28/4/116 (notes of loans raised by
the committee to avert mutiny) and SP. 28/253B (examinations by the accounts sub-
committees of soldiers who had served at Warwick).
[9] P.R.O., SP. 28/121A (musters of the county forces, 1643-44).
[10] Acts and Ordinances, I, pp. 88-100; P.R.O., SP. 28/136 (the accounts of Major James
Castle (foot) and Captains Thomas Layfield and Richard Creed (horse), showing the
system at work).
[11] Based on an analysis of soldiers' accounts in P.R.O., SP. 28, and on P.R.O.,
E. 121 (certificates for the sale of crown lands which include details of soldiers' arrears).
[12] Bodleian Library, Tanner MS. 60, fos. 127-8.

conflicts between military and civilian authorities seen in many counties, for many of the committeemen served also as officers in the army.

The drawbacks to this organization are predictable. The understandable reluctance of the troops to move far from their source of income will be indicated below. The burdens imposed on the local population were extremely heavy. The sum officially levied on the county was £600 per week; this can be compared to the ship money levy of £4,000 in a year, but in fact nearer £1,000 per week was collected for much of the war.[13] Many local people suffered from quartering, plunder, forced labour and kidnapping, too, particularly if they lived near one of the county's many garrisons. George Purefoy, the unsavoury Governor of Compton House, addressed his warrants to the 'most malignant constable and towne of Tysoe' and ordered the inhabitants to work on his fortifications on 'paine of death'.[14] The close relationship between the committee and its soldiers meant that it was difficult to obtain redress for such suffering, especially as Quarter Sessions did not sit between 1642 and 1645.

Hence the committee was very unpopular. Two thousand people signed a petition of August 1644 in support of Denbigh despite the military dominance of the earl's opponents. All the non-royalist senior gentry signed this petition: men like Sir Simon Archer and Sir Henry Gibbes who had remained neutral in 1642, but also those like Thomas Boughton and William Combes who had supported Brooke in 1642 but had soon withdrawn from the parliamentarian leadership. The petition revealed the main objections to the committee's rule: the level of weekly tax; the heavy charges through quarter and plunder; the committee's sitting at Coventry rather than Warwick; and the impossibility of obtaining redress for such grievances when committeemen were also military officers. For the established gentry these grievances were exacerbated by their being imposed by obscure committeemen and even more obscure officers. Soldiers behaved in a 'harsh and insolent manner' towards gentlemen and freeholders while the committeemen were 'men of inconsiderable fortunes, others of little or noe estate, and strangers in our county and therefore cannot be sensible of our Burthens and payments'.[15] The degree of support gained by this petition, and the committee's failure to obtain the return of their candidates in the county 'Recruiter' election of October 1645, despite considerable military intimidation of the electorate,

[13] This total is estimated from surviving parish accounts and assessment orders of the committee in P.R.O., SP. 28.

[14] P.R.O., SP. 28/184 (parish accounts of Tysoe).

[15] For the petition, with signatures, see House of Lords Record Office, Main Papers, 21 August 1644.

indicates that opposition to military rule extended far beyond the leading gentry.[16]

This is to anticipate, however, for there is no sign of any immediate hostility between Denbigh and the committee. Rather, in the panic of mid-1643 induced by the fall of Bristol, the siege of Gloucester and the feeling that Coventry was next, the committeemen initially welcomed a powerful commander. In July they wrote to Denbigh, urging him to come down to Warwickshire and asking him to obtain additional supplies from Parliament.[17] Denbigh did not in the event reach Coventry until December 1643 and in the interim the position changed. Much of the delay was caused by doubts about Denbigh's political stance. In August the earl and his newly raised troops were hastily recalled from their march to the midlands when a letter from Denbigh's mother was intercepted, begging her son to 'leve thoys that murthered your deere father ... let me knowe and I shall make your way to your best advantage'. Denbigh vindicated his loyalty before the Committee of Safety, but further delays arose when he demurred at taking the Covenant.[18] In addition the county committee began to realize how the demands of the Association would affect their own embryonic military organization. Denbigh's troops, sent ahead from London, competed for scarce resources at Coventry and, lacking pay and senior officers, they became disorderly. In October, many were unilaterally disbanded by the committee, who informed Denbigh that it did not 'beleive your Lordship ment them a sole charge to this county who we conceived came down for the service of the Association'.[19]

This determination to put the needs of Warwickshire before those of the Association consistently characterized the committee's attitude towards Denbigh. Immediately on the earl's arrival in Coventry, the committee refused to accept his authority over the Warwickshire troops, claiming they were part of Essex's army. Thus, by virtue of a commission from Essex as Governor of Coventry, Barker was Denbigh's superior in the city while Purefoy's regiment was confined to Warwickshire by Major General Skippon's orders.[20] Denbigh's

[16] For the Recruiter election see *The Scottish Dove*, 7-12 November 1645, and *The Life, Diary and Correspondence of Sir William Dugdale*, ed. W. Hamper (London, 1827), p. 83.

[17] Bodleian Library, Tanner MS. 62, fo. 201.

[18] Denbigh Family Letters (microfilm at Warwick County Record Office), vol. 1/24, no date, but the most compromising of a series of reproachful letters, and very probably the one intercepted. For Denbigh's vindication, see *C.J.*, III, p. 226. For his doubts about the Covenant, see *ibid.*, p. 249. His stance was typical of 'peace party' adherents (Valerie Pearl, 'Oliver St John and the "Middle Group" in the Long Parliament, August 1643-May 1644', *Eng. Hist. Rev.*, lxxxi (1966), 497-8).

[19] Denbigh Civil War Letters, 1/33.

[20] *L.J.*, VI, pp. 325-6; Denbigh Civil War Letters, 1/13, 2/133-4.

attempts to relieve Shropshire were continually sabotaged by the committee. After long discussion, it was apparently agreed that Denbigh could 'call in the country' to raise horse, but when he went to Warwick to implement these arrangements, the committee sent a warrant after him authorizing voluntary contributions only.[21] Neither could Denbigh use any of the committee's best troops to help Shropshire; he was offered only 'broken companies ... of little use', the committee arguing that defence of Warwickshire and aid for Gloucester were the priorities.[22] Denbigh finally limped north from Warwickshire in late April 1644 with a few unpaid troops, raised through voluntary contributions, complaining of his usage in the county:

> 'Colonel Barker's troope, contrary to your Lordships order and my summons is gone the second time with Colonel Purefoy to Glocester, and with him another troope of Major Bridges, without my privity or consent, and if whole counties must be thus expos'd to ruine, and your Lordships orders neglected to maintaine persons (who have no great interest in this county, and lesse in theire affections) in that power and authority which is conferr'd upon me by ordinance of Parliament, I know not what can be expected but ruine and confusion to these parts.'[23]

III

The cooperation of the Warwickshire horse in the relief of Gloucester might suggest that the committee's localism was directed against Denbigh only. But although no other commander met 'localist' resistance to the same degree as Denbigh, the committee was usually reluctant to allow its forces out of the county. After much prompting from the Committee of Both Kingdoms, the county forces served with Massey and Waller in 1644 and with Massey and Brereton in 1645-46. Until the closing stages of the war, however, the troops were swiftly followed out of the county by appeals from the committee for their return.[24] It is unnecessary to assume an automatic loyalty to the local community in order to explain the committee's approach; certainly

[21] P.R.O., SP. 16/501/59 (Denbigh to the Committee of Both Kingdoms, 2 April 1644). See H.M.C., *Sixth Report*, Appendix, p. 8a (Humphrey Mackworth to Denbigh, 13 March, explaining the committee's attitude).

[22] P.R.O., SP. 16/501/75, 79 (Denbigh to the Committee of Both Kingdoms, 15 & 16 April).

[23] P.R.O., SP. 16/501/98 (the same to the same, 28 April).

[24] For examples see P.R.O., SP. 21/18, p. 103 (the Committee of Both Kingdoms to the Coventry committee, May 1644, urging it to allow its horse to stay with Massey); SP. 21/16, p. 94 (Waller to the Committee of Both Kingdoms, July 1644, complaining that Coventry wanted their troops 'home againe').

the Yorkshiremen on the committee, who were as localist as any, were unlikely to have felt such loyalties. In the first place, simple military commonsense dictated a constant concern for local defence in Warwickshire. The county was ringed by powerful royalist garrisons and parish accounts indicate that border areas paid contribution to royalist forces until the fall of Banbury and Lichfield in 1646.[25]

The committee's localism stemmed as much from political considerations, however. Holmes has suggested that radical and socially obscure parliamentarians tended to put national before local considerations because they owed their positions to the commissions of Parliament rather than to any power base in county society.[26] This was often true, but it assumes that only the gentry could provide such a power base, which was not necessarily the case during the civil war. The Warwickshire committeemen were radical and comparatively obscure, and had no standing with the gentry who had dominated the county before 1642, but they had won control because of the support they had received from the ranks below the gentry. Much of this support evaporated as ordinary people as well as gentlemen felt the burdens of war; but it survived amongst those who received rather than paid the local taxes—the county's soldiers. Here is the key explanation of the committee's general approach in which localism and militancy were coherent rather than conflicting parts. The committee's radicalism lost it any hope of local influence based on the leading gentry so its political control was dependent on military force. Indeed the committee was in a vicious circle because the more it enforced the taxation necessary to recruit and pay the troops, the more unpopular it became, and then the more reliant on the military for survival. It should be emphasized that the committeemen were not preying on a helpless county merely to preserve their own tyrannical power. They believed that 'they who are now assailed by neuters were those who in the first breaking out of the war saved the county from the cavaliers'.[27] From the committee's standpoint there was much justification in this view. Denbigh's political stance was open to question, as we have seen, while his gentry supporters had either shown no commitment to parliament before 1644 or had only briefly been active.

Denbigh's Association was thus met with particularly intense localist resistance because, unlike the loan of troops to Massey or Waller, it was a potentially permanent threat to the committee's own power

[25] For examples see the parish accounts of Grendon (P.R.O., SP. 28/183/18), Wishaw (SP. 28/185, fos. 390-401), Brailes and Priors Hardwick (SP. 28/184).
[26] Holmes, 'Colonel King', 483.
[27] H.M.C., *Sixth Report*, Appendix, pp. 27b-28a (the committee's Remonstrance to the parliament, 23 September 1644, in answer to the charges of the petitioners).

and possibly to parliament's whole control of the county. Several of the committee's officers accepted new commissions from Denbigh in the spring of 1644. In most cases this was probably just a precaution to ensure continued employment should circumstances in Warwickshire change,[28] but others seem to have switched for political reasons. When Captain Richard Turton joined Denbigh's army, his men lost the assignations which had kept them in constant pay for a year but Turton continued to serve the Earl.[29] Denbigh wrote that the Warwickshire committeemen acted 'as if they fear'd and apprehended nothing so much as my raising forces', and he was absolutely correct.[30] The committee's obstructions did indeed ensure that Denbigh never assembled an army that could threaten its control of Warwickshire or one that could be militarily effective. Denbigh's total receipts for his Association were £5,300, a sum the Warwickshire committee received in six months,[31] and the accounts of his officers make sad reading, especially when compared to those of the Warwickshire county forces. Colonel Edward Peyto's command, for example, lasted but two weeks, then[32] 'for want of further supply some of them ran away with horses and armes. And the rest, for the like reason, ... were dispersed under severall other comanders.'

The committeemen were not purely involved with local needs, however. They were aware of the demands of the national war effort, but because their resources were limited and their military and political position precarious, they were in a continual dilemma, performing a balancing act between local and national needs. This dilemma emerged clearly in the committee's relationship with Sir William Brereton in 1645-46. From October 1645 much of the Warwickshire horse served with Brereton in Cheshire, and from November the usual letters from the committee begged for the return of the troops, 'whose absence is the cause of such misery to this Country'. The postscript to one of the most pathetic appeals, however, read: 'if you judg theire stay necessary to the effecting yor present designe, let the issue bee what it will bee, wee shall consent to it', and the horse remained with Brereton until the end of the war.[33]

[28] An example is Captain Waldive Willington, Governor of Tamworth, who in the autumn of 1644 summarily ejected Denbigh's troops from his garrison (see P.R.O., E. 113/1/2 (Willington's account of his service, 1661), and B.L., Add. MS. 28,175, fo. 114r (*Collections for a History of Tamworth*)).

[29] H.M.C., *Denbigh*, p. 78.

[30] P.R.O., SP. 16/501/59.

[31] Denbigh's receipts (P.R.O., SP. 28/34/290); the committee's (SP. 28/247/2-3). The contrast is even greater when it is remembered that much of the money raised in Warwickshire did not go to the committee's treasurer but was received directly by the troops.

[32] P.R.O., SP. 28/136 (Peyto's accounts).

[33] B.L., Add. MS. 11,332, fo. 98r; 11,333, fo. 15r, (Brereton's letter books).

In this connection perhaps some qualification is necessary to the prevailing view that parliament had to overcome 'localism' to win the civil war.[34] Obviously major battles could best be waged by a nationally organized army, but much of the civil war was a war of attrition, with minor garrisons struggling for control of their immediate areas. In Warwickshire a purely local form of organization proved most effective for this type of war. In 1642–43 the county was dependent on handouts from London which were never sufficient; after 1643 the committee established a system which secured Warwickshire for the parliament despite royalist predominance in many of the neighbouring counties. The Committee of Both Kingdoms appreciated the need to conduct the struggle on both a local and a national level. In April and May 1645 the Committee bombarded Warwickshire with requests for troops to help Massey, to garrison Evesham, and to join a rendezvous at Aylesbury. Then Leicester fell and Coventry was urged to 'strengthen your guarisons'.[35] What the national authorities do not seem to have appreciated was that local resources were finite.

If the military localism of the committee was not absolute, discussion of the political aspects of its struggle with Denbigh also reveals the difficulty of separating local and national issues. Local developments do not fully explain Denbigh's failure to raise an effective army. The Earl of Manchester initially faced similar problems in the Eastern Association but, as Holmes has shown, by January 1644 Manchester had obtained legislative backing in parliament which enabled him to establish centralized control over the military and financial resources of his region.[36] Denbigh's ordinance of appointment gave him only vague powers and he suffered, too, from lukewarm backing from the Committee of Both Kingdoms.[37] Denbigh fully realized the need for more legislative power and he frequently pressed for an ordinance giving the same powers as Manchester had.[38]

[34] Morrill, *Revolt of the Provinces*, p. 55; Holmes, *Eastern Association*, p. 2.

[35] P.R.O., SP. 21/8, pp. 171, 285, 289; SP. 21/20, p. 320.

[36] Holmes, *Eastern Association*, pp. 89–108.

[37] See *L.J.*, VI, p. 92, for Denbigh's ordinance which specifically confirmed existing officers in their posts—a clause which the county committee exploited to the full in December 1643. In the spring of 1644 the Committee of Both Kingdoms agreed with the Warwickshire committee that the relief of Gloucester took precedence over Denbigh's Shropshire expedition and often showed impatience with the earl's complaints (P.R.O., SP. 21/18, pp. 60–1: the Committee to Denbigh, 12 April 1644).

[38] In May 1644 Denbigh complained to the Committee of Both Kingdoms that he could never be effective while the Warwickshire revenue was 'wholly and only disposed of by the Committee of Coventry' (P.R.O., SP. 16/501/125). In December 1643 he wrote to 'Mr Moore' (probably John Moore of Liverpool) asking him to consult with John Wilde of Worcestershire and Michael Noble of Staffordshire about the passing of a new ordinance (Bodleian Library, Tanner MS. 62, fo. 402).

There were two main periods in which these disputes in Warwick-shire were intimately related to parliamentary politics. In November and December 1643 both Denbigh and the committee appealed to Westminster to settle the question of Denbigh's power to command Barker and Purefoy. Partly because of the slipperiness of Denbigh's personal politics, but mainly because of the fluid and confused nature of groupings in parliament, local and national divisions do not dove-tail in any clear-cut way. Rather, the adversaries in Warwickshire manipulated national political divisions, seeking backing wherever they could. In the summer of 1643, the military setbacks suffered by parliament had encouraged the more radical members of the Com-mons to attack the authority of the Earl of Essex and to support the creation of armies independent of him. Waller was initially the main beneficiary, but Denbigh and Manchester to some extent owed their commands to these moves. More moderate members—the 'middle group'—attempted to combine conciliation of Essex with support for other commanders, in the interests of military efficiency, while less political members supported commanders who would help their par-ticular region.[39] Thus at Westminster in 1643-44 the local moderate, Denbigh, was backed by radical M.P.s like Sir Peter Wentworth and John Wilde,[40] while the radical county committee appealed to Essex and the House of Lords. As an M.P., William Purefoy was increasingly identified with a 'war party' that was suspicious of Essex, but as a local committeeman he headed the signatories of a letter to Essex in which the committee disingenuously claimed that Denbigh's attempt to command Purefoy and Barker was 'derogatory to your Excellency's Power'.[41]

Hence the attitudes of the two Houses were not as might be ex-pected. The Lords saw Denbigh's command as a threat to Essex and, at a conference with the Commons on 2 December 1643, they wanted to write abruptly to Denbigh to ask 'why he did protest against Mr. Purefoy's submitting to the Lord General's command'. But most of the Commons were anxious to preserve unity and to promote a variety of military forces: the diarist Whitaker reported, 'we thought fit only

[39] J. H. Hexter, The Reign of King Pym (Cambridge, Massachusetts, 1941), pp. 118-32; Ashton, English Civil War, pp. 109-10; Pearl, 'Oliver St John and the "Middle Group"', pp. 494-5.
[40] Wentworth took Denbigh's ordinance for raising £6,000 to the Lords on 20 June 1643 (C.J., III, p. 137). For Wilde see above, n. 38. Throughout this essay, information on the national political affiliations of M.P.s is taken from D. Underdown, Pride's Purge: Politics in the Puritan Revolution (Oxford, 1971), Appendix; Lotte Glow, 'Political Affilia-tions in the House of Commons after Pym's Death', B.I.H.R., xxxviii (1965), 48-70, and Lotte Mulligan, 'Property and Parliamentary Politics in the English Civil War', Historical Studies, 16 (1975), 341-61.
[41] L.J., VI, p. 321.

to write unto the Earl of Denbigh to understand the truth of those things'. The Commons did not want to send the committee's complaints on to Denbigh, 'lest it cause some further distemper that would not easily be appeased'.[42] The support Denbigh received in the Commons was half-hearted, however. He remained politically suspect and was never conspicuous for military skill. An ordinance empowering him to execute all the money-raising measures previously passed was given a second reading on 2 November 1643 when, according to Whitaker,[43] 'which Commission, being thought too large, it was recommitted'. The ordinance never emerged from committee although the powers it gave Denbigh were no greater than those given Manchester.

After his experience in Warwickshire and the other counties of his Association, Denbigh decided in July 1644 on a concerted attempt to improve his position in a campaign conducted on the local and the national levels. In Warwickshire a petition was organized by Denbigh's allies.[44] We have seen above how the petition revealed the discontent in Warwickshire with the nature and personnel of the committee's administration, but the petitioners also called for 'all possible Encouragement' to be given to Denbigh and his Association, asking that the Earl be given control of the revenue raised in the county.[45] In Warwickshire it was thus the moderate or neutralist gentry who were most anxious to see the county involved in the wider war effort, but from motives entirely consistent with their political stance, for they regarded the local troops as the prop of an oppressive, upstart committee.

Denbigh opened his campaign with a Remonstrance against his opponents, presented in the Lords on 3 August 1644, while the Warwickshire petition was delivered on 21 August, once again to the Lords.[46] It is worth emphasizing, in view of the accepted picture of civil war conflicts, that this second resort to the national arena was initiated by the moderates in Warwickshire. There are two main reasons for this: in the first place, Denbigh and his allies were being out-manœuvred on the local level; but secondly, it was clear that it was the moderates who had local popular opinion, if not military strength, on their side: only Denbigh's allies could conduct a credible

[42] *C.J.*, III, pp. 326-8; *L.J.*, VI, pp. 320-1; B.L., Add. Ms. 31,116, fo. 98r (Laurence Whitaker's diary of proceedings in the House of Commons). The conflict of authority became bogged down in a committee that never reported (*C.J.*, III, pp. 335, 337, 352; *L.J.*, VI, pp. 324-6, 335-6, 354).
[43] B.L., Add. MS. 31,116, fo. 89r; *C.J.*, III, p. 298.
[44] Denbigh Civil War Letters, 2/20 (Thomas Leving to Denbigh, 23 July, on the organization of the petition).
[45] House of Lords Record Office, Main Papers, 21 August 1644.
[46] *L.J.*, VI, pp. 651-4.

petitioning campaign in the counties. In defending themselves against Denbigh's charges, the committeemen had to rely on allies in the Commons and on militants on the committees of Shropshire and Staffordshire who had also fallen foul of Denbigh. A series of Remonstrances answered the specific charges against them and, in turn, accused Denbigh and his supporters of 'neutralism'.[47]

This second period of parliamentary concern with Warwickshire is interesting also because it reveals how national politics had shifted since the previous winter, although there was still no absolute correspondence between local and national divisions into radicals and moderates. The House of Lords was now firmly behind Denbigh: the criticisms of aristocratic generals in the autumn of 1644 meant that Essex, Manchester and Denbigh were now allies rather than rivals.[48] Thus William Purefoy argued strongly on 14 August that Denbigh's accusations against the county committee should be dealt with by a committee of the Commons alone, not one that included the Lords. When it was clear that the mood of the House was against this, Purefoy and Bosvile moved, unsuccessfully, for the matter to be deferred, and not committed at all.[49] On 8 November the Lords accepted all the conclusions of the committee of both Houses which reported in Denbigh's favour.[50]

In the Commons, though, Denbigh's support had declined, especially amongst the more militant members. When the Commons were informed of the Lords' votes of 8 November, D'Ewes reported that the 'war party' adherent, William Strode, 'did very impudently condemne the house for referring it at first to a Committee of Lords and Commons . . . for now they saw the fruit of it, with some more of such unsavoury stuff'.[51] On 20 November the Commons devoted most of the day to the Denbigh's committee's report and held four divisions on the affair. All but one of the tellers against Denbigh were probably identified with the more radical wing of the Commons; they included

---

[47] House of Lords Record Office, Main Papers, 3 August 1644; H.M.C., *Sixth Report*, Appendix, pp. 27b-28a. The Warwickshire committee claimed it had not organized a counter petition because it would increase divisions, but its lack of popular support caused some derision in the Commons. D'Ewes described Purefoy's delivery of a counter petition to a Staffordshire petition with 3,000 signatures calling for Denbigh's return to the midlands, 'pretending to be the petition of Staffordshire, Shropshire and Warwickshire but that proved false in the issue for it was a private petition made in Towne here, framed by some nine persons' (*C.J.*, III, p. 646; B.L., Harleian MS. 166, fo. 126v (D'Ewes' Journal of the House of Commons), 30 September).

[48] M. Kishlansky, 'The Creation of the New Model Army', *Past & Present*, 81 (1978), p. 58.

[49] B.L., Harleian MS. 166, fo. 107r.

[50] *L.J.*, VII, p. 51.

[51] B.L., Harleian MS. 166, fo. 153r.

Sir Peter Wentworth, a supporter of Denbigh in 1643.[52] Denbigh's allies were a more heterogeneous group, mainly moderates like Sir Philip Stapleton and Sir John Potts, but also more militant members like Sir William Strickland.[53] Regional considerations were important here: some members who wanted a more effective army in the north-west still supported Denbigh. In August John Moore of Liverpool had been the chief opponent of Purefoy's attempt to exclude the Lords from the committee to discuss the disputes in the Association. He is usually identified with the 'war party', but here he argued on regional grounds: the obstruction of Denbigh in Coventry 'was the cause of losse in Cheshire'.[54]

In general the Commons seem to have seen little point in rehabilitating Denbigh's Association on the eve of military reform, although many M.P.s wished to avoid condemning him. When the Commons considered the Lords' vote that Denbigh was cleared of any 'breach of the trust reposed in him', the division over whether the question should be put passed by just one vote; on the substantive motion a majority of fifteen voted that Denbigh was not so cleared; while the decision that he should not be sent back to his Association passed without a division.[55] Finally, in an attempt to conciliate the Lords, the Commons tactfully resolved that 'this house is of opinion that the Earl of Denbigh is deservedly employed upon the service of going with the propositions for a safe and well grounded Peace to his Majesty'.[56]

IV

Denbigh's Association thus received its death blow at the national level. The conflict illustrates how local disputes became tangled up with national politics as adversaries in the counties sought reinforcement for their local positions from parliament. What is not found is any necessary correspondence between local divisions and groupings at Westminster. However, the links between local and national issues became clearer at the end of the war with the revulsion against county committees and all their rule implied. It was a commonplace in 1645–

[52] C.J., III, p. 700. The tellers were Strode, the younger Vane, Wentworth, Sir Henry Heyman, Sir Robert Pye and William Heveningham. Pye was a very moderate member and little is known about Heveningham's views at this time, although he was to sit in the Rump.

[53] C.J., III, p. 700. The tellers were Stapleton, Potts, Strickland, Henry Darley, Simon Thelwall and Robert Reynolds.

[54] B.L., Harleian MS. 166, fo. 107r. For the importance of regional considerations, see Mulligan, 'Property and Parliamentary Politics'.

[55] C.J., III, p. 700. There is a tradition that the first vote only passed because some of Denbigh's supporters were at dinner (Ashton, English Civil War, p. 222).

[56] C.J., III, p. 700.

47 that the tyranny of county committees was worse than anything
suffered in the 1630s: 'every Committee is a Star Chamber, a High
Commission', declared one pamphleteer.[57] Such views were current
in Warwickshire, as is shown in a sermon preached in December 1646
by the Coventry minister, John Bryan, a supporter of the committee:

> 'we are displeased and murmur at taxes and Impositions whereat
> we should not quarrel seeing we enjoy our lives, Liberties, Privileges,
> Estates and Religion (all which were at stake and almost lost), for
> so great a Difference is there betwixt these Taxes the Parliament at
> present imposeth and those which formerly our Taskmasters laid
> upon us. Those were in design to ruine and enslave us to Arbitrary
> power, these are to preserve us from it.'[58]

After Denbigh's eclipse the attacks on the county committee were
led by the sub-committees of accounts which sat at Coventry and
Warwick. All the accounts committeemen had been supporters of
Denbigh while the Warwick committeemen were senior gentry of
conspicuously higher status than the county committeemen. With
great industry the sub-committeemen hunted down financial irregu-
larities in the work of the county committee and its officers, and
showed an almost fanatical concern to draw up details of all the
charges imposed on the county since 1640.[59] They wished to lessen
the burdens brought by war and to ensure that orderly, legal procedures were followed, even where royalists were concerned. Predictably, these attitudes led to bitter conflict with the county committeemen who felt, with Bryan, that it was worth while sacrificing traditional procedures to win the war. It is not possible to follow the local
course of these conflicts here; rather I am concerned to highlight the
links with national developments.

Professor Ashton has argued that such conflicts were, in part, a
conflict between localist county committees and sub-committees
which, as the subordinates of a London committee, were a 'very
important agency of centralised control'.[60] This again suggests that
moderates were as likely as militants to be 'nationally minded', for in

[57] *England's Remembrancer of London's Integrity or Newes from London* (London, 1647),
p. 17; *cf.* Colonel King's view of the Lincolnshire committee (Holmes, 'Colonel King',
p. 467). For a modern criticism of committee rule see Morrill, *Revolt of the Provinces*,
pp. 52–3, 64–6, 73–80.

[58] John Bryan, *A Discovery of the Probable Sin* (London, 1647), p. 3.

[59] For a full discussion of the Committee for Taking the Accounts of the Whole
Kingdom and its local sub-committees, particularly in Warwickshire, see D. H. Pennington, 'The Accounts of the Kingdom', *Essays in the Economic and Social History of
Tudor and Stuart England in Honour of R. H. Tawney*, ed F. J. Fisher (Cambridge, 1961),
pp. 182–203; see also, Hughes, 'Politics, Society and Civil War', pp. 383–93.

[60] Ashton, *English Civil War*, pp. 276–7.

Warwickshire, as in many other counties, the sub-committees represented a classic moderate position, attempting to restrict the upheavals
brought by civil war.[61]

It is difficult, though, to fit such conflicts into any framework that
opposes local to national concerns. Both sides in Warwickshire automatically appealed to London for help: the sub-committees complained of the obstructions of the county committee in letters to their
London committee and to sympathetic local M.P.s. Thomas Boughton, one of the Recruiter knights of the shire and a long standing
opponent of the county committee, was the main recipient of such
complaints, while Purefoy and Bosvile continued to act as the defenders of the county committee at Westminster.[62]

Purefoy and Boughton were not simply involved in a factional
struggle for the control of one county but represented two profoundly
different attitudes to the prosecution of the war. The intimate connections between local and national concerns become clearer after
1645 as the House of Commons became increasingly separated into
two organized 'parties' divided on the same lines as men were locally.
From the spring of 1646 Holles and the 'Presbyterians' followed a
national policy similar to that of the accounts committees in Warwickshire and other counties: they wanted financial reform, the disbanding of military forces, and in general sought to limit the disruption
caused by war.[63] The struggle between 'Presbyterians' and 'Independents' focused on supposedly 'local' issues like the composition of
committees and the disbanding of county forces, as well as on attitudes
to the New Model or to settlement with the king.[64] M.P.s like Thomas
Boughton began with specific experiences of the arbitrary actions of
obscure committeemen, but when these experiences were voiced in

---

[61] Lincolnshire and Somerset are examples (Holmes, 'Colonel King', pp. 474–5;
Morrill, *Revolt of the Provinces*, pp. 69–70).

[62] For appeals from the sub-committees of accounts to London, see P.R.O., SP. 28/
254/5, fos. 70r, 99v, 108v, 122r, 130r. Boughton often attended the Committee for
Taking the Accounts of the Whole Kingdom when the misdeeds of the Warwickshire
county committee were under discussion (SP. 28/252 (Order Book of the Accounts
Committee), pp. 2, 195). Bosvile and Purefoy transmitted the county committee's
objections to many of the newly nominated accounts committeemen in 1644 (*ibid.*
(Warrant and Letter Book of the London Accounts Committee), fos. 10r–v).

[63] M. Kishlansky, 'The Emergence of Adversary Politics in the Long Parliament',
Journal of Modern History, 49 (1977), 617–40.

[64] Divisions concerning Warwickshire support Professor Underdown's view that such
issues were approached on party lines, rather than Dr. Morrill's argument that there
was no clear correspondence between local and national issues (Underdown, *Pride's
Purge*, pp. 38–9; Morrill, *Revolt of the Provinces*, pp. 122–4). See, for example, the votes
on whether there should be an addition to the county committee (November 1646)
and on whether Coventry should be 'disgarrisoned' (March 1647) (*C.J.*, IV, p. 722;
V, p. 104; Holmes, 'Colonel King', 481–2).

the Commons they became generalized into an attempt, on principled grounds, to abolish such committees altogether.[65] The Lords gave three readings to an abolition ordinance in August 1646, while the majority in the Commons agreed that it was essential to 'bring things into the old course and way of government' and gave two readings to an ordinance removing the arbitrary power of committees in February 1647.[66]

Parliament's function as a blender of local into national issues is well known, but in the 1640s the press, too, acted as a generalizing mechanism. Many newsbooks must have had good sources for provincial information, for they carried detailed accounts of local incidents that can be confirmed from other sources.[67] On the other hand, newspapers provided for a provincial audience an account of parliament's proceedings as well as examples of parallel experiences in other counties. Many newsbooks attacked county committees in 1646-47; one of the most virulent was the *Scottish Dove* which often publicized the misdemeanors, real and imagined, of the Warwickshire authorities. In May 1646 the *Dove* described how Major George Purefoy had ridden into a tree in Hyde Park, knocking himself out and losing a hat decorated with diamonds worth £150. Thus in two sentences Purefoy's corruption and his incapacity as a cavalry officer were suggested. The *Dove* also called for the abolition of county committees and commented in January 1646 that 'no committees of counties ... do as good service as Committees for accounts, which other Committees seeke to obstruct'.[68]

In 1647 the issue of county committees was overshadowed by the conflict over the New Model, while in 1648 the committees were needed to organize local defence during the second civil war. Although the Rump limited the powers of committees, in general the Purge was decisive in local as in national events, confirming the supremacy of militant parliamentarians in the counties. One of the casualties of the Purge was the militia ordinance of 2 December 1648 which attempted to return local government to the traditional élite.[69]

---

[65] B.L., Add. MS. 31,116, fo. 305v, gives an example of Boughton's criticisms of the Warwickshire county committee (March 1647).

[66] *L.J.*, VIII, p. 474; *C.J.*, V, p. 85.

[67] The Warwickshire Recruiter election is one example. For the use of the press by rivals in Lincolnshire, see Holmes, 'Colonel King', 455, n. 20, and 457.

[68] *Scottish Dove*, 13-20 May 1646, 21-29 January 1646. See also *Weekly Account*, 20-27 January 1647, and *Perfect Occurrences of Everie Daie Journall in Parliament*, 9-16 April 1647. There were also many specific satires on county committees like *The Poore Committee-man's Accompt* (London, 1647) or the play by Samuel Sheppard, *The Committee-Man Curried* (London, 1647).

[69] The militia ordinance was repealed on 15 December 1648 (*Acts and Ordinances*, III, pp. lxv-lxvi).

Thomas Boughton was imprisoned by Pride while William Purefoy and Godfrey Bosvile became prominent 'Rumpers'.

It would be invidious to attempt definitive conclusions on the basis of one county's experience. However, this account of Warwickshire politics suggests that the current picture of civil war conflicts should not always be accepted. 'Localism' as an active policy, rather than a mere sentimental loyalty, was not an automatic reflex on the part of the county gentry but an approach that served particular ends. In many areas it was the moderate gentry whose aims were best attained through a localist stance, but in Warwickshire the militant parliamentarians, out of military and political necessity, were the localists while the moderate gentry, for equally valid reasons, supported a wider approach to the conduct of the war. The local–national dichotomy itself may not be the only fruitful way of examining the disputes of the 1640s. Provincial disputes almost automatically became caught up in national conflicts as local rivals sought allies at Westminster, and vice versa, while by the end of the war there was much political and ideological coherence between the divisions in parliament and those in the counties. The widespread attacks on military dominance and committee rule were not only localist phenomena but part of a national campaign conducted in parliament and the press.

THE PROBLEM OF POPULAR ALLEGIANCE IN THE ENGLISH CIVIL WAR*

The Prothero Lecture

By Professor David Underdown,
M.A., B.Litt., F.R.Hist.S.

READ 2 JULY 1980

THE belief that the common people of England had little real sympathy for either side in the civil war—that they were mere cannon-fodder, targets for plunder, at best deferential pawns—has a long and respectable ancestry. Many of the combatants believed it, noting the automatic changes of local attitudes when news came of distant victories or defeats. In postwar politics too they knew it was 'safest to be in favour with the strongest side'.[1] When they fought, it was because they had no alternative. How often, Anthony Ascham lamented, 'ambitious or angry men forme subtilties and pretences, and afterwards the poore people (who understand them not) are taken out of their houses . . . to fight and maintaine them at the peril of one anothers lives'.[2] Survival on the margin of subsistence was the universal motive. 'The people,' Sir Arthur Haselrig declared, 'care not what Government they live under, so as they may plough and go to market.' Looking back after 1660, men as various as Hobbes and Baxter took the same line. 'There were very few of the common people that cared much for either of the causes, but would have taken any side for pay or plunder,' Hobbes tells us. Baxter has been as often quoted: 'The poor plowman understood but little of these Matters; but a little would stir up their Discontent when Money was demanded.'[3]

* The research on which this paper is based was begun with the help of a grant from the American Council of Learned Societies, and is currently supported by one from the National Council for the Humanities; both are gratefully acknowledged. I am also indebted to Ms Susan Amussen, Dr. John Morrill and Professors Clive Holmes and Lawrence Stone for their helpful comments on an earlier draft.

[1] B.L., T[homason] T[racts], E. 346 (10): *Scotish Dove*, no. 144 (22–31 July 1646). For examples of local reactions to changing military fortunes, see *The Letter Books 1644-45 of Sir Samuel Luke*, ed. H. G. Tibbutt (London, 1963), pp. 304, 306.

[2] Anthony Ascham, *Of the Confusions and Revolutions of Governments* (London, 1649), p. 144.

[3] *Diary of Thomas Burton*, ed. J. T. Rutt (London, 1828), III, p. 257. Thomas Hobbes, *Behemoth or the Long Parliament*, ed. F. Tönnies and M. M. Goldsmith (London, 2nd edn. 1969), p. 2. *Reliquiae Baxterianae*, ed. M. Sylvester (London, 1696), p. 17.

From all this we might naturally conclude that the lower orders of rural England participated in the war only if compelled to do so, and that, left to themselves, their behaviour would be determined by a localist, community-centred neutralism. That neutrality and localism were among the common denominators of popular politics in the 1640s is undeniable: recent historians have done much to illuminate them.[4] Even the gentry, with their broader horizons, often tried to stay out of the conflict. Both sides had sworn to uphold the Protestant religion, Jonathan Langley remarked, 'what reason have I therefore to fall out with either?'[5] If the gentry regarded disputed national issues as less pressing than the preservation of good order and community, it would be absurd to expect their inferiors to see things differently. The cry of the Wiltshire countryman, 'Yt were noe matter yf the Kinge and Queene and all were hanged unles the price of corne doe fall', comes from many years before the wars, but the 1640s abound with similar expressions of popular agnosticism. When the Sherborne Royalists demanded of a suspected spy which side he was for, the answer was easy: for both.[6]

For most people survival was bound to take precedence over a choice between two remote, only half-relevant ideologies. Free quarter and plundering, these were the realities, not the echoes of distant arguments about episcopacy and the militia. The worst situation was to be caught in the middle between rival garrisons. A newsbook recounts the plight of villages near the Northampton–Oxfordshire border in 1645:

'When Banbury men come to gather their money, they observe a time when their Enemies of Northampton are at home, then they come in, and with a loud cry, say, where are these Roundheads? wee'll kill them all for raysing money of you, you shall pay to none but us: when Banbury men are gone, then comes the other party, where are the Cavaliers? wee'll kill them all, you shall pay to none but us, we will protect you; but hardly in a year doth the one interrupt the others collections.'[7]

---

[4] The starting-point is A. Everitt, *The Community of Kent and the Great Rebellion 1640–60* (Leicester, 1966). Besides many other valuable local studies, see especially J. S. Morrill, *The Revolt of the Provinces* (London, 1976).

[5] 'The Ottley Papers relating to the Civil War', ed. W. Phillips, *Trans. Shropshire Arch. and Nat. Hist. Soc.*, 2nd ser., vii (1895), 264.

[6] 'Extracts from the Records of the Wiltshire Quarter Sessions: Reign of King James the First', ed. R. W. Merriman, *Wilts. Arch. Magazine*, xxii (1885), 33. A. R. Bayley, *The Great Civil War in Dorset 1642–1660* (Taunton, 1910), p. 46.

[7] B.L., T.T., E. 298 (17): *Moderate Intelligencer*, no. 26 (21–28 August 1645). For the impact of plundering, see also I. Roy, 'England Turned Germany? The Aftermath of the Civil War in its European Context', *T.R. Hist. S.*, 5th ser., xxviii (1978), 127–44.

'You cannot but know how terrible troopers are to country people,' Sir Samuel Luke reminded a fellow officer. Luke's own troopers knew it, too, as they listened to the neighbourhood mutterings and feared that they 'may rise and cut our throats, if an enemy approach'.[8] Soldiers could be persuaded to behave by a determined authority-figure, as the lady of the manor, Elizabeth Wheate, showed at Glympton in Oxfordshire in 1648. But she had not done it alone: 'I perceived thay are affraid of the countrey lest thay should rise one them,' she told her absent husband.[9]

So here we have one widespread view of civil war allegiance, or rather the absence of it: that the common people were essentially neutral, moved primarily by the impulse to protect home and community from plundering soldiers and tax-gatherers. But there was another, and still familiar, assumption. It is the constant refrain of Clarendon's *History of the Rebellion*: that the people were overwhelmingly parliamentarian, largely through envy of the rich and, in the towns especially, out of a 'natural malignity' derived from hatred of authority. Spurred on by the preachers, there arose that 'fury and license of the common people, ... that barbarity and rage against the nobility and gentry'.[10] Rival propagandists might differ on the motives underlying this popular support for Parliament, but most agreed that it existed, among both the broad social groups to be considered in this paper: the respectable 'middling sort', and the propertyless poor. Royalists tended to emphasize their enemies' dependence on the latter element, to dismiss them as a mutinous rabble intent only on lining their pockets. Thus in 1642 Hertford explained the great rising which drove him out of Somerset as having been assembled by the promise of plunder, 'as rifling of the Palace of Wels doth make manifest'. After the second civil war, the anonymous historian of the siege of Colchester concluded that 'under cover of zeal to the cause, the poore levelled the rich of both parties'.[11] In the years between, the theme was incessantly repeated. Conservative Parliamentarians took the same cynical, or frightened, view of their followers. In the riots along the Essex–Suffolk border in 1642 the Earl of Warwick's secretary, Arthur Wilson, noted that the mob claimed to be attacking the houses of

[8] *Letter Books of Sir Samuel Luke*, pp. 291, 514-15.

[9] *Glympton: The History of an Oxfordshire Manor*, ed. H. Barnett (Oxfordshire Rec. Soc., V, 1923), pp. 58-9.

[10] Clarendon, *The History of the Rebellion*, ed. W. D. Macray (Oxford, 1888), *passim*, esp. II, pp. 226, 318. See also Christopher Hill, 'Lord Clarendon and the Puritan Revolution', in Hill, *Puritanism and Revolution* (London, 1958), pp. 199-214.

[11] B.L., T.T., E. 118 (31): *A Declaration Made by the Lord Marquesse of Hartford* (12 Aug. 1642). H.M.C., *12th Report, Appendix IX* (Beaufort MSS.), p. 28.

Catholics: 'They made that their pretence, but spoyle and plunder was their ayme.'[12]

Officially, Parliament was more sanguine about the quality of its supporters. Baxter's familiar picture of the sober, godly 'middling sort' ranged against the corrupt gentry and godless poor has been immensely popular with later historians. His version of the alignment echoes that of many parliamentarian writers and is a central feature of much of Parliament's wartime propaganda.[13] The central assumption is that Parliament's cause is that of reason and religion, and that its typical adherents (yeomen, freeholders and craftsmen) are literate, rational and religious. The deluded countrymen on the King's side, it was supposed, would be susceptible to rational arguments if only they were exposed to them, at any rate the 'better, and more understanding sort': hence the persistent use of the anti-Catholic line, intensified when the King brought over Irish troops in 1644, and the sermons to royalist prisoners.[14]

But the preaching often fell on deaf ears, and the respectable freeholders showed a distressing tendency to ignore their rational interest—to mutiny or run away. Even this awkward fact could be squared with the belief in a parliamentarian middling sort. John Vicars excused the massive desertions before Sherborne in September 1642 because many of the volunteers 'having Wives and estates, were loath to loose or hazard them in such an apparently difficult and obscure way'; others noted that they were prudently afraid of retaliation by royalist landlords.[15] The Committee of Both Kingdoms had long experience of the problems caused by citizen soldiers, 'men of trade and employment', regularly sending them home after representations by county committees. Early in 1645 Myddleton's forces on the Welsh border were reported to be 'much wearied', many of them being 'of the Yeomandry and Husbandmen of the Country'

[12] Arthur Wilson, 'Observations of God's Providence', in *Desiderata Curiosa*, ed. Francis Peck (2 vols., London, 2nd edn. 1779), II, p. 474.

[13] *Reliquiae Baxterianae*, pp. 30–3. See also, for example, John Corbet, 'A True and Impartial History of the Military Government of the Citie of Gloucester', in *Somers Tracts*, ed. Sir W. Scott (London, 2nd edn. 1809–15), V, pp. 302–7; T. May, *The History of the Parliament of England, which began November 3, 1640* (Oxford, 1854); John Rushworth, *Historical Collections* (7 vols., London, 1659–1701). The most uncompromising recent exposition of the 'middling sort' argument is by B. Manning, *The English People and the English Revolution 1640–1649* (London, 1976).

[14] B.L., T.T., E. 4 (1): *A Continuation of Certain Speciall and Remarkable Passages*, no. 4 (24 July–1 Aug. 1644). The use of the Irish issue in parliamentarian propaganda is discussed by Joyce L. Malcolm, 'The English People and the Crown's Cause, 1642–1646', Brandeis University Ph.D. thesis, 1977, ch. 6. Preaching to royalist prisoners is stressed in B.L., T.T., E. 309 (24): *Scotish Dove*, no. 109 (12–19 Nov. 1645).

[15] John Vicars, *Jehovah-Jireh, God in the Mount* (London, 1644), p. 146. See also Manning, *The English People*, p. 233.

who had 'estates of their owne, which must needs sometimes be lookt unto'.[16]

*   *   *   *

Neither of these versions of popular behaviour is entirely satisfactory. The first—localist neutralism—requires us to believe that both sides in the civil war relied on impressed men, half-hearted militia forces, and the reluctant dependants of peers and gentry, supplemented in Parliament's case by a few zealous Puritans, mainly from London. The second—middling-sort parliamentarianism—at least explains how Parliament got an army, but not how the King managed to do so, except by adding to the aforementioned categories levies from Ireland, Wales and other 'dark corners of the land'.[17] Both explanations assume that large numbers of men were coerced into fighting for causes in which they had no interest. Yet there were contemporaries who doubted this. 'Plentifull experience teacheth,' a newsbook proclaimed in 1644, 'that none but Volunteers doe the work on both sides.'[18] It is fairly clear that some parts of England were more parliamentarian, some more royalist, than others, and that these differences did not always coincide with the loyalties of the local élites. There therefore appears to be room for further investigation of the subject.

This paper summarizes the progress of part of such an investigation, focussing on the counties of Dorset, Somerset and Wiltshire. In the course of an attempt to chart the geographical distribution of support for King and Parliament respectively, some tentative suggestions about the determinants of popular allegiance will be offered, along with some even more tentative suggestions about grass-roots perceptions of the conflict. The inherent difficulties are all too obvious. Sources like memoirs and correspondence are often maddeningly uninformative and always full of pitfalls for the unwary. Newsbook accounts of campaigns sometimes provide clues to popular involvement, but are inevitably coloured by propagandist intentions. Petitions, regularly proclaimed as evidence of popular support, have been shown to be highly misleading.[19] Still, granting all the difficulties, the

[16] B.L., T.T., E. 269 (14): *A Diary, or an Exact Journall*, no. 39 (6-13 Feb. 1645). Examples of similar statements by the Committee of Both Kingdoms are in *Cal. S. Papers Dom., 1644*, pp. 346, 366.
[17] For a recent argument on these lines, see Joyce L. Malcolm, 'A King in Search of Soldiers: Charles I in 1642', *Historical Journal*, xxi (1978), 251-73.
[18] B.L., T.T., E 44 (14): *A True and Perfect Journall*, no. 2 (30 April 1644).
[19] Everitt, *Community of Kent*, pp. 86-7, 271-2. J. S. Morrill, *Cheshire 1630-1660: County Government and Society during the English Revolution* (Oxford, 1974), pp. 46, 53. Luke often expresses scepticism about petitioning. (*Letter Books of Sir Samuel Luke*, pp. 145, 279, 281, 291.)

historian using conventional tools—common sense and a critical approach to sources—can obtain at least a general impression of group
behaviour in the civil war.

One further caution is necessary. It has often been pointed out that
only the finest of lines separated the moderates of the two sides; that
even among the élite, allegiance was often largely accidental, a reluctant response to immediate circumstances such as the temporary local
predominance of one party or the other.[20] If this is a wise caution for
historians of gentry politics, it is doubly so for one attempting to
analyse the lower orders. Adam Martindale was among those who
'would have been quiet and meddled on no side', but with his brother
Henry fled to the parliamentarian camp to avoid impressment by the
Earl of Derby's officers. Servants and labourers, on the other hand,
had virtually no defence against such pressure. Denying that he had
ever borne arms for the King, friends of George Hemynge admitted
that 'his servants were compelled soe to do as most of the Cittie of
Worcester did'.[21]

*　　*　　*　　*

Neutralism, localism, individual circumstance: all must be
accepted. Yet people fought and killed one another in England in the
1640s, with greater readiness for the King in some areas, for the
Parliament in others. I have argued elsewhere that in the greatest
popular movement of the entire civil war, the outward neutralism of
the Clubmen concealed distinct local differences in their attitudes to
the two sides. The 'parliamentarian' Clubmen came from the wood-
pasture textile region of north Somerset and north-west Wiltshire, and
from the pasture lands of west Dorset and the Somerset levels; the
'royalist' Clubmen came from the nucleated villages of the chalk
downlands and the adjacent region of Blackmore Vale.[22] The question
remains whether this pattern prevailed, not only in 1645, but throughout the war.

The regional contrasts are clear enough. The northern dairying and
textile area was characterized by relatively dispersed settlements, weak
manorial structures, rapid population growth, high rates of migration
and vulnerability to food shortages in bad harvest years. Between

[20] D. H. Pennington, 'County and Country: Staffordshire in Civil War Politics, 1640-
44', N. Staffs. Journal of Field Studies, vi (1966), 15. See also Morrill, Cheshire, p. 74, and
Morrill, Revolt of the Provinces, p. 46.
[21] The Life of Adam Martindale, ed. R. Parkinson (Chetham Soc., IV, 1845), pp. 31-2, 35:
P.R.O., S.P. 20/12 (Sequestration Committee papers (Certificate on behalf of George
Hemynge, 4 Jan. 1647)).
[22] D. Underdown, 'The Chalk and the Cheese: Contrasts among the English Clubmen', Past & Present, no. 85 (1979), 25-48.

1590 and 1640 population pressure in the Wiltshire 'cheese' country
led to a marked increase in the proportion of small landholders,
and to corresponding increases of both internal and out-migration.
Recurrent food shortages provoked riots, repeated petitions to the
J.P.s, and anxious appeals to the Council. Beset by depression in the
cloth industry and by the disruptive impact of disafforestation, the
wood-pasture region was the scene of constant instability and disorder.[23] The downland villages of south Wiltshire and Dorset were
very different. Physically compact, with few detached farms and hamlets, they tended to occupy parishes of smaller size. Manorial controls
remained strong: as late as 1780 it was noted that in this area 'very
few manors have been dismembered'. Like the dairy country, the
downlands had been affected by the growth of a market economy,
and by the consequent trend to partial enclosure.[24] But through it all,
the bonds of neighbourhood, institutionalized in church and manor
court, ritualized in village feasts and revels, seem to have survived.
The fielden villages were both more stable and less individualistic
than those of the pasture lands.[25] This dualism does not exhaust all
the community types that existed in the three counties—we shall find
elements of both field and pasture in Blackmore Vale—but it is a
sufficient preliminary to a review of the civil war experience of the
region.

The war in the three counties reveals a probably familiar impression
of the distribution of allegiance.[26] Most of the gentry, when forced out
of the neutrality they would undoubtedly have preferred, supported
the King, though there were prominent exceptions: Erles and Tren-
chards in Dorset, Horners and Pophams in Somerset, Bayntons and

---

[23] E. Kerridge, 'Agriculture c. 1500–c. 1793', in *V.C.H.*, *Wiltshire*, IV, ed. E. Crittall
(London, 1959), pp. 43–64; A. Salerno, 'The Social Background of Seventeenth-Cen-
tury Emigration to America', *Journal of British Studies*, xix, no. 1 (1979), 31–52; G. D.
Ramsay, *The Wiltshire Woollen Industry in the Sixteenth and Seventeenth Centuries* (Oxford,
1943), chs. 5–6; E. Kerridge, 'The Revolts in Wiltshire against Charles I', *Wilts. Arch.
Mag.*, lvii (1958–60), 64–75; D. G. C. Allan, 'The Rising in the West, 1628–1631', *Econ.
H.R.*, sec. ser., v (1952–3), 76–85. Morrill, *Revolt of the Provinces*, pp. 102–3.

[24] William Camden, *Britannia*, ed. and enlarged by Richard Gough, I (London,
1806), p. 138; Kerridge, 'Agriculture c. 1500–c. 1793'. For an illustration of capitalist
farming in arable Wiltshire, see 'The Note Book of a Wiltshire Farmer in the Early
Seventeenth Century', ed. E. Kerridge, *Wilts. Arch. Mag.*, liv (1951–2), 416–28.

[25] L. Stone, *The Family, Sex and Marriage in England 1500–1800* (London, 1977), p. 143.
For a doubtless idealized account of a downland village, c. 1700, see 'A Document from
Great Cheverell', ed. H. C. Brentnall, *Wilts. Arch. Mag.*, liii (1949–50), 430–40.

[26] The following summary is based mainly on Bayley, *Civil War in Dorset*; D. Underdown, *Somerset in the Civil War and Interregnum* (Newton Abbot, 1973); *Memoirs of Edmund
Ludlow*, ed. C. H. Firth (2 vols., Oxford, 1894), I, pp. 439–81 (Appendix of documents);
and G. A. Harrison, 'Royalist Organization in Wiltshire, 1642–1646', London University Ph.D. thesis, 1963.

Hungerfords in Wiltshire. Parliament's greatest strength lay unmis-
takably in the northern clothing district near Bath and Chippenham,
with the addition of a few other clothing or port towns such as
Taunton, Wellington, Dorchester and Lyme. The northern region
rose overwhelmingly to drive away Hertford's Cavaliers in August
1642, was hostile to Hopton's army in the following year, and rallied
strongly to Fairfax in 1645.[27] Evidence of the places of origin of
Parliament's soldiers is scanty, but it seems likely that they were drawn
heavily from the clothing parishes. Royalists commonly assumed that
this was where their enemies came from. After the fall of Wardour in
May 1643 a hostile observer sneered that the Roundheads sold off
lead piping from the castle at 6d. a yard, 'as these men's wives in
North Wiltshire do bone-lace'.[28]

The arable areas provide a striking contrast. Through all the sieges,
the skirmishes, the marches and counter-marches, downland Dorset
and south Wiltshire shared (or followed) the neutralist or mildly
royalist bent of the gentry. When the Royalists gained control after
the taking of Bristol in July 1643 they could enlist popular support
only in the downlands, this being the only part of Wiltshire where
their Oath of Association was effectively imposed. Until the emergence
of the Clubmen there was nothing in this region to rival the parliamentarian rising of 1642, but a few signs of popular royalism can be
detected: at Blandford, for instance, and in the participation of downland villagers in the attempt on Weymouth in February 1645.[29]

The contrast is, of course, too simple, for neither neutralism nor
royalism was confined to the downlands. The Somerset levels show
few signs of attachment to either side before the Club rising, while the
thinly populated hill country to the west was royalist throughout. And
the mixed farming country of south-east Somerset—from Bruton south
to Yeovil and on into Blackmore Vale in Dorset—was almost as
consistently for the King.[30] The situation is further complicated by
the drastic changes of attitude that accompanied military reversals.
Taunton and Dorchester well deserve their Puritan reputations, yet
in 1643 both promptly surrendered to overwhelming force. Everywhere the initial enthusiasm for Parliament quickly waned as the
realities of war sank in; not until 1644, after the King began employing

[27] Underdown, 'Chalk and Cheese', 37–9. The behaviour of south Gloucestershire
was very similar (I. Roy, 'The English Civil War and English Society', *War and Society,
A Yearbook of Military History*, ed. B. Bond and I. Roy (London, 1975), pp. 35–41).
[28] *Ludlow*, I, p. 450.
[29] Harrison, 'Royalist Organization', pp. 243–7. Bulstrode Whitelock, *Memorials of
the English Affairs* ... (4 vols., Oxford, 1853), I, p. 179. W. B. Barrett, 'Weymouth and
Melcombe Regis in the Time of the Great Civil War', *Proc. Dorset Nat. Hist. and Antiq.
Field Club*, xxxi (1910), 212–13.
[30] Underdown, 'Chalk and Cheese', 45–6.

Irish troops, did Parliament regain the popular initiative.[31] Yet none of this refutes the contention that Parliament's greatest appeal was to the inhabitants of the clothing towns and the northern wood-pasture parishes. When circumstances permitted, they supported Parliament; when circumstances did not, they kept quiet. Even when he personally orchestrated a propaganda campaign in the area in 1644, the King had little success with them.

All this, however, is totally impressionistic. Is there any way of plotting more exactly the distribution of allegiance in these counties, for example by statistical methods? Alas, there is not. But it is possible to determine the geographical origins of some of the men who served in the King's army. The availability of recruits cannot necessarily be correlated with the allegiance of a given area, but since some evidence of royalist recruiting exists it is worth examining it. As in all statistical exercises using seventeenth-century sources, the attempt to do even this is fraught with technical hazards. Nevertheless, some interesting conclusions emerge.

Under an act passed in 1662, the J.P.s of each county were required to pay small pensions to indigent royalist ex-soldiers.[32] Somerset's pensions cannot be studied because of a gap in the Quarter Sessions records during the crucial years before 1666. But for Dorset and Wiltshire petitions and orders for pensions are plentiful, involving 815 individuals from identifiable places in Dorset and 327 from Wiltshire.[33] The much larger number of pensioners in Dorset, a smaller county, at once raises doubts about the completeness of the Wiltshire records, but in fact the contrast is explained by the different policies followed by the two county benches. The Dorset justices were less inclined to insist on total indigence, and chose to make many small awards (usually £1 per annum) rather than the smaller number of

---

[31] Malcolm, 'The English People', chs. 9–10.

[32] 14 Car. II, c. 9 (*Statutes of the Realm*, V (1819), pp. 389–90). Pensions had also been awarded to parliamentarian soldiers in the 1650s, but the surviving records for Somerset and Wiltshire contain too few names to make analysis worthwhile. Dorset has no extant Quarter Sessions records between 1638 and 1663.

[33] Pensions awards continued in Somerset after 1666: *Q[uarter] S[essions] R[ecords for the County of] Somerset*, IV: *Charles II 1666–1677*, ed. [M. C. B. Dawes] (Somerset Rec. Soc., XXXIV, 1919), *passim*. But it would be unsafe to draw conclusions from them, given that so many from 1662–6 are missing. The Wiltshire and Dorset awards have been extracted from Wilts. R.O., Q.S. Order Book, 1654–68; and Dorset R.O., Q.S. Order Book, 1663–74. Some of the Dorset pensions are tabulated in R. G. B[artelot], 'Dorset Royalist Roll of Honour, 1662', *Somerset and Dorset N[otes and] Q[ueries]*, xviii (1924–6), 89–93, 165–7, 200–3; xix (1927–9), 43–6, 139–42. However, Bartelot lists only 712 names, compared with 815 in the original order book. The awards used in this analysis date from 1661 for Wiltshire, from 1663 for Dorset, and include all those made down to the end of 1667 in each case. Awards continued after 1667, but too sporadically for the effort of extracting them to be worth while.

TABLE I: *Wiltshire*

	Estimated population (1676)	Royalist pensioners	Pensioners per 1,000 population
Cheese country			
Rural	17,500	44	2.54
Towns under 1,000	3,000	16	5.33
Towns and villages over 1,000	17,000	20	1.18
Total	37,500	80	2.13
Intermediate parishes			
Rural	12,500	36	2.88
Towns under 1,000	500	0	0
Towns and villages over 1,000	9,000	55	6.11
Total	22,000	91	4.14
Chalk country			
Rural	37,000	91	2.46
Towns under 1,000	4,200	21	5.00
Towns and villages over 1,000	14,000	44	3.14
Total	55,200	156	2.83
Total: Wiltshire	114,700	327	2.85

pensions of a shilling a week that was the policy in Wiltshire.[34] Armed with a Grand Inquest presentment demanding that only the 'truly indigent' be relieved, the Wiltshire magistrates appear to have scrutinized applications more carefully.[35] But even if the Wiltshire J.P.s were rigorous, there is no evidence that they were more so for one part of the county than for another. The procedures in both counties, and the existence of pensioners in all the main regions of each, suggest that the listings are reasonably complete. It might be argued, though, especially for Wiltshire, that the pensions are as much a guide to the location of poverty as to the location of Royalists, and this possibility will have to be considered. One other likely element of distortion should also be noted: the help of a conscientious squire or parson,

[34] The Dorset J.P.s began by making these £1 awards as a temporary measure, while they considered further 'how to settle pensions on them' (B[artelot], 'Dorset Royalist Roll of Honour', 90). But these temporary orders were often annually repeated, effectively becoming annual pensions: at the July 1665 sessions, for example, many awards went to men who had been granted the same sums a year earlier.

[35] Wilts. R.O., Q.S. Great Rolls, Michaelmas 1662 (Presentment of Grand Inquest). The Wiltshire J.P.s often refused or revoked pensions on unspecified grounds. In a case at Michaelmas 1661 they did so because the applicant had been in the service of Parliament.

TABLE II: *Dorset*

	Estimated population (1641–2)	Royalist pensioners	Pensioners per 1,000 population
Chalk country			
Rural	29,000	146	5.03
Towns under 1,000	3,600	64	17.78
Towns and villages over 1,000	7,000	98	14.00
Total	39,600	308	7.75
South and west Dorset			
Rural	11,750	87	7.40
Towns under 1,000	—	—	—
Towns and villages over 1,000	6,600	68	10.30
Total	18,350	155	8.44
Heathlands			
Rural	4,250	10	2.35
Towns under 1,000	—	—	—
Towns and villages over 1,000	3,500	27	7.71
Total	7,750	37	4.77
Blackmore Vale			
Rural	10,500	110	10.48
Towns under 1,000	850	9	10.59
Towns and villages over 1,000	4,800	196	40.83
Total	16,150	315	19.50
Total: Dorset	81,850	815	9.96

concerned for his dependants to get what was due to them, may have been important in some places.[36]

The geographical distribution of pensioners has been compared with the estimated population of the principal regions of the two counties.[37] For this analysis, Wiltshire has been divided into three: the wood-pasture, cheese, and clothing parishes of the north-west, with the addition of a handful of parishes in the 'butter' country of the south-west and in the south-eastern woodlands; secondly, the down-land sheep-corn country; and a third, geographically indefinite, intermediate category which includes the north-western Cotswold fringe, where a mixture of sheep-corn and pastoral agriculture prevailed, along with some large, scattered parishes containing nucleated

[36] Particularly at Sherborne: see below p. 82.
[37] See Appendix.

cores (sometimes towns like Warminster and Westbury) and a few rural parishes like Edington which also shared both types of economy.[38]

The pensioners amount to 2.85 per thousand of the population of Wiltshire. Taking the three categories as wholes, with no distinction between rural and urban parishes, the differences between them are not particularly striking, apart from a possibly significantly higher figure for the intermediate category.[39] Only when distinctions are made between urban or large parishes (of over 1,000 population) and smaller places do clear differences emerge. The rural areas show a rough uniformity across the three zones. But in the towns, large and small, and in the more populous villages, there are some obvious variations. The small market-towns of the cheese country, most of them outside the main clothworking area, show surprising royalist strength, though this is largely accounted for by two places: High-worth (for some time a royalist garrison) and Wootton Bassett. Pensioners seem to have been somewhat less common in the small towns of the chalk country, though again there are wide variations: Hindon and Ludgershall contained about fifteen per thousand, Amesbury and Heytesbury hardly any.[40]

These places are so small that generalization is hazardous. With the larger towns and heavily populated villages, however, greater confidence is possible. First, the statistics clearly contradict the notion that we are dealing solely with an indicator of poverty, at least as far as the clothing towns are concerned. These were the places where poverty was most serious, yet such towns as Bradford-on-Avon, Calne, Chippenham and Trowbridge contained only a trivial scattering of pensioners.[41] Only Devizes, where there had been a garrison, makes a respectable showing. Even the fragmentary records from the 1650s disclose more roundhead pensioners than Royalists in such places.[42] The conclusion is clear, though scarcely surprising: few royalist soldiers were recruited in the larger clothing towns.

[38] For the main Wiltshire agricultural regions, see Kerridge, 'Agriculture c. 1500–c. 1793', p. 43. I have adapted this classification to my own purposes, making use of information on parishes in V.C.H., Wilts. 'Towns' are those listed as such in [John] Adams, Index Villaris ... (London, 1680).

[39] See Table I.

[40] Highworth: 12.73 per thousand. Wootton Bassett: 7.82. Hindon: 15.44. Ludgershall: 14.19. Amesbury: 1.18. Heytesbury: 1.43.

[41] For poverty in the clothing towns, see Ramsay, Wiltshire Woollen Industry, pp. 72–84; P. Slack, 'Poverty and Politics in Salisbury 1597–1666', Crisis and Order in English Towns, ed. P. Clark and P. Slack (London, 1972), pp. 168–73; M. J. Ingram, 'Communities and Courts: Law and Disorder in Early Seventeenth-Century Wiltshire', Crime in England 1550–1800, ed. J. S. Cockburn (Princeton, 1977), pp. 133–4.

[42] Devizes: 3.27 Royalists per thousand. Chippenham: 3 Roundheads, 2 Royalists. Melksham: 3 Roundheads, 0 Royalists.

Indigent Royalists were somewhat more common in the larger towns of the chalk country. But much more impressive are the concentrations in the towns of the intermediate category: Downton, Mere, Warminster and Westbury.[43] What do these places have in common? They were all market-towns set in large rural parishes that straddled the downland and wood-pasture zones. They contained both nucleated cores and rural hinterlands of scattered settlement, with areas of both pasture and sheep-corn husbandry. Mere, Warminster and Westbury all had important corn markets, Warminster's being one of the biggest in the western counties. Downton, on the edge of the woodlands, was a borough in decay, while both Warminster and Westbury had extensive cloth industries, Westbury's being in a state of particularly acute depression.[44] Here, therefore, poverty may indeed affect the statistics, indicating either a higher ratio of indigent to other royalist soldiers, or possibly heavier recruitment in places where economic life—in both the corn markets and the cloth industry—was disrupted by the war. Warminster was in an area troubled by more frequent fighting than was the case in much of Wiltshire, and also received more of the recorded parliamentarian pensions than any other place in the county.[45]

This evidence from Wiltshire suggests that the political sympathies of the population limited royalist recruiting only in the region where Puritanism was most deeply entrenched—the larger clothing parishes—and does little to support the hypothesis that settlement patterns by themselves had much to do with it. The Dorset evidence enables us to refine these conclusions. It should first be remembered that numerical comparisons between the two counties cannot be made, the generosity of the Dorset magistrates rewarding more than three times as many people, relative to population, as in Wiltshire. However, this very fact may make the Dorset returns a more useful guide to the distribution of royalist soldiers, and a rather less automatic indicator of the distribution of poverty.

What, then, do the Dorset figures disclose? First, perhaps surprisingly, they indicate rather heavier royalist recruitment in the pasturelands of south and west Dorset than in the downlands.[46] But once again it is the towns that provide the real contrasts. The bigger towns

[43] Downton: 8.67 per thousand. Mere: 11.90. Warminster: 2.80. Westbury: 4.39.

[44] V.C.H., Wilts., VIII, pp. 110-11, 115-16, 168-9, 175. In none of these cases is it possible to determine how many of the pensioners were from the town and how many from the out-parish. In a very few cases occupational descriptions are given: the thirteen pensioners from Westbury include two weavers, a fuller, a tiler and a husbandman, as well as a man from the hamlet of Chapmanslade.

[45] Eight. Several were granted to widows of men hanged by Sir Francis Dodington at Woodhouse in 1644. See Underdown, Somerset in the Civil War, p. 75.

[46] See Table II.

of the Dorset chalk and chalk-edge contained significantly more Royalists than those of the pasture region, with especially high concentrations at Shaftesbury and Blandford. Puritan Dorchester, by contrast, contained very few. Among the smaller chalk towns there are high figures for Bere Regis, Corfe Castle (a garrison) and Milton Abbas, a very low one for Cranborne. The west and south Dorset towns also vary widely, but at a level generally below that of the chalk towns. Lyme, in keeping with its Puritan reputation and long months of siege, harboured only one pensioner. Weymouth and Melcombe Regis are also below the average for towns in this region, Bridport, on the other hand, much above it. The inland towns of west Dorset, Beaminster and Netherbury—perhaps better classed as large villages—follow the pattern of Wiltshire places like Wootton Bassett in showing moderately high concentrations of Royalists.[47] In Dorset, as in Wiltshire, royalist recruitment thus appears to depend more on economic activity (though Dorset parliamentarianism was more maritime than industrial) than on settlement patterns. And once again the royalist soldiers are concentrated in market towns which contained large numbers of the recruitable poor in times of wartime depression.

Of the remaining Dorset regions, little can be said about the sparsely populated heathlands, and it may be that this area is under-represented in the returns. The sharpest departures from the country-wide average occur in Blackmore Vale, the region of mixed farming and stock-rearing to the south and south-east of Sherborne. Some of the Vale's distinctiveness is accounted for by a huge concentration of pensioners at Sherborne: 141 in a population of just under 2,500, or 57.72 per thousand. There is nothing like it in any other place in either Dorset or Wiltshire, but it is easy to explain. Sherborne was garrisoned for the King for long periods, while the authority of the Digbys at the castle would ensure that virtually every able-bodied male was in arms at one time or another, and that those eligible were both encouraged to apply for, and likely to receive, their pensions. But even without Sherborne, Blackmore Vale is impressively royalist, with more than twice the proportion of pensioners found in the chalk country. Gillingham, the scene of earlier violent protests against disafforestation, contradicts expectations by its relatively large number of pensioners; their presence may reflect poverty among people displaced by enclosure.[48] But this does not dispose of the smaller villages of the Vale.

[47] Shaftesbury: 30.86 per thousand. Blandford: 29.10. Dorchester (including Fordington): 2.94. Cranborne: 0.87. Weymouth and Melcombe Regis: 4.74. Bridport: 16.00. Beaminster: 14.29. Netherbury: 13.42. Bere Regis: 19.59. Corfe Castle: 21.07. Milton Abbas: 22.08.
[48] Gillingham: 22.00 per thousand. Sturminster Newton, with 25.00, is still higher.

The fact is that in this region mixed farming, with cattle-grazing rather than dairying predominating, had not led to the collapse of traditional community ties. Many Blackmore villages contained nucleated centres, though they were less nucleated than the downland villages, with outlying hamlets and farms carved out of the woodland long after the original open-field settlements had been established.[49] Throughout the area, big royalist landlords like the Digbys and, across the Somerset border, the Berkeleys had extensive manorial holdings. It was also, as we shall discover, an area of marked cultural conservatism. Bruton and Wincanton, a roundhead newsbook lamented, lay at 'the Center and heart of all the Malignants' of Somerset. The verdict is confirmed by the region's entire history during the civil war.[50]

Statistical analysis thus seems to contradict the hypothesis that parliamentarian sentiment was stronger in the scattered settlements of the pasturelands than in the nucleated villages of the sheep-corn country. It may suggest that economic rather than settlement patterns were the determinants of allegiance: that (as we knew already) Parliament did best in the clothing towns, the King (which perhaps we did not know already) in economically depressed market towns. It certainly demonstrates the continuing force of social deference in places with a strong aristocratic presence, and the effect a protracted period as a garrison might have, as at Sherborne, Devizes and Corfe Castle.

But before we discard completely the field-pasture hypothesis, we should again remember that we have been measuring, at best, only military recruitment. Armies were recruited from the poor and the marginal, and this seems to have been particularly true of the King's army. Richard Gough's classic account of Myddle, Shropshire, records twenty men who fought in the wars, almost all for the King. They included a small farmer heavily in debt, the bastard son of a cooper, a man whose father had been hanged for horse-stealing, a ruined weaver, a vagrant tailor, and a man and his three sons who were so marginal that they lived in a cave.[51] Whether as volunteers or

[49] C. Taylor, *The Making of the English Landscape: Dorset* (London, 1970), pp. 95-7, 120.

[50] B.L., T.T., E. 240 (12): *England's Memorable Accidents*, no. 17 (19-26 Sept. 1642). See also Underdown, *Somerset in the Civil War*, pp. 116-17; Underdown, 'Chalk and Cheese', 45-6. The manorial influence of the Berkeleys is evident in J. Collinson, *History and Antiquities of the County of Somerset* (3 vols., Bath, 1791), I, pp. 215, 221, 229; that of the Digbys in J. Hutchins, *History and Antiquities of the County of Dorset*, 3rd edn. with additions by W. Shipp and J. W. Hodson (4 vols., Westminster, 1861-73), IV, pp. 136-7, 200-1, 303, 444-5, 450.

[51] Malcolm, 'The English People', pp. 274-5. Richard Gough, *Antiquityes and Memoyres of the Parish of Myddle*, ed. W. G. Hoskins (Fontwell, 1968), pp. 39-40, 67, 80-1, 147,

impressed men, such people were available in numbers sufficient to make up armies in all types of communities and regions. The ability to recruit, in other words, depended as much on local military predominance as on popular sympathies. So once again the distinction between the propertied householders and the poor has to be kept in mind. The distribution of pensioners may seem to contradict the previous impression of parliamentarian loyalty in the rural parishes of north Wiltshire and the Dorset pasturelands, but does not necessarily invalidate it. The poor and marginal from those regions may have been drawn into the King's army in much the same proportions as those from the downland villages, but it does not automatically follow that the more established residents who stayed behind were correspondingly royalist. An inclination to withhold supplies and intelligence, as Hopton discovered in north Wiltshire in 1643, may be more symptomatic of the outlook of a region than the Royalists' success in recruiting some of the poorer inhabitants.

*　　　*　　　*　　　*

By combining the results of this analysis of royalist recruitment (in other words, the behaviour of the poor), with the evidence presented earlier from other sources (illustrating mainly the behaviour of the propertied), we may reach some general conclusions about the pattern of allegiance in the three counties. It indicates strong parliamentarianism in the northern textile region (to which we can add such towns as Dorchester, Taunton and Wellington), more muted roundhead strength in the pasture country of central Somerset, west Dorset and north-east Wiltshire; royalism in the chalk and chalk-edge regions, especially in the market towns, in the mixed farming country of south-east Somerset and Blackmore Vale, and in the thinly settled western hills. The textile towns and villages need not detain us. These were the Puritan strongholds, the places where, in the 1630s, resistance to Laudian innovations had been most vigorous, and the popularity of itinerant preachers and illegal conventicles most evident.[52] The connection between Puritanism and the clothing districts is wearisomely familiar, and although historians have differed widely about its causes, this is not the place to reopen the argument. It is enough to conclude that, for whatever reasons, industrial development and the

---

151, 162. D. G. Hey, *An English Rural Community: Myddle under the Tudors and Stuarts* (Leicester, 1974), pp. 195-7.

[52] Margaret F. Stieg, 'Church and Community: The Diocese of Bath and Wells in the Early Seventeenth Century' (Bucknell University Press, forthcoming), ch. 10: I am grateful to Dr. Stieg for enabling me to read her work in typescript. See also Marjorie E. Reeves, 'Protestant Nonconformity', *V.C.H., Wilts.*, III, pp. 99-101.

kind of society it produced can be associated with parliamentarian loyalties.

Let us turn instead to the fielden and the royalist wood-pasture regions. Close-knit downland communities, we might easily suppose, would exhibit strong attachments to the traditional order in church, state and everything else. But might not royalism, in the downlands or in Blackmore Vale, simply reflect the outlook of the squires and parsons who were the natural leaders of their communities? Certainly people depended on their landlords for protection: 'Unles Sir Edward Nicolas stand for the hundred, wee are all undun,' a tenant told Nicholas's steward in 1644.[53] Equally certainly, many of the poorer sort obeyed orders to enlist, as is strikingly evident at Sherborne. Those who lacked security of tenure, like those on Sir John Stawell's estates in west Somerset, were particularly likely to contribute money, men or their own persons to the King's cause.[54] But it is possible to exaggerate the magnates' ability to control their inferiors, whether yeomen or marginal poor. Excessive harshness might be counterproductive and drive tenants into the opposite camp in spite of their vulnerability. Wartime conditions made it more difficult for landlords to exert control. In 1644 the parliamentarian Earl of Denbigh complained that plundering roundheads, not under his command, had made even his own tenants unwilling to enlist.[55] One who proved too unresponsive might find himself with empty lands, as William Wheate was warned. Unless he paid the contributions demanded by the Dudley garrison, his Warwickshire tenants were 'resolved to throw up your land at Michaelmas'.[56] Or he might find the inhabitants gleefully assisting when his court rolls were destroyed, as happened when Maurice's troops sacked the Earl of Salisbury's mansion at Cranborne. The ties of deference were much strained in all regions. 'As for the Commonality,' an anonymous writer declared in 1654, 'They will not stirr ... the Landlord not beinge able to doe that he did in Former time unto them in Feasting and protecting them, hath no power with them.'[57]

[53] B.L., Egerton MS. 2,533, fo. 388 (W. Woolfe to T. Fry, 1 Dec. 1644).

[54] Such at least was the prevailing belief (*Exceeding joyfull newes from the Earl of Bedford* (1642), quoted in R. Ashton, *The English Civil War: Conservatism and Revolution 1603–1649* (London, 1978), p. 175). However, Malcolm argues that west-Somerset landlords were more benevolent than those of the east ('The English People', p. 151).

[55] *Cal. S. Papers Dom., 1644*, p. 97. For counterproductive behaviour by a landlord, see B. G. Blackwood, 'The Lancashire Cavaliers and their Tenants', *Trans. Hist. Soc. Lancs. and Cheshire*, cxvii (1965) 23.

[56] Bodleian Library, Oxfordshire V.C.H. Office: Glympton Papers, 7 July 1645 (J. W[heate] to William Wheate).

[57] B.L., Add. MS. 4,159, fo. 236v (R.B. to —, [1654]). For the Cranborne episode, see H.M.C., *Salisbury*, XXII, p. 375; and L. Stone, *Family and Fortune: Studies in Aristocratic Finance in the Sixteenth and Seventeenth Centuries* (Oxford, 1973), pp. 148–9.

So while the authority of the downland squires, or landlords like the Digbys and Berkeleys in the Blackmore Vale region, is a partial explanation of the royalism we find there, it may not be the only one. The relationship of patrician and plebeian always had reciprocal elements, and it is possible that some of the differences in regional behaviour that we have observed came from below, from differences in the cultures of the regions. Politics is part of culture, and unless we assume that an entire culture is imposed by the élite, it is plausible to suppose that cultural variations might be reflected in differences in political outlook. The historian John Oldmixon, who grew up in the Puritan household of the Blakes at Bridgwater, regarded cultural attitudes as central to civil war allegiance. In 1642, he asserted, Somerset was 'Protestant and sober', thus hostile to the Cavaliers, 'excepting those Gentry and Peasantry who had oppos'd the putting down Revels and Riots'.[58] Oldmixon exaggerated, no doubt. But hatred of popular festivals was certainly one of the distinctive marks of the Puritans, so the subject is therefore worth pursuing. If in one place we find a more tenacious survival of traditional rituals, in another a different set of symbols being more commonly employed, it may be easier to explain contrasts in political behaviour. Were there in fact significant differences between the cultures of the regions under discussion?

John Aubrey certainly thought so. The people of the Wiltshire cheese country, he tells us, were 'melancholy, contemplative, and malicious', addicted to Puritan fanaticism, witchcraft beliefs and litigiousness; their downland counterparts had none of these attributes and were little inclined 'to read or contemplate of religion'.[59] Aubrey records many village feasts and revels in north Wiltshire, but he was writing after the Restoration and rarely indicates whether they had survived earlier attacks, or had been revived after 1660.[60] The question of survival or revival is crucial, and can rarely be decided on the evidence of local customs assiduously collected by later folklorists. However, other sources permit at least some tentative conclusions about the relative effectiveness of the campaign against church-ales and revels in the three counties.

There had been earlier official moves against them, but the parish feasts first received the magistrates' serious attention in the 1590s. A

[58] John Oldmixon, *History of England, During the Reigns of the Royal House of Stuart* (London, 1730–5), I, p. 208.
[59] John Aubrey, *The Natural History of Wiltshire*, ed. J. Britton (London, 1847), pp. 11–12. See also *Wiltshire: The Topographical Collections of John Aubrey*, ed. J. E. Jackson (Devizes, 1862), p. 266.
[60] See, for example, *Topographical Collections of Aubrey*, pp. 128, 139, 146, 185, 198, 272–4; and Aubrey, 'Remaines of Gentilisme and Judaisme', in John Aubrey, *Three Prose Works*, ed. J. Buchanan-Brown (Fontwell, 1972), pp. 137–8, 143, 192–4, 212.

series of ill-enforced sessions and assize orders eventually ran headfirst into the contrary Laudian policy that culminated in the Book of Sports.[61] While the campaign's success was mixed, it was clearly most effective in the clothing parishes. Very few church-ales disturbed the authorities in this area, though one caused a riot at Coleford, in the disorderly Mendip mining district, after the lifting of the prohibitions in 1633.[62] The argument from silence should not be pressed too far: it may be that church-ales were still held, but with sufficient discretion to escape official displeasure. But the silence of the record must surely have some significance.

In the Wiltshire downlands and the adjacent 'intermediate' parishes there is somewhat more evidence of survival. Ales were still being held at Donhead St. Mary in 1612, while at Mere festivities presided over by a 'Cuckoo King' continued until 1621. By after that date, however, repairs to the church were being financed by the Puritan alternative, a parish rate. Rates appear in other downland parishes; even so, at Winterslow the church-ale survived them, though without the earlier minstrels and morris-dancers. And at Broad Chalk midsummer revels still flourished in 1639, with a 'dauncinge match' featuring a mock bishop and a lot of nocturnal horseplay.[63]

The pasturelands outside the northern textile area display a clearer pattern of cultural survival. Much depended on local circumstances: a pious squire like Francis Hastings at North Cadbury, a determined preacher like Richard Allein at Ditcheat and Batcombe, might establish islands of Puritan conformity.[64] But where zealous reformers in authority were absent, enforcement was distinctly erratic. This was especially so in the parishes north and west of Yeovil, the scene of nearly all Somerset's recorded church-ales in the early seventeenth century, and in the nearby parts of Dorset. Several of the forbidden festivals came to light in 1607 during an investigation of an itinerant bull-keeper: at Yeovil a riotous charivari procession had been led

---

[61] The relevant orders for Somerset are listed by T. G. Barnes, 'County Politics and a Puritan Cause Célèbre: Somerset Church-ales, 1633', *T.R. Hist. S.*, 5th ser., ix (1959), 109 and n.

[62] Barnes, 'County Politics', p. 116, n. For references to other early seventeenth-century church-ales in north Somerset and north-west Wiltshire, see *Q.S.R. Somerset*, I: *James I, 1607–1625*, ed. E. H. Bates (Somerset Rec. Soc., XXIII, 1907), p. xlix (Cameley); *Records of the County of Wilts ... Extracts from the Quarter Sessions Great Rolls of the Seventeenth Century*, ed. B. H. Cunnington (Devizes, 1932), p. 91 (N. Bradley). Dorset's lack of Sessions records before 1625 should again be noted.

[63] *Records of Wilts.*, ed. Cunnington, pp. 35, 131–2; T. H. Baker, 'Notes on the History of Mere', *Wilts. Arch. Mag.*, xxix (1896–7), 269–70; 'The Churchwardens' Accounts of Mere', *ibid.*, xxxv (1907–8), 266–76; W. Symonds, 'Winterslow Church Reckonings, 1542–1661', *ibid.*, xxxvi (1909–10), 29–33.

[64] *Letters of Sir Francis Hastings 1574–1609*, ed. C. Cross (Somerset Rec. Soc., LXIX, 1969), pp. 117–18; Stieg, 'Church and Community', ch. 10.

88 TRANSACTIONS OF THE ROYAL HISTORICAL SOCIETY

by a lord of misrule. The replacement of ales by parish rates was common in south Somerset in the next decade, but revels still survived there more openly than in the north of the county.[65] Culturally as well as politically the Yeovil–Sherborne area resembled the sheep-corn country far more than it did the northern cheese and textile zone.

The northern region was more likely to suppress wakes and revels. It had at least two other distinctive cultural features. One is that after 1645 there appears to have been a curious reversal, with signs of a defiant assertion of traditional culture in the very area where it had previously been effectively put down. Bull-baiting, cock-fighting, riotous outbreaks at fairs, even the reappearance of ales and revels, all aroused the authorities' concern in the area south of Bath and along the Wiltshire–Somerset border.[66] Few such incidents were reported in the chalk country, though there were some in west Somerset parishes like Langford Budville where the old customs had flourished before 1640, and in the Vale of Pewsey, a region with characteristics of both chalk and cheese countries.[67] However we may explain this surprising revival of traditional customs in the Puritan areas, the development (if it is not an illusion caused by fragmentary record survival) again points to the cultural peculiarity of the northern parishes.

The other distinctive feature also suggests the greater individualism of the cheese country. All over Europe festive processions, charivari, had long been employed to ridicule deviant members of communities.[68] 'Ridings' accompanied by rough music were part of the common

[65] *Q.S.R. Somerset*, I: *James I*, pp. 5–6. Barnes, 'County Politics', p. 107, n. G. R. Quaife, *Wanton Wenches and Wayward Wives: Peasants and Illicit Sex in Early Seventeenth Century England* (New Brunswick, N.J., 1979), p. 86. For the fortunes of church-ales in south Somerset, see *Q.S.R. Somerset*, I: *James I*, p. xlvii (Yeovilton); *V.C.H., Somerset*, III, ed. R. W. Dunning (1974), pp. 119 (Kingsdon), 264 (Tintinhull); IV, ed. R. W. Dunning (1978), p. 60 and n. (Merriott); Barnes, 'County Politics', p. 108, n. (E. Coker); and William Prynne, *Canterburies Doome* ... (London, 1646), p. 378 (Beer Crowcombe, Montacute).

[66] B.L., T.T., E. 441 (22): *Perfect Weekly Account*, no. 9 (3–10 May 1648); *Cal. S. Papers Dom., 1652–3*, p. 301; *Q.S.R. Somerset*, III: *Commonwealth, 1646–1660*, ed. E. H. Bates Harbin (Somerset Rec. Soc., XXVIII, 1912), pp. 285, 302, 324.

[67] M. B. McDermott, 'Church House at Langford Budville', *Somerset and Dorset N.Q.*, xxix (1968–73), 129–30. *Q.S.R. Somerset*, III: *Commonwealth*, pp. xxxv–xxxvi (Kingweston), xlix–l (Langford Budville), 303–4 (Staple Fitzpaine); Somerset R.O., C.Q.3, 1/82 (2), no. 20: Sessions Rolls, 1650 (Hillfarrance); *Records of Wilts.*, ed. Cunnington, pp. 221 (Woodborough), 222 (apparently Marden).

[68] Natalie Z. Davis, 'The Reasons of Misrule', in Davis, *Society and Culture in Early Modern France* (Stanford, 1975), pp. 97–123; P. Burke, *Popular Culture in Early Modern Europe* (London, 1978), pp. 198–204; E. P. Thompson, ' "Rough Music": Le Charivari Anglais', *Annales E.S.C.*, xxvii (1972), 285–312; Violet Alford, 'Rough Music or Charivari', *Folklore*, lxx (1959), 505–18.

stock of popular culture in both urban and rural areas. But north-west Wiltshire and north Somerset had their own peculiar form of chari-vari, the 'skimmington', distinctive in both its targets and ritual. 'Skimmingtons' were of two kinds: public and domestic. In the former, men and women, or men disguised as women, expressed community disapproval of outsiders who had enclosed commons or otherwise violated customary rights: well-known examples are the riots against disafforestation around 1630 led by the mythical 'Lady Skimming-ton'.[69] The distinctiveness of the domestic 'skimmington' is perhaps less obvious, but even more suggestive. Its almost invariable target was the couple which had inverted the patriarchal order through the wife beating the husband. Nowhere in England does the attempt to affirm traditional domestic values appear to have been as common as in Wiltshire and north Somerset; nowhere else did it involve as elab-orate a ritual.

In its fully developed form, rarely seen outside this area except in urban settings, the 'skimmington' procession was led by a mounted figure wearing horns, followed by a horse bearing surrogates for the offending couple, with the humiliated 'husband' facing backwards while the 'wife' beat him with a skimming ladle, the procession being accompanied by a noisy crowd making rough music.[70] The custom is akin to other 'riding' forms such as the north-country one of 'riding the stang', but with different targets (stang ridings being usually directed at simple cases of marital infidelity) and with a more dramatic ritual. That ritual is clearly related to the economy of the cheese country (hence the skimming ladle), and involves the playing of specific theatrical roles in a way suggesting a greater sense of individual identity.[71] The geographical concentration and the relative frequency

[69] See Kerridge, 'The Revolts in Wiltshire'; Allan, 'The Rising in the West'.

[70] The best description is in the depositions for the incident at Quemerford in 1618 (B. H. Cunnington, '"A Skimmington" in 1618', *Folklore*, xli (1930), 287–90; also in *Records of Wilts.*, ed. Cunnington, pp. 65–6). For other cases around this time, see *Records of Wilts.*, pp. 79–80 (Marden); *Q.S.R. Somerset*, I: *James I*, p. xlix (Cameley); III: *Commonwealth*, p. 1 (Leigh-on-Mendip); Quaife, *Wanton Wenches*, p. 200. Urban exam-ples include a threatened 'skimmington' at Dorchester, 1630 (*Municipal Records of the Borough of Dorchester*, ed. C. H. Mayo (Exeter, 1908), p. 655) and one at Greenwich described by Marvell (*Poems and Letters of Andrew Marvell*, ed. H. M. Margoliouth (Oxford, 3rd edn. 1971), I, pp. 156–7). See also *The Diary of Samuel Pepys*, ed. R. Latham and W. Matthews (London, 1970–), VIII, p. 257. That both the custom and the term 'skimmington' were originally associated with north Wiltshire is made clear in G. E. Dartnell and E. H. Goddard, *A Glossary of Words used in the County of Wiltshire* (London, 1893), pp. 145–6.

[71] E. K. Chambers, *The Mediaeval Stage* (Oxford, 1903), I, p. 154. C. R. B. Barrett, 'Riding Skimmington and Riding the Stang', *Journal of British Arch. Assoc.*, new ser., i (1895), 58–68. The 'Skymmety' panel at Montacute House involves the same target as the cheese country 'skimmington', but with a more primitive ritual.

of 'skimmingtons' in this period raise interesting questions outside the scope of this paper. But however we choose to explain it, the 'skimmington' is a further mark of the cultural peculiarity of the cheese country.[72]

*   *   *   *

These regional contrasts suggest that variations in popular political behaviour may be related to plebeian culture as well as patrician leadership. They also compel us to look more closely at the ways in which political and cultural attitudes reinforced each other. It was an Interregnum commonplace that tolerance of popular recreations automatically implied political unreliability. Thus Edward Curle of Batcombe, the radical sequestrator of Catsash Hundred in Somerset, broadened the attack on the Presbyterian M.P., William Strode, by alleging that Strode had obstructed the campaign against alehouses and had helped 'Enemies of reformation' to get licences 'by Clandestine wayes'.[73] Further down the scale, the constable and tithingman of West Monkton were assumed to be disaffected for 'countenancing drunkennes, multiplicity of alehouses and prophanation of the Sabbath', while John Sheppard of Kilton was regarded as subversive even though he had served the Parliament, because he allowed drinking and card-playing in his house, rarely went to church, and spent Sunday afternoons gambling and corrupting youths by supplying them with 'bowls, balls, or cudgels'.[74] Correspondingly, people encountering officious interference with their small pleasures easily translated resentment into political terms; hence all the seditious words in taverns.[75]

Some of these cases reveal how the civil war was perceived by ordinary people. At Stoke St. Mary in 1650, William Mansfield was refused a drink by William Helyar's wife, she 'knowing him to be a leud fellow'. He forced his way into the house, smashed a pot with a billhook and said 'that in like manner he hoped to cut downe the Roundheaded Rogues'. Soldiers away from their units were tempting

[72] A possible explanation may be that in this area women as dairy producers had more direct access to the market than women in traditional communities, and hence greater independence which men found threatening.

[73] Somerset R.O., Q.S. 164: Petitions (Petition of Edward Curle [1648-9?], with supporting petition from the Batcombe area).

[74] *Q.S.R. Somerset*, III: *Commonwealth*, p. 239. *Cal. S. Papers Dom., 1648-9*, pp. 31-2. Sheppard had a bad record as a plunderer and was said to have served both sides in the civil war.

[75] Among many other possible examples of tavern sedition, see *Q.S.R. Somerset*, III: *Commonwealth*, pp. xxxii-xxxviii, 298-9, 347, 370-1. P. Clark ('The Alehouse and the Alternative Society', *Puritans and Revolutionaries: Essays in Seventeenth-Century History presented to Christopher Hill*, ed. D. Pennington and K. Thomas (Oxford, 1978), pp. 66-7) minimizes the importance of the alehouse as a centre of sedition.

targets. On the revel day at Kingweston in 1653 two blacksmiths started a fight by trying to make a trooper drink the Queen's health.[76] Village outcasts might identify with enemies of *de facto* authority and be goaded into sedition, much as others were goaded into witchcraft in search of revenge. Joan Walton of Chelwood was a poor, embittered woman, full of brooding hatred for her neighbours. In 1650 Thomas Stone suspected her of stealing his wood. Now Stone's brother Richard was steward to Alexander Popham, the rich and powerful Commonwealth magnate of those parts. Questioned about the wood, Walton denounced Richard Stone as 'a fat gutted roague', declaring 'she would make his gutt as poore as hers before she had donne, and though they had now the power of the Countrie in their hands yet they should be glad with a bitt of bread as well as she, when the Kings Armie did come'. Others remembered her threats to 'be revenged on the parish of Chelwood if ever the wind did turn', especially on the parson, and her claim 'that she had them in the other Armie that would doe it'.[77]

Such outbursts show how far the civil war had penetrated the popular consciousness. For every one reported there must have been dozens that were not, when the circumstances lacked the necessary ingredients—a prior antagonism to provoke an informer, an unusually vigilant minister or constable. Among other things they demonstrate how localist and personalized these perceptions of the war were. The war enabled participants in village quarrels to settle old scores; it also created new divisions. The constable of Burbage requisitioned two of Francis Barber's carts for Waller's army. But Barber had two sons on the other side and when the tide turned they had the constable's horses seized in retaliation, threatening 'not to leave him while he was worth a groat'.[78] Victory permitted the settling of other kinds of old scores. The Protestant inhabitants of Nunney long resented Richard Prater's colony of recusants in the castle. Before the war they were unable to 'contradict' them, but afterwards they petitioned to have the Catholics removed and punished.[79] These incidents contain frequent reminders of the strength of community ties, in pasture and field areas alike. Eleanor Butt's husband died in the service of Parliament, her house was destroyed, and she settled at Isle Brewers, her late husband's birthplace. But she then rashly informed a neighbour-

[76] Somerset R.O., C.Q.3, 1/82 (2), no. 91: Sessions Rolls, 1650. *Q.S.R. Somerset*, III: *Commonwealth*, pp. xxxv–xxxvi.
[77] Somerset R.O., C.Q.3, 1/82 (2), nos. 103–5: Sessions Rolls, 1650. A later case similarly combining enmity to neighbours with political (in this case anti-royalist) feeling is in C.Q.3, 1/102, no. 23: Sessions Rolls, 1665.
[78] 'The Falstone Day-Book', ed. J. Waylen, *Wilts. Arch. Mag.*, xxvi (1892), 365.
[79] Somerset R.O., Q.S. 164: Petitions, 'N'.

turned her out and refused her any other accommodation.[80]

*   *   *   *

This paper has touched on only a few of the possible variables
affecting popular allegiance in the civil war. Nothing has been said,
for instance, about the impact of rival propaganda-systems and the
results of varying literacy-rates. The country gentry may have been
less isolated than sometimes supposed, but even they often confessed
bewilderment. 'I live in darknes and ignorance,' Nathaniel Tovey
wrote from Leicestershire in 1642, 'and know not which end of the
world stands upwards, unless it be by pedling rumours in the country
wherof a man can believe scarce one of an hundred.'[81] For the un-
educated, vulnerability to rumours was obviously much greater. John
Corbet says that the Royalists made Welsh peasants believe 'that we
came to put man, woman, and child to the sword, and filled their
fancies with as many strange conceits of the Roundheads, as the poore
Spaniards had of the English after their revolt from Rome; it being
easier to perswade an irrational and stupid people'.[82]

The conclusion is predictable: we are still a long way from a full
understanding of the motives of the English people in taking up arms
(or avoiding doing so) in the civil war. We may learn something from
the symbols they chose or attacked, not only in such obvious instances
as the destruction of altar rails and church ornaments, but also in
playful episodes like the one at Winchester in 1643 when soldiers broke
into the muniment room and threw some of the records in the river,
while others were 'made kytes withall to flie in the aire'.[83] As we
pursue these and other subjects we shall undoubtedly find great variations in the comparative strengths of deference and popular independence. Although in the western counties we are more likely to find
Royalists in traditional field areas and in towns on their borders, there
are obvious contrasts in other parts of the country: in East Anglia, for
example.

Even in the wood-pasture textile regions we shall rarely find more
than a handful of genuine radicals. Preaching soldiers were as likely
to provoke abuse as respectful attention, just as Quakers were soon to
encounter angry mobs as well as enthusiastic converts.[84] It is certainly

[80] Somerset R.O., Q.S. 164: Petitions, 'I'.

[81] P.R.O., S.P. 46/83: Warner MSS., 1636-44, fo. 51 (N. Tovey to G. Warner, 28
Jan. [1642]).

[82] Corbet, 'True and Impartial History', *Somers Tracts*, V, p. 358.

[83] *Documents Relating to the History of the Cathedral Church of Winchester in the Seventeenth
Century*, ed. W. R. W. Stephens and F. T. Madge (Hants. Rec. Soc., 1897), p. 57.

[84] Defenders of preaching soldiers tended to discount the interruptions as being
instigated by Royalists or papists, as at Wookey, Somerset, in 1652 (*Q.S.R. Somerset,*

true that radical Puritanism was strongest in the forest and urban areas. But the attitude of the common people on both sides was more generally traditionalist and socially conservative. Two examples must suffice. One is from a royalist parish, Yarlington, near Bruton. When a Protectorate proclamation was read at the Court Leet, a resident gave the succinct retort: 'Wee will have no new laws here.'[85] The other comes from the leader of the parliamentarian Clubmen in Somerset, Humphrey Willis. The title page of his pamphlet denouncing the County Committee bears a representation of an inverted globe surmounted by a committeeman (obviously Colonel Pyne) caught in the act of tyranny, with the caption *Heu quantum mutatus ab illo*[86] Royalists were not alone in lamenting 'The World Turned Upside Down'.

Appendix: Population Estimates

Estimates of population for Dorset are based mainly on *The Dorset Protestation Returns preserved in the House of Lords, 1641–2*, ed. E. A. Fry (Dorset Records, XII, 1912), with the addition of those from Abbotsbury in *Somerset and Dorset Notes and Queries*, xxviii (1961–7), 59–61. For parishes where no Protestation returns survive, estimates have been made from *Dorset Hearth Tax Assessments, 1662–1664*, ed. C. A. F. Meekings (Dorchester, 1951), and J. Hitchcock, 'Statistics of Dorset Parishes, c. 1600', *Proc. Dorset Nat. Hist. and Arch. Soc.*, lxxxix (1967), 231–2. Poole has been excluded because of its separate county status: the Dorset pensions lists contain none from Poole. Estimates for Wiltshire are more difficult, as the Protestation returns survive from only a small group of downland hundreds: they are printed in 'The Wiltshire Protestation Returns of 1641–2', ed. E. A. Fry, *Wilts. Notes and Queries*, vii (1911–13), 16–21, 79–84, 105–10, 162–7, 203–8, 260–5, 309–13, 343–7, 418–21, 450–2, 496–9. For most of Wiltshire recourse has to be made to the Compton Census of 1676, printed in 'A Census of Wilts. in 1676', ed. C. Simpson and C. S. Ruddle, *Wilts. Notes and Queries*, iii (1899–1901), 533–9; and in *Original Records of Early Noncon-*

III: *Commonwealth*, p. xxxix). Royalists naturally regarded them as spontaneous expressions of popular feeling. See the case at Wimborne 1646 (J. M. J. Fletcher, 'A Dorset Worthy: William Stone, Royalist and Divine (1615–1685)', *Proc. Dorset Nat. Hist. and Antiq. Field Club*, xxxvi (1915), 18–19).

[85] *Q.S.R. Somerset*, III: *Commonwealth*, p. xxxvii.

[86] B.L., T.T., E. 374 (10): Hum. Willis, *Times Whirligig, or The Blew-new-made-Gentleman mounted* [9 Feb. 1646–7], title page (reproduced in Underdown, *Somerset in the Civil War*, p. 134). The image was common in popular royalist literature. See, for example, B.L., T.T., 669 f. 10 (47): *The World is Turned Upside Down* [8 April 1646]. The ballad was to be sung to the tune of 'When the King enjoys his own again'.

formity, ed. G. L. Turner (3 vols., London, 1911–14), I, pp. 127–33. The problems raised by the Compton Census are well known, notably the virtual impossibility of deciding whether a parish's figure represents the number of communicants or an estimate of total population (see L. Bradley, *A Glossary for Local Population Studies* (*Local Population Studies*, Supplement, 1971), p. 61, and 'The Compton Census—Peterborough', *Local Population Studies*, x (1973), 71–4). The far from perfect solution adopted has been to compare the 1676 figures with those from the 1801 census (*V.C.H. Wilts.*, IV, pp. 339–61). Where the 1676 figure multiplied by 10/6 exceeds the 1801 figure, the former has been as an estimate of total population; where it is smaller, it has been taken as number of communicants and has been multiplied by 10/6 to obtain total population. Checking this method in parishes which have both Protestation and Compton Census returns suggests that it is accurate to within plus or minus 5%, being confirmed by the Protestation figures in 34 of the 49 parishes checked. For Wiltshire parishes which have neither Protestation nor Compton Census returns, rough estimates based on Hearth and other tax assessments in P.R.O., E. 179, have been made. These Wiltshire estimates for 1676 ought ideally to be converted to 1641–2, in the light of estimated population growth during the interval. There undoubtedly were different rates of growth in, for example, the downland villages and the clothing towns, but the latter display such wide variations and the problems involved in determining them are so complicated and require so many assumptions that to attempt it would more likely compound rather than reduce the existing errors. It should therefore be noted that while Dorset's population estimates are for 1641–2, Wiltshire's are for 1676. I am most grateful to Dr. Anthony Salerno and Dr. Anne Whiteman for their advice on Wiltshire population problems.

FROM STRANGERS TO MINORITIES IN WEST AFRICA*

By Professor J. D. Hargreaves, M.A., F.R.Hist.S.

READ AT THE SOCIETY'S CONFERENCE 11 SEPTEMBER 1980

I

I am somewhat daunted by the honour of opening this conference; for what I have to offer is not the product of intensive scholarship but a broad and possibly contentious argument about the whole sub-continent of West Africa (roughly bounded by the Senegal river, Lake Chad and Mount Cameroon). My underlying hypotheses will be that many so-called minority problems in contemporary Africa derive from changes introduced by the creation of colonial states, rather than from some exotic African malady called 'tribalism'; and that African experience over the last millennium may sometimes be more relevant to contemporary problems than the received wisdom of western political science. I have some fear that, to adapt a phrase of Sir Keith Hancock, these may prove no themes for scholars.

Let me begin by recalling one official attempt to apply western concepts. In September 1957, when British policy required that Nigeria should follow Ghana to independence with the least delay, Mr. Lennox-Boyd appointed a Commission under Sir Henry Willink whose primary duty was

> 'To ascertain the facts about the fears of minorities in any part of Nigeria, and propose means of allaying those fears whether well or ill founded.'[1]

This now seems a somewhat curious formulation; would not the Commissioners have felt embarrassed if required to help allay fears which they believed to be well founded? Fortunately optimism prevailed. They concluded that minority interests could be adequately safeguarded by constitutional draftmanship: by distributing 'powers and functions in such a way that it may be to the interest of the party in

* This paper has greatly benefited from comments on earlier drafts by Dr. Roy Bridges, Dr. Alan Short, Mr. Robert Smith, and members of the Aberdeen University African Studies Group.

[1] Parliamentary Papers, 1957–8, Cmnd. 505. *Nigeria: Report of the Commission appointed to enquire into the fears of Minorities and the means of allaying them*, p. iii.

power to pay due attention to the interests of others',[2] and by incorporating a constitutional declaration of Fundamental Rights. The practice of liberal democracy and the general process of modernization were expected progressively to erode ethnic differences in favour of common Nigerian loyalties. During the next ten years, however, this clearly failed to happen.

It would be unfair to blame the Civil War of 1967–70 on the inadequacies of Willink's analysis; it was due less to the grievances of min orities than to conflicts among the ethnic majorities which dominated the three regions of colonial Nigeria. And although in consequence of that war some minorities may have achieved solid guarantees within the new nineteen-state Federation, the problems of ethnic relations clearly remain enormous. In 1957, when the British government was working under pressure to shorten the dangerous period of shared responsibility, the Willink Commission was intended to provide reassurances about these long-term problems, rather than to resolve them. But its attempt to do so by appeal to recent European experience was hardly felicitous.

The term 'minority'—in its modern sense of 'a small group of people separated from the rest of the community by a difference in race, religion, language, etc.' as distinct from the losing side in a parliamentary vote—did not reach the *O.E.D.* until the Supplement of 1976. The earliest reference there given is to Temperley's *History* of the 1919 peace conference, and although earlier usages can be found,[3] it is clear that this concept derives from nineteenth-century thinking about the nation-state. The assumptions underlying its use seem to be that it is an unfortunate anomaly if the boundaries of a modern state include permanently resident populations who do not identify themselves with the dominant nationality; but that when this is unavoidable legal safeguards for the civic rights of the minority, and for their access to public resources, should be incorporated in the constitution or guaranteed by the central government.

If European minority problems in their modern form derive from the rise of nation-states, in Africa we must look to the formation of colonial states—though related phenomena may be observed earlier in Ethiopia and other centralizing monarchies. I distinguish three problems. First, the partition of Africa created minorities by the same method as the roughly contemporary partitions of eastern Europe— by driving boundaries through existing cultural or political unities in order to serve the interests of external powers. Some of these minority

---

[2] *Ibid.*, p. 88.

[3] E.g. '... guarantees ... for ... the fair treatment of the minority by the majority' (Mrs. K. O'Shea to W. E. Gladstone, 5 Aug. 1886: F. S. L. Lyons, *Charles Stewart Parnell* (London, 1977), p. 292).

problems may yet be alleviated by agreed frontier rectifications; but the 1963 Charter of the Organisation of African Unity, by proclaiming respect for the territorial integrity of member states, has made these no easier to promote.

Secondly, the partition brought together, within boundaries which frequently bore little relation to earlier history, peoples of differing language and culture. Only Somalia and Lesotho approximate to the Mazzinian ideal of a homogeneous nation-state whose citizens share a common language, culture or ethnic identity. Nigeria, where over two hundred languages can be identified, provides the extreme example of ethnic pluralism; and it was with these peoples turned into minorities by agglomeration that Willink was chiefly expected to deal. After independence, this problem of ethnic pluralism was made more serious by new expectations about the fruits of political power. Those who could claim majority status—within the post-colonial state, within the regions of Nigeria, or within such smaller units as might thereafter be created—came to expect that the distribution of the resources of modern technology—roads, electricity and water, hospitals, schools and scholarships—would follow the arithmetic of the ballot-box. The 'relative deprivation' of the new minorities was thus certain to increase.

Thirdly—and this is the problem on which I hope to focus this paper—the hard lines of colonial and post colonial boundaries turned into aliens communities of people who had previously enjoyed a relatively secure status as strangers, under well-established systems of international customary law.[4] There have been many examples in the last twenty years of such communities suffering from being treated as minorities, and Ghana provides the classical case. When on 19 November 1969 the Ghanaian government gave all aliens not possessing residence permits fourteen days to leave the country, as many as 400,000 Africans may have been affected. There were many ironies in this: that the laws which had turned long-term residents into aliens had been passed under the government of the great pan-African Kwame Nkrumah; that he had been moved to do so by the support which some of them gave to political rivals, the very people who were later to carry out the expulsion of 1969; that the non-African aliens commonly known as expatriates were (having ready access to residence permits) largely unaffected.

The achievement of African independence undermined the position of many such 'strangers'. All over West Africa there existed communities of sojourners or more transient visitors who, although unconnected by kinship, had by agreement with the host community

---

[4] For a general view of pre-colonial international relations, see R. S. Smith, *Warfare and Diplomacy in Pre-Colonial West Africa* (London, 1976), chs. 1 and 2.

established the terms of continued residence. Not all stranger communities, of course, enjoyed perfect security; in Asante itself this expulsion of foreign traders seems to have been foreshadowed as early as 1844, when Asantehene Kwaku Dua I is said to have tried to 'nationalize' the kola trade.[5] But strangers do seem to become more vulnerable when regarded as minorities within a modern nation-state.[6]

Until recently, problems concerning the status of strangers in African communities interested social anthropologists more than historians; but the balance may now be changing.[7] I have a feeling, without the learning to develop it, that some of the questions that have been posed might fruitfully be asked about some stranger communities of early modern Europe—foreign merchants in sixteenth-century Antwerp, or the trade diaspora of the Hanseatic League—or about the changing fortunes of European Jews during the transition to the national state. But I have already committed myself to a wider range of generalization than a wise historian normally attempts . . .

II

West African ideas of the state have traditionally been based on notions of common ancestry, and people frequently perceive their rights and obligations through the metaphors of kinship. In most cases these are metaphors; for centuries states have existed which claim rights of sovereignty over land as well as people and control populations of diverse ethnic origins. The problem of defining the political status of resident aliens or strangers thus long predates the establishment of colonial rule.

Most African languages contain a number of words referring to different categories of stranger, some of which define their relationship to the host community with considerable subtlety. For the purpose of this paper I suggest a crude distinction between those aliens whose relationship with the host community needs to be defined on some enduring basis, and those who are resident for the purpose of playing distinctive and specific roles. Typically, the former situation may originate in conquest, or in migration and resettlement as a result of

---

[5] I. Wilks, *Asante in the Nineteenth Century* (Cambridge, 1975), pp. 267–9.

[6] For other examples, see M. Peil, 'The Expulsion of West African Aliens', *Journal of Modern African Studies*, ix (1971), 205–29.

[7] See, for example, E. P. Skinner, 'Strangers in West African Societies', *Africa*, 33 (1963), 307–20; M. Fortes, 'Strangers', *Studies in African Social Anthropology*, ed. M. Fortes and S. Patterson, (London, 1975), pp. 229–53; *Strangers in African Societies*, ed. W. A. Shack and E. P. Skinner, (Berkeley, 1979). For an early example of collaboration by historian and anthropologist, see V. R. Dorjahn and C. H. Fyfe, 'Landlord and Stranger; Change in Tenancy Relations in Sierra Leone', *Journal of African History*, iii (1962), 391–7.

ecological change: the latter, in commerce. The former situation is typically dealt with by subordination, which may lead to eventual incorporation into the polity of kinship: the latter, by what I shall call the enclavement of the stranger community. This paper will primarily be concerned with changing forms of enclavement during recent centuries. But since my distinction is not an absolute one, I should first say a little about the subordination of strangers.

This could take various forms. Manding society, for example, included endogamous groups who were associated with specialized occupations, known as *nyamakala*—or, roughly, castes. The region of Wasulu was controlled by Mande-speaking Fulas, bearing one of the four clan-names which denoted descent from a mythical common ancestor; collectively these free citizens enjoyed a special joking relationship, said to originate in a form of blood-pact called *senanyuka*, with the whole caste of smiths, or *numu*. Jean-Loup Amselle has studied a group of people called the Kooroko, originally refugees from the wars which followed the break-up of the Mali empire, who in Wasulu were received into this subordinate status of *numu*. Though regarded as smiths, this did not mean that they learned to work in metal; instead they took to trading, finding a distinctive place within Wasulu which, though it subordinated them to the ruling Fulas, cannot be described as slavery.[8]

There are many groups of strangers in Africa whose status can only be readily described by that word, slavery. But what did this imply, in societies which had not yet felt the pressures of external commerce? Ever since Mungo Park's oblique commentary on the abolitionist hypothesis,[9] Europeans have been speculating on this question; and like Park they have usually been obliged by lack of evidence to extrapolate backwards from their own observations and enquiries. The current tendency among many Africanists is to emphasize the open, almost benign, nature of some of the institutions through which rights in persons were exercised; many contributors to a recent symposium edited by Suzanne Miers and Igor Kopytoff seem to regard African slavery as essentially a method of defining the status of marginal persons, strangers without kin, and in some cases of facilitating the absorption of their descendants into kinship structures.[10] Slavery, Maurice Bloch suggests, 'is not a status but the absence of a status.'[11] Failing such devices as the *senanyuka*, strangers may be regarded as slaves because there is no other way of regarding those

[8] J.-L. Amselle, *Les négociants de la savane* (Paris, 1977), esp. pp. 45-8.

[9] Mungo Park, *Travels in the Interior Districts of Africa* (London, 1799), ch. XXII.

[10] *Slavery in Africa: Historical and Anthropological Perspectives*, ed. S. Miers and I. Kopytoff (Madison, 1977).

[11] *Asian and African Systems of Slavery*, ed. J. L. Watson (Oxford, 1980), pp. 130-1.

who are not kinsmen. This need not imply any intention to exploit or oppress.

It need not; but of course it may. Slavery may be essentially the absence of a status; but in practice the obligations, rights and general felicity of African slaves varied enormously, and it would be absurd to attempt any wide generalization in a paper on another subject. Fifty years ago R. S. Rattray noted five different Twi words denoting types of servitude among the Asante; among the Duala of Cameroun, Ralph Austen counts six; in Wasulu the word for slave varied according to the generation of residence in the family, and so did the rights of the owner.[12] For our purposes, it is relevant only to note that the 'open' nature of slavery was most evident in those societies which wished to absorb strangers; this might be related to the ratio of population to land, to the value placed on slaves as a source of social prestige and military strength, or—often the decisive factor since the seventeenth century—their value as a labour-force producing materials for export, or as an article of export themselves. Juridically, then, some strangers were regarded as slaves, people with few rights, because they had no kinsmen; but what this meant in practice depended on the use which the host community, at a particular period, wished to make of their services.

III

So slavery—whether benign or exploitative, open or closed—may be regarded as one method by which kinship societies defined the position of strangers. But it was clearly inappropriate when the strangers were recognized as agents of commerce. Trading strangers were not men without kin; their kinsmen lived elsewhere, and it was by maintaining these trans-territorial links that they developed mutually advantageous long-distance exchanges. Some form of extra-territorial status was needed to regulate the conditions of their residence: what I am calling enclavement.

Islam, of course, has always recognized a legal status appropriate to resident non-Muslim strangers: that of *dhimmi*. Some of our earliest and best-known documentary sources for West Africa show such a system working in reverse, in order to accommodate Berbers or Arabs trading in African states to the south of the Sahara desert. An often-quoted account of Ghana in 1068 by the Andalusian al-Bakri describes a separate town inhabited by Muslims (generally assumed to be strangers from the Maghreb) six miles from the walled town of the

[12] R. S. Rattray, *Ashanti Law and Constitution* (London, 1929), pp. 33-46; R. Austen, in Miers and Kopytoff, *Slavery in Africa*, pp. 307-9; Amselle, *Les négociants*, pp. 31-2.

animist ruler; this Muslim town had its own legal authorities, and twelve mosques, each with its imam.[13] Similar conditions are described at Gao.[14] Besides enjoying religious autonomy these strangers were allowed to regulate their internal property relationships; Ibn Battuta describes Berber communities in the towns of fourteenth-century Mali accepting responsibility for housing their countrymen, and administering their estates if they happened to die.[15]

Until recently, many Europeans tended to assume that this was privileged treatment for a racially distinct (if not racially superior) minority. It is not always understood that the medieval trading network extended into gold- and kola-producing regions far to the south where—though they cannot be documented at such early dates— comparable arrangements were made for the reception of strangers. Philip Curtin's important study of the economic history of eighteenth-century Senegambia shows the importance, far beyond that region, of the commercial network or diaspora of Mande-speaking traders who became known collectively as *juula* (or *dyula*).[16] Its strength lay partly in the reciprocal trust made possible by the common ethnicity of this dispersed population (reinforced and indeed partially defined by their Islamic allegiance), but also in the readiness of host communities to respect the institutions through which these strangers regulated their affairs.

The crucial figure in this system of international trade was a man generally known as the landlord—though perhaps some such clumsy compound as landlord-patron would be a better translation of *ja-tigi*, the Mande word prevalent throughout the western half of our region. Similar persons, known as *masugida* (sing. *maigida*), are found in the widely dispersed but culturally coherent settlements of Hausa-speaking peoples, which formed a complementary network in the eastern part of the region.[17] Such a landlord has been defined by Polly Hill as 'a settled stranger who makes it his business to accommodate long-distance stranger-traders and to assist them in selling, and usually storing, their goods',[18] and writers on other areas have described the system in essentially similar terms. I again take as example the Kooroko—for, after Wasulu was conquered by Samori in 1882 and so

---

[13] For a French translation of al-Bakri's text, see J. M. Cuocq, *Recueil des sources arabes concernant l'Afrique occidentale du viiie au xvie siècle* (Paris, 1975), p. 99.

[14] *Ibid.*, p. 77 (al-Muhallabi).

[15] *Ibid.*, pp. 299, 301, 311 (Ibn Battuta).

[16] P. D. Curtin, *Economic Change in Precolonial Africa: Senegambia in the Era of the Slave Trade* (Madison, 1975).

[17] For a general view, see Mahdi Adamu, *The Hausa Factor in West African History* (Zaria, 1978).

[18] Polly Hill, 'Landlords and Brokers: a West African Trading System', *Cahiers d'Etudes africaines*, vi, 23 (1966), 350.

drawn more solidly into the Mande trading network, their status as *numu* enabled them to move further afield as relay traders. Their role now was to buy kola in the forests of the Ivory Coast and exchange it for salt, livestock and cotton cloth in various markets in the middle valley of the Niger, and later along the Dakar–Bamako railway. The Kooroko who has adopted the métier of *juula*, says Amselle, finds with his landlord accommodation with a 'family atmosphere' and a congenial cuisine; warehousing facilities where bulk consignments can be broken; interpreters and introductions to potential customers, with relevant commercial intelligence; banking facilities and guarantees of credit.[19]

Around the houses of the landlords in the major market centres, strangers' quarters (*zongos*, in Hausa) might develop. Local rulers were usually happy to encourage this, allowing the strangers substantial liberty to regulate their own affairs; apart from the direct benefits of commerce (being able to exchange an abundant resource, like kola, for scarce items of diet or consumption goods) they derived revenue from market dues and taxes. When—as was usually the case—the traders were united by common allegiance to Islam, their religious and cultural identity was likewise respected. In most circumstances, strangers were careful to avoid involvement in local politics; but this did not prevent them putting valuable skills—as accountants, scribes, physicians, artisans, musicians—at the disposal of their political overlords. Only when a wave of Muslim militancy threatened the legitimacy of the rulers was the autonomy of such enclaves seriously jeopardized.[20]

Europeans, when they tried to establish their own footholds within West African trading systems, found that they could settle on the coastline under broadly comparable conditions, enjoying substantial autonomy within small territorial enclaves in return for regular payments or rent, tribute or taxes. Philip Curtin goes so far as to describe the chartered companies of France, England and the Netherlands as 'European *juula*'; and even into the nineteenth century it seems more useful to regard the fortified trading posts of Senegambia, the castles of the Gold Coast, even the settlements of African repatriates in Sierra Leone and Liberia, as stranger enclaves with marked cultural differences and fairly strong defensive technology rather than as miniature empires. Certainly those European brokers who settled on the coast as isolated individuals or discrete communities—like the Portuguese

---

[19] Amselle, *Les négociants*, pp. 203–4.

[20] For the example of Suluku of Biriwa Limba, threatened by the co-operation with Samori of 'Mohammedan children born in their country', see Sierra Leone Archives, Government Interpreter's Letter Book, Report by Momodu Wakka and Weeks, 2 Dec. 1886.

lançados in Senegambia,[21] or the Owen brothers, impoverished Irish gentry reduced to slave brokerage in the Sherbro estuary[22]—had initially to accept the rights and obligations of strangers as locally understood, though eventually they might become integrated by marriage into the host community themselves. As Dorjahn and Fyfe realized when in 1962 they examined the procedures which Europeans had to follow to obtain the patronage of a 'landlord' in the Guinea rivers in the 1780s, these were adaptations of 'a set of relationships ... that arose in a tribal setting where immigrants sought to gain rights to hunt, farm, or follow their trade'.[23] Europeans were only the most conspicuous set of strangers enjoying extra-territorial privileges within their enclaves.

IV

During the nineteenth century commercial development caused more movement of people within West Africa. This was not solely due to the impact of western capitalism; the establishment of Muslim theocracies in the savanna increased the demand for kola from the forest. (This was what gave the Kooroko their opportunity.) Hausa caravans came increasingly to buy kola in transit markets in the northern provinces of the Asante empire—Yendi and Salaga, later in Kintampo and Atebubu; and during the first half of the century the Asante authorities allowed them to penetrate the producing areas around Kumasi itself. New *zongos* were established in the major market towns, where landlords and brokers of different ethnic groups not only catered for the commercial needs of their kinsmen, but elected *sarakai* or headmen. These officers not only exercised extra-territorial jurisdiction according to Islamic or customary law, but performed consular functions by representing the interests of their communities to the local authorities. Alan Short, who has recently studied their development, sees these institutions, 'designed to attract traders to the area, facilitate temporary residence and solve the problems of conflict of laws', as reflecting the existence of 'an international customary law operating in the middle Volta basin and within Asante.'[24] And similar developments

[21] Curtin, *Economic Change*, pp. 95–100.
[22] Nicholas Owen, *Journal of a Slave-Dealer*, ed. Eveline Martin (London, 1930).
[23] Dorjahn and Fyfe, 'Landlord and Stranger', 397.
[24] A. W. Short, 'Continuity and Change in West African Foreign Relations: Problems of some Stranger Communities in Ghana in the Nineteenth and Twentieth Centuries', Ph.D. thesis, University of Aberdeen, 1978, p. 29. Two other important studies of strangers in Asante are Enid Schildkrout, *People of the Zongo* (Cambridge, 1978), which concentrates on problems of ethnic identity, and Kwame Arhin, *West African Traders in Ghana in the Nineteenth and Twentieth Centuries* (London, 1979), which is particularly valuable for economic organization.

of international customary law were taking place elsewhere in West Africa.

During the nineteenth century one of the most important junctions between the internal trading networks and the oceanic export sector was the British colony of Sierra Leone. Freetown grew as a cosmopolitan city almost entirely composed of strangers; the indigenous Temnes were submerged in a new community dominated by Black repatriates from the Americas and by Liberated Africans of diverse origins. The relationship of Yoruba, Igbo, Congo minorities to the emerging Creole society is a fascinating subject in itself.[25] But Africans from the surrounding region were also drawn voluntarily to the city. As early as 1816 the British established a reservation called Kru Town, for seamen and labourers from the Liberian coast; this distinctive (and for many years exclusively male) community chose its own headman, who received immigrants, negotiated with employers, and adjudicated domestic disputes. Later in the century the British gave somewhat intermittent recognition to the Kru headman, sometimes enrolling him in the colonial police.[26]

Continuity with pre-colonial custom is more evident in the behaviour of the long-range caravan traders of various ethnic groups who brought their hides, gold, ivory and cattle to Freetown to exchange for firearms or other European goods. Here as elsewhere they found *ja-tigi* to render the traditional services, and protect them against the sharp practices of colonial capitalism. Anxious to encourage this commerce, the British authorities appointed a remarkable African interpreter, T. G. Lawson, to supervise the welfare of the strangers, and he founded a small 'Aborigines department' whose records throw much light on the growth of these enclaves.[27] Later in the century, when Temnes, Mendes and other neighbouring peoples began to seek employment in Freetown, they too elected 'tribal headmen' who rendered political and judicial as well as social and economic services to their people, and, with varying degrees of official recognition, acted as intermediaries with the colonial government. Most of these short-range immigrants, unlike the caravan traders, did not come from Muslim societies; but once in Freetown they tended to join mosques, which in some cases assumed specific ethnic identities. The

[25] A. T. Porter, *Creoledom* (London, 1962); J. Peterson, *Province of Freedom* (London, 1969). Both works draw heavily on C. H. Fyfe, *A History of Sierra Leone* (Oxford, 1962).
[26] Barbara E. Harrell-Bond, A. M. Howard and D. E. Skinner, *Community Leadership and the Transformation of Freetown (1801–1976)* (The Hague, 1978), pp. 31, 70–5; G. E. Brooks, Jr., *The Kru Mariner in the Nineteenth Century* (Newark, Delaware, 1972).
[27] J. D. Hargreaves, 'The Evolution of the Native Affairs Department', *Sierra Leone Studies*, n.s. 3 (1954), 168–84. These records have been well utilized in Harrell-Bond et al, *Community Leadership*, which forms the principal source for this paragraph.

generic title by which these communities were known—*jamat*—reflects the importance of Islam in integrating strangers into city life.

Sierra Leone became a source of new stranger communities as well as a centre for their reception; as missionaries, clerks, but above all as commercial agents or independent traders, Sierra Leoneans followed, and often pioneered, the expansion of European commerce through the coastal regions of western Africa. In 1839 some of them chartered a ship and landed at Badagry, which became the base for substantial return migration into their Yoruba homeland.[28] Yet their experiences in Sierra Leone—their conversion to Christianity, the literacy in English which made them valuable commercial and cultural intermediaries—seem to have turned these repatriates into strangers, half in and half out of the society of their own kinsmen; often they became known by the Yoruba word for white man—*oyinbo*. Similarly, Africans from the four communes of French Senegal were called *toubab* by the Wolof.

Africans who identified themselves with European enclaves might thus become strangers among their own kinsmen. In Dahomey, a centralized kingdom which claimed virtually totalitarian powers over its subjects, the European forts were surrounded by African settlements known as *salaams*, whose extra-territorial status was generally respected in peacetime. (These may have been modelled on the settlements of Hausa-speaking Muslims, which had been developing since the early eighteenth century.)[29] Christian missionaries were allowed to work in nineteenth-century Dahomey, but they ministered chiefly to repatriates from Brazilian slavery; their rare Fon converts had to sever their links of kinship and become strangers. '. . . From the moment when . . . an individual is regarded as being attached to a creole, a mulatto or one of those blacks who call themselves whites because they live in the manner of the whites,' wrote Father Borghero in 1864, 'there is no more opposition . . . Christians are considered as foreigners living among the blacks.'[30]

The increased scale of nineteenth-century migrations sometimes strained the systems of 'international customary law'. Demands for export crops created labour shortages which might be met by renewed commerce in slaves, to supply both European and African masters. In other cases, new tenancy arrangements provided for labouring strangers to be accommodated in a subordinate status. The revolutionary growth of groundnut production in the lower Gambia valley during

[28] J. H. Kopytoff, *A Preface to Modern Nigeria: the Sierra Leonians in Yoruba, 1830–1890* (Madison, 1965).

[29] Adamu, *The Hausa Factor*, pp. 113–16.

[30] Diary of Fr. Borghero, April 1864, quoted in J. M. Todd, *African Mission* (London, 1962), pp. 82–3.

the later nineteenth century was made possible by seasonal migrants known as *navetanes*, or 'strange farmers'. Too numerous to be absorbed under a traditional system of land tenancy known as *lungtango*, the strangers were 'taken into the compound by the compound head and given a portion of compound land to farm for themselves in return for an agreed number of labour days on the compound head's farm'.[31] Economically, this is clearly a form of share-cropping, but socially it recalled the position of the slaves, or *jaam*; the *navetane*, say Martin Klein, 'simply assumed the obligations of a *jaam* or an unmarried son'.[32] These strangers were in social subordination, though not in compulsory servitude; the current of voluntary migration continued to grow, with the encouragement of British colonial authorities. Nowadays 20,000–40,000 farmers find seasonal employment within the Gambia,[33] an underprivileged minority, no doubt, but not so far as I know a discontented one.

V

The extension of colonial rule in the later nineteenth century did not have any marked impact on the general status of African strangers, whether subordinated or enclaved. Though some colonial administrators felt a general responsibility to ensure respect for the human rights of under-privileged groups, this was generally outweighed by fears of jeopardizing the colonial *pax* by disturbing the social order; when they did intervene in stranger–host relations it was usually an improvised response to some local difficulty. Each colony moved, more or less gradually, towards a legal proscription of slavery, but few Governors paid more than lip-service to ideals of social equality or the elevation of under-dogs. Strangers in general remained peripheral to their local society.

But the numbers of such peripheral strangers were vastly increased by population movements. Some of these involved relatively articulate people, versed in European ideologies. The growing needs of colonial governments and commercial companies for clerks, storemen and artisans meant that in developing towns existing settlements of Sierra Leoneans were supplemented by groups of educated men from missionary centres in the Gold Coast, southern Nigeria, Senegal and

[31] A. A. O. Jeng, 'An Economic History of the Gambia Groundnut Industry, 1830–1924: the Evolution of an Export Economy', Ph.D. thesis, University of Birmingham, 1978, pp. 37–40.
[32] M. Klein, 'Servitude among the Wolof and Sereer of Senegambia', *Slavery in Africa*, ed. Miers and Kopytoff, p. 355.
[33] K. Swindell, 'Serawoollies, Tillibunkas and Strange Farmers: the Development of Migrant Groundnut Farming along the Gambia River, 1848–95', *Journal of African History*, xxi (1980), 93–104.

Dahomey.[34] More numerous were the migrations of labourers, who often crossed colonial as well as ethnic boundaries in search of seasonal or long-term employment in the export sector. African cocoa farms in the southern Gold and Ivory Coasts attracted thousands of workers from densely populated states in the upper Volta region; established networks of *masugida* found new roles as recruiters and travel agents.[35]

Trading strangers increased too; despite the erection of new frontiers and customs-posts the old trading networks found that colonial rule opened new routes, and sometimes new modes of transport. The formation of British Nigeria encouraged Hausa merchants to move south to sell cattle; in 1916 the chiefs of Ibadan, under British pressure, allocated them the strangers' quarter known as Sabo (or *sabon gari*) which had an initial population of about four hundred.[36] Similarly, British rule allowed Hausa and Mossi traders again to penetrate the forest areas of central Asante; officials encouraged them to establish new *zongos* in the hope of stimulating free trade. Considerable continuity can be traced in many of these population movements, and in the methods by which strangers and hosts regulated their relationships; but their new scale, added to the tendency of colonial bureaucracies to classify strangers as aliens, created political hazards for future African statesmen. The Ghana census of 1960 would identify 1 in 8 of adult Africans as born abroad.[37]

Colonial attitudes towards stranger enclaves vacillated. The British concept of Indirect Rule, as it evolved, envisaged the reconstruction of Native Authorities as agents of local administration, exercising jurisdiction according to local custom over all residents within a defined territory (except Europeans and their clients, who would retain a privileged form of extra-territoriality). Yet many practitioners of Indirect Rule also believed in respecting ethnic identity, and were prepared to do so where stranger settlements clearly served the local economy. Many compromises resulted. In Ibadan, for example, the British strengthened the autonomy of the Sabo, while insisting that the overlordship of local Yoruba authorities should be strictly respected in form; even orders to keep Hausa cattle off the golf-course had to pass through the Olubadan and Council.[38]

After the conquest of Asante, both British administrators and their Akan collaborators recognized the advantages of encouraging the

[34] See H. S. Challenor, 'Strangers as Colonial Intermediaries: the Dahomeyans in Francophone Africa', *Strangers in African Societies*, ed. Shack and Skinner, pp. 67–83.

[35] Short, 'Continuity and Change', pp. 171–6.

[36] A. Cohen, *Custom and Politics in Urban Africa: A Study of Hausa Migrants in Yoruba Towns* (London, 1969), pp. 103–19. In Ibadan the term 'Zongo' is kept for the cattle-market itself.

[37] Peil, 'The Expulsion of West African Aliens', 208.

[38] Cohen, *Custom and Politics*, pp. 115–17.

Northern stranger enclaves. In Kumasi the *zongo* area was physically reconstructed after 1905 and the *sarkin zongo* dealt with the British Chief Commissioner as successor to the deposed Asantehene; while in former provinces of metropolitan Asante (*aman*) and elsewhere, new *zongos* were established under the patronage of the *amanhene*, who generally stood to gain thereby.[39] In some of the older savanna *zongos* the position of the northerners was greatly strengthened; in Kintampo, where the strangers over-shadowed their Brong hosts, *sarkin zongo* Fanyinama I (a former warrior under Samori) 'gradually assumed the position of an autonomous chief'.[40] The balance struck between hosts and strangers thus often depended more upon local relationships than on any consistent British policy.

Many immigrants who expected to remain permanently resident in Asante still wished to maintain their own ethnic identities or, as in the case of the Asante-born young men who formed a body called 'Members of Islam' in 1924–5, to merge them into the wider identity of a multi-ethnic enclave.[41] Sallo, an able and energetic Hausa who became *sarkin zongo* of Kumasi in 1919, succeeded in persuading the colonial authorities to extend the jurisdiction of his court over those of the seven tribal headmen. But thereafter British policy moved, though erratically, against enclavement. The orthodoxy of Indirect Rule indicated extending the jurisdiction of the territorial chiefs; Prempe's reinstatement as chief of Kumasi in 1924 and the recognition of his nephew as Asantehene in 1935 reflected this. In 1932 Sallo was deposed, having alienated the non-Hausa communities; and although the headmen chose a new *sarkin zongo* to represent the whole enclave in its external relationships, he was no longer officially recognized. Headmen had to answer directly to the Asante authorities for the affairs of their communities and the proceedings of their courts. In 1943 strangers became liable to taxation by the Native Authorities, usually without acquiring any right to representation upon them. The British were now seeking to create organs of local government under which all residents would have similar responsibilities and similar rights, in preparation for a transfer of power in the distant future. But

[39] Short, 'Continuity and Change', ch. 3. J. Simmensen, 'Commoners, Chiefs and Colonial Governments. British Policy and Local Politics in Akim Abuakwa, Ghana, under Colonial Rule', Ph.D. thesis, University of Trondheim, 1975, contains an important discussion of the attempts by Ofori Atta I to extend his territorial jurisdiction over Akan immigrants who were obtaining land in Akim Abuakwa; but as Short points out (pp. 225-6, 385-8), he remained apparently content to respect the extra-territorial status of his Hausa strangers.
[40] Arhin, *West African Traders*, pp. 115-20 and 81-4.
[41] Short, 'Continuity and Change', p. 336 and ch. 5, *passim*, for the basis of this paragraph. There is a somewhat different interpretation in Schildkrout, *People of the Zongo*, pp. 194-206.

in practice this policy was not fully implemented; *amanhene* continued to deal with their strangers on special terms, where these seemed justified by custom or expediency.[42]

These general tendencies, and these vacillations in practice, could be paralleled in other colonies. In Freetown, British long-term objectives, on the rare occasions when they were made explicit, seemed to be assimilationist; this colonial city would eventually be ruled by a Municipal Council, elected on some uniform franchise, but in practice no doubt directed by educated Creoles. Since few Governors ever felt much confidence in the Creoles they knew (and many Creoles were far from enthusiastic about the institutions offered them), headmen of the various *jamat* did secure sporadic recognition, notably in the Tribal Administration (Freetown) Ordinance of 1905.[43] Once decolonization was accepted as a real though distant objective, however, continued enclavement of strangers (whether potential fellow-citizens of Sierra Leone or immigrants from across colonial borders) seemed anomalous. In 1944 a government committee declared that

> 'the ideal to which we look forward is a Freetown of intelligent and independent citizens, not an agglomeration or even a federation of tribal detachments. The aim should be to instil a civic sense into the individual and to avoid any course which might perpetuate tribal consciousness. The Tribal Administrations of Freetown, we feel, may have their places as friendly societies and nurseries of sentiment alongside the Caledonian Societies, and Liverpool-Irish battalions, but not as an integral part of the local government.'[44]

In reality 'tribal detachments' continued to provide immigrants, and indeed long-term urban residents, with essential support within the city; during the early 1950s the pioneer anthropological researches of Michael Banton suggested that the system of tribal headmanship 'might be utilized more systematically as a means of organizing self-help ... and training the newcomers in citizenship'.[45] Nevertheless, British policy was now tending towards the creation of nation-states in which strangers would turn into minorities, as a step towards full integration.

VI

This desire to reproduce the European nation-state in Africa was warmly taken up by African political leaders. Their Mazzinian

[42] Short, 'Continuity and Change', pp. 394–6.
[43] Harrell-Bond et al, *Community Leadership*, App. C and *passim*.
[44] C.O. 267/688/32348, Part 1. Sessional Paper No. 4 of 1944, Reconstitution of the Freetown City Council.
[45] M. P. Banton, *West African City: A Study of Tribal Life in Freetown* (London, 1957).

rhetoric commonly called for the unification of peoples into new nations, whose citizens would enjoy equal access to resources and owe equal loyalty. In practice, where the bonds of kinship remained strong, citizens continued to expect favoured treatment from their kinsmen. These expectations were heightened rather than reduced by the advent of electoral politics; for in Africa as elsewhere it could be assumed that the triumph of a party would be followed by rewards for its supporters. Majority peoples were tempted to keep marginal groups down so that they would not compete for public resources. At best, this was but a short-term expedient, for ethnic identity is quickly strengthened by a sense of relative deprivation. When communities confined to proleterian roles perceive that they are being treated as slaves once more, strangers have become minorities.

To allay their new fears, minorities did engage in electoral politics, as Willink suggested. But such tactics proved most effective when conducted from a secure base in an enclave with a well-seasoned relationship with its neighbours. The Hausa of Western Nigeria, though numbering over 40,000, were not among those expressing fears to the Willink Commission. Within the Ibadan Sabo, their response to political change had been to redefine and intensify their own identity, by processes which Abner Cohen describes as 'retribalization'. During the 1940s many Ibadan Hausa distinguished themselves from Yoruba Muslims by adopting the Tijanniyya order, and in 1952 they took the radical step of holding Friday prayers in their own mosque. Meanwhile they sought to protect their position within the Western Region by bargaining with political parties. Rejecting the strategy of joining their kinsmen in the Northern Peoples' Congress, which could not hope to win seats in the West, the Sabo leaders weighed the alternatives and decided to support the Action Group (whose leader, Obafemi Awolowo, came down to ask for it). When that party split in 1963 they hastened to make terms with the new regional government of S. L. Akintola.[46] Corporate flexibility seems to have provided a viable strategy for protecting the interests of this distinctive stranger enclave.

Within the city of Freetown, the *jamat* have also preserved their identities, despite the commitment of successive governments to ideals of uniform law and citizenship within a modern Sierra Leonean state. African politicians inherited the British ambivalence, which continued to the last; an official committee of 1952 noted that 'The system of organisation of tribal communities has undeniable advantages, but … these … are not those which it is the intention of the law to provide.'[47] Consciousness of the practical utility of sectional jurisdic-

---

[46] Cohen, *Custom and Politics*, esp. ch. 5.
[47] Report of the Committee appointed to examine the working of the Tribal Administration (Colony) Ordinance, 1952. Copy in writer's possession.

tions was strengthened by services rendered to party politicians; a remarkable Temne headman, Kandeh Bureh, enabled the provincial-based Sierra Leone Peoples' Party to secure a foothold in the capital, and in 1957 was rewarded with ministerial office. But the civil service, largely led by Creoles, retained its dislike of the system, and in 1967 a military regime declared the office of tribal headman abolished.[48]

This, however, was not easily achieved. Immigrants still looked to headmen as patrons and spokesmen in the complex world of the city; their unrecognized courts continued to judge minor criminal offences, charges of witchcraft, questions of family law and 'woman damage', according to concepts of 'African law' which were increasingly becoming accepted across tribal lines. And those headmen who represented strangers with homelands beyond the boundaries of Sierra Leone—the Kru and the Fula—proved more effective than regular diplomatic channels in handling minority problems. In 1968 the Ministry of the Interior tried to persuade the Kru that 'As your country Liberia is represented by an Embassy in Sierra Leone . . . all affairs concerning your tribe should pass through him for the time being'; but it was not easy to by-pass channels established for a century and a half, and on 1 January 1969 the Kru headman was reinstated. A Fula headman was elected next year, the government hoping that he would help control a current of immigration which had been greatly intensified by the diamond boom in Sierra Leone and by the policies of Sekou Touré in Guinea.[49] Meanwhile the Temne and other indigenous communities also wanted their headmen back. In 1975 these offices were restored, doubts about the effects on 'unity and social cohesion' outweighed by their evident utility as political intermediaries and tax-collectors. This apparently untidy form of enclavement now seems stronger than ever.

Stranger communities in Asante have been less fortunate in their involvement with Ghanaian national politics. Initially, many young men from the *zongos* responded to the social and ideological appeal of Nkrumah's Convention Peoples' Party; but the community leaders still sought to defend their special interests, and specifically to promote Islamic education, by independent action through immigrant pressure groups. In 1953 they shifted their focus from local to national politics by forming the Muslim Association Party, which allied with other largely sectional opposition groups and four years later merged into the United Party led by Kofi Busia. This was an attempt to reconcile membership of trans-African communities, on which their commerce in kola and cattle still depended, with citizenship in the new Ghana;

[48] These two paragraphs are based on Harrell-Bond et al, *Community Leadership*, which quotes from unpublished documents as well as personal observations.

[49] Harrell-Bond, *Community Leadership*, pp. 267–79.

but to Nkrumah it seemed to identify the Muslim strangers as one of several minorities which threatened his vision of a unitary nation-state. Soon after independence a Ghana Nationality Act turned most of the strangers (including many born in Ghana) into aliens, and two M.A.P. leaders (Ahmadu Baba and Othman Lardan) were deported to Nigeria. The local C.P.P. leader Mutwakilu was appointed *sarkin zongo* of Kumasi by the Cabinet; but when he attempted to revive the extra-territorial status of the *zongo*, his office was suspended as part of a campaign against 'tribalism'. However, Nkrumah's commitment to pan-Africanism helped to prevent mass expulsions, and the long-established relationships by which strangers regulated their position within local communities largely continued to operate.

As we saw, the strongest attack on the enclaves came in 1969, when the government of their former ally Busia faced pressure for 'indigen-ization' from Ghanaians who saw the strangers as successful compet-itors in times of unemployment and business depression. Yet those affected by expulsion orders seem to have had considerable success in maintaining or recovering their residence in Ghana. To a limited degree they may have been assisted by diplomatic or consular officers representing their 'home' governments (e.g. over residence permits);[50] but more important seem to have been evasions of the law, connived at by host communities which still derived benefit from the presence of the strangers. In 1976 Dr. Short found the headmen in the Kumasi *zongo* still adjudicating internal cases, and discharging quasi-consular functions in regard to relationships with local Ghanaian authorities. Many of the latter, it seems, accept the contention of young Kumasi Muslims in 1968, that 'a patriotic stranger is better than a rebelled citizen'.[51]

There is one category of stranger which has survived the transition to the African nation-state well, though not usually because of con-spicuously patriotic loyalty to the country of residence. European strangers like ourselves, unless they have seemed to be competing with indigenous Africans for political power, still fall into the especially favoured category of expatriate. This may be because, as in the days of the slave-trade, they represent international business enterprises which offer advantages to some at least of their hosts, or because they are regarded as bringers of desirable skills or expertise. Even where,

[50] The efforts of the Yoruba are described in Niara Sudarkasa, 'From Stranger to Alien: the Socio-Political history of the Nigerian Yoruba in Ghana, 1900-1970', *Strangers in African Societies*, ed. Shack and Skinner, pp. 141-68.

[51] Short, 'Continuity and Change', p. 469; see also ch. 6 and app. 2, *passim*, for the argument of these paragraphs. See also J. Adomako-Sarfoh, 'The Effects of the Ex-pulsion of Migrant Workers on Ghana's Economy, with Particular Reference to the Cocoa Industry', *Modern Migrations in Western Africa*, ed. S. Amin (London, 1974), pp. 138-55.

as in Senegal or the Ivory Coast, Europeans are in serious competition with citizens for employment and other resources, they can still count on extensive extra-territorial immunities. At the price of various inconveniences and financial disbursements, expatriates continue to enjoy considerable comfort and privilege within air-conditioned enclaves. If the desire to recreate economic unities across the modern frontiers of West Africa, expressed by the creation of the international body known as ECOWAS, come to fruition, it may yet seem equally advantageous to retreat from nationalist orthodoxy by restoring some extra-territorial privileges to African strangers too.

RELIGIOUS BELIEF AND SOCIAL CONFORMITY: THE 'CONVERSO' PROBLEM IN LATE-MEDIEVAL CÓRDOBA

By J. H. Edwards, M.A., D.Phil.

READ AT THE SOCIETY'S CONFERENCE 11 SEPTEMBER 1980

THE fact that Spain is, to date, the only western European country which has ever been an Islamic colony still seems to banish her to the fringe of her neighbours' historical consciousness. Much of the responsibility for this state of affairs rests with the Spaniards themselves. In most cases and in most periods, the inhabitants of the Iberian peninsula have, with varying degrees of enthusiasm, used the Pyrenees as an intellectual, as well as a physical, barrier, and considered the Peninsula's problems as distinct from those of the rest of the European continent. A strong reason for adopting this approach is the remarkable co-existence of Islamic, Christian and Jewish civilization between 711 and 1492, which placed Spain and Portugal within both medieval Christendom and the Islamic world of North Africa and the eastern Mediterranean. The successes of co-operation between the three religions which were achieved during this period are worthy of greater recognition than they generally receive, but the intention here is to investigate the causes of the failures which brought co-existence to an end, concentrating on the relationship between Judaism and Christianity in a large, late-medieval Castilian town.

Córdoba, the city on the right bank of the Guadalquivir, in the southern region of Andalusia, which had once been the capital of the Muslim caliphs, was captured by the armies of Ferdinand III, king of Castile, in 1236. After this, it became the capital of the kingdom of Córdoba, a purely theoretical territorial unit which none the less remained as one of the royal titles and gave the city two seats in the Castilian Cortes. Following the pattern already established in earlier phases of the Christian reconquest of the Peninsula, Ferdinand granted Córdoba a charter, or *fuero*, and entrusted the government of the city and the surrounding region to magistrates and councillors who represented the parishes. Knowledge of the thirteenth-century constitutional arrangements is hazy, but it appears that both the magistrates and the parish councillors were elected annually by the citizens, until the fourteenth century brought the creation of an inner council of *regidores*, who were appointed for life by the Crown. In the late fifteenth century, Córdoba was governed by the *regidores* and by magistrates, who were also appointed by the Crown. The parish councillors had been relegated to a subordinate role. By this time, many of the lands, towns and castles which had originally been given to Córdoba had been transferred to the secular nobility as lordships, with attendant immunities, but the council still ruled over about two-thirds of the land in the kingdom of Córdoba, though only about half its population. There is no census for the area before 1530, but in that year the city is said to have contained 5,845 households.[1] Córdoba was thus one of the larger Castilian towns of the period. Although it had a high-quality textile industry, its economy was largely agrarian and dominated by the seignorial aristocracy.

After the reconquest of 1236, the existing population of Córdoba seems to have been expelled and replaced by Christian settlers from further north. The vacant urban and rural properties were distributed among them by royal officials, in the years after 1241. Some Muslim artisans were soon invited back to the city to carry on specialized trades, particularly in the building industry, and a small Muslim community remained in Córdoba until the Crown ordered the expulsion of Muslims from Castile in 1502. There was also a Jewish community in Córdoba throughout this period, though little is known about it. Jews in Córdoba are mentioned in secular and ecclesiastical legislation from the years immediately after 1236. Various thirteenth-century documents refer to the buying and leasing by Jews of urban property and lands in the area. In 1250, Pope Innocent IV ordered the bishop of Córdoba to investigate complaints that the Jews of the city had constructed a synagogue which was excessively ostentatious and a danger to the Christian faithful, while in the fourteenth century, the local Jewish community was forced to pay an annual tax of thirty *dineros* to the cathedral chapter, as a reminder of the thirty pieces of silver paid to Judas by the Jewish authorities in return for his betrayal of Jesus. The Jewish quarter was to the north-west of the Great Mosque (the cathedral after 1236) and the bishop's palace, the central administrative area of the city.[2] It is impossible to make an accurate assessment of the numbers in Córdoba's Jewish community (in Hebrew, *kahal*, in Castilian, *aljama*). It was insignificant in comparison with that of Toledo and smaller than that of Seville, which is said by Jewish sources to have contained two hundred families around 1290.

[1] Emilio Cabrera, 'Tierras realengas y tierras de señorío a fines de la Edad Media. Distribución geográfica y niveles de población', *Actas del Primer Congreso de Historia de Andalucía (1976), Andalucía Medieval*, i (Córdoba, 1978), 295-308.
[2] F. Baer, *Die Juden im christlichen Spanien* (Berlin, 1929-36), I, pt. 2, pp. 9, 27-8, 53-4, 220; Francisco Cantera Burgos, *Sinagogas de Toledo, Segovia y Córdoba* (Madrid, 1973), pp. 153-4.

Probably it never numbered more than five hundred people, this being a point worth noting in view of the furore which surrounded it. Taxation evidence from the period of Ferdinand and Isabella's Granada campaigns, during which Jewish communities were forced to make special and disproportionately large contributions, suggests that Córdoba's *aljama* was no bigger than that of many much smaller towns.[3]

There is no doubt, however, that Córdoba's Jewry went into a permanent decline as a result of the attacks made upon it by Christian citizens in 1391. Riots against the Jews had been fomented in Seville in the earlier part of that year by the preaching of the archdeacon of Ecija, Ferrand Martínez, and soon spread to Córdoba, as well as other cities. The main motive seems to have been robbery, but although the Crown took the part of its traditional protégés, the Jews, with Henry III ordering an investigation of the violence and the payment of compensation to the victims, the Córdoba Jewry never recovered from the attack, so that, although a small number of Jews remained in the city until their expulsion from Andalusia in 1483, the last written reference being in a tax document in 1485, the Jews who remained faithful to the old religion were never again the focus of serious social tension in the city.[4]

Although some Jews were killed in 1391 and many others fled the city, most responded to the attacks by becoming Christians. In this way they clearly sought to avoid in future the anti-Jewish feelings of their fellow citizens and become fully integrated into local society. By the act of passing, at least metaphorically, through the waters of baptism, Córdoba's Jews would automatically lose the legal and social disabilities which were the lot of Jewish communities wherever they lived in medieval Europe. They would henceforth be subject to the city's magistrates, instead of their own communal judges, and their lives would therefore be regulated by Córdoba's charter, the Visigothic *Fuero Juzgo*, and the same royal legal and administrative dispositions as those of the Christian majority. Above all, they would no longer be barred from public office, ecclesiastical or secular. Although sources for the history of Córdoba in the early and mid-fifteenth century are somewhat sketchy, it none the less appears that the first sign of serious difficulty in the reception of Jewish converts as Christians was the outbreak of rioting in the city in 1473.

[3] Baer, *A History of the Jews in Christian Spain* (2 vols., Philadelphia, 1961–66), I, pp. 191–6. Luis Suárez Fernández, *Documentos acerca de la expulsión de los judíos* (Valladolid, 1964), p. 67.
[4] Manuel Nieto Cumplido, 'Luchas nobiliarias y movimientos populares en Córdoba a fines del siglo XIV', in Manuel Riu Riu, Cristóbal Torres, Manuel Nieto, *Tres estudios de historia medieval andaluza* (Córdoba, 1977), pp. 43–6; Baer, *Die Juden*, I, pt. 2, pp. 232–3, 245, 348–9; Suárez Fernández, *Documentos*, pp. 35–6.

The trouble began when a child spilt some water from a balcony on to a statue of Our Lady which was being carried in a Lenten procession by the most powerful of Córdoba's Christian confraternities, the Brotherhood of Charity. It was said that the liquid was urine and that the act was deliberate. The supposed insult to the Mother of God led immediately to violence and, since the relevant house belonged to a New Christian, or *converso*, that is, a Christian of Jewish origin, large-scale looting of *converso* property began throughout the city. The current chief magistrate, or *alcalde mayor*, Don Alonso de Aguilar, who was the senior member of the local nobility, decided that he did not have the forces to stop the rioting and retired to the Alcázar, or castle. When the looters reached exhaustion, after three days, he emerged to decree that no *converso* should ever again hold public office in the city.[5] The next step was the introduction of the Inquisition.

Córdoba was the second city, after Seville, to receive the re-founded Castilian Inquisition of the Catholic Monarchs, Ferdinand and Isabella. On 4 September 1482, the cathedral chapter agreed to allow the three inquisitors, who had been appointed by the Crown and the Pope and who were also canons of Córdoba, to be absent from choir services on official business.[6] The effects of the Holy Office's activities were quickly felt by the *conversos* of the city. Sadly, the records of the Córdoba tribunal for this period do not survive, but fragments of evidence may be found in local and royal administrative sources. Thus it is known that least two parish councillors (*jurados*) and two public notaries lost their offices as a result of conviction by the Inquisition for 'judaizing', between 1484 and 1486. In the period 1484–92, ten citizens of Córdoba who had been 'reconciled' to the Church after 'judaizing' were released from their debts by the Crown, because their goods had been confiscated.[7] Throughout the last two decades of the fifteenth century, there was a steady stream of trials, leading in most cases to conviction and penalties which always included confiscation of goods and loss of any public office, but might also involve death by burning, in person or in effigy.

It may seem extraordinary that the attitude of the Christian

[5] Diego De Valera, *Memorial de diversas hazañas*, ed. Juan de Mata Carriazo (Madrid, 1941), pp. 240–3; Alfonso de Palencia, *Décadas*, trans. A. Paz y Melia (Madrid, 1904–9), III, pp. 107–16; M. Nieto, 'La revuelta contra los conversos de Córdoba en 1473', *Homenaje a Antón de Montoro en el V centenario de su muerte* (Montoro, 1977), pp. 31–49.

[6] Archivo Catedralicio de Córdoba (ACC), Actas capitulares, iv, fo. 142v.

[7] Archivo General de Simancas, Registro General del Sello, entries for 8.2.1484, 21.2.1484, 20.12.1484, 20.2.1485, 15.2.1485, 15.6.1486, 4.4.1487, 4.1487, 7.4.1487, 8.4.1487, 29.8.1487, 26.2.1490, 30.4.1485, 24.9.1491, 27.1.1492; ACC, Cajón L No. 513 (28.3.1487), Cajón G No. 247 (17.2.1492).

majority in Córdoba towards its fellow citizens who converted from Judaism after 1391, and their descendants, should have changed from acceptance to violent rejection, at some point in or before 1473. After all, fifty years or more had passed without the existence of Jewish Christians being, apparently, a cause of dissension in the city. In order to understand the change, it is necessary, first of all, to place the foundation of the Córdoban Inquisition in its national and regional political context. Castilian politics in the reigns of John II (1406-54) and his son, Henry IV (1454-74), are noted for their complexity, but their main feature is generally said to have been a growth in the power and influence of the secular nobility at the expense of other groups, including the towns, and above all the Crown. Whether or not seignorial power was either as great or as harmful as is often assumed, it is undoubtedly true that these two successive kings had very little control over what happened in Córdoba and district. The main beneficiaries from this state of affairs were the local magnates, nearly all of whose families had first settled in the area after the thirteenth-century reconquest, but had come to real prominence as a result of the accession of the Trastamaran dynasty to the Castilian throne in 1369, with French help and after a civil war. Don Alonso de Aguilar, who was in charge of Córdoba during the 1473 anti-*converso* riots, had been appointed to his post as chief magistrate by Henry IV, but he owed his dominance of the city and much of the surrounding region to the victory of his house of Aguilar over the rival house of Baena, in a long-standing dispute which had led to violence on many occasions. The Aguilar and Baena parties, or *bandos*, were the only political groupings of any importance in city and region. They were led by the heads of two different lines of the Fernández de Córdoba family, Don Alonso de Aguilar and the count of Cabra, and it was difficult for citizens of Córdoba to avoid connections with one or the other. In the absence of effective royal authority, the *bandos* virtually had a free hand and this situation only changed after the accession of Isabella to the Castilian throne in 1474 and the intervention of her husband Ferdinand in the government of the kingdom.

From the point of view of Córdoba's *converso* minority, the arrival of Isabella and Ferdinand was not, in practice, an improvement. For about two years after Henry IV's death little changed, because the new queen had to fight for her throne against Henry's daughter, Joanna, and her Portuguese allies. The Andalusian magnates, including Don Alonso de Aguilar and the count of Cabra, were unwilling to declare themselves until they knew which side would win. The vital battles and diplomacy, which led to Isabella's victory in 1476, took place elsewhere in the Peninsula, so that Don Alonso continued to dominate Córdoba and *conversos* were still excluded from public office until the Catholic Monarchs found time to visit Andalusia, in 1477–78. The visit's success, from the royal point of view, is still not entirely explicable, but it is certain that the magnates who governed the main towns of the region, including Don Alonso, were all suspended from the exercise of their offices, though they retained the title of *alcalde mayor*, and were replaced by teams of royal officials, headed in each case by a *corregidor*, who acted as the Crown's personal representative in the area under his control. In the case of Córdoba, Don Alonso left the city and seems not to have returned between 1478 and his death during a Muslim rebellion near Málaga in 1501.[8]

Whether the submission of Córdoba's magnates to royal authority was due to an extraordinary strength of will on the part of the Monarchs or simply to exhaustion and stalemate in the struggle between the *bandos*, the fact remains that politics of the traditional kind, in which nobles sought to dominate the municipal government by methods which ranged from marriage alliances with council members to straightforward intimidation, either ceased altogether or, more commonly, continued, without the visible presence of the noble leaders, under the watchful and fearful eye of the *corregidor*. A vital part of the settlement which Ferdinand and Isabella achieved in 1478 was, however, the exclusion of Jewish Christians from public life and often, in the case of those found guilty of reverting to their ancestral faith, from any life at all.

The new arrangements seem to have stood the test of the Granada campaigns, between 1482 and 1492. Like other Castilian towns, Córdoba was required on a number of occasions to supply armies that consisted of a few hundred cavalry and several thousand infantry, which supplemented the largely mounted contingents which the local nobles maintained and generally led in person. It was the period of relative peace, after Granada fell in 1492, which brought out latent tensions and questioned the efficacy of the Catholic Monarchs' earlier work. The difficulties after 1500 included a partial breakdown of royal authority, when Isabella died in 1504, Philip I soon followed and the incapacity of his widow, Joanna, led to disputes about the role of Ferdinand in the government of Castile. There was a series of challenges to the Crown's authority in Córdoba, as personified by the *corregidor*, which were led by Don Alonso de Aguilar's son, the marquis of Priego, and culminated in a brief revolt in the summer of 1508, which was ended by Ferdinand's intervention, with a large professional army. In the years after 1501, there were seven bad harvests in Andalusia and expensive foreign grain had to be bought. There was pestilence, particularly in 1507, and the Córdoban nobility took

[8] More on Córdoba's politics in this period in my forthcoming book, *Christian Córdoba*.

advantage of the situation to re-assert its political influence.[9] Córdoba's *conversos* and the Inquisition were intimately involved with these problems.

The strains which the Inquisition caused in the fabric of local society were concentrated in the person of Diego Rodríguez Lucero, a canon of Seville, who became inquisitor in Córdoba in 1500. The fact that the introduction of the Holy Office to Córdoba coincided with a decline in noble control over local politics indicated the possibility of aristocratic opposition to the tribunal's activities. In the event, resistance focused on the supposed excesses of Lucero and was led, in a rare show of unanimity, by the upper nobility, the town council and the cathedral chapter. As early as 1501, a council official was banished by the Crown for assaulting an Inquisition notary, but matters came to a head in 1506, when Joanna and Philip, trying to gain support in Castile at the expense of Ferdinand, acceded to a demand from Córdoba that the Holy Office's activities should be suspended until Lucero's conduct had been investigated. This instruction was never implemented, but the city continued with vigour its campaign against the inquisitor. The burden of the accusations against Lucero was that he convicted innocent people of 'judaizing', using false confessions, frequently extracted under torture. It appears that, in Lucero's mind, Córdoba was a kind of national centre for Jews who masqueraded as Christians, while at the same time continuing to practise Judaism secretly, in synagogues and led by rabbis. Lucero was even said by Córdoba's council to have taught Jewish prayers to Christian children whom he had imprisoned, so as to make the charges against them appear more plausible.[10] It may seem surprising that Lucero supposedly applied the techniques of a show-trial when the Inquisition's proceedings were always secret, but whatever the truth concerning this accusation, most of Córdoba's charges against Lucero were eventually held as proved by a Catholic Congregation, which Cardinal Cisneros had summoned and which gave sentence on 9 July 1508.[11] It appears that the cardinal, who by this time was regent of Castile for Joanna, was concerned at the instability which Lucero's activities were causing in the city and by their possible wider repercussions, and therefore took the matter out of the hands of the initial investigator, the Inquisitor-General, Don Diego Deza, who was also archbishop of Seville. After the 1508 congregation, there seem to have been no more

[9] The problems of the Andalusian economy in the early sixteenth century are discussed in *Christian Córdoba*.

[10] Biblioteca Municipal de Jerez de la Frontera, MS. 81, *Libro de istorias ... de lo qual da testimonio Juan Román*, fo. 3; Archivo Municipal de Córdoba, Actas capitulares, 1.2.1514.

[11] H. C. Lea, 'Lucero the Inquisitor', *American Historical Review*, ii (1896-97), 611-26.

major incidents in Córdoba involving the Inquisition, but it must be obvious that, for whatever reason, the presence in the city of Christians of Jewish origin produced extreme reactions from other citizens.

The association between Ferdinand and Isabella's reassertion of royal authority in Andalusia in 1477-8 and the foundation of the Inquisition in Seville and Córdoba has already been stressed, but the use of this tribunal in the task of maintaining Christian orthodoxy was far more than a response to local and temporary political difficulties. Myth has an essential and commonly underestimated part to play. Glick has argued that, because historians select and approach their evidence in ways which are inevitably determined by their own cultural and social values, they are in fact engaged in a kind of myth-making.[12] John Robinson and other theologians have pointed out that there is nothing shameful in admitting the role of myth, both in historical events and in historical writing. Myth is 'true' and the commonly made distinction between 'myth' and 'reality' is, in those terms, false. Myth may or must be used where direct evidence is unobtainable and the truth of a myth does not depend on whether it is historically accurate but on whether it adequately represents the data to be explained. If it does not, then it must be abandoned.[13] These concepts have recently been applied to late-medieval Spain by Hillgarth. In the late fifteenth century, most Spaniards saw their society as multi-cultural, though they would never have used such a word. For seven centuries co-existence between Christians, Jews and Muslims, however painful, had been at least an assumption, if not an ideal, and in some cases it was undoubtedly a reality. After 1492, the new belief came to prevail that Spain was or should be a country of one religion, a uniformly Christian society in which dissenters had no place. The expulsion of unbaptized Jews and Muslims and the attempt to remove Jewish belief and practice from the Church by means of the Inquisition were intended to achieve this aim. The prevailing myth had changed and social conditions had to be forcibly altered to match the new theory.[14]

The fate of Jewish Christians in cities such as Córdoba in the late Middle Ages is thus of considerable theoretical and practical significance for the modern interpreter, as well as the participants in the action. The councillors, notaries, churchmen and artisans who had their careers destroyed, lost all their goods, often went into exile or

[12] T. F. Glick, *Islamic and Christian Spain in the Early Middle Ages. Comparative perspectives in social and cultural formation* (Princeton, 1979), p. 3.

[13] J. A. T. Robinson, *In the End God* (London, 1968), pp. 45-6; M. Wiles, 'Myth in Theology', in *The Myth of God Incarnate* (London, 1977), pp. 148-66.

[14] J. N. Hillgarth, *The Spanish Kingdoms, 1250-1516, II. 1410-1516. Castilian hegemony* (Oxford, 1978), pp. 624-8.

even to the flames, and left their families and descendants to suffer a stigma for generations felt in their lives the power of the intellectual over the material. The introduction of the Inquisition to Castile was the result not only of certain economic, political and social conditions, but also of the beliefs which certain men held about themselves and hence about the nature of their society. It is thus inevitable that religious history must be accepted as a vital part of the explanation of the phenomena of conversion and Inquisition in late-medieval Spain. It must also be clear that the kind of religious history which is needed is not 'ecclesiastical history', in the sense of a study of the institutional and material aspects of the Christian Church, the business of lands and benefices and the relationship between papal and governmental bureaucracies. What is required is a recognition and, if possible, an understanding of the inner life of men—the asking of the fundamental questions about the nature of life and death, which underpin all philosophy and theology—and its realization in human society. A philosopher, Professor Atkinson, has recently observed that for most present-day practitioners, the terms of historical explanation are taken without question from current scientific assumptions. The rights and wrongs of religious revelations are not regarded as relevant to the work of the historian and thus the claims of religions such as Judaism, Christianity and Islam are automatically ignored in modern attempts to explain events in which their adherents participated. The historian proceeds as though his personal beliefs were entirely separate from his professional work.[15] It would be difficult to dissent from this view of observable reality, but the usefulness of such an approach to the study of a society's treatment of a religious minority is, to say the least, questionable.

The supreme test of the historian's skill and effectiveness in interpreting the relations between Old and New Christians is the phenomenon of conversion. It is here that his own assumptions, not only about his professional activities but also about his view of the nature of the world and his place within it, must be subjected to scrutiny. Religious minorities, and majorities, are of course groups with a particular identity, but they consist of individuals. Both Judaism and Christianity claim to be based on the revelations of Himself which God has at certain times chosen to offer to particular human groups— the people of Israel and the Christian Church. Both religions are therefore 'social' or 'community' religions, with their own structure of law and administration as well as sacred texts and cult practices. However, both religions also speak to the individual human being and demand from him or her a response. The Word must be heard

[15] R. F. Atkinson, *Knowledge and Explanation in History. An introduction to the philosophy of history* (London, 1978), pp. 90-1.

but it must also be done, and this action involves participation in a human society with some form of communal organization. The impetus which causes the believer to behave in a certain way in public must, in the case of a revealed religion, be expected to arise from personal communication with the Creator. It is in this area that the historian's customary methods are most inadequate, but the difficulties are particularly stark and unavoidable in the case of those who change from one religion to another.

When Solomon Halevi, chief rabbi of Burgos, converted to Christianity in 1391, apparently during a time when his community was under attack, his own justification of the step was commented upon by Joshua Halorki. Both these men later had distinguished careers as Christians and their views of conversion are of assistance in understanding possible personal motives for such a change, in the absence of similar evidence from Córdoba in the later period. In attempting to understand Halevi's action, Halorki suggested four possible motives for conversion. These were a quest for honours and wealth, a rejection of faith in Judaism resulting from the study and acceptance of the tenets of rationalist philosophy, the belief that the current misfortunes of Israel, notably the 1391 attacks, were a sign that God had finally abandoned His people, and, lastly, receipt by the convert of a new revelation from God that the Jewish religion was false.[16] The distinguished converts of the period after 1391 themselves asserted their acceptance of the Christian revelation and the claims made for it, first by the apostle Paul and then by the Church. They accepted Jesus as the Messiah and the Church as the New Israel, and without regarding these individuals' testimony as entirely false it is difficult to assert that no converts were genuine or that personal conviction was irrelevant to the conversion process.[17] Nevertheless, it is equally certain that political, economic and social conditions provided the impetus for many conversions. The violence of 1391 had an immediate effect, just as panic was instantly created among the existing converts of Córdoba and other cities, when the riots began in 1473. Obviously, force might make individuals take a step which was out of line with their personal convictions. Particularly interesting is Halorki's reference to scepticism as a cause of conversion. This factor was clearly important in Spanish Jewry, which had been heavily involved for centuries with the rationalistic tendencies of Greek and Arab philosophy. Thus, three of Halorki's proposed motives for conversion—acceptance of a new revelation, awareness of the misfortunes of Israel as illustrated by discrimination and violence, and a lapse into intellectual scepticism which permitted the lukewarm adoption of the majority religion—

---

[16] Baer, *History*, II, p. 143.
[17] Various cases in Baer, *History*, II, pp. 130-224.

were clearly relevant to the creation of the *converso* minority in late-medieval Spain. None of them however, can be considered without reference to Halorki's fourth point, the quest for wealth and honours. In recent years, the material explanation of the *converso* phenomenon has been effectively advocated by Wolff, MacKay and others. The argument connects attacks on the Jews with times of economic difficulty and social stress, and explains the conversion of Jews to Christianity in terms of a response to intimidation and a desire to escape discrimination.[18] The intimate connection between the fate of Córdoba's *conversos* and the problems of the region has been both assumed and described in the preceding discussion, but certain difficulties remain and no monocausal explanation can hope to cover the case. Perhaps the best way into the problem is to examine more closely the origins and nature of the Inquisition. Ferdinand and Isabella's foundation of the Holy Office in Castile arose not only out of the material circumstances which have already been noted but also out of an impassioned theological debate about the nature of conversion and the place of converts of Jewish origin in a Christian society. In 1449, the city council of Toledo, in rebellion against John II, provided the prototype for Córdoba's action in 1473 by banning *conversos* from public office in perpetuity. This revival of the repressive measures of the Church councils of the Visigothic period provoked a theoretical controversy, involving *converso* officials and churchmen such as Bishop Alonso de Cartagena, Fernán Díaz de Toledo and Cardinal Juan de Torquemada.[19] The issue was specifically that of office-holding, but while Pope Nicholas V and the *converso* authors all reasserted the power of baptism to remove both pre-existent sins and the distinctions between men, contemporary writers, Old Christian, New Christian and Jewish, seem to have agreed unanimously that, whatever happened to genuine converts from Judaism to Christianity, false converts were worthy of the severest punishment, even death by burning, and that an Inquisition was the most effective way of carrying out this operation.[20]

[18] P. Wolff, 'The 1391 Pogrom in Spain. Social crisis or not?', *Past & Present*, 50 (1971), 4–18; A. MacKay, 'Popular Movements and Pogroms in Fifteenth-Century Castile', *Past & Present*, 55 (1972), 33–67.

[19] B. Blumenkrantz, *Juifs et Chrétiens dans le monde occidental (430–1096)* (Paris/The Hague, 1960), pp. 105–35; Alonso de Cartagena, *Defensorium unitatis christianae*, ed. Manuel Alonso (Madrid), 1943); Fernán Díaz de Toledo, *Instrucción del relator*, in Cartagena, *Defensorium*, pp. 343–56; Juan de Torquemada, *Tractatus contra madianitas et ismaelitas*, ed. Nicolás López Martínez and Vincente Proaño Gil (Burgos, 1957). For the 1449 statute and other texts and commentaries, see also Eloy Benito Ruano, *Los orígenes del problema converso* (Barcelona, 1976), and Hillgarth, *Spanish Kingdoms*, II, pp. 410–69.

[20] The best Old Christian source is Andrés Bernáldez, *Memorias del reinado de los Reyes Católicos*, ed. Manuel Gómez-Moreno and Juan de Mata Carriazo (Madrid, 1962), pp.

There was no doubt in the minds of contemporaries that what was called 'judaizing' was going on extensively among the newly converted Jewish Christians and even their second- and third-generation descendants. Although the specific model for the Castilian Inquisition had been developed in the thirteenth century to repress dualist belief among the Christians of Languedoc, the notion of religious dissent as a threat to both Church and State, which needed to be suppressed, even by force, had become accepted by ecclesiastical and secular authorities as early as the time of Constantine.[21] The best evidence of what late-medieval Spaniards meant by 'judaizing' may be found in the charges brought against *conversos* by the Inquisition. Twenty-three such charges may be identified in the trials held in Ciudad Real between 1483 and 1512, and their most striking feature is that only six of them can properly be described as doctrinal, the rest being concerned with ritual practices.[22] This is a highly significant point, as it suggests that the threat which the new converts were believed to pose to the Old Christian majority lay primarily in their public and private behaviour, rather than any doubts they may still have had about Christian doctrine.

Thanks to the prevalence, even among non-specialists, of the functionalist approach to the study of human societies, it is often assumed that ritual actions must have some specific, practical purpose, so that apparently irrational religious and social customs in fact serve as bonds of social cohesion. If such a purpose cannot be found, the practice is condemned as 'primitive'.[23] In no religion does ritual play a more essential part than in Judaism, for the God of Israel not only revealed Himself to specific individuals at certain times, but He also prescribed, thorugh the law of Moses, the detailed conduct of a specific human society. The Torah contains no provision for its repeal and here lies the heart of the tensions between Jews and Gentiles throughout history. Castilian Jews in the late fifteenth century, like their ancestors and their successors, could not, and believed that they should

94–103. *Converso* views include Cartagena, *Defensorium*, p. 109; Fernán Díaz, *Instrucción*, p. 350; Fray Alonso de Espina, *Fortalitium fidei*, quoted in Américo Castro, *The Structure of Spanish History* (Princeton, 1954), p. 539. Rabbinical sources are surveyed in H. J. Zimmels, *Die Marranen in der rabbinischen Literatur* (Berlin, 1932). The view that most converts became genuine Christians is advocated, on the basis of similar sources, by B. Netanyahu, *The Marranos of Spain from the Late Fourteenth to the Early Fifteenth Centuries* (New York, 2nd edn. 1973).

[21] H. Maisonneuve, *Etudes sur les origines de l'Inquisition* (Paris, 2nd edn. 1960), esp. pp. 9–11, 29–58, 71–9.

[22] *Records of the Trials of the Spanish Inquisition in Ciudad Real*, I, *1483–85;* II, *1494–1512*, ed. H. Beinart (Jerusalem, 1974–7).

[23] F. C. T. Moore, 'Thresholds of coherence. An inaugural lecture', *Supplement to the University of Hong Kong Gazette*, xxvii (1980), 4.

not, distinguish between their religious beliefs and their behaviour in the world. Many would not have understood what such a distinction might mean.[24] Christianity, on the other hand, had a contradiction within it from the moment when the texts now included in the New Testament began to be produced. The conflict is most clearly seen in Paul, the first great *converso*, who tried to separate the Covenant from the Law, in a way which has never been done in Judaism. A dualist outlook replaced, in Christianity, the Hebrew understanding of the unity of Man's nature under the one, omnipotent God. In Christian thought, the 'flesh' became in itself wicked, the 'spirit' was separated from it and elevated to an ideal. The material realization on earth of God's kingdom of justice was postponed to the future, leaving humanity without hope of earthly reform, and trembling before an arbitrary God, who might, inscrutably, 'save' His elect by removing them from material existence. Thus clergy came to rule over laity and monastic withdrawal became the only approved model for Christian practice.

Jews who remained faithful to the revelations once given to Abraham and Moses were inevitably an obstacle to this Christian view of the world. Jewish rejection of the claims made for Jesus, combined with the dualism and triumphalism of the Christian Church, condemned the Jews to a kind of eschatological limbo, which came to justify any degree of atrocity against them. Jews had to suffer for their blindness and guilt in the rejection and death of Jesus, to remain on the margin of Christian society as perpetual wanderers and outsiders, until their conversion ushered in the era of the Messiah's second coming. Not surprisingly, some Christians tried to hasten this coming, while many Jews have sought, at various times, to escape from this terrible burden by abandoning that indissoluble unity of faith in God and social order which is Israel's historic calling. It is necessary here to distinguish clearly between the concepts of 'acculturation' and 'assimilation'. Spanish Jews were certainly able successfully to adopt many of the external features and even thought-forms of Islamic or Christian society, but the abandonment of one personal and social identity for another, which assimilation demands, was impossible without the deepest internal and external disturbance. When the violence of 1391 applied the pressure, conversions were inevitable and it was equally certain that the Inquisition, when it arrived, would not lack for business.

It is, however, important to remember that the problems of minorities are primarily problems for the majority. In the case of Spain, the Christians were incapable of allowing Jews either to remain faithful

---

[24] On the irrelevance to Judaism of the Christian charge on 'legalism', see B. S. Jackson, 'Legalism', *Journal of Jewish Studies*, xxx, no. 1 (1979), 1–22.

to their calling or to convert. The Jews were expelled and the *conversos* were persecuted because Spanish Christians, like the rest of the Church, had failed to come to terms with their own identity. Thus, not only did Jews and *conversos* suffer, like any other minority, the consequences of the injustice and instability of contemporary society, but their belief in the unique calling of Israel, and their determination to realize that belief in material terms, brought them into violent conflict with a Christian society which, neither publicly nor privately, could come to terms with its origins or its nature. In late-medieval Spain, as elsewhere, the stereotype of the Jew took on a life of its own, but its effect on real Jews, assimilated or otherwise, was all too dreadfully tangible.

FROM MONOPOLY TO MINORITY: CATHOLICISM IN EARLY MODERN ENGLAND

By Christopher Haigh, M.A., Ph.D., F.R.Hist.S.

READ AT THE SOCIETY'S CONFERENCE 12 SEPTEMBER 1980

ROBERT PARSONS, the Jesuit, compiled his account of the transition of English Catholicism from monopoly to minority status in 1599-1600, and called it 'A story of domestical difficulties which the Catholic cause and promoters thereof hath had in defending the same, not only against the violence and persecution of the heretics but also by sundry other impediments among themselves, of faction, emulation, sedition and division, since the change of religion in England'. This version of Tudor ecclesiastical history supplements Nicholas Sander's attention to evil Protestants and politicians by an examination of the Catholic response to the Reformation. The Parsons story has two groups of villains, the bishops and the parish clergy, who betrayed their faith to hold on to their livings; it has two groups of heroes, who rescued the faith by their self-sacrifice, the Jesuits and the seminary priests they inspired, and the Elizabethan Catholic gentry; and it goes something like this. The early Tudor monopolistic Church was weakened by spiritual decadence and mere conformism, and its leadership divided by ambition and faction, so it could not resist the challenge of heresy. In the reign of Mary a legal monopoly of religion was restored to the Catholics, but the clergy carried through no spiritual or institutional reforms and the laity held tightly to their ill-gotten monastic gains. In 1559, though the bishops passively refused to bow to Elizabeth's supremacy, there was no crusade against heresy and the parish clergy and laity quietly conformed: through the 1560s, medieval Catholicism slowly died. The spineless, moribund, hierarchical and monopolistic Church had succumbed to a fast and easy Reformation, and had dragged the Catholic faith down with it. But, to the rescue, as the Protestant dragon was about to devour the Catholic damsel, came the Jesuits and the seminary priests! The missioners converted the lax conservative gentry to a reformed Catholicism of interior commitment, and gave them determination to resist official persecution and protect their loyal tenants. The anaemic, formalist religion of the monopolistic medieval Church had been replaced by the vibrant new Catholicism of a devoted minority.[1]

[1] 'The Memoirs of Father Robert Persons', ed. J. H. Pollen, C[atholic] R[ecord] S[ociety], ii (1906), pp. 48-63; R. Parsons, *A Briefe Apologie or Defence of the Catholike*

This story will be familiar even to those who have not heard it in its original Parsons form, since it has become part of the received historiography of Tudor England, accepted by Protestant historians explaining what they see as the popular appeal of the Reformation and by those Catholics who, like Parsons, wish to disown the ramshackle medieval Church. But in its origin and structure, the story has two main defects. First, it is a partisan, propagandist version, designed by Parsons to defend the novelty of his own order and the missionary method, and to discredit the conservative, hierarchically minded clergy who attacked the Jesuits and their ways: it is significant that Parsons' opponents were driven to defend the villains of his story and produce an alternative Catholic history.[2] Second, it has the flaw of so many historical explanations: it presupposes the result and, by a form of 'Catholic whiggery', explains how this conclusion inexorably came about. English Catholicism became a very small, seigneurially structured, sectarian body, and the Jesuit and seminarist mission can be seen as a dynamic success because it created that form of Catholicism: the bishops and parish clergy may be dismissed as medieval relics, since they appear to have contributed little to the outcome. But there were alternatives to the kind of Catholic community which the mission fostered, and perhaps English Catholicism reached its post-Reformation characteristics by failure and loss in the missionary period rather than by success and growth. It is not yet possible to attempt the full revision of Reformation history which may be needed, but we may usefully re-examine the villains and heroes of the story, the bishops and parish clergy of the declining monopolistic Church and the missionaries and gentry of the fervent new minority—like Parsons, we may for the moment ignore the commons.

First, is it true that the Catholic bishops of Tudor England were content with routine administration of their Church and failed to respond to political and social change? The episcopate of Wolsey's years, though largely composed of lawyers, produced a number of diocesan reformers: at Chichester, Ely, Lincoln, Norwich, Rochester and Winchester there was vigourous attention to pastoral supervision, clerical standards, and the disciplined fulfilment of spiritual duties by priests and people.[3] Such bishops protested to Henry VIII against early attacks on their Church and, when political action failed, some turned, like Longland of Lincoln, to administrative obstruction, pro-

---

Ecclesiastical Hierarchie (n.p., ?1601), fos. 1–4; *The Jesuit's Memorial for the Intended Reformation of England*, ed. H. Gee (London, 1690), pp. 2, 4, 20–2, 49–51.

[2] H. Ely, *Certaine Briefe Notes upon a Briefe Apologie* (Paris, ?1603), pp. 65–8.

[3] R. Houlbrooke, *Church Courts and the People during the English Reformation, 1520–1570* (Oxford, 1979), pp. 10–11, 21–2, 30–1, 175–9, 185, 210, 222–7.

tecting their dioceses from the full implementation of Reformation measures.[4] Mary's episcopate of theologians also included a number of reforming activists: again there was stress on discipline and pastoral care, but there was also an official encouragement of lay piety and understanding by books of homilies and religious guides.[5] In 1559 and after, these bishops were examples of dignified resistance, while the next generation of prelates-to-be, the middle-rank administrators and academics of the Marian Church, fled to Louvain, Rome and Douai to begin the polemical attack on the Elizabethan Church and, in the case of Allen, to train young missionaries.[6] Perhaps the Tudor Catholic bishops were not battling ecclesiastical warriors, but nor were they unimaginative bureaucrats. The contribution to Catholic survival of Gardiner as a conforming Henrician bishop of Winchester may have exceeded that of the executed papalist Fisher, whose principled stand yielded Rochester to the Protestant zealot Hilsey. The conservative bishops slowed the pace of Reformation in the dioceses and, by their emphasis upon clerical standards and lay piety, they strengthened Catholic resistance.

The conservative parish clergy have had as bad a press as their bishops and, though the grosser calumnies of idleness, ignorance and immorality have generally been abandoned they are still the 'mere conformists' and 'vicars of Bray'. But many priests tried to insulate their parishes from religious change, especially from the royal injunctions, and Cranmer in Canterbury and Latimer and Hooper in Worcester found their protestantizing efforts blocked by clerical non-compliance.[7] Thus there were many parts of England where the attack on traditional religion made little progress, and where the Elizabethan settlement saw the beginning and not the end of the Reformation in the parishes, while, especially in the North and West, conservatism and 'counterfeiting' remained problems until the Marian generation had died out.[8] Some parish priests, like their episcopal superiors,

[4] M. J. Kelly, 'The Submission of the Clergy', *T. R. Hist. S.*, Fifth Series, xv (1965), 109-17. For Longland, I am grateful to Margaret Bowker for allowing me to read the typescript of her forthcoming book on the diocese of Lincoln 1521-1547.

[5] D. M. Loades, *The Reign of Mary Tudor* (London, 1979), pp. 329-31, 341-7, 351-2; P. Hughes, 'A Hierarchy that Fought, 1554-1559', *Clergy Review*, xviii (1940), 25-39; G. Alexander, 'Bonner and the Marian Persecutions', *History*, lx (1975), 384-8; A. Bartholomew, 'Lay Piety in the Reign of Mary Tudor' (unpublished University of Manchester M.A. thesis, 1979), especially pp. 1-42.

[6] A. Morey, *The Catholic Subjects of Elizabeth I* (London, 1978), pp. 27, 99-102; J. Bossy, *The English Catholic Community, 1570-1850* (London, 1975), pp. 12-19.

[7] *Letters and Papers of Henry VIII*, xviii (2), no. 546, pp. 292-7, 299-309; F. D. Price, 'Gloucester Diocese under Bishop Hooper, 1551-3', *Trans. Bristol and Glouc. Arch. Soc.*, lx (1938), 119-21, 123-5, 133.

[8] C. Haigh, 'The Continuity of Catholicism in the English Reformation', *Past & Present* (forthcoming), and references in notes 8-15 therein.

delayed the impact of the Reformation upon the localities, and many also contributed in a positive way to the re-organization of Catholicism. In upland England, where government was weak and the parochial structure of the established Church ineffective, recusant Catholicism was created in the 1560s and 1570s by local clergy who led their people into separation, and by migrant priests from the South in search of safer opportunities for Catholic action: in the Lancashire deanery of Blackburn a group of ex-chapel-curates was in successful competition with the official Church by 1571.[9] Elsewhere, in cathedral cities and peculiar jurisdicitions, in isolated pockets over much of England, recusant priests provided Catholic sacraments for growing numbers of recusant laypeople, before the mission from the seminaries had any impact.[10]

It seems clear that, after they lost their monopoly of legal worship in 1559 and the slow imposition of Protestantism was resumed, English Catholics would, without political change, become a minority. I am not convinced that Tudor government was characterized by Eltonian efficiency, but the state could certainly prevent a majority of its subjects joining an opposition Church. But the issues of the size, the social structure and the geographical distribution of the Catholic community remained to be decided, and, until the mid-1570s at least, the signs were, from a Catholic point of view, promising: especially in the ill-governed regions of England, and in virtually all Wales, conservative attachment remained strong and the construction of a separated Church was well under way. The task of the seminary priests and later the Jesuits who crept into England from 1574 was not the creation of a new form of Catholicism, but the sustaining of existing loyalties: they inherited, if not a safe seat, at least a strong minority vote in need of careful constituency nursing, and their success should be measured by their ability to maintain party allegiance.[11] As we know, Catholicism in England became a very small and distinctively structured minority, but 'The English Catholic Community', as brilliantly characterized by John Bossy, was not the successful product of a missionary triumph in the face of Protestantism and persecution. It was a rump community, the residue of a process of failure and decline in which whole regions and social groups were neglected and betrayed by the heroes of Robert Parsons' story.

If its main task was the servicing of an existing Catholic group, the mission got off to a poor start. Though the majority of the early

[9] *Ibid.*; C. Haigh, *Reformation and Resistance in Tudor Lancashire* (Cambridge, 1975), pp. 247-59.

[10] Haigh, 'Continuity of Catholicism', and references in notes 47-66 therein.

[11] I have set out some of the evidence for this view in my 'Continuity of Catholicism'.

missioners were from the North and West, they had forged new
relationships at Oxford and in exile, and their natural 'invasion route'
from Douai and Rheims was through Calais and Dieppe to Dover and
Rye.[12] The new priests therefore concentrated in the South and East
of England, though Protestant advance and effective government
made pastoral effort in these areas difficult. In 1580 half the missionary
priests working in England were in Essex, London and the Thames
Valley, districts which together had only a fifth of detected recusants,
and though the North had two-fifths of detected recusants (and,
because of poor detection, certainly a larger proportion of total recusants) it had attracted only one-fifth of the priests.[13] Parsons reported to Rome that on his arrival in England in 1580 there were no
seminary priests in Wales and the Far North, where the Catholic
potential was considerable, and Robert Southwell noted in 1586 that
'there are many counties, each containing not a few Catholics, in
which there is not a single priest', while 'the priests actually working
in the harvest betake themselves in great numbers to one or two
counties, leaving the others devoid of pastors'. John Cornelius recognized the demand for priests in the North and wanted to serve there
or in Ireland, but his education had been financed by Sir John
Arundell and he was obliged to act as family chaplain and spiritual
director in Dorset and London.[14] While the Arundells and their aristocratic friends profited from the talents of Cornelius, the Catholics of
Malpas in Cheshire had three masses in two years, a Cleveland couple
had to go to Lincolnshire for a priest to marry them, and Richard
Danby of Masham had to baptize his six children himself.[15] Parsons
tried to remedy matters by directing newly arrived priests to neglected
counties, and later Henry Garnet used some of the funds under his

[12] *First and Second Douai Diaries* ed. T. F. Knox (London, 1878), *passim;* G. Anstruther,
The Seminary Priests, i (Ware, n.d.), *passim;* ii (Great Wakering, 1975), *passim*; J. Bossy,
'Rome and the Elizabethan Catholics: a Question of Geography', *Historical Journal*, vii
(1964), 136–7; *Unpublished Documents relating to the English Martyrs*, ed. J. H. Pollen
(C.R.S., v, 1908), pp. 21, 33, 123, 124, 173; R. Parsons, 'Of the life and Martyrdom of
Father Edmund Campion', *Letters and Notices*, xii (1878–9), pp. 16–17.
[13] The distribution of priests is calculated from Anstruther, *Seminary Priests*, i, *passim*,
omitting those arrested on or soon after arrival; the distribution of recusants is drawn
from a conflation of returns of 1577 (*Miscellanea XII*, C. R.S., xxii (1921), pp. 6–9) and
1582 (P.R.O., SP 12/156, fo. 78).
[14] *Letters and Memorials of Father Robert Persons*, ed. L. Hicks (C.R.S., xxxix, 1942), p.
108; *Unpublished Documents relating to the English Martyrs*, ed. Pollen, p. 309; H. Foley,
Records of the English Province of the Society of Jesus (7 vols., London, 1877–84), iii, pp.
435–8, 449, 451.
[15] Foley, *Records*, iii, pp. 439–40, 449; K. R. Wark, *Elizabethan Recusancy in Cheshire*
(Chetham Society, 1971), pp. 42–4; J. C. H. Aveling, *Northern Catholics* (London, 1966),
p. 191.

control to send men to the poorer parts of England.[16] Their efforts
were assisted by the renewal of religious conflict in France, which
made the cross-Channel route less attractive in the 1590s, and land-
ings in East Anglia and at the mouth of the Tyne became common:
Richard Holtby established a reception centre near Durham, and
distributed incoming priests across the North-East.[17] The position in
the western counties and Wales seems to have been helped by the
foundation of English seminaries in Spain, which for obvious geographical reasons were less likely to send their missionaries to the
South-East. There may even have been the beginning of an overflow
from the South: in 1590 Thomas Stransham moved north from his
native Oxfordshire 'for want for harbour and entertainment'.[18] But
most priests still came in through Sussex, Kent and London and,
as we shall see, the distribution network which many of them used
sent them to Hampshire, Sussex, the Thames valley, East Anglia and
the Midlands. By 1603 the maldistribution of priests had been less-
ened, but was still a major problem: the South-East and East had
20% of the secular priests to serve 14% of detected English recusants,
while the North had 38% of the priests to work with 48% of detected
recusants. Thereafter, the distribution of secular clergy deteriorated
somewhat, and the apportionment of the growing Jesuit element in
the mission was disastrous: in 1635 the South-East and East had 23%
of seculars but 42% of Jesuits, and the North had 35% of the secular
clergy but only 25% of the Jesuits. Half of the Jesuits and seculars on
the mission in 1635 served in the less-promising South and East sector
of England, which had, despite better detection, barely a quarter of
known recusants.[19] In 1633 the Carmelite Christopher Lee complained of Oxfordshire that 'there are so many priests in this country
it is difficult to find shelter for them all', and there was fierce competition for scarce chaplaincies between regulars and seculars. While
priests in the South-East had little to do and were getting in each
other's way, it was claimed in the 1630s, elsewhere clerical shortages
left the laity to die without sacraments.[20]

[16] Parsons, 'Life and Martyrdom of Father Edmund Campion', *Letters and Notices*, xii,
p. 38; *Letters and Memorials of Father Robert Persons*, ed. Hicks, p. 108; P. Caraman, *Henry
Garnet, 1555–1606, and the Gunpowder Plot* (London, 1964), p. 45.

[17] Bossy, 'Rome and the Elizabethan Catholics', 138–40; Aveling, *Northern Catholics*,
pp. 159–60; Foley, *Records*, iii, pp. 2, 5–6.

[18] Bossy, 'Rome and the Elizabethan Catholics', 138–9, 141–2; A. Davidson, 'Roman
Catholicism in Oxfordshire, c. 1580–c.1640' (unpublished University of Bristol Ph.D.
thesis, 1970), pp. 416–17.

[19] The distributions for 1603 are calculated from Anstruther, *Seminary Priests*, i, *passim*,
and B. Magee, *The English Recusants* (London, 1938), p. 83; those for 1635 are from
Anstruther, *Seminary Priests*, i and ii, *passim*, and Foley, *Records*, vii (1), analytical
catalogue.

[20] B. Stapleton, *A History of the Post-Reformation Catholic Missions in Oxfordshire* (London,

Though the North of England produced large numbers of recruits for the seminaries, there was a serious leakage of priests from the region: only two-thirds of the northern-born seculars who came to England on the mission returned to the North, and few clerical outsiders ventured there. The Benedictines lost some of their northern monks to the South, and attracted hardly any southerners north in return.[21] Wales and the border counties were also net suppliers of priests: North Wales lost particularly heavily, and only one of over twenty Elizabethan recruits for the mission from Worcestershire returned to his native shire.[22] Until, by the 1630s, saturation in the South-East forced missioners back to their own counties, it is clear that the London area exercised a strong attraction. Thomas Somers, a Westmorland schoolmaster, sent his pupils to Douai so they could return as local pastors, but after he had trained as a priest himself he went to work in London. John Bennett, a Flintshire Jesuit, worked in North Wales for many years, but towards the end of his career he moved south to serve plague victims in London.[23] The magnetic effect of London was partly the result of the Catholic communications network centred there and partly of a recognition that if Catholicism was to have a political future then a substantial metropolitan presence was essential, but it also owed something to the growing martyr cult. It is difficult to escape the conviction that some priests, such as Richard Thirkeld who prayed for eight years that he might die for his faith, actually wanted to be caught, and the risks were highest in London: in 1586 John Low sighed as he walked near London Bridge 'I see the heads of my brothers and I will never be happy until it happens to me to be of that blessed number'. Low's wish was granted after he was overheard and arrested, but a more practical view of the missionary task suggests that he would have been better occupied serving quietly in Hereford-

---

1906), p. 127; Anstruther, *Seminary Priests*, ii, 203; Bossy, *English Catholic Community*, pp. 210, 220–1; P. Hughes, *Rome and the Counter-Reformation in England* (London, 1942), p. 410.

[21] Anstruther, *Seminary Priests*, i, and ii, *passim;* Aveling, *Northern Catholics*, pp. 236–7; D. Lunn, *The English Benedictines, 1540–1688* (London, 1980), p. 155.

[22] M. Cleary, 'The Catholic Resistance in Wales, 1568–1678', *Blackfriars*, xxxviii (1957), 116, 122; *The Welsh Elizabethan Catholic Martyrs*, ed. D. A. Thomas (Liverpool, 1971), pp. 32, 36–9; F. Pugh, 'Monmouthshire Recusants in the Reigns of Elizabeth and James I', *South Wales and Monmouth Rec. Soc. Publ.*, iv (1957), p. 64; V. Burke, 'Catholic Recusants in Elizabethan Worcestershire' (unpublished University of Birmingham M.A. thesis, 1972), p. 90.

[23] Aveling, *Northern Catholics*, p. 244; R. Challoner, *Memoirs of Missionary Priests*, ed. J. H. Pollen (London, 1924), pp. 321–2; *Welsh Elizabethan Catholic Martyrs*, ed. Thomas, p. 45.

shire or Staffordshire, even if he could not force himself into the wilds of Wales or the North.[24]

Another reason for the geographical concentration of priestly effort was the tendency, pronounced from the earliest stages of the mission, to devote most attention to the substantial gentry, who were most numerous in the prosperous counties of the South and might spend part of each year in London. Though poorly paid chapel-curates in the North who withdrew from the Church of England after 1559 might serve circuits of poor hamlets for alms, the recusant priests of the South seem rather to have become chaplains to the gentry when they resigned their benefices:[25] not surprisingly, several of the first seminary priests, Cúthbert Mayne, John Paine, Thomas Stamp and William Hanse among them, followed their example, and by 1580 the Yates at Lyford had two resident seminarist chaplains.[26] It is arguable that the high risk of arrest forced missionaries in southern England to seek protection in gentry households, but it seems that persecution was never fierce enough to push priests to the safer North and West. Indeed, when a frightened regime regarded Catholic gentry as a political danger, priests may have found less safety in manor-houses than in peasant households, and a concentration on the gentry seems a deliberate strategy rather than a tactic of evasion. The instructions given to the first Jesuit missioners in 1580 urged attention to the gentry above all, and John Gerard thought this the most sensible approach, at least in southern England: 'The way, I think, to go about making converts is to bring the gentry over first and then their servants, for Catholic gentlefolk must have Catholic servants.'[27] From the beginning, the leaders of the mission envisaged a reconstruction of English Catholicism along seigneurial, rather than parochial or congregational, lines. In an account of the mission in 1575-6, Allen noted that the priests came from the gentry and returned to serve with gentry families, and, Parsons noted, Allen intended missionaries to work 'in private houses after the old example of the Apostles in their days'. In

[24] Challoner, *Memoirs*, p. 79; *Unpublished Documents relating to the English Martyrs*, ed. Pollen, p. 290; Aveling, *Northern Catholics*, p. 156; Anstruther, *Seminary Priests*, i, p. 215. See also Southwell's comment at London Bridge: 'Oh, my Lord, if God grants it you will see *my* head sometimes on one of those' (C. Devlin, *The Life of Robert Southwell, Poet and Martyr*, London, 1956, p. 235).

[25] Haigh, *Reformation and Resistance*, pp. 254-9; Aveling, *Northern Catholics*, pp. 34, 40-5; J. E. Paul, 'The Hampshire Recusants in the Reign of Elizabeth I' (unpublished University of Southampton Ph.D. thesis, 1958), pp. 171-2; Burke, 'Catholic Recusants in Elizabethan Worcestershire', pp. 37-9.

[26] Anstruther, *Seminary Priests*, i, pp. 147-8, 225, 266, 331, 345; Foley, *Records*, iii, p. 27.

[27] *Letters and Memorials of Father Robert Persons*, ed. Hicks, p. 320; J. Gerard, *Autobiography of an Elizabethan*, ed. P. Caraman (London, 1951), p. 33.

1580-1, Campion and Parsons, 'at the request of certain principal Catholic gentlemen', moved round the houses of the conservative gentry, preaching, advising on cases of conscience and reconciling to the faith: they attracted to their service a number of young gentlemen, led by George Gilbert, who acted as guides and naturally led the priests to the homes of their own gentry relations.[28] But what may have begun as a pastoral technique, aiming at the poor through their masters and landlords, seems to have become an end in itself. John Gerard gave much of his attention to London society and to courtiers, and moved his lodgings near the Strand to be closer to his fashionable friends: his missionary journeys to the North were not directed to the poor, but to the noble benefactors of his order. The Jesuit annual reports to Rome deal almost entirely with the conversion and piety of 'one of high position', 'the head of a distinguished family', 'a lady of rank', 'a lady of noble birth', 'a certain gentleman', and 'a lady of no mean condition'.[29]

When Parsons arrived in England, he found that most of the priests who had preceded him were peripatetic, staying little more than one night with a gentry family before moving on. In areas of clerical shortage this pattern remained usual, but elsewhere there were soon strong pressures against itinerancy: increasingly, the missioners devoted themselves not merely to the gentry but to individual gentry households. Though the recusant gentry had been nervous earlier, by December 1588, Southwell reported, they were anxious for priests to settle with them, and a skilled household director such as John Gerard was in great demand.[30] A domestic chaplaincy was clearly what many priests wanted: it guaranteed comfort and financial security, and it may have offered greater safety. In 1581-2, John Chapman wandered aimlessly from Rye to London, then to Devon and around Somerset, till he found himself a niche with Mrs. Bullacre at Warblington in Hampshire. After William Freeman came to England in 1587 he worked, with 'weariness of body and sundry perils' according to a contemporary account, among 'the meaner sort' of Worcestershire and Warwickshire, but only 'until an honest gentlewoman in the country

---

[28] 'Some correspondence of Cardinal Allen', ed. P. Ryan, *Miscellanea VII*, C.R.S., ix (1911), pp. 65, 67; Parsons, 'Life and Martyrdom of Father Edmund Campion', *Letters and Notices*, xi (1876-7), p. 325; xii (1878-9), pp. 21, 29, 51; 'Memoirs of Father Robert Persons', pp. 27, 29-30; *Letters and Memorials of Father Robert Persons*, ed. Hicks, pp. 59, 61, 67, 83-4, 331, 335; E. Waugh, *Edmund Campion* (London, 1947), pp. 136-7.

[29] Gerard, *Autobiography*, pp. 39-40, 175-88; 'Annual Letters of the Vice-Province of England, 1619', *Letters and Notices*, xi (1876-7), pp. 274-88; Foley, *Records*, vii (2), pp. 985-6, 1095.

[30] *Letters and Memorials of Father Robert Persons*, ed. Hicks, p. 86; W. Weston, *Autobiography of an Elizabethan*, ed. P. Caraman (London, 1955), p. 28; Devlin, *Robert Southwell*, p. 181; Gerard, *Autobiography*, pp. 15-16, 22-3, 29, 146.

was willing to entertain a Catholic servingman, whose service she might use in such affairs she had to be done, but especially in teaching a son she had, of which offer Mr. Freeman, in his distress, was contented to accept and so was admitted to her service'.[31] It was not merely exhaustion and fear which drove such priests from itinerancy to chaplaincy, but a particular conception of the missionary task and of the kind of Catholicism to be encouraged. In the seminaries they had shared the intense spirituality of an institutional spiritual life, and the Jesuits and their friends had taken the 'Spiritual Exercises': in England, many of them tried to recreate their student experience in the religious round of the reformed Catholic gentry household. The devotional works printed for English Catholics were designed for the gentry family, and Loarte's *Exercise of a Christian Life*, Parsons' *Christian Directory*, Southwell's *Short Rule of Good Life* and Lascelles' *Little Way How to Heare Masse* enjoin a life of piety and a regularity of sacramental practice which necessitated a resident chaplain. The priests fostered a brand of piety which created a demand for domestic chaplains, and the pattern of intense family religiosity, established by John Gerard and reaching its highest points with the Wisemans at Braddocks and the Babthorpes at Osgodby, was followed, not always with success, in manor-houses across the country. The Devonshire Jesuits reported in 1624 that 'The missioners, as far as the severity of the times permitted, were usefully employed, chiefly among some families of the gentry in which they lived, instructing and training them to all piety, repressing bad habits, healing dissensions, etc.'[32] The informed, determined and highly charged family piety which some gentry households offered was clearly more attractive to most priests than the laxer observances of peasant religion, and John Gerard pointed the contrast:

'There is a great difference between these counties where I was now working [East Anglia] and other parts of England. In other places, where a large number of the people are Catholics and nearly all have leanings towards Catholicism, it is easy to make many converts and to have large congregations at sermons. For instance, in Lancashire I have seen myself more than two hundred present at mass and sermon. People of this kind come into the Church without difficulty, but they fall away the moment persecution blows up. When the alarm is over, they come back again. By contrast, in the districts I was living in now, Catholics were very few. They

---

[31] *Unpublished Documents relating to the English Martyrs*, ed. Pollen, pp. 33–4, 345, 347–8.

[32] Gerard, *Autobiography*, pp. 28–32, 150, 168–9; *The Chronicle of the English Augustinian Canonesses Regular of the Lateran, at St. Monica's in Louvain*, ed. A. Hamilton (London, 1904, 1906), i, p. 80; *Troubles of our Catholic Forefathers*, ed. J. Morris (London, 1872–7), iii, p. 468; Foley, *Records*, vii (2), p. 1111.

were mostly from the better classes; none, or hardly any, from the ordinary people, for they are unable to live in peace, surrounded as they are by most fierce Protestants.'[33]

As one solution to the evangelist's dilemma of 'quality or quantity', a preference for the resolute and reverent gentry was defensible, but if, as I have suggested, the mission should be judged by its ability to sustain existing commitment, it was a strategy for disaster, for it dictated a concentration upon the least promising areas and a neglect of the majority of Catholics.

If priests became private chaplains because of the brand of religion they preferred, they did so too because of the kind of men they were and their conception of clerical dignity. The missioners were not the priested proletariat of the medieval Church: half of the first hundred had some university education, a third at Oxford, and all had professional training in the seminaries. Robert Parson claimed in 1584 that 'major pars' of the priest came 'ex nobilitate', and in the next decade half the recruits to the seminaries were sons of gentlemen.[34] Few of such men would become peripatetic pastors to the rural poor. Robert Southwell wrote to an itinerant colleague, 'I am much grieved to hear of your unsettled way of life, visiting many people, at home with none. We are all, I acknowledge, pilgrims, but not vagrants: our life is uncertain, but not our road.' For the first four years after his arrival in 1578, William Anlaby worked on foot among the poor of Yorkshire, dressing appropriately and carrying his mass-equipment in a bag, but then, 'humbly yielding himself to the advice of his brethren', he bought a horse, improved his clothes, turned his attention to the gentry and, for a time, moved south.[35] Such attitudes probably became even more common later, for Humphrey Ely claimed in 1601 that diversion of funds to the new seminaries in Spain led Douai to turn away poor scholars and accept only the sons of the rich and influential: certainly recruits from the gentry came to outnumber commoners by two to one. By 1634 Leander Jones was proposing that, with exceptions for unusual talent, entry to the priesthood should be restricted to the financially independent sons of gentry, to preserve the status of the clergy in England.[36]

The social predilections of most missioners were reinforced by the

---

[33] Gerard, *Autobiography*, pp. 32–3.

[34] *Douai Diaries*, ed. Knox, pp. 24–7; Anstruther, *Seminary Priests*, i, *passim*; *Letters and Memorials of Father Robert Persons*, ed. Hicks, p. 230; Bossy, *English Catholic Community*, p. 415.

[35] *Unpublished Documents relating to the English Martyrs*, ed. Pollen, p. 338; Challoner, *Memoirs*, p. 232; Anstruther, *Seminary Priests*, i, p. 9.

[36] Ely, *Certaine Briefe Notes*, pp. 209–13; A. C. F. Beales, *Education under Penalty* (London, 1963), p. 120; Bossy, *English Catholic Community*, pp. 198–201, 220–1, 415.

mechanics of the clerical employment agency operated by the Jesuits from the mid-1580s. Only a formal distribution network could protect priests from the fate of John Brushford who, when he arrived in 1585, 'found everybody so fearful as none would receive me into their houses', and then spent more than two years hiding away in garrets in London and cottages in the West Country, until finally he gave up and went back to France.[37] Parson established lines of communication through France into England by 1584, but the network in England was instigated by his colleague William Weston in 1585–6. Weston seems to have decided that the mission could only work by close cooperation with the Catholic gentry, and in 1585 he called leading laymen to a meeting at Hoxton, where a fund was established for the support of incoming priests. By the meeting at Hurleyford in 1586, Weston had a list of safe Catholic houses to which new priests could be sent, and a corps of guides to lead them: the supervision of this network for the next twenty years fell to Henry Garnet, assisted by Southwell and Gerard. It is probable that the Weston–Garnet scheme saved many priests from arrest, but it also did much to determine the social and geographical structure of early modern English Catholicism.[38] The network was first constructed from the relatives and friends of the first Jesuit missionaries and their patrons, and was for several years restricted to a coterie of gentry families in East Anglia, the Thames valley, the Sussex–Hampshire border, Northamptonshire and Leicestershire, and Worcestershire and Warwickshire.[39] Priests were supported in London or nearby on their arrival in England, until they were found specific placements, and it was the character of these placements which was crucial for the future of Catholicism. In 1591 Thomas Wiseman of Lincoln's Inn was helping Southwell with the distribution centre in London, and when James Younger and Richard Blount made contact with him he provided clothes and hid them for three days, before sending them off, Younger to Lady Throckmorton's house in Essex and Blount to the Darrells at Scotney Castle in Sussex, where he stayed as chaplain for seven years. When Oliver Tesimond arrived in London in 1598 he sought out his Jesuit superior Henry Garnet and stayed with him for some weeks, 'until a request came that I should go to the house of a person of note'.[40] Henry Garnet explained the method in a report to Rome in 1596:

---

[37] *Dodd's Church History of England*, ed. M. A. Tierney (London, 1839–43), iii, 136n–7n.

[38] *Letters and Memorials of Father Robert Persons*, ed. Hicks, pp. 223, 235–6, 243; Weston, *Autobiography*, pp. 28, 71–2, 77; Caraman, *Henry Garnet*, pp. 32–6, 45–6; Devlin, *Robert Southwell*, pp. 114, 116, 161, 220–1; Gerard, *Autobiography*, p. 82.

[39] Devlin, *Robert Southwell*, pp. 11, 114, 129; M. Hodgetts, 'Elizabethan Priest-Holes', *Recusant History*, xi (1972), 280, 286; xii (1973), 100.

[40] Devlin, *Robert Southwell*, pp. 225–6; *Troubles*, ed. Morris, i, pp. 177–9, 181, 207.

'When the priests first arrive from the seminaries, we give them every help we can. The greater part of them, as opportunity offers, we place in fixed residences. This is done in a very large number of families through our offices. The result now is that many persons, who saw a seminary priest hardly once a year, now had one all the time and most eagerly welcome any others.'

The intention was to place priests in 'fixed residences' with gentry families, and the point was confirmed by Garnet in 1597: 'Very many priests take up residence on our recommendation, it is true, at fixed stations in which now and then they are maintained at our expense.' The domestication of the mission, which had begun almost by accident, was now deliberate policy, and Gerard saw it as the task of the Jesuits to found 'ecclesiae domesticae'.[41]

George Gilbert's experience as a misssionary guide in 1580-1 had convinced him that a peripatetic pastorate was not the most effective use of clerical resources: in 1583 he advised the use of fixed bases:

'It will be necessary also for the priests to be stationed in various parts of the country and for each of them to stay at the house of some gentleman or other, as though he were a relation, friend or steward, or in some office of dignity but little work, so as not to interfere with his own calling; and he should also undertake the charge (unless the family with whom he is staying is a very large one) of a certain district in the neighbourhood, or of a number of neighbourhood families, because it will be very difficult to find priests enough for every family.'[42]

The proposal was for household chaplaincies with additional parochial responsibility: this remained Garnet's theory, and the practice of energetic priests such as Edward Oldcorne, but it was achieved infrequently.[43] As we shall see, many gentlemen were reluctant to allow 'their' priest to work outside the family and its servants, and a chaplain was expected to move about the country with his patron.[44] The wider clerical task could become a low priority: Thomas Stanney had a base with a gentry family in Hampshire, and went on a circuit of the local villages only once a month. Some families, such as the

[41] Caraman, *Henry Garnet*, p. 45; *The Wisbech Stirs*, ed. P. Renold (C.R.S., li, 1958), p. 289; Gerard, *Autobiography*, pp. 82, 161, 168-9; *The Condition of the Catholics under James I: Father Gerard's Narrative of the Gunpowder Plot*, ed. J. Morris (London, 1872), p. 283.

[42] *Letters and Memorials of Father Robert Persons*, ed. Hicks, p. 332.

[43] Caraman, *Henry Garnet*, pp. 215-16; Foley, *Records*, iv, pp. 210-13; *Condition of the Catholics*, ed. Morris, pp. 283-4; W. M. Brady, *The Episcopal Succession in England, Scotland and Ireland* (3 vols., Rome, 1876-7), iii, pp. 83-4.

[44] J. A. Williams, *Catholic Recusancy in Wiltshire, 1660-1791* (C.R.S., Monograph Series, i, 1968), p. 103; Gerard, *Autobiography*, pp. 39-40; Foley, *Records*, iii, pp. 449, 451.

Babthorpes at Osgodby, kept two priests, one for household duties and another for the tenants and local Catholics, while the Abingtons at Hindlip and the Vaux at Harrowden each had two Jesuits, one acting as family chaplain and the other as regional organizer of the mission, but it is difficult to justify such duplication when there were serious shortages elsewhere and, from a missionary point of view, the placing of two chaplains with Lord Stourton and three with Lady Montagu was indefensible.[45] The gentry household may have been envisaged as a base, but it soon became a chaplaincy and, in the minds of many priests, a benefice: Garnet complained in 1596 of the priests who found profitable niches and tried to prevent further missionary efforts round the houses where they lived.[46]

As the system which placed priests in gentry houses was devised and run by Jesuits, it is not surprising that they were accused of attending only to the needs of the rich and powerful and neglecting the souls of the poor, and, indeed, the defence Garnet produced against this charge seems decidedly lame.[47] But this was merely an egalitarian stick with which the Appellant secular clergy could beat the Jesuits, and they themselves thought in similar terms. The proposals for an 'association' of seculars, produced in 1596, tackled some weaknesses in the Jesuit network, but it, too, envisaged a system of fixed, single-household chaplaincies.[48] By 1609-10 it appears that the main concern of Archpriest Birkhead was a reduction of the supply of priests in England to a number which could conveniently be accommodated by the gentry, and his agent in Rome thought it a defect rather than an economy that one priest could serve forty households. The priority of the mission had changed, from the provision of priests for Catholics to the supply of Catholics for priests, and the necessary dependence of priests upon gentlemen was unquestioned: 'For take away patrons and you will take away priests at the same time; and all this holy enterprise which we have in hand will collapse.'[49]

The Jesuit Richard Cowling reported in 1600 that in the Lancashire

[45] Challoner, *Memoirs*, p. 595; *Troubles*, ed. Morris, iii, p. 467; Hodgett, 'Elizabethan Priest-Holes', *Recusant History*, xii, 193-4; Gerard, *Autobiography*, pp. 31, 33, 194-5; Foley, *Records*, iii, p. 444; *An Elizabethan Recusant House: the Life of Lady Magdalen, Viscountess Montagu*, ed. A. C. Southern (London, 1954), pp. 39, 42-3.

[46] Caraman, *Henry Garnet*, pp. 215-16.

[47] T. G. Law, *A Historical Sketch of the Conflicts between Jesuits and Seculars in the Reign of Queen Elizabeth* (London, 1889), pp. 97-8, 105-6; *The Archpriest Controversy*, ed. T. G. Law (Camden Society, n.s., lvi, lviii, 1896, 1898), i, 205-6; *Wisbech Stirs*, ed. Renold, pp. 289-95.

[48] Westminster Cathedral Archives, A.6, no. 77, pp. 274-5 (I am grateful to Miss Elizabeth Poyser for a transcript of this document); *Dodd's Church History*, ed. Tierney, iii, 45n; J. Colleton, *A Just Defence of the Slandered Priests* (n.p., 1602), pp. 122-3.

[49] *Letters of Thomas Fitzherbert*, ed. L. Hicks (C.R.S., xli, 1948), pp. 53, 100, 121-2, 135-6, 144-5.

Fylde 'Catholics are so numerous that priests can wander through the villages and countryside with the utmost freedom', and laypeople openly knelt for a blessing when they met a priest: but he lived with the widow of a leading gentleman, and his masses and sermons were mainly for the gentry. In the relative peace of Jacobean Durham, the secular clergy still focussed their attentions on the gentry: they came from the gentry, they lived with the gentry, and any commons they served were almost always tenants of their patrons.[50] But even in southern England 'seigneurial Catholicism' was not the only variety needing clerical support: there were individual Catholic peasant families, and pockets of Catholic survival in out-of-the-way districts, but there were few priests to serve them. About 1590, the Jesuit Thomas Stanney replied to a request to go round Hampshire villages to minister to poor Catholics 'That I had been not long since in those parts, where I was very much fatigued with preaching, hearing confessions and administering the sacraments, the more because I was obliged to watch whole nights and to celebrate mass twice in the day, so that I had not, as yet, been able to recover myself'. 'Well, but Master,' he was told by his guide, 'we still have a great many hungry souls that want bread, and there is no-one to give it to them; we have many also that would be glad to shake off the yoke of bondage, heresy, and embrace the Catholic faith, and I can find none to help them and receive them into the Church. What then must I say to them?' It was a good question, and the Catholic leadership had no answer. The position was much the same in Suffolk in the 1620s, where a sister of Mary Ward's Institute complained that there were too few priests, and those there were were prevented by their gentry hosts from working among the poor: she claimed it took her six months to find a priest to reconcile three converts, and even then she had to travel twelve miles to get him.[51] When many gentry families had daily masses and weekly confession, the lower orders were less well served: in 1624 the Jesuits reported that 'none delay beyond a month, unless from the want of priests', and Thomas Churchill wrote that in 1665 'most of the poor farmers in Kent, Sussex, Surrey and Middlesex were under my charge and, God be praised, in all that sad time there was not a child of thirteen years of age but once in the month or five weeks I saw at the sacraments.'[52] What could happen when clerical provision was inadequate was demonstrated in North Wales and in Cumbria: in both areas Protestantism had made little impact by the middle of

[50] G. Anstruther, *A Hundred Homeless Years: English Dominicans, 1558–1658* (London, 1958), p. 70; J. A. Hilton, 'Catholicism in Jacobean Durham', *Recusant History*, xiv (1977), 80, 81.

[51] Challoner, *Memoirs*, pp. 595–6; M. C. E. Chambers, *The Life of Mary Ward* (2 vols., London, 1882, 1885), ii, pp. 28, 35.

[52] Foley, *Records*, vii (2), p. 1101; Anstruther, *Seminary Priests*, ii, p. 55.

the reign of Elizabeth and, under the leadership of recusant priests and one or two early seminarists, the shift from 'survivalism' into recusancy was under way in the 1580s. But when the old clergy died out they were not replaced by new missioners, and the recusant-potential of the regions was lost: in 1599 the bishop of Carlisle noted that few priests were left in his diocese and his problem now was not popery but popular ignorance.[53]

But on the fringes of England, where government was weaker, the possibilities for successful Catholic action were immense. Roger Cadwallader devoted himself to the poor Catholics of Herefordshire from 1593 to 1610, and from 1601 until his arrest two years later John Sugar worked in the West Midlands 'to serve, help and comfort the meaner and poorer sort of Catholics with the sacraments of the Holy Catholic Church'.[54] In Lancashire in the 1620s, the Jesuit John Layton served a large, popular congregation, which met in an extended and decorated barn for masses and sermons, and the Benedictine Ambrose Barlow lodged with a poor farmer and ministered to the poor Catholics of his district.[55] In the 1630s Ralph Corby worked on foot round the villages of the North-East, concentrating upon Catholics without regular access to a priest. He became known as 'the priest of the poor', and a colleague wrote later that, 'He was so beloved of the poor people and so reverenced and esteemed for his pious labours and functions that he was commonly called by them the Apostle of the Country.' In Lancashire and Yorkshire, above all, missionary activity was never confined to the gentry, and there are signs that by the 1620s available chaplaincies had been filled and some priests were forced to turn to the poor and adopt a more populist approach. In Yorkshire under Charles I there were Jesuits who were private chaplains, Jesuits who moved round circuits of gentry households from which they provided services for the poor, and Jesuits who were entirely dependent on the alms of their poor congregations.[56] But, in national terms, it is hard to escape the conclusion that the reputation of men such as Corby was partly the result of their singularity, and the martyrological collections certainly stress the self-sacrifice of the few priests who slummed among the poor. Even in the North the balance was seriously awry: in Lan-

[53] Haigh, 'Continuity of Catholicism'; J. A. Hilton, 'The Cumbrian Catholics', *Northern History*, xvi (1980), pp. 41–7; *Calendar of State Papers, Domestic 1598–1601*, p. 362.

[54] Challoner, *Memoirs*, pp. 299–300, 275.

[55] Foley, *Records*, vii (2), p. 1108; 'The Apostolical Life of Ambrose Barlow', ed. W. E. Rhodes, *Chetham Miscellanies II* (Chetham Society, n.s., lxiii, 1909), pp. 4–5, 6, 10, 12.

[56] Foley, *Records*, iii, pp. 70, 91, 92, 93, 122, 253; vii (2), pp. 1111–12; Hilton, 'Catholicism in Jacobean Durham', 80; P. Caraman, *Henry Morse, Priest of the Plague* (London, 1957), p. 161. There was also a more populist approach in Wales at this time (Foley, *Records*, iv, pp. 441, 447).

cashire in 1639 it seems that half the Benedictines, two-thirds of the
Jesuits and virtually all the seculars had fixed bases. While the chaplains had little to do, the congregational priests were worked to exhaustion. Nicholas Postgate was chaplain to various noble ladies for
most of his career, but when his last patroness died he turned to the
poor of Cleveland. He was soon driven to cry for assistance: 'At this
moment I have quite six hundred penitents, and could have more if
I wished; or rather, what I lack is not the will, but help; I am working
to the limits of my strength.'[57] There were too few priests tramping
the Yorkshire moors: there were too many relaxing in plush Oxfordshire manor-houses.

The Catholic gentry, the second group of heroes of the Parsons
version of English Catholic history, arrogated to themselves an
inappropriate share of the clerical resources of the post-Reformation
mission. The gentlemen have been credited with ensuring 'the survival
of the faith'—and so they did, but their faith, at the expense of
everyone else's! The fact that English Catholicism became more and
more seigneurial in structure does not demonstrate the crucial role of
the gentry in its survival: that was the way it was, but not the way it
had to be. Some priests did manage long and successful missionary
careers among the people, supported by the alms of the poor, but most
turned to the gentry for sustenance and became chaplains. As the risk
of punishment and the weight of fines increased, the gentry became,
as the Jesuit Robert Jones complained in 1613, less willing to allow
their homes to be used as missionary centres. Thus, unless priests were
able to establish safe, independent bases and forsake their patrons, the
range of pastoral activity was severely restricted. In 1635 Thomas
Green commented on the general ignorance of Catholics in Essex,
because most of them could not afford to support priests and wealthy
Catholics would not permit their chaplains to attend the poor for fear
of provoking the government, and Panzani thought such limitations
were quite common. Green's proposed solution was a fund, financed
by the gentry, to support priests among the poor, but such a reallo-
cation had been tried several times, from Henry Garnet to Richard
Smith, with little success. When leading lay Catholics were generous,
as were the Petres in Essex and the Vaux sisters in the East Midlands,
they usually wanted their gifts used in their own regions and the
imbalance in the distribution of clergy worsened.[58] Yorkshire Jesuits

[57] Challoner, *Memoirs*, pp. 232, 275, 300, 322, 359, 394, 596; G. Anstruther, 'Lancashire Clergy in 1639', *Recusant History*, iv (1958), 38–46; Anstruther, *Seminary Priests*,
ii, p. 250; Aveling, *Northern Catholics*, p. 348.

[58] Foley, *Records*, iv, pp. 385–6; ii, p. 6; Brady, *Episcopal Succession*, iii, pp. 83–4; M. J.
Havran, *The Catholics in Caroline England* (London, 1962), p. 78; Williams, *Catholic
Recusancy in Wiltshire*, p. 103; Bossy, *English Catholic Community*, pp. 55–6, 229–30, 233,
235.

146   TRANSACTIONS OF THE ROYAL HISTORICAL SOCIETY

tried to raise money in the South-East for poor Catholic prisoners, but, it was said in 1610, 'it hath been so little and we so wearied with asking it, that it hath scarce been worth the labour', and Birkhead reported in 1611 that 'scarcely anything comes for the general needs of the poor, who cry in vain for bread'.[59] The Catholic consciences which the gentry paraded before the Council and the courts when charged with disobedience did not extend to assisting their poorer co-religionists, and in 1604 several of them tried to negotiate a settlement with the government which would permit the practice of Catholicism within gentry houses alone, and all priests but their chaplains were to be harried out of the country.[60]

The concentration of recusancy around the houses of the Catholic gentry, revealed in many official surveys, was the result, and not the cause, of the attention priests gave to gentlemen. The grand enterprise which some saw as a mission for the conversion of England from heresy became an agency for the provision of private chaplains for the gentry: over much of England those Catholics outside the orbit of a Catholic manor-house slipped into conformity to the Church of England. The lost opportunities were demonstrated in parts of Lancashire, Yorkshire, the High Peak and the South Wales borders, where small numbers of itinerant and congregational priests could maintain Catholicism as a popular force. But the brand of religion which appealed to illiterate peasants offered little satisfaction for the priestly products of the seminaries, Jesuits colleges and reformed Benedictine monasteries, who preferred the spiritual life of an educated household. By the 1630s, however, with too many priests chasing too few patrons, even the piety of the gentry family seems to have been in decline: it was claimed that priests were willing to overlook the sins and laxity of their masters to secure comfortable billets. Several reports to Rome in the 1630s paint the same general picture of English Catholicism: priests sought comfort and security with rich gentlemen rather than risk poverty and danger in the open, and as the wealthy were numerous in the Home Counties the priests settled there. Elsewhere, there were fewer priests but many more Catholics, pastoral provision was inadequate and the spiritual needs of the commons were not met.[61]

The origins of this situation can be seen in the 1580s, when strategic and logistical errors led to a social and geographical maldistribution of the clerical workforce. The errors were not made, I should add, by

[59] *Troubles*, ed. Morris, iii, pp. 453–4; Westminster Cathedral Archives, A. 8, no. 160.
[60] *A Petition Apologeticall, presented to the Kinges Most Excellent Maiesty by the Lay Catholikes of England* (Douai, 1604), pp. 34–5; *The Supplication of Certaine Masse-Priests falsely called Catholics* (London, 1604), pp. 2–3, 49; Bossy, *English Catholic Community*, p. 38 & n.
[61] Hughes, *Rome and the Counter-Reformation*, pp. 410–12, 417, 419, 426–7; Bossy, *English Catholic Community*, pp. 210, 220–1; G. Albion, *Charles I and the Court of Rome* (Louvain, 1935), pp. 111–14.

Robert Parsons, who was well aware of the needs of Wales and the North—and, in any case, no Balliol man would deliberately favour the rich against the poor. No, the social selectivity of the mission might be ascribed, as one could have guessed, to William Weston of Christ Church! Perhaps it was always likely that the attempt to practice Counter-Reformation piety in conditions of proscription would lead the missioners into the arms of the gentry, and that the Catholic minority would become a seigneurially structured minority. The history of the post-Reformation Catholic mission has been written as if it was made by saints, and perhaps, in a few cases, it was. But, especially after the Armada scare, when persecution abated except for occasional crises and the risk in a clerical career was much less, the Jesuits and seminarists were men, not saints. Perhaps we should not be too surprised if they chose to spend their time with their social and educational equals, in the relative safety of a manor-house, rather than tramp the cold moors from one hovel to the next. It is not for a historian, especially a non-Catholic historian and coward, to criticize those who chose to be live private chaplains and not dead popular evangelists. If a historian is to offer criticism, it should not be of these clerical realists, but of his colleagues who for 380 years have believed Robert Parsons' fairy story.

THE IRISH IN NINETEENTH-CENTURY BRITAIN: PROBLEMS OF INTEGRATION

By M. A. G. Ó Tuathaigh, M.A., F.R.Hist.S.

READ AT THE SOCIETY'S CONFERENCE 12 SEPTEMBER 1980

UNLIKE their American cousins, the Irish immigrants in nineteenth-century Britain have, until recently, received comparatively little scholarly attention from historians. This is not to say that their presence in Victorian Britain has gone unnoticed; far from it. Throughout the nineteenth century the doings and, much more often, the misdoings of the immigrant Irish were logged in massive detail by an army of social investigators, philanthropists, clergymen, royal commissions and parliamentary committees. But, with very few exceptions,[1] the scholarly analysis of the data has only begun in earnest during the last two decades, and especially during the past few years. In a growing body of local and regional studies,[2] and in studies of particular aspects

[1] The exceptions include A. Redford, *Labour Migration in England, 1800–1850* (London, 1926; revised edn., Manchester, 1964); J. E. Handley, *The Irish in Scotland* (Cork, 1943), and *The Irish in Modern Scotland* (Cork, 1947); J. A. Jackson, *The Irish in Britain* (London, 1963); R. Lawton, 'Irish Immigration to England and Wales in the Mid-Nineteenth Century', *Irish Geography*, iv (1959–63), 35–54. It would be absurd to exclude from this list the far from scholarly, sadly dated, but splendidly informative J. Denvir, *The Irish in Britain* (London, 1892).

[2] The growing volume of work includes Lynn H. Lees, 'Patterns of Lower-Class Life: Irish Slum Communities in Nineteenth-Century London', *Nineteenth-Century Cities*, ed. S. Thernstrom and R. Sennett (New Haven, 1969), pp. 359–85; 'Mid-Victorian Migration and the Irish Family Economy', *Victorian Studies*, xx (1976), 25–43; *Exiles of Erin: Irish Migrants in Victorian London* (Manchester, 1979); R. D. Lobban, 'The Irish Community in Greenock in the Nineteenth Century', *Irish Geography*, vi (1971), 270–81; W. J. Lowe, 'The Irish in Lancashire, 1846–71: a Social History', *Irish Economic and Social History*, ii (1975), 63–5 (thesis abstract); 'The Lancashire Irish and the Catholic Church, 1846–71', *Irish Historical Studies*, xx (1976), 129–55; 'Social Agencies among the Irish in Lancashire during the Mid-Nineteenth Century', *Saothar*, 3 (1977), 15–20; E. D. Steele, 'The Irish Presence in the North of England, 1850–1914', *Northern History*, xii (1976), 220–41; C. Richardson, 'Irish Settlement in Mid-Nineteenth Century Bradford', *Yorkshire Bulletin of Economic and Social Research*, xx, 40–57; 'The Irish in Victorian Bradford', *The Bradford Antiquary*, 9 (1976), 294–316; R. J. Cooter, 'Lady Londonderry and the Irish Catholics of Seaham Harbour: "No Popery" out of Context', *Recusant History*, 13 (1975–6), 288–98; J. V. Hickey, 'The Origin and Growth of the Irish Community in Cardiff' (unpublished M.A. thesis, Univ. of Wales, 1959); *Urban Catholics* (London, 1967), pp. 56–134; J. M. Werly, 'The Irish in Manchester, 1832–49', *Irish Historical Studies*, xviii (1973), 345–58; J. H. Treble, 'The Place of the Irish Catholics in the Social Life of the North of England, 1829–1851' (unpublished Ph.D. thesis, Univ. of Leeds,

149

of the Irish presence,[3] the literature on the Irish immigrants is becoming not only more plentiful but also conceptually more sophisticated. Two recent collections[4] concentrate on providing a comparative framework for discussing the presence and problems of various groups of immigrants and minorities in British society during the past two centuries. This growing body of scholarly writing is to be welcomed, and it is especially to be hoped that further local studies will follow, to enable us to test more rigorously our assumptions and generalizations about the Irish in nineteenth-century Britain.

Perhaps it is not altogether surprising that there should have been for so long this relative neglect of the immigrant Irish in nineteenth-century Britain. For one thing, the Irish in Britain constituted a somewhat peculiar minority. Indeed, Mr. E. P. Thompson asserts with some force that 'the Irish were never pressed back into ghettoes. It would have been difficult to have made a people who spoke the same language and were British citizens under the act of union into a subject minority.'[5] A 'subject' minority they may not have been; but, in their own perception of themselves and in the way the natives of the host society perceived them, the immigrant Irish were undoubtedly a minority of some kind. Yet it is difficult to fit them into the more conventional or accepted typology of minorities. Without becoming enmeshed in unhelpful semantics about what constitutes a minority, we may (as A. C. Hepburn has done recently)[6] identify two main types of minority. The first kind is that minority, usually immigrant, which seeks the maximum degree of assimilation and integration into

---

1969); Brenda Collins, 'Aspects of Irish Immigration into Two Scottish Towns during the Mid-Nineteenth Century', *Irish Economic and Social History*, vi (1979), 71–3 (thesis abstract). Miss Collins kindly allowed me to read the original M.Phil. thesis.

[3] See, for instance, A. O'Day, *The English Face of Irish Nationalism: Parnellite Involvement in British Politics, 1880–86* (Dublin, 1977); S. Gilley, 'The Roman Catholic Mission to the Irish in London, 1840–1860', *Recusant History*, 10 (1969–70), 123–45; 'Protestant London, No Popery, and the Irish Poor, 1830–60', *ibid.*, 210–30; 'The Catholic Faith of the Irish Slums: London 1840–70', *The Victorian City*, ed. H. J. Dyos and M. Wolff (2 vols., London, 1973), ii, pp. 837–53; 'Heretic London, Holy Poverty and the Irish Poor, 1830–1870', *Downside Review*, 89 (1971), 64–89; 'English Attitudes to the Irish in England, 1780–1900', *Immigrants and Minorities in British Society*, ed. C. Holmes (London, 1978), pp. 81–110. See also H. W. Benjamin, 'The London Irish: a Study in Political Activism, 1870–1910' (unpublished Ph.D. thesis, Princeton, 1976), and E. P. M. Woolaston, 'The Irish Nationalist Movement in Great Britain, 1886–1908' (unpublished M.A. thesis, Univ. of London, 1958).

[4] *Immigrants and Minorities*, ed. Holmes; K. Lunn, *Hosts, Immigrants and Minorities* (London, 1980). For the process of migration itself, see *Migration*, ed. A. Jackson (Cambridge, 1969).

[5] E. P. Thompson, *The Making of the English Working Class* (1976 edn.), p. 480.

[6] *Minorities in History*, ed. A. C. Hepburn (London, 1978), pp. 1–2.

the majority society, but which regards itself as the object of collective discrimination by the majority. In short, a minority whose urge to integrate is resisted. Secondly there is the European-type minority (based on religious, ethnic or linguistic grounds) which finds itself (through the accident of war or geography) in a minority status and which seeks to retain its distinctiveness and to resist assimilation into the majority community. The Irish in nineteenth-century Britain, as we shall see, shared certain characteristics of both of these types, while fitting snugly into neither mould.

A second explanation for the relative lack of scholarly interest in the immigrant Irish may be the fact that within the context of Irish emigration in general in the past two centuries, the emigration to Britain was very much the smaller part of the story. Throughout the nineteenth century the volume of Irish emigration to Britain was small in relation to the total volume of Irish emigration.[7] Nevertheless, in absolute numbers it was quite significant. Of course, Irish emigration to Britain did not begin with the nineteenth century. For centuries previously the Irish had been travelling and settling in Britain—and it is worth pointing out that from the outset they were officially 'visible' as a problem group, cropping up in enquiries into vagrancy and the like. By the late eighteenth century there were already sizeable Irish settlements in some British towns and cities, particularly London and Lancashire, and their presence had already produced varieties of social tension and occasional violence.[8]

However, the really heavy influx of immigrant Irish only intensified in the early decades of the nineteenth century, and at an accelerating rate from 1815 to 1845, by which time it had firmly established its predominantly urban character.[9] The influx reached its climax during and immediately after the great famine of 1845–51 in Ireland. Already in 1841 there were some 419,256 Irish-born residents in Britain, and a decade later (as a consequence of the famine influx) the figure had climbed to 727,326. These settlers reached their maximum figure in 1861, when the total number stood at 806,000. Thereafter, the decennial figure for Irish emigration to Britain declined continuously from the 1870s to 1939 (with the exception of the early 1900s which saw a

[7] Though the figures for Irish emigration to Britain have, it seems, hitherto been underestimated, see C. Ó Gráda, 'A Note on Nineteenth-Century Irish Emigration Statistics', *Population Studies*, 29 (1975), 145–8; 'Some Aspects of Nineteenth-Century Irish Emigration', *Comparative Aspects of Scottish and Irish Economic and Social History, 1600–1900*, ed. L. M. Cullen and T. C. Smout (Edinburgh, 1977), pp. 65–73.
[8] See, for example, Dorothy George, *London Life in the Eighteenth Century* (London, 1930).
[9] See Redford, *Labour Migration*, pp. 150–64. The most detailed source of opinions on the pre-famine Irish immigrants is G. Cornwall Lewis's report on the state of the Irish poor in Britain in the early 1830s (*Parliamentary Papers*, 1836 (40), xxxiv, app. G).

sharp rise in Irish emigration from the north-east to Britain). By 1901 the total figure for the Irish-born immigrants was down to 632,000.[10]

As a proportion of the total population of Britain these figures were quite modest—the Irish constituting under 3.5% of the total population in 1861, at its maximum, and as low as 1.7% in 1901.[11] These national averages, however, conceal the wide regional variations in the density of Irish settlement.

The 1851 census revealed the following figures for select British towns and cities:[12]

	% Irish-born
Liverpool	22.3
Dundee	18.9
Glasgow	18.2
Manchester and Salford	13.1
Paisley	12.7
Bradford	8.9
London	4.6

A few towns (e.g. Greenock) reached their maximum percentage of Irish-born later in the century.[13] Of course, these figures relate only to the Irish-born; and as such represent the minimum volume or density of Irish immigrant settlement. The inclusion of at least the second-generation Irish would give a more realistic picture of the actual size of the Irish immigrant minority in nineteenth-century Britain.

The overwhelming majority of these immigrants came from rural Ireland, though there was also an artisan and small middle-class urban element. The three main emigrant routes were (1) the northern route, from Ulster and North Connacht to Scotland; (2) the midland route, from Connacht and most of Leinster via Dublin to the north of England and the midlands; and (3) the southern route, from South Leinster and the Munster counties to London, often via Bristol. In addition to the young, single, adult emigrant (i.e. in the age-group 15–40) Irish emigration to Britain in the first half of the nineteenth century featured a substantial amount of family migration, particularly to the textile towns where prospects were most favourable for the employment of women and children as well as the household head. Again, in the pre-famine decades at least, the Irish emigration to

[10] Derived from statistical tables in Jackson, *Irish in Britain*, p. 11.

[11] *Ibid.* See also B. R. Mitchell and P. Deane, *Abstract of British Historical Statistics* (Cambridge, 1962), p. 6.

[12] Cited as percentages by Brenda Collins, 'Aspects of Irish Immigration' (unpublished M.Phil. thesis, Univ. of Edinburgh, 1978), p. 22.

[13] Lobban, 'Irish Community in Greenock', 270-1.

Britain comprised the least well-off elements of the Irish emigrant stream, the more comfortable elements going to North America. From the 1860s onwards, however, these differences began to disappear; the young and single came to dominate the Irish migration flow to Britain as well as to the United States, and there was a general levelling in the condition and circumstances of the Irish emigrants irrespective of their destination.[14] Finally, in terms of sex-ratio, while there were some regional variations (reflecting differences in economic and occupational structure between different British towns and cities), generally there was a preponderance of males in the total Irish immigrant stream up to the 1890s, after which the female element achieved a slight majority.[15]

With few exceptions (such as the few settlements of Irish agricultural labourers in Scotland) the immigrant Irish concentrated in the main cities and towns of industrial Britain—in London, Liverpool (a quarter of whose population was Irish born in 1861), Glasgow, Tyneside, Cardiff, Bradford and other industrial areas of Lancashire, Yorkshire, the English midlands, and the east and west of Scotland. The three main clusters of concentrated Irish settlement were in Lancashire, the west of Scotland and London. By 1851 more than 80% of the Irish-born in Britain were resident in towns with a population of more than 10,000. Of course, in talking of 'settlement' it is worth remembering that for certain categories of Irish immigrants in Britain permanent settlement in any real sense was often a very late development; these categories would include not only the seasonal labourers (ranging from c. 60,000 to 100,000 per annum in the decades 1840-1860, after which their numbers declined drastically),[16] but also certain categories of labourers with an exceptionally high mobility rate—in construction and railway navvying.[17]

Within their new habitat the Irish were heavily concentrated in what one commentator, speaking of more recent immigrants, has described as 'the most disadvantaged parts of the social structure of

[14] Lees, *Exiles*, pp. 39-40, 42-4; Ó Gráda, 'Aspects of Irish Emigration', pp. 66-7.

[15] *Reports of the Commission on Emigration and Other Population Problems (1948-54)*, P.R. 2541 (Dublin, 1965), Table 90, p. 120.

[16] For seasonal migrants and their impact, see B. M. Kerr, 'Irish Seasonal Migration to Great Britain, 1800-38', *Irish Historical Studies*, iii (1942-3), 365-80; C. Ó Gráda, 'Seasonal Migration and Post-Famine Adjustment in the West of Ireland', *Studia Hibernica*, 13 (1973), 48-76; E. J. T. Collins, 'Migrant Labour in British Agriculture in the Nineteenth Century', *Econ. Hist. Rev.*, 2nd ser., xxix (1976), 38-59.

[17] For Irish railway navvying see, for example, T. Coleman, *The Railway Navvies* (London, 1965); J. E. Handley, *The Navvy in Scotland* (Cork, 1970); J. H. Treble, 'Irish Navvies in the North of England, 1830-50', *Transport History*, 6 (1973), 227-47; D. Brooke, 'Railway Navvies on the Pennines, 1841-71', *Journal of Transport History*, new ser., 3 (1975-6), 41-53.

British cities'.[18] Rent levels, proximity to work-place, transport costs (where, as in London, these were relevant) were all important determinants of the settlement habits of the immigrant Irish. As it happened, they were heavily concentrated in city-centre areas, or in dockside settlements, 'where residential competition was least intense'.[19] Their living conditions were generally the very worst which the Victorian industrial slum could offer. Some of these inner-city Irish settlements became bywords for industrial slum living. The 'little Ireland' ghetto in Manchester, the London courts and rookeries, the Glasgow tenements, the Liverpool cellars and similar quarters in Cardiff, Bradford and other centres of British industry, displayed the full spectrum of social evils—appalling over-crowding, little or no sanitation, open sewers and cesspools, unhealthy diet, inadequate clothing, vagrancy, disease, alcoholism and general squalor; a high quota of unemployed paupers, or of underemployed casual labourers; and a high incidence of casual violence (very often provoked by drink). These were the conditions which appalled Engels, terrified Carlyle, and absorbed the attention of a generation of social investigators and commentators from the 1830s to the 1860s. What is remarkable is that they survived in many cities not only into the last years of Victoria's century, but indeed well into the present century. Booth's description of the rat-infested Irish ghetto of dockside London at the close of the nineteenth century is as chilling as anything penned in the worst years of the famine influx.[20]

Turning from habitat to occupational structure, the immigrant Irish were disproportionately concentrated in the ranks of the semi-skilled and unskilled casual labour force—in construction, transportation, dockside labour (as stevedores and casual labourers), in food distribution and in railway construction. Again, in certain industries such as sugar refining, textiles (especially where the Irish acted as sweated labour in declining trades), in gasworks and paper-making, as sawyers, coal-heavers and porters—in all of these categories the Irish were disproportionately numerous. John Denvir (an invaluable contemporary chronicler of his fellow immigrants in nineteenth-century Lancashire and, indeed, in Britain in general) asserted that in

---

[18] K. Boyle, 'The Irish Immigrant in Britain', *Northern Ireland Legal Quarterly*, 19 (1968), 422.

[19] Lees, *Exiles*, p. 55.

[20] F. Engels, *The Condition of the Working Classes in England* [1845], ed. W. O. Henderson and W. H. Chaloner (Oxford, 1958), esp. pp. 30–87, 104–7; T. Carlyle, *Chartism* (London, 1839), esp. pp. 28–33; H. Mayhew, *London Labour and the London Poor* (4 vols., London, 1861–2: reprinted New York, 1968); C. Booth, *Life and Labour of the People in London* (London, 1902–3), esp. ser. 3, 'Religious Influences'. It should be noted that the Irish did not bulk as large as a social problem in Booth's work as they had done for Mayhew a generation earlier.

the mid-nineteenth century, and for long afterwards, it was unusual to find a stonemason's labourer who was not an Irishman.[21] There was also an Irish labour element in the coal-fields of South Wales, the west of Scotland and, to a lesser extent, in the English north-east and the midlands, and in the unskilled labour sectors of the heavy industries.

The occupations most common among female Irish immigrants were in textile factories, laundry work and domestic service (though here the supply always ran ahead of demand, and in certain areas, such as in certain towns in Scotland and the north of England, Irish girls faced strong local competition in domestic service).[22] Many Irish women survived, or contributed to the family income, through earnings from piece-work (such as needlework, sewing or rag-picking) in their own homes. Both male and female Irish immigrants were heavily involved in hawking and street-trading in the larger centres of population, while the keeping of lodgers was an important source of income for the enterprising immigrant family, both because of the rent and the laundry services often rendered for cash by the woman of the house.

The army and navy was an important source of employment among Irish immigrants. It has been calculated that in 1830 the Irish accounted for 42.2% of the non-commissioned ranks of the British army, and while this proportion gradually declined in succeeding decades, it was still 14.0% as late as 1891. In round figures, the Irish presence in the army ranged from 55,000 in 1868 (the maximum figure) to around 25,000 as late as 1896.[23]

Not all Irish immigrants belonged to the ranks of the unskilled labouring classes. There was a sizeable Irish artisan or tradesman element in most of the larger British towns, especially during the first half of the nineteenth century, with tailors, masons and shoemakers being particularly numerous.[24] Moreover, though not very numerous, there was a middle-class element among the immigrant Irish—doctors and lawyers, writers and journalists, with a sprinkling in the world of business and finance.[25] But the Irish presence in these higher reaches of the occupational structure was disproportionately small, whether

---

[21] J. Denvir, *The Life Story of an Old Rebel* (Dublin, 1910), p. 50.

[22] Lobban, 'Irish Community in Greenock', 272.

[23] See the excellent paper by H. J. Hanham, 'Religion and Nationality in the Mid-Victorian Army', *War and Society: Essays in Honour and Memory of J. R. Western*, ed. M. R. D. Foot (London, 1973), pp. 162, 176-7.

[24] Some of these are noted in passing in *Parliamentary Papers*, 1836 (40), xxxiv, app. G.

[25] It is difficult to quantify this element. They emerge from Denvir's survey of the immigrant Irish (*Irish in Britain*), and particularly in the study of the political leadership of the immigrant Irish in the studies of Benjamin and Woolaston (see n. 3 above). See also Richardson, 'Irish in Victorian Bradford', 303-4.

this disproportion is measured in terms of the occupational structure of the Irish immigrants themselves, or in terms of the occupational structure of the communities in which they settled. For example, Lawton found in Liverpool in 1851 that some 6.5% of merchants, bankers and business men in sample areas of Liverpool were Irish-born—whereas the Irish-born in Liverpool at this time were of the order of 23%; similarly in Greenock, whilst the Irish-born comprised 16.1% of the population as late as 1881, the percentage of Irish-born among the higher white-collar category jobs was only 5.3%.[26] Even within general categories, there were marked variations. Thus, for example, among settled traders with premises, Irish publicans were numerous, but Irish shopkeepers were not as plentiful as one might expect.

It would be wrong to suggest that this was a static picture throughout the nineteenth century. Undoubtedly in the second half of the century, and at a moderately accelerating pace from the 1880s, there was some demonstrable improvement in the general status of the immigrant Irish—in terms of both jobs and of living conditions. Some mobility did take place—outward from the inner-city ghetto and upward from the chronically congested ranks of the unskilled labour force. Some of the changes in occupational structure were forced changes—forced by structural changes in the economy. The completion of a railway line or of a major construction job obliged some immigrants to seek new jobs—very often as maintenance men on railways or in some other 'settled' job in the manual labourer category. Though the evidence is unsatisfactory, it seem likely that there was only a very limited penetration of the white collar jobs by second-generation Irish.[27]

The commercial directories of some British towns in the 1890s show a modest increase in the number of Irish names when compared to the names listed in the 1850s. Irish penetration of the skilled trades, especially the highly unionized trades, appears to have been much slower. Indeed, it seems most likely that it was easier for the modestly educated son of an unskilled labourer to move into the white-collar ranks of the clerks and book-keepers than to join the ranks of the skilled tradesmen in the occupational category most closely related to his father's job. Nevertheless, there was unquestionably some degree of upward social mobility, and at the turn of the century John Denvir perceptively noted that it was 'a sure sign that our people are rising on the social scale', when the local Irish in Lancashire no longer

[26] Lawton, 'Irish Immigration', 48–54; Lobban, 'Irish Community in Greenock', 274–7.
[27] See Lees, *Exiles*, pp. 88–122, for the general discussion of mobility. See also the sources cited in n. 25 above for non-quantified but relevant data.

monopolized the job of bricklayer's labourer.[28] Indeed some of this improvement in status occurred even among the first-generation Irish immigrants—an ambitious and prudent labourer might, with the assistance of the earnings of his wife, or other kin, be able in his mature years to set himself up in business—as a lodging-house keeper, a publican or, more rarely, as a shopkeeper. The accumulation of a modest amount of capital was all that was required.

In the same way, in social and particularly residential circumstances no less than in occupational structure, the Irish as a group improved their position during the final third of the nineteenth century. Improvements in public health provisions, municipal activity in housing, the impact of railways, roads and other major construction works on slum clearance and on city-centre settlement generally—these were some of the important developments which led to some dispersal of the Irish from the inner-city slums during the closing decades of the nineteenth century. However, it would be unwise to exaggerate the pace of this dispersal and consequent improvement in housing and social conditions. Depending on structural changes in the economy, slum clearance and general urban renewal could be, and was in fact, a rather protracted business—coming as early as the 1860s and 1870s in some places (London and Birmingham), but as late as the 1930s in others (Greenock).[29] Nor should it be imagined that dispersal from inner-city slums and resettlement in more periphal areas automatically meant accelerated assimilation for the immigrant Irish. The evidence for London, for example, suggests that in short-distance migration or dispersal within the city, the immigrant Irish succeeded to a remarkable degree in reproducing in their new neighbourhoods the cohesion and self-segregation of their original slum. As Lynn Lees concludes in this context, 'mobility did not produce geographic assimilation'.[30] For all that, however, it may be conceded that during the closing decades of the nineteenth century some improvements did take place in the living conditions of sections of the immigrant Irish.

While this evidence of increasing Irish mobility, of immigrant adaptability to changing conditions of employment and accommodation, is of considerable interest (especially for the purposes of comparisons with experiences in other countries, such as the United States),[31] what is far more remarkable is the fact that such a relatively

[28] Denvir, *Life Story*, p. 50.

[29] Lobban, 'Irish Community in Greenock', 277-8. Hickey (*Urban Catholics*, pp. 99-113) discusses dispersal in Cardiff, for which see also M. J. Daunton, *Coal Metropolis: Cardiff 1870-1914* (Leicester, 1977), pp. 89-105, 125-46. See also Richardson, 'Irish in Victorian Bradford', 301-2, and, for the impact of railways and other construction on cities, *The Victorian City*, ed. Dyos and Wolff, esp. chs. 10-15.

[30] Lees, *Exiles*, p. 63.

[31] See particularly the work of S. Thernstrom, *Poverty and Progress: Social Mobility in*

large proportion of the immigrant Irish remained tied for so long to the old pattern of jobs and localities. This remarkably conservative pattern of occupational and social structure among the immigrants is worth examining more closely.

There are, of course, many obvious and common-sense explanations for this conservatism among the immigrants. It is reasonable to accept the view that 'kinship relations between emigrant and would-be emigrant in many cases probably determined both the place he went to and his choice of work'.[32] In more general terms, effective Irish control of recruitment in certain occupations soon established a tradition for immigrants' sons, or eased the initiation of the newly arrived immigrant into his new situation. A ganger on a building site or on the dockside might easily establish a recruitment pattern from among his fellow countrymen, or indeed his fellow county-men. There is abundant evidence, for example, that among stevedores on dockside London, or in the sugar-refining factories in Greenock, the establishment of a dominant Irish influence soon led to the operation of something approaching an 'Hibernian closed shop' in subsequent recruitment of workers.[33]

Again, familiar faces and accents, a general ease of social intercourse, familiar landmarks (such as pubs and shops), all these undoubtedly helped in creating a sense of cohesion among the immigrant community and in reinforcing their social and occupational conservatism.

Finally, it is likely that the very high illiteracy rate of successive waves of Irish immigrants (the available data suggest an illiteracy rate among Irish immigrants about twice as high as the average for their social equivalents among the indigenous population in the 1860s) further retarded the mobility, social and otherwise, of the Irish immigrants as a whole.[34]

However, while acknowledging these conservative patterns of settlement and occupation it seems that there were certain more fundamental factors inhibiting the early and successful integration of the immigrant Irish into their host society. Some of these factors relate to

---

a *Nineteenth-Century City* (Cambridge, Mass., 1964); *The Other Bostonians* (Cambridge, Mass., 1973), pp. 45–75, 111–44, 145–75, 220–6, which highlights the disappointingly limited mobility of second-generation Irish-Americans relative to certain other immigrant groups.

[32] Boyle, 'Irish Immigrant', 429.

[33] Lobban, 'Irish Community in Greenock', 273–4; J. Lovell, 'The Irish and the London Dockers', *Society for the Study of Labour History: Bulletin, 35* (1977), 16–18; *Stevedores and Dockers: a Study of Trade Unionism in the Port of London, 1870–1914* (London, 1969).

[34] The estimate is from Steele, 'Irish Presence in the North of England', 224. See also Lobban ('Irish Community in Greenock', 279) who suggests that the percentage may have been higher. For a note on the Irish-speaking immigrants, see below, n. 53.

the attitudes of the immigrant; to the strength or weakness of his desire to integrate. Others relate to the willingness or otherwise of the host community to accept and absorb him. In the case of the Irish immigrant, there were strong currents running against the desire to integrate. These currents were in the first instance psychological. The very proximity to home, the disappointment of those whose original aspirations had centred on a passage to America, the high mobility of a section of the Irish labour force; all these factors combined to encourage among many immigrants an attitude of refusal to accept the permanency of their exile. Furthermore, the Irish immigrant communities had, deriving from their historical sense, an unusually ambivalent attitude towards their host society. While acknowledging that Britain was providing them with the means to live, and while always ready to acknowledge the better wages and hopes of improvement which prompted emigration in the first place, among the immigrant Irish the sense of obligation or of gratitude for these benefits was nullified, to a considerable extent, by their belief that it was Britain's misgovernment of Ireland which had caused them to be uprooted in the first instance. These attitudes contributed to a situation where the primary loyalty of the immigrant Irish was to their homeland or to the immigrant community itself, and only lastly, if at all, to their new society.

While granting the Irish tendency towards self-segregation—the understandable clannishness of immigrants and the manner in which this was facilitated and reinforced by social and economic structures in industrial Britain—there can nevertheless be no doubt but that the Irish in nineteenth-century Britain encountered very strong opposition from many elements in the host society in their efforts to gain acceptance, not to speak of integration. David Steele is surely correct in asserting that 'nowhere else, save in Orange Canada, did the Irish abroad meet with such sustained antagonism' as in nineteenth-century Britain.[35]

There were many reasons for this antagonism. Anti-Irish prejudice (or, more correctly, attitudes) in British society had a long and complicated history, and its sources are a matter of some controversy.[36] That this antagonism was an odd compound of religious, social and political elements, of the rational and the irrational, is not in dispute. However, some recent American writing has described this set of attitudes and antagonisms, which sections of British opinion showed

[35] Steele, 'Irish Presence in the North of England', 226.
[36] A reasonably scrupulous backward glance would go at least as far as Geraldus Cambrensis, *Expugnatio Hibernica*, ed. A. B. Scott and F. X. Martin (Dublin, 1978). For Elizabethan attitudes, see D. B. Quinn, *The Elizabethans and the Irish* (Ithaca, N.Y., 1966).

towards the Irish at home and abroad, as evidence of a clear example of racial prejudice.[37] In the case of Professor Curtis, his examination of these attitudes has concentrated on sections of the mid- and late-Victorian intelligentsia, chiefly literary men and cartoonists, among whom he detects the emergence, c. 1860–80, of a firm set of anti-Irish prejudices based on 'the assumption or conviction that the "native Irish" were alien in race and inferior in culture to the Anglo-Saxons'.[38] In essence, this was a set of racist assumptions.

Professor Curtis's analysis has been strongly disputed by, among others, Dr. Sheridan Gilley.[39] Gilley very properly insists on the adjective 'racial' being used with some precision and consistency, and he takes Curtis to task not merely for imprecision, but for clear contradictions in his use of the racial stereotype to describe English 'prejudices'. More positively, Gilley sees the British stereotype of 'Paddy' as having a benign as well as a menacing face, and as being every bit as much an Irish as a British creation (with Irish elements of self-image contributing heavily to the making of the stereotype). Finally, Gilley argues that it was only on specific politico-religious issues that anti-Irish attitudes became dominant among the British and, furthermore, that there were very understandable social and economic reasons for much of the popular hostility shown to the immigrant Irish, reasons which do not deserve to be described as prejudices.[40]

There is much sense in many of Gilley's arguments and, certainly, the attitudes of the Victorian intelligentsia towards Irish political demands are too complex for the procrustean frame of simple anti-Celticism. However, it may be that Dr. Gilley underestimates the extent, the pervasiveness and the endurance of this antagonism towards the Irish immigrants. And, while he acknowedges that 'anti-Celtic racism became a partial, and temporary component of English nationalism as a fleeting mood in the euphoria of the hey-day of the Anglo-Saxon "lords of human kinds" ',[41] this does not go far enough in conveying the extent to which the vocabulary of race was resorted to in popular discussions of the 'Irish problem'—in the press and the journals—from at least the 1840s. While 'national' rather than racial may be a more accurate description, as Gilley would have it, of anti-Irish attitudes, there was an almost universal tendency from the 1840s

[37] L. P. Curtis, Jr., *Anglo-Saxons and Celts* (Bridgeport, Conn., 1968); *Apes, Angels and Victorians* (Newton Abbot, 1971); R. W. Lebow, *White Britain and Black Ireland* (Philadelphia, 1976).

[38] Curtis, *Anglo-Saxons and Celts*, p. 5.

[39] Gilley, 'English Attitudes to the Irish', pp. 81–110. See also W. L. Arnstein, 'Victorian Prejudice Re-examined', *Victorian Studies*, xii (1969), 452–7.

[40] This bald summary does scant justice to Gilley's carefully argued case.

[41] Gilley, 'English Attitudes to the Irish', p. 94.

onwards to describe the immigrant Irish and their problems in distinctly racial terms. The balance or emphasis here is crucial. The idealized Ireland—the suffering but beautifully melancholy lady of *Punch* cartoons, or good-natured 'Pat'; these are idealized types so far as the cartoonists were concerned. They are somewhat unreal, and are certainly not the stereotype likely to be related to the bulk of the immigrant Irish. In short, it seems that, on balance, from the 1840s immigrant Irish benefited much less from the idealized and benign elements of the 'Paddy' stereotype in cartoons and elsewhere than they suffered from its malign elements.

Whatever may have been the balance between the 'good' and 'bad' images of the Irish prior to 1800, the antagonisms against the Irish intensified and became more widespread from the early decades of the nineteenth century, as the social and economic problems of pre-famine Ireland and the transformation of the British labour market, under the impact of the industrial revolution, combined to send an increasing volume of the unemployed Irish to Britain. Anti-Irish feeling had its rational side; to a certain extent it did rest on an indisputable 'body of social fact'. The Irish did indeed represent a major social problem. British rate payers resented the heavy burden of Irish paupers on their poor-rates, and further feared them as disease-carriers. The British working man had reason to resent the Irish immigrant labourer, who was prepared to work harder and longer and for lower pay, and to live in more brutalizing conditions than his British counterpart. Again, the use of the Irish as strike-breakers, though its incidence was probably exaggerated, left a long and bitter legacy, dividing the native labouring classes from the Irish.[42] Some other aspects of the Irish immigrant impact on the British labour market are less clear. For example, E. H. Hunt's study of inter-regional wage variations in early nineteenth-century Britain suggests that the Irish influx may have increased or widened these variations,[43] a view at variance with what historians have until now accepted to be the case.[44] It has also been argued that by flooding the casual labour market the Irish, even if unintentionally, were responsible for the native British labourer's becoming more skilled or otherwise moving up a rung on the ladder of the labour hierarchy. Finally, in this context of the British labour market, the point was made as early as the 1830s by Cornwall Lewis that the Irish were concentrated heavily in employment which required exceptionally high mobility, and were an indispensable part of

---

[42] For examples see Redford, *Labour Migration*, pp. 161-2, and E. H. Hunt, *Regional Wage Variations in Great Britain, 1850-1914* (Oxford, 1973), p. 296.

[43] Hunt, *Wage Variations*, pp. 286-323.

[44] But for doubts on Hunt's thesis, see Ó Gráda, 'Aspects of Irish Emigration', 65-6, 71, n. 6.

a dynamic economy.[45] But, in the case of attitudes and prejudices, what is demonstrable is very often of less consequence than what is feared; and the Irish were generally perceived as a threat, a nuisance, a contagion. Indeed, writing as late as the 1930s the late J. H. Clapham wrote of 'the decisive and degrading influence of the early nineteenth-century Irish immigration on housing habits and housing conditions', and further stated that those areas where the Irish had not settled 'had been spared a social disease'.[46]

The huge famine influx of Irish brought native fear and resentment to fever pitch. The flooding of ghetto areas by impoverished and disease-ridden Irish, and the violence and social misery which was a by-product of such a brutalizing environment, together with a ready acceptance of the notion that Irish peasant society was inherently violent, formed for sizable sections of the British public an explanation for all Irish troubles and misfortunes which rested on 'the fundamental weaknesses of the Irish national character'. A stereotype of the brutal-ized 'Paddy' was formed, in greater detail and enjoying wider cur-rency than ever before: intemperate, improvident, violent, totally innocent of any notions of hygiene, mendacious and undependable—not so much a lovable rogue as a menacing savage. The popular imagination had, in general, little time for reflection on the environ-mental factors which dictated the over-representation of the immi-grant Irish on the poor-law and crime lists, and in the alcoholic gutters.[47] Weaknesses in the national character was an easily accepted explanation. During the middle decades of the nineteenth century these prejudices were systematized within a somewhat crude anthro-pological typology.

The *Punch* cartoons of the late nineteenth century illustrate very well that caricature of what a Glasgow newspaper referred to as 'the ape-faced, small-headed Irishman', who showed 'the unmistakable width of mouth, immense expanse of chin, and "forehead villainous low"', so characteristic of the lowest Irish'.[48] And, of course, the vast majority of the Irish in nineteenth-century Britain belonged to 'the lowest Irish'. While the ineluctable fact of colour is missing here, it is still difficult to describe this kind of language as other than racial.

The intensity of these prejudices and this hostility towards the Irish immigrant community varied from time to time, from place to place, and between different classes. In south-west Scotland, anti-Irish preju-

[45] See *Parliamentary Papers*, 1836 (40), xxxiv, app. G, esp. pp. xxx–xxxviii.
[46] J. H. Clapham, *An Economic History of Modern Britain* (3 vols., Cambridge, 1926–38), ii, p. 494.
[47] Richardson ('Irish in Victorian Bradford', 310–12) shows that the Irish received special notice in the Chief Constable's annual reports.
[48] Cited in Handley, *Irish in Modern Scotland*, p. 105.

dice was especially bitter, with large areas of urban Lancashire not far behind.[49] Not surprisingly, the prejudices were almost everywhere directed against 'the lowest Irish', the Irish immigrant working class. Irish birth or extraction does not seem to have hindered in any significant way the prospects of the Irish professional man in Britain. British journalism presented plenty of opportunity for talented Irish pens—in the late Victorian era some of the most respected names in Fleet Street, Justin McCarthy, William O'Malley and the legendary T. P. O'Connor ('Tay Pay') were Irish.[50] Likewise, Irish entertainers and music-hall artistes added a welcome dash of provincial colour to the Victorian and Edwardian stage.[51] Even among certain 'blue-collar' communities (such as in some industrial areas of Tyneside) the local work-situation, and the dominant modes of political and religious behaviour, seem to have been adequate defence against discord, even where the Irish immigrant influx was substantial.[52] Nevertheless, it remains true that, whether dormant or roused by accidental circumstances, a deep-rooted set of anti-Irish attitudes was widespread in British society throughout the nineteenth century.

Both the Irish reluctance to integrate and the host society's reluctance to accept can be seen as functions of a more fundamental and more complex problem underlying the relations between the two communities. This was the 'cultural distance' separating the Irish immigrant community from the native population. This cultural distance proved, in the event, very difficult to bridge. Despite being white and, for the most part, English-speaking,[53] the sense of identity of the Irish immigrant, his consciousness of himself and of his history, was

[49] These were the areas of heaviest Irish settlement and also the areas with a substantial Orange immigrant element from Ulster, two factors which increased the likelihood of communal tension and violence. See Denvir, *Irish in Britain*, pp. 406–9, 429–38, 446–58.

[50] T. P. O'Connor, *Memoirs of an Old Parliamentarian* (2 vols., London, 1929); W. O'Malley, *Glancing Back* (London, 1933).

[51] For contrasting views on the 'stage Irishman', see G. C. Duggan, *The Stage Irishman* (New York, 1969), and J. M. Nelson, 'From Rory and Paddy to Boucicault's Myles, Shaun and Conn: The Irishman on the London Stage, 1830–60', *Eire-Ireland*, 13 (1978), 79–105.

[52] See J. Keating, 'History of the Tyneside Irish Brigade', *Irish Heroes in the Great War*, ed. F. Lavery (London, 1917), which is useful but written with wartime recruitment in mind; Cooter, 'Lady Londonderry', 288–98; T. P. MacDermott, 'Irish Workers on Tyneside in the Nineteenth Century', *Essays in Tyneside Labour History*, ed. N. McCord (Newcastle-upon-Tyne, 1977); R. Moore, *Pit-Men, Preachers and Politics* (Cambridge, 1974), pp. 64–77, 179–80.

[53] From Ó Gráda's revised figures for Irish immigrants to Britain (above, n. 7) and their provenance, it may be inferred that the number of Irish speakers in the immigrant stream to Britain was higher than has been allowed for. This, of course, has implications for literacy, social isolation and religious life among the immigrants.

sufficiently acute to present considerable difficulties in the way of early or successful integration.

To the social and economic forces making for self-segregation we must also add some other cultural features which increased internal cohesion within the immigrant community while simultaneously working against its assimilation.

It is easy to enumerate some of the ways in which this determination of the immigrant community to retain its identity manifested itself. The full spectrum of immigrant associations dedicated to the cultivation of Irish music and song, Irish debating and literary clubs, Gaelic League branches, G.A.A. clubs in the 1880s and 1890s, and the growth of informal and formal countymen's associations—all these constituted a mosaic of ties binding the immigrant community to the homeland. The ultimate celebration of this distinct group identity was the annual St. Patrick's Day celebrations in British towns. In Sheffield, for example, at the Patrick's Day concert in 1891, there was a large and representative gathering of well-to-do Irish; distinguished guests from the local community were there to be impressed by the good representation of professional and white-collar Irish. The hall was decorated with shamrocks and other recognizably Irish bunting, and the rendering of Moore's melodies and especially T. D. Sullivan's *God Save Ireland* (a kind of immigrant anthem) was especially enjoyed.[54] This, of course, was the high point of the nostalgic graph. But the Irish pubs on Saturday nights regularly saw the collective nostalgia of the labouring 'Paddies' indulged to the full, albeit with a more earthy flavour.

These activities, however, are but the simple manifestations of group identity not uncommon among many immigrant groups in many lands. There would seem to be no particular reason why they could not have been accommodated without any great difficulty by the host community, as indeed they are at the present time. However, the two main cultural props of the immigrant community conflicted directly with the norms of behaviour acceptable to wide sectors of British society. These were the religion and the political allegiance of the Irish immigrants.

The fidelity, or at least the emotional loyalty, of the Catholic Irish to their religion has been attested by historians and social commentators alike. But it is not enough simply to say that the Catholic Church was a central institution in the lives of the immigrant Irish in Britain.[55] The extent of its influence, and the ways in which this

[54] Programme of St. Patrick's Day concert in the Albert Hall, Sheffield, 1890 (Sheffield Central Library: H. J. Wilson Papers).

[55] The most thorough attempt to investigate this subject is the work of Gilley, cited n. 3 above.

influence manifested itself, call for some elaboration. While it is true that, unlike their spiritual brothers in America, the Irish never succeeded in capturing the commanding heights of the Catholic Church in Britain,[56] nevertheless, through sheer weight of numbers, the Catholic Church in Britain in the nineteenth century became, at a popular level, very much the church of the immigrant Irish. By a permeation, or rather saturation, of its structures, the Catholic Irish succeeded in moulding the shape of an institution which, although it differed in crucial respects from the Catholic Church they had known in rural Ireland,[57] was nevertheless an institution much closer to being an Irish Catholic Church than the majority of the native hierarchy, or the vast majority of indigenous British Catholics, would have desired. As Lynn Lees has put it, 'support for an ultramontane Church and for moderate brands of Irish nationalism permeated Roman Catholic rhetoric, rituals and social life'.[58] Some of the attempts made by English priests to marry Irish nationalist-type popular religious practices to more universally 'Roman' habits of Catholic worship produced an amusing litany of incongruities. Such, for example, was the spectacle of a well-drilled religious procession of Catholic children after Sunday school briskly stepping it out to the strains of *The Wearing of the Green* or, more incongruously still, *God Save Ireland* (the hymn to the Manchester Martyrs).[59] Attempts to infuse Irish Catholic habits and pieties with a Smilesian dose of sobriety and self-help, and indeed a more general drive to 'raise the tone' of the Catholic Irish, did not always meet with the success which its idealistic sponsors hoped for.[60]

The Catholic Church in Britain encountered considerable problems in ministering to the immigrant Irish. Human, physical and financial resources were intolerably over-strained during the famine influx, and in the post-famine decades there was a chronic and constant shortage both of priests (particularly of Irish priests, though their numbers undoubtedly increased in the final third of the nineteenth century)[61]

---

[56] A point noted, self-consciously and defensively, by D. Gwynn, 'The Irish Immigration', *The English Catholics, 1850–1950*, ed. G. A. Beck (London, 1950), pp. 265–90.

[57] For which see E. Larkin, 'The Devotional Revolution in Ireland, 1850–75', *American Historical Review*, lxxvii (1972), 625–52; D. Miller, 'Irish Catholicism and the Great Famine', *Journal of Social History*, ix (1975–76), 81–98.

[58] Lees, *Exiles*, p. 194.

[59] See Steele, 'Irish Presence in the North of England', 231.

[60] For amusing examples, see Lees, *Exiles*, p. 196.

[61] On the crucial role of Irish-speaking priests in administering the sacraments (especially confession), see the letter sent in November 1865 to Mgr. Kirby, Rector of the Irish College in Rome, by the Rev. George Montgomery of the parish of Wednesbury in south Staffordshire, where 'nineteen twentieths of my flock' came from Connacht (Irish College, Rome, Kirby Papers, Kirby/65/269). See also Richardson, 'Irish Settlement in Mid-Nineteenth Century Bradford', 56.

and of money, shortages which severely hampered the English Catholic mission to the immigrant Irish from the 1840s onwards. Failure in any aspect of this mission added further to what gradually emerged as the central problem for the Catholic Church in nineteenth-century Britain, the problem of 'leakage' of baptized Catholics out of the Church. Leakage in this sense did not mean a repudiation of Catholic teaching, or conversion to an alternative faith, or an explicit profession of atheism. It simply meant ceasing to practise regularly.

The precise extent of this 'leakage' among Irish Catholic immigrants in nineteenth-century Britain is difficult to calculate, though by the third quarter of the century it was deemed to be considerable enough to cause great anxiety to the hierarchies of Britain and Ireland, and indeed in Rome itself. Catholic commentators, like Edward Lucas of *The Tablet*, and bishops, such as Vaughan of Salford (who collected statistical data on the 'leakage' problem), were unaminous in their view that 'leakage' was the major challenge facing the Catholic Church in Britain, and that it was increasing as the century got older.[62] What they meant, of course, was that regular attendance at Mass and the sacraments, and particularly the performance of Easter duties, was not satisfactory when related to the total number of nominal Catholics resident in Britain.

But even the alarmists acknowledged that in the case of many of the immigrant Irish, relative 'indifference to Catholic ritual' should not be confused 'with indifference to Catholicism'.[63] And even if we accept that there was a relatively low level of regular attendance at Mass among working-class Catholics in particular, two points are none the less worth keeping in mind. First, that, low as it was, religious observance among the labouring Irish Catholics was considerably higher, as K. Inglis has shown, than religious observance among other sectors of the native British working-classes.[64] Secondly, even those whose attention to the repeated exhortations of the Catholic hierarchy to attend Mass and the sacraments regularly was, to say the least, indifferent, seldom lost their emotional loyalty to the Catholic Church. This is well attested both by the rueful testimony of disappointed evangelical Protestant missionaries and by the fact that even for those Catholics who were not regular attenders, the key dates in the life-cycle (birth, marriage, death) were seldom celebrated without the Church's benediction.[65]

In talking of 'leakage' historians generally accept the contemporary

[62] K. S. Inglis, *Churches and the Working Classes in Victorian England* (London, 1963), esp. pp. 119–30.
[63] Lees, *Exiles*, p. 184.
[64] Inglis, *Churches and the Working Classes*, pp. 16–18, 119–30.
[65] Lees, *Exiles*, pp. 180–2.

view that the main problem was in the second and subsequent generations of immigrants. E. D. Steele's comment that 'whenever the Irish settled, the first generation rarely lost all contact with their religion, but the second and third generations did so' is not untypical of the late-Victorian period and of later historians.[66] Sheridan Gilley, for example, sees two contradictory forces as contributing to this 'leakage'; the one, upward social mobility, rendering old values irrelevant or obsolete, the other, 'a total submersion in the common culture of poverty'.[67]

However, even in the face of such a consensus there is need for caution. The evidence on marriage behaviour is of relevance here. The view that 'mixed' marriages were on the increase, at least in the 1880s and 1890s, was voiced by contemporary Catholic leaders, and has been accepted by historians.[68] Such dense smoke makes it highly unlikely that there was no fire. Yet there is independent evidence of an extraordinary incidence of intra-group marriages among the immigrant Irish. Lynn Lees, for example, basing her findings on data from 1851 to 1861, concludes that 'the London Irish generally married within their own ethnic group; there was little inter-marriage with people of English ancestry or with continental Catholics.... First and second generation Irish ... would seem to have intermarried freely.'[69] Similarly, in analysing data for Greenock, R. B. Lobban found a high degree of intra-group marriages among the immigrant Irish in 1851 and again in 1891. And while there was a weakening in the intra-group pattern in the years between 1851 and 1891 (from 86% of Irish men and women finding partners within their own group in 1851, to 72.4% in 1891), the weakening was not dramatic, and the group solidarity was still remarkably strong by 1891.[70]

While the evidence is patchy, and clearly requires further local studies on this particular aspect of the problem, nevertheless these figures for intra-group marriage patterns are a further warning to us not to take at face value all the dire forecasts of Catholic observers during the late-Victorian era. As with attendance figures, so also with marriage patterns, the evidence suggests that there was a much stronger emotional loyalty to the Catholic Church than many commentators suspected; and, furthermore, that nominal, occasional or symbolic membership of the Catholic Church was a psychological necessity for a much greater number of immigrant Irish

[66] Steele, 'Irish Presence in the North of England', 220.

[67] Gilley, 'English Attitudes to the Irish', 92–3.

[68] In theory, of course, a 'mixed' marriage was as likely to lead to the 'gain' of the non-Catholic partner as to the 'loss' of the Catholic.

[69] Lees, *Exiles*, p. 153.

[70] Lobban, 'Irish Community in Greenock', 278–9.

Catholics than were prepared to attend regularly at Mass and the sacraments.

While group solidarity in marriage patterns was, perhaps, the most crucial way in which the Catholic Church sought to preserve its congregation intact, there were also many other ways in which a self-contained, almost self-segregated community was encouraged by the Church and its activities. The system of Catholic schools, the litany of social, recreational and educational societies sponsored by the Church for its Catholic children, all of these were part of a general strategy whose purpose was the creation, as far as possible, of a self-contained Catholic community of sobriety and solid good behaviour. In short, the Catholic Church was a crucial force inhibiting, indeed actively discouraging, the assimilation of the Irish immigrants in the working-class culture of the native majority.

In another sense, too, a negative sense, the Catholic Church, whatever spiritual or social comfort membership of it may have given to the immigrant, raised a barrier between the immigrant Irish and his host society. This was because Catholicism in itself, without any exertions on the part of its leaders, was suspect in the eyes of major sections of British public opinion. It is not necessary here to analyse in detail the sources of anti-Catholicism in Britain, particularly in the Victorian era.[71] Papal interference and Jesuitical intrigues in international politics, sacerdotalism and excessive priestly influence in private and public matters, vestigial elements of medieval superstition and idolatry in Catholic rites, authoritarianism in Catholic teaching and organization—these were some of the main planks in the anti-Catholic platform. Moreover, anti-Catholicism was, in a sense, an integral part of the national myth of both the English and the Scots since the sixteenth century. Loyalty to Rome was seen as compromising loyalty to the national state, involving, as it did, the acknowledgment of a jurisdiction, albeit a spiritual one, outside the state.

While the violent 'No Popery' campaigns of earlier times found relatively faint echoes in late-Victorian Britain, there was, nevertheless, a strong anti-Catholic prejudice present in many levels of British society for most of the nineteenth century. As the *Salford Weekly News* wrote in 1868:

> 'Nobody who has not the sublime audacity of Mr. Disraeli dare now raise the old anti-social "No Popery" cry; but there are a great many left who have a lingering instinctive dread of Roman Cath-

[71] E. R. Norman, *Anti-Catholicism in Victorian England* (London, 1968); G. A. Cahill, 'Irish Catholicism and English Toryism', *Review of Politics*, 19 (1957), 62–76; G. F. A. Best, 'Popular Protestantism in Victorian Britain', *Ideas and Institutions of Victorian Britain*, ed. R. Robson (London, 1967), pp. 115–42.

olicism gaining ground. It is not easy work combating a feeling of this kind.'[72]

This was in 1868, and far from being a 'lingering instinctive dread', anti-Catholicism had, if anything, been experiencing something of a temporary revival during the previous twenty years. The Irish influx in these crucial decades probably helped to heighten fears of Roman Catholicism gaining ground, at least numerically, in Britain, and in this suspicious and fearful mood the violence of the denunciation of Catholic pretensions which followed the reconstitution of the Catholic hierarchy in Britain in 1850 was hardly surprising.[73] It has been noted that on relatively few occasions did this anti-Catholic mood result in overt violence, in attacks on Catholics, especially when compared to the story in America.[74] Notwithstanding such notorious exceptions as the Stockport riots of 1852 or the Murphy riots of the late 1860s, this contention is substantially true.[75] Nevertheless, the long list of public agitations which accompanied every airing of the Catholic question, from Brunswick Club opposition to Catholic emancipation in the 1820s to the political storm over Peel's Maynooth grant in 1845, to the Durham letter of 1852, and finally to the outrage at papal claims as asserted in the syllabus of errors and the infallibility decree—all these represent a continuous, enduring and deep-seated popular British suspicion of Rome, its influence and intentions.

However, anti-Irish attitudes were not simply varieties of anti-Catholicism, though religious prejudice undoubtedly entered into it. It was not only the non-Catholic British who had misgivings, or worse, about the Catholic Irish. Many of the native British Catholics found their Irish co-religionists a decidedly uncomfortable presence among them. There were class and cultural factors involved here. British Catholics were, by historical circumstances, an ultra-loyal minority, with (at least in England) a leadership drawn from aristocratic and intellectually patrician circles. In their long struggle to win acceptance as full political members of their state, loyalty and discretion (and, of course, tenacity) had been their invaluable weapons.[76] Many of them

---

[72] *Salford Weekly News*, 18 April 1868, cited in R. L. Greenall, 'Popular Conservatism in Salford, 1868-1886', *Northern History*, ix (1974), 131.

[73] The materials for popular anti-Catholicism were plentiful enough without taking the immigrant Irish into account at all. See Gilley, 'Protestant London', 210-30.

[74] Steele, 'Irish Presence in the North of England', 226.

[75] For Murphy, see W. L. Arnstein, 'The Murphy Riots: a Victorian Dilemma', *Victorian Studies*, xix (1975), 51-71. For a good example of the combustible materials of religious and national antagonism at work in Wales in 1882, see Denvir, *Irish in Britain*, pp. 296-314.

[76] See *The English Catholics*, ed. Beck, and, for a sympathetic portrait over a longer period, D. Mathew, *Catholicism in England, 1535-1935* (London, 1936). The outstanding recent account is J. Bossy, *The English Catholic Community, 1570-1850* (London, 1975).

found it extremely difficult to come to terms with the hordes of Irish Catholics who came among them during the nineteenth century. They found some of the transplanted forms of peasant piety embarrassing. Their intellectual no less than their social snobbery was, in turn, deeply resented by the Irish. True, Manning managed to reach across this cultural divide; but Mannings were in relatively short supply.[77] It is also true, of course, that many English Catholics found in the mission to the Irish poor the ideal, and idealized, outlet for their Christian witness.[78] But there remained a number of major issues which soured relations between the leaders of the Catholic Irish immigrants and the British Catholic establishment. The most serious of these issues was the political role of the immigrant Irish. In fact, it was the peculiarly strong political connotations of Irish Catholicism which caused the tensions and divisions within the Catholic ranks in Britain. Where Irish experience encompassed an easy, indeed natural, fusion of religion and politics, the English Catholic required that they be kept separate. Or, more correctly, since political exertions in the interests of Catholic education were quite legitimate, he did not want his Catholicism compromised through association with Irish nationalist politics. And yet, as the immigrant Irish permeated 'the rhetoric, rituals and social habits' of the Catholic Church in Britain, there was a constant danger of just such an association. It remains for us to offer an explanation for this problem of Irish political demands and their implications for the immigrants in Britain.

For most of the nineteenth century the majority of Irish immigrants had a political objective—the broad nationalist one of redefining in some way Ireland's constitutional relations with Britain—which lay outside the range of objectives accepted as legitimate by British public opinion. This Irish deviance was resented. When it intruded violently on the British domestic scene (as, for example, in the Fenian escapades in Manchester and Clerkenwell) native indignation and anger were widespread and deep. Furthermore, not only in objectives, but also in political organization, the Irish were to a considerable extent a self-contained political entity, at least up to the 1880s. There was no Irish-based political organization, clandestine or constitutional, from at least the Repeal movement of the 1840s, which did not have affiliated, if not always fully obedient, branches from all centres of Irish settlement in Britain.[79] Neither was there any shortage of local leadership among the immigrant Irish, chiefly 'professional men', as Denvir noted.[80]

[77] For Manning, see V. A. McClelland, *Cardinal Manning: His Public Life and Influence, 1865-92* (London, 1962).

[78] Gilley, 'Heretic London', 64-89.

[79] See Denvir, *Irish in Britain, passim,* and the theses by Benjamin and Woolaston cited in n. 3 above.   [80] Denvir, *Life Story,* p. 177.

In electoral terms, at local and parliamentary level, the immigrant Irish 'fifth column' was an interesting element in late-Victorian and Edwardian politics. Yet it is important not to exaggerate the electoral strength of the Irish in late Victorian Britain.[81] True, the Irish gained from the extension of the franchise in 1867 and again in 1884. Indeed, after the creation of largely single-seat constituencies in 1884, the Irish vote was probably crucial in a small number of constituencies.[82] But against that, it ought to be remembered that the Irish working classes, partly because of their relatively high rate of mobility, partly because of the general inadequacy of their accommodation and education, were especially prone to disqualification from voting owing to their failure to satisfy some of the difficult qualifications laid down in the franchise acts.[83] The dominance of the 'national question' in Irish immigrant political behaviour severely retarded, indeed almost entirely precluded, significant Irish participation in domestic British politics for the greater part of the nineteenth century. True, it is possible to identify a thin green line of Irish participation in the various streams making up the British radical tradition during the nineteenth century—from the correspondence societies of the 1790s to the early advocacy of general unionization by John Doherty, and the more significant, if short-lived, attempt at fusing Irish nationalist and British democratic demands in the Chartist campaign of the 1840s.[84] But the religious and cultural modes of Irish nationalism could not be made to fit easily into the mould of British radical politics. Indeed, even where opportunities were most favourable for Irish participation in domestic British politics (such as within elective school boards in the 1870s), there was remarkably little Irish participation in such domestic politics up to the 1880s.[85]

But, as in other areas, the political obstacles to the more successful integration of the immigrant Irish into British society began to weaken during the last two decades of the nineteenth century. In this context, Gladstone's 'conversion' to Home Rule in 1886 was the decisive turning point, and its significance has not been sufficiently appreciated by

[81] There is a useful discussion of this in O'Day, *English Face of Irish Nationalism*, pp. 108–25. See also H. Pelling, *The Social Geography of British Elections, 1885–1910* (London, 1967), *passim*.

[82] Nor should it be forgotten that T. P. O'Connor sat as an Irish Nationalist M.P. for the Scotland Division of Liverpool from 1885 to 1929.

[83] N. Blewett, 'The Franchise in the United Kingdom, 1885–1918', *Past & Present*, No. 32 (1965), 27–56.

[84] Thompson, *Making of the English Working Class*, pp. 82, 146, 179, 183–8, 483–4, 523–6, 557–8, 632, 650, 653–5, 707, 771; R. G. Kirby and A. E. Musson, *The Voice of the People: a Biography of John Doherty, 1798–1854* (Manchester, 1975); Rachel O'Higgins, 'The Irish Influence in the Chartist Movement', *Past & Present*, No. 20 (1961), 83–96.

[85] But for an early breakthrough, see Denvir, *Life Story*, pp. 155–6, 172.

historians writing on the immigrant Irish, since it effectively legit-imized their political aspirations and objectives. They could now ad-vocate moderate nationalist demands (anything short of separation) without incurring the charge of treason or subversion of the empire. In the short term, the Liberal–Irish alliance of 1886–92 broke down many psychological barriers in British constituencies, as Liberal and Irish nationalist leaders shared the same election platforms, advocat-ing the 'union of hearts'. Admittedly, not all Liberals (even the most loyal) could share in the Pauline conversion of 1886, and in the aftermath of Parnell's downfall and death, with the Liberal imperial-ists firmly in the party saddle, there were times when the thread of Liberal commitment to 'Ireland' was very thin indeed. But the decisive break-through had been made. After Gladstone's conversion there could be no going back to the pre-1886 consensus. The Irish national-ist case was no longer automatically damned as heretical in British politics.[86]

Gladstone's 'conversion' had further political repercussions. By stitching Home Rule into the Liberal party banner he ensured the continued support of the majority of the Irish in Britain for the Liberal party up to the outbreak of the Great War. This loyalty to the Liberals was, on the whole, strong enough to withstand both the enticing carrot of Conservative education policies, and the more natural pol-itical claims of a nascent Labour party on a largely working-class community.[87] It was not until the third decade of this century, after the war, the Liberal collapse and the drastic reconstruction of Anglo-Irish relations had transformed the political landscape, that mass Irish support for Labour became a feature of British politics.

In the industrial context, however, Irish involvement in the Labour movement was already increasing in the closing years of the nineteenth century. With the growth of 'new Unionism' among the unskilled, the Irish for the first time *en masse* began to play a major part in the general struggles of the British working classes. This was well attested by the strong Irish participation (right up to leadership level) in the London Dock Strike of 1889.[88]

Finally, with the arrival in the late nineteenth century of a wave of new immigrants from central and eastern Europe, the Irish were

[86] The writer hopes to explore some of these aspects of the subject in greater detail in a forthcoming work on British public opinion and Irish Home Rule in the Gladstonian era.

[87] For a perceptive view of this dilemma, see T. W. Moody, 'Michael Davitt and the British Labour Movement, 1882–1906', *T.R.Hist.S.*, 5th ser., iii (1953), 53–76.

[88] B. Tillett, *Memories and Reflections* (London, 1931). See also H. A. Clegg, A. Fox and A. F. Thompson, *A History of British Trade Unions since 1889* (Oxford, 1964), i, pp. 55–96.

eclipsed as the most visible and problematic minority group in British society.[89]

These developments in industrial and political life, together with the blunting of the edge of religious prejudice consequent upon the spread of religious indifference, meant that by the early twentieth century the Irish immigrant working man had gradually, if at times grudgingly, won a wide measure of acceptance in British society. But the process had been a slow one. Many anti-Irish attitudes were very slowly abandoned, and were likely to surface at times of public excitement, as, for example, in the reaction to Irish republican bombings in Britain during the Second World War. Moreover, the 'no Irish need apply' notice in advertisements for jobs and accommodation served constant notice, long after 1922, that old prejudices die hard.[90]

One last point. For the Irish immigrants in nineteenth-century Britain, as for their American cousins,[91] expatriate nationalism may have served an important and complex psychological function, giving, as it did, an exalted sense of purpose to lives which were otherwise spent in adverse social circumstances and, by demanding freedom for the homeland, allowing immigrants to engage in a kind of revolt by proxy against their own depressed condition. On this reasoning, the achievement of national independence, the creation of a national state in the homeland, might be expected to act as a kind of liberation, a collective rise in self-esteem for the expatriates. The establishment of an Irish national state (whatever its shortcomings) in 1922 signalled the end of an era in Irish immigrant history. Thereafter, the Irish immigrant in Britain could devote his entire energy and his full attention to making his way and making the best of his chances in his new society.

[89] For which see the essays in *Immigrants and Minorities*, ed. Holmes, and *Hosts, Immigrants and Minorities*, ed. Lunn.

[90] See Jackson, *Irish in Britain*, pp. 97-8, 124.

[91] L. J. McCaffrey, *Irish Nationalism and the American Contribution* (New York, 1976), and, particularly, T. N. Brown, *Irish-American Nationalism, 1870-1890* (Philadelphia: New York, 1966), pp. 17-34, 178-81.

HISTORIANS, THE NATIONALITY QUESTION, AND THE DOWNFALL OF THE HABSBURG EMPIRE

By Alan Sked, M.A., D.Phil.

READ AT THE SOCIETY'S CONFERENCE 13 SEPTEMBER 1980

WAS the Habsburg Empire doomed to collapse, and if so, at what point did its collapse become inevitable? This is a question which has been debated consciously and unconsciously by historians ever since 1918. Today, it is true, Austrian historians are warning against it—Professor Wandruszka even a decade ago advised us to do our 'duty' and accept 'the tragic element in history'[1]—yet the issue is still discussed. Alexander Gerschenkron, for example, in his last work on Austrian history[2] chose a counter-factual theme, and in the introduction to his book condemned historians—presumably those like Professor Wandruszka—who were 'anxious to prevent people from asking pertinent and interesting questions and [had] neither the wit nor the imagination for asking those questions themselves'. Whether Professor Gerschenkron himself employed too much imagination is only one of the issues to be examined in this paper.

At the heart of the debate over the viability of the Habsburg Empire has always been the 'Nationality Question'. No historian of any eminence has failed to recognize in this a life-or-death issue for the Monarchy. Yet, as we shall see, some historians have examined that issue in more interesting ways than others. Most of them have been concerned to discover whether the Habsburgs could have solved the nationality problem. Could they have altered their system of government to have satisfied the demands, just and unjust, of the fourteen or so nationalities which made up the population of the Empire? This quest among historians has led to two strands of historiography, both of which are strongly represented not merely in the modern historical

---

[1] See A. Wandruszka, 'Finis Austriae? Reformpläne und Untergangsahnungen in der Habsburger Monarchie', *Der österreichisch-ungarische Ausgleich von 1867. Seine Grundlagen und Auswirkungen* (Buchreihe der Sudostdeutschen Historischen Kommission, 20, Munich, 1968), p. 112.

[2] A. Gerschenkron, *An Economic Spurt That Failed. Four Lectures in Austrian History* (Princeton, 1977).

literature of Austria[3] but also in that of the United States,[4] where—
and I shall be discussing this later—a remarkable blossoming of Habsburg studies has taken place since the Second World War. The first
strand of this historiography is that which examines not merely the
conditions—primarily cultural and constitutional, but nowadays also
social and economic—of the nationalities themselves, but which also
examines and outlines the plans put forward by many people in the
nineteenth and twentieth centuries to reform the Habsburg Empire.
Thus historians such as Robert A. Kann[5] in America and Rudolf
Wierer[6] in Vienna have catalogued all the proposals for reform from
the Kremsier draft constitution of 1849, through the various schemes
of Fischof, Renner, Popovici, Radic and others, including those of the
Social Democrats, Christian Socialists and Liberals, to those of the
Belvedere Circle, ending finally with the Emperor Charles's *Manifesto
to his Peoples* of 16 October 1918—that supreme example in history of
'too little, too late'. This strand of historiography, necessary though
it no doubt is, represents a sort of archaeology or anthropology of the
Habsburg Empire and is based, to quote A. J. P. Taylor's famous
review[7] of Kann's *Multinational Empire*, on the 'delusion that if only we
know enough facts, we shall arrive at the answer'. Kann's books are,
in Taylor's view, 'an anatomy in Burton's sense, not an analysis'.[8]

Analysis is more in evidence in the second strand of Austro-American historiography. This is the truly counter-factual one, whose latest
representative, already referred to, is Alexander Gerschenkron. Historians of this school—if I can use that word—ask themselves at what
point did the Habsburgs lose control of their empire? At what stage
in history did it become clear that the Habsburg Monarchy was no

---

[3] One survey of the literature which is readily available to British readers is
A. Novotny, 'Austrian History from 1848 to 1938 as seen by Austrian Historians since
1945', *Austrian History Notebook*, 3 (1963), 18–50.

[4] Surveys of American writing on Austria-Hungary include R. J. Rath, 'Das amerikanische Schrifttum über den Untergang der Monarchie', *Die Auflösung des Habsburgerreiches. Zusammenbruch und Neuorientierung im Donauraum*, ed. R. G. Plashka and
K. Mack, Vienna, 1970), pp. 236–48; Arlie Hoover, 'The Habsburg Monarchy, Austria
and Hungary as treated in other U.S. Journals than the *Journal of Central European
Affairs*', *Austrian History Notebook*, 3 (1963), 51–72; I. Deák, 'American (and Some
British) Historians look at Austria-Hungary', *New Hungarian Quarterly*, 41 (1971) 162–
74; Paula S. Fichtner, 'Americans and the Disintegration of the Habsburg Monarchy:
the Shaping of an Historiographical Model', *The Habsburg Empire in World War I. Essays
on the Intellectual, Military, Political and Economic Aspects of the Habsburg War Effort*, ed.
R. Kann, B. K. Kiraly and P. S. Fichtner (New York, 1977), pp. 221–34.

[5] See, in particular, his *The Multinational Empire, 1848–1918* (2 vols., New York, 1950).

[6] See his *Der Föderalismus in Donauraum* (Graz and Cologne, 1960).

[7] A. J. P. Taylor, 'The Failure of the Habsburg Monarchy', *Europe: Grandeur and
Decline* (Harmondsworth, 1967), pp. 127–32.

[8] *Ibid.*, p. 128.

longer capable of surviving? Having then selected their date, they usually tell us, or at least imply, that all would have been different— and usually better—had only this or that occurred instead. There are a number of key dates involved and something must be said about most of them. In all fairness, however, it should be added that at least one British historian should be ranked in this tradition. For powerful support for the first date favoured by the counter-factualists comes from C. A. Macartney, until his recent death the doyen of British scholars of Hungary. In his last book, *The House of Austria*, Macartney wrote:[9] 'The turning point in the central Monarchy ... can without extravagance be dated to a day: 28 January 1790 ...' That was the day on which, as he had put it in his *Habsburg Empire*, 'the time turned in Central Europe'.[10] Joseph II had been forced to revoke most of his reforms and, thereafter, the Habsburg Monarchy entered a period of decline. In Macartney's words, 'the territorial advance gives way to a retreat in which one outpost after another is lost. At the same time, the forces of absolutism and centralism are driven back on the defensive until at last the peoples of the monarchy allied with its foreign enemies, repudiate not only the character of the Monarch's rule, but the rule itself. The end has come.'[11]

The whole period 1790-1815 has been singled out by Austrian historians as portentous for the Monarchy's decline. Professor Wandruszka also discussed the death of Joseph II as a turning point, although, as the celebrated biographer of Leopold II, he laid more emphasis on the year 1792 and the death of that monarch.[12] Not only did Leopold's death usher in the reactionary reign of Francis I, which, combined with the outbreak of war against revolutionary France and the discovery in 1794/5 of the 'Jacobin Plot' in Hungary and Vienna, put paid to Leopold's plans for imperial reform; the year 1792, Wandruszka reminds us, also witnessed that resumption of diplomatic relations between Austria and Turkey which ended three centuries of hostility and warfare. But with the resumption of normal relations between these states, it can be argued, the House of Austria had fulfilled its historic mission, which had been to protect Europe from the Turks. Danilevski and other Russian Panslavs in the later nineteenth century were certainly to maintain that, on this ground alone, the Monarchy had forfeited its right to survive.

The period 1790-1815 contains still more possible turning points— 1804, for example, with the assumption by Francis I of the simple

[9] C. A. Macartney, *The House of Austria: The Later Phase, 1790-1918* (Edinburgh, 1978), p. 1.
[10] C. A. Macartney, *The Habsburg Empire, 1790-1918* (London, 1968), p. 1.
[11] *Ibid.*, p. 1.
[12] Wandruszka, 'Finis Austriae?'

title, 'Emperor of Austria'; or 1806, with the end of the Holy Roman Empire. Berchtold Sutter has pointed out that the Archduke John believed that the 'fatal day for the young Austrian Empire' was 6 July 1809, when Napoleon won the battle of Wagram.[13] There is something in this, because it was with Wagram that the only attempt to defeat Napoleon by rousing the German and European peoples under Austrian leadership was thwarted, and it was after Wagram that the reform party at the Vienna court, led by the brothers Stadion and the Archdukes Charles and John, had to relinquish their control of Austrian policy to Metternich.

In the nineteenth century the two dates most favoured by historians have been 1849 and 1867. The first indeed represents the most famous 'missed opportunity' in the history of Austrian constitutionalism. For the so-called Kremsier Constitution of that year, drawn up by the National Assembly, succeeded, in the opinion of most scholars, in establishing the fairest possible constitutional arrangements for Austria. It declared, for example, that 'all sovereignty proceed[ed] from the people and [was] to be exercised in the manner prescribed by the constitution';[14] it vested real power in the people's representatives; it deprived the Emperor of absolute veto power; it abolished Catholicism as a state religion; and it abolished all titles of nobility. It did not presume to regulate Hungarian affairs, since Hungary was regarded as already in possession of a constitution; and with regard to the nationality question, the relevant paragraph (No. 21) ran:

'All peoples of the Empire are equal in rights. Each people has an inviolable right to preserve and cultivate its nationality in general and its language in particular. The equality of rights in the school, administration and public life of every language in local usage is guaranteed by the state.'[15]

Little wonder, therefore, that the Austrian historian and statesman, Joseph Redlich, compared this document to the American constitution and the French Constitution of 1791.[16] Little wonder, either, that Prince Schwarzenberg and Franz Joseph never allowed it to see the light of day.

The other date in the nineteenth century which arouses much interest is predictably enough that of 1867, the year of the 'Compromise' or 'Ausgleich' with Hungary. Some historians prefer to use the word 'Settlement' instead of 'Compromise', but if settlement it was,

[13] B. Sutter, 'Erzherzog Johanns Kritik an Österreich', *Mitteilungen des Österreichischen Staatsarchivs*, 16 (1963), 165 seq.

[14] Macartney, *The Habsburg Empire*, p. 417.

[15] *Ibid.*, p. 418.

[16] A. Murad, *Franz Joseph of Austria and his Empire* (New York, 1968), p. 130.

it was hardly a final one. Most historians, in fact, like most contemporaries, have scarcely a good word to say for the 'Ausgleich'. Nor is it difficult to understand why. In the first place, it was an agreement made, not between the representatives of the various parts of the monarchy, but between Franz Joseph and the Magyar leadership. Having reached this agreement, the Emperor then forced it on the 'Austrian half' of his monarchy, despite its unpopularity with most of his subjects there. Even his Hungarian subjects, however, were displeased with it because, as György Szabad, the Hungarian scholar, has recently demonstrated,[17] the Magyar parliamentarians who drew it up had failed to address themselves 'to the questionable legality of the 1865 elections and [had] failed also to take into account the fact that the conditions of the proposed settlement were hardly known to the electors who had given [Deák's] party its parliamentary majority. For not a word had been said in the course of the 1865 elections about revising the 1848 Laws to extend the sovereign's prerogatives, and even the section of Deák's May programme discussing joint affairs had not yet been published in Hungary.'[18] The Hungarian leaders, on the other hand, had obviously seen the chance to strike an excellent bargain. For Franz Joseph, it appears, had agreed to the 'Ausgleich' in a hurry.[19] In fact, he may never have read the document's fine print, with the result that the Hungarian Law embodying the 'Compromise' included important clauses which suggested that Hungary not only retained the right to an independent army but also to a separate foreign policy. These clauses, it is true, were excluded from the Austrian law embodying the settlement, but this merely meant that the Monarchy was to be run on the basis of two fundamental laws which were textually different. Even worse, the assumptions underlying these laws were also different. The Austrians assumed the existence of some sort of 'overall state' or 'Oberstaat' called the 'Austrian Monarchy' to which the two 'halves', or 'Reichshälfe', would be subordinated. Such an interpretation was totally alien from Hungarian constitutional thought, which was still anchored to the concept of a separate, constitutional Hungarian state which shared a ruler—or rather the person of a ruler—with the Austrians, but which had merely entered into certain specific constitutional arrangements with them. The 'Compromise', finally, left a number of hostages to fortune by decreeing that the so-called 'economic compromise' between Austria

[17] See his *Hungarian Political Trends between the Revolution and the Compromise (1849–1867)* (Budapest, 1977).
[18] *Ibid.*, pp. 166–7.
[19] The following analysis is based on B. Sutter, 'Die Ausgleichsverhandlungen zwischen Österreich und Ungarn 1867–1918', *Österreichisch-ungarische Ausgleich von 1867*, pp. 71–111.

and Hungary should be renegotiated every decade. This arrangement covered not only tariffs and trade but also the amount of money each country would contribute to the joint exchequer—the so-called Quota. Needless to say, these negotiations led to regular clashes between both 'halves' of the Monarchy. By 1895, therefore, Karl Lueger's views on the 'Compromise', as delivered to the Lower House of the Austrian Parliament, represented those of the majority of Austrian Germans: 'I consider Dualism,' he said, 'as a misfortune, indeed as the greatest misfortune which my fatherland has ever had to suffer, a greater misfortune even than the wars we lost.'[20] The spokesmen of the nationalities would have added their agreement also. The 'Compromise' of 1867 had surrendered them to the master races, despite all their efforts on behalf of the dynasty in 1848. Andrássy is supposed to have summed up their position in his notorious words to an Austrian colleague' 'You look after your Slavs and we'll look after ours.'[21]

The 'Ausgleich', consequently, has had few defenders. Its main one has been Macartney who, in an extremely interesting article on the subject, adopted the viewpoint that in the first place everything else had been tried; and secondly, for all its faults, the Compromise lasted for half a century: 'The proof of the pudding ... is in the eating and by that test the "Compromise", if not generally palatable, at any rate contained enough vitamins to support fifty million people for fifty years.'[22] There are two objections to his defence: first, despite a long list of experiments, it is simply untrue—take Kremsier, for example— to suggest that everything else had been tried; and, secondly, there is no reason to approve of poor—occasionally even starvation—diets in history.

Nearly all non-Hungarian historians have argued that through the 'Compromise' of 1867 the Hungarians took control of the Monarchy. For whereas the Magyars kept their Slavs under control and displayed great solidarity when faced with possible encroachments by, or, more often, resistance from Vienna, in Cisleithania—one of the official names for the 'Austrian half' of the Monarchy—on the other hand, the bitter struggle between Czechs and Germans fatally undermined the bargaining strength of the 'Austrian' government when it came to negotiating with the Magyars. The result, in the words of one Austro-American historian, was that 'Hungary in effect ruled and exploited the entire Monarchy ... With every ten year renewal of the "Settlement", Hungarian demands became bolder ... If it had not been for

[20] *Ibid.*, p. 90.
[21] The saying is apocryphal.
[22] C. A. Macartney, 'The Compromise of 1867', *Studies in Diplomatic History; Essays in Memory of David Bayne Horn*, ed. Ragnhild Hatton and M. S. Anderson (London, 1970), pp. 287–300, esp. p. 299.

the First World War, it is likely that Hungary would have become independent by the time of the next renewal of the "Settlement" in 1917.'[23] One of the latest studies by a distinguished Austrian historian has reached the same conclusion. Under Koloman Tisza after 1875, it claims, Hungary changed the nature of Dualism: 'According to [Tisza's] formula, Hungary took the lead in the "Dual Monarchy" and the Magyars were masters in Hungary.' The same historian points out that the fall of the Badeni ministry in Austria in 1897, an event which practically led to the suspension of parliamentary government there, came about not least as a result of Badeni's efforts to secure Czech agreement for a further settlement with Hungary. The general point he makes, however, is this: 'Austrian internal politics in these years cannot be understood without the permanent pressure being exerted by Hungary. Much of what was and is chalked up to Austrian governments was none other than one of the consequences of Dualism, none other than the insidious and ominous consequences of Dualism, none other than the notion of keeping the Hungarians in the system at any price.' Once the First World War broke out, according to this historian, Hungarian predominance in all diplomatic and economic matters became 'unambiguous'.[24] Worst of all, Tisza closed Hungary off from Austria completely, ruled it almost as a foreign country, and denied starving Austria essential food supplies.

How true, then, is this picture of Dualism as provided by Austrian historians? A more balanced assessment may be found in an article written by the Hungarian scholar, Péter Hanák, in which we are treated to the fruit of modern Hungarian historical research.[25] Hanák first of all reminds us that under the 'Compromise', arrangements regarding Hungary fell into three groups including: (a) purely internal matters in which, according to the 'Ausgleich', Hungary was independent, in which decisions were reached by the Hungarian government, were approved by the Hungarian Parliament and sanctioned by the Hungarian King; (b) the so-called 'unpragmatic agreements' (i.e. those not stemming from the Pragmatic Sanction of 1723), arrangements which represented 'an agreement of interests' based 'on common principles', and which included the Quota and the tariff and trade agreements of the economic 'compromises', were to be negotiated by the governments of Austria and Hungary whose approved formulae were then to be submitted to their respective parliaments and to the sovereign; (c) the final group of arrangements were those

[23] Murad, *Franz Joseph*, p. 176.

[24] Sutter, 'Die Ausgleichverhandlungen', esp. pp. 81, 92-3, 106.

[25] P. Hanák, 'Die Stellung Ungarns in der Monarchie', *Probleme der Franzisko-Josephinischen Zeit 1848-1916*, ed. F. Engel-Janosi and H. Rumpler (Vienna, 1967), pp. 79-93.

stemming from the Pragmatic Sanction and handled by the common imperial-royal ministry. The constitutional position regarding these were quite unclear. For, legally, the common ministry was simply in charge of all matters which did not belong to the governments of either Austria or Hungary. Moreover, the relationship of the common ministers to those of Austria and Hungary was also unclear, the common Minister of Foreign Affairs, for example, being legally obliged 'to proceed only with the understanding and approval of the ministries of both parts (of the Empire)'.[26] Common policies were supposed to be prepared by the joint ministry, then presented to the separate delegations of both parliaments for a vote, after which they were to be presented to the monarch for approval. From all this then it might be assumed that Hungary was independent regarding her own affairs and had achieved parity in joint affairs. In practice, however, as Hanák points out, the system worked very differently. In domestic affairs, for a start, there were two important divergences from the legal model. The Hungarian government in the first place had to lay its proposals not before parliament in the first instance, but—and this was in accordance with a very precise formula—before the King. The latter, in other words, had a veto on legislation. This might be regarded as a feudal survival rather than a sign of Hungarian dependence were it not for the fact that Franz Joseph discussed the proposals of his governments with unofficial groups of courtiers, especially if such proposals might affect the Monarchy as a whole. These groups of courtiers included members of the imperial family, the aristocracy and the armed forces, who served the dynasty rather than either of the governments concerned. In this way Franz Joseph could subordinate even Hungarian internal affairs to the needs of the Monarchy as a whole.

Regarding 'common matters' there was a similar divergence from the juridical model. Policy here was not determined by negotiations between governments and parliaments, but between the monarch and the governments concerned. If a clash took place between monarch and government, in most cases, the government had to defer or to depart. In cases of a clash between Austria and Hungary, the monarch once again decided the outcome. As far as the common ministry was concerned, policy was also arrived at by discussions between the ministry and the sovereign. The role of the delegations was purely formal and only in matters of extreme importance could the constitutional influence of the Austrian and Hungarian premiers be brought to bear. Meanwhile, the soldiers and the courtiers from whom the monarch sought advice continuously influenced decision-making. All these points, therefore, materially alter the traditional picture of the

[26] *Ibid.*, p. 88.

Magyars running the Monarchy. There are two more points, however, which Hanák would have us bear in mind. The first is that although Hungary exercised much influence on foreign policy—about 25-30% of the diplomatic corps, not to mention at least three foreign ministers of the period were Hungarian, all following a foreign policy which, in fundamentals, had been established by Andrássy—the Hungarians had no influence on the army. Indeed, this body was distinctly antipathetic towards the Hungarians and often acted within Hungary as an army of occupation. It was an independent power within the Hungarian state and made Hungary dependent on the dynasty. Hanák's description of it as the 'Achilles Heel of Dualism' is well borne out by the many clashes which took place between Austria and Hungary over military affairs, not to mention the constitutional crisis of 1903-6 during which a detachment of troops expelled the deputies from the Hungarian Parliament and the imperial army was given orders, albeit never executed, for an invasion and occupation of Hungary.

The final point Hanák makes is that one should always remember the emotional factors involved. Thus no matter how well economically, for example, the Hungarians did out of Dualism—and it is now clear that economically they did very well indeed[27]—Hungarian public opinion considered Hungary to be oppressed. Conversely, however weak the Hungarian position may have been constitutionally, in many respects, Austrian public opinion resented what it took to be the sinister and predominant role of Hungary within the Monarchy.

So much then for Hanák's assessment of Dualism. It goes a long way to balance the picture painted by Austrian and other historians. However, it should not be forgotten, especially in the context of the nationality question, that the minorities in Hungary itself were meanwhile being oppressed by the Hungarians. Linguistic restrictions were carried to outrageous lengths; elections were gerrymandered in Magyar interests; the judicial system was regularly abused to deny the nationalities their rights. In 1906, a former Hungarian premier justified all this in a well-received speech to the Hungarian Chamber. 'The legal State is the aim,' he said, 'but with this question we can only concern ourselves when we have already assured the national State ... Hungary's interests demand its erection on the most extreme Chauvinist lines.'[28] The final picture which one has of Dualism, therefore, is of a state of affairs in many ways unsatisfactory, but one in which perhaps the monarch had not yet lost control to the Hungarians, although he might not really be in control of events.

[27] *Ibid.*, p. 84.
[28] Quoted by R. W. Seton-Watson, 'Austria-Hungary and the Southern Slavs', R. W. Seton-Watson, J. Dover Wilson, E. Zimmern and A. Greenwood, *The War and Democracy* (London, 1915), pp. 136-7.

Ironically, the real trouble with 'Ausgleich', as it turned out, was to be the monarch's inability to alter it. For short of independence the Hungarians would agree to nothing else. They had no interest in Trialism, which would have upset the balance with Austria, lost them Croatia and access to the Adriatic; they would not agree to the creation of an associated Polish Kingdom when Poland was conquered in the First World War; and they had no desire to lose Slovakia to the Czechs. Yet the twentieth century was to bring enormous pressure for all these changes, which pressure the Magyars successfully resisted.

The final date which has to be discussed in any list of possible turning points in the history of the Habsburg Monarchy is undoubtedly 1914. That is a date, however, which will be discussed in a different context later on. In the meantime we should examine this counter-factual tradition in historical literature, more specifically in the light of American studies of Habsburg history. I do this mostly by way of praise, although partly by way of rebuke. Praise because, thanks to the efforts of scholars such as Professor Béla Király, Professor John Rath, Professor István Deák, Professor Robert Kann, Professor Gunther Rothenberg, and many, many others, Habsburg studies are now flourishing in the United States to a degree unthinkable in this country. One just has to point, for example, to the *Austrian History Yearbook* and the many specialized monographs published through the Columbia University Press. Rebuke, because a certain amount of the literature produced betrays traces of nostalgia and special pleading.

In a survey of American writing on the Monarchy,[29] John Rath himself pointed out that more than half of the authors concerned had, significantly, been born, or were the sons of parents who had been born, in Central Europe. The list of names just mentioned should have made the reader suspect this anyway. In fact, most of the historians writing on Habsburg history in the United States today have very strong connections with the countries of the former Monarchy itself. The American historiographical tradition, in other words, is to a large extent based on the writings of exiles. In particular, it stems from the work of Oscar Jászi, the Hungarian political scientist whose book, *The Dissolution of the Habsburg Monarchy*,[30] can, in Rath's words,[31] be regarded as the 'Old Testament' of U.S. Habsburg studies, and which, according to Paula Fichtner,[32] 'has become almost paradigmatic in [U.S.] thinking about the Austro-Hungarian Empire'. Jászi described the aims of the Habsburgs as 'unification, Germanization,

[29] Rath, 'Das amerikanische Schrifttum', p. 236.
[30] O. Jaszi, *The Dissolution of the Habsburg Monarchy* (Chicago, 1929).
[31] Rath, 'Das amerikanische Schrifttum', p. 239.
[32] Fichtner, 'Americans and the Disintegration of the Habsburg Monarchy', p. 226.

Catholization . . .' and created what is now the standard model of the Monarchy as a political structure in which the so-called 'centripetal', or unifying, forces were opposed by ultimately stronger 'centrifugal' or disintegrating ones. The centrifugal forces were able to destroy the Monarchy in the end, according to Jászi, because the Habsburgs failed to introduce 'a well-balanced federalism' [33] at some point in the nineteenth century. The works of Professor Kann, it has been suggested, now represent the 'New Testament' of Habsburg scholarship.[34] To a certain degree this may be true, but, on the other hand, as in the Bible, the Old and New Testaments are intimately related. Kann's concern for constitutional problems, reform plans, integrative and disintegrative forces in many ways echo Jászi, although in all fairness it should be pointed out that, in contrast with the latter, Kann believes that the centrifugal forces only became dominant during and as a result of the First World War. Both men, however, have reinforced the tendency among American scholars of thinking of the Habsburg Monarchy primarily in terms of missed opportunities for survival.

Although not often enough admitted, another factor is important in this context, namely that not only has the American historiography of Central Europe been influenced by the writings of exiles and by Jászi in particular, but several of these exiles have been victims of, or refugees from, Europe's totalitarian upheavals and, wittingly or unwittingly, have been writing Cold War history in America. One should not overemphasize this point, but it is no doubt true that the majority of the historians concerned would at least endorse the viewpoint expressed, for example, by George Kennan in his latest book,[35] that 'The Austro-Hungarian Empire still looks better as a solution to the tangled problems of that part of the world than anything that has succeeded it.'[36] The occasional result of this sort of attitude has been an historiography which asserts, first, that the Monarchy wasn't nearly as bad as it was depicted, and, indeed, that it always enjoyed popular support; and, secondly, that in many ways it was simply unlucky. The people who were its potential saviours were unable to execute their reforms.

These trends can be illustrated with a few examples. It would be tedious to list the many politicians and cultural leaders who can be quoted in 1914 in support of the Monarchy, and unprofitable to cite the large number of writers who have used such statements to support the case that the Monarchy was a popular one. Of more interest has

[33] *Ibid.*

[34] Rath, 'Das amerikanische Schrifttum', p. 239.

[35] G. Kennan, *The Decline of Bismarck's European Order. Franco-Russian Relations 1875–1890* (Princeton, 1979).

[36] *Ibid.*, p. 423.

been a recent attempt by an American scholar of Hungarian extraction to demolish the traditional belief that the Magyars oppressed
their nationalities. I refer to Andrew J. János' study, 'The Decline of
Oligarchy: Bureaucratic and Mass Politics in the Age of Dualism
(1867–1918)',[37] in which the author argues that it is wrong to judge
nineteenth-century Hungarian society and politics by western standards and models. Instead, one should apply the criteria used today
for developing countries. This makes it easier, perhaps, for him to
affirm the grip of the aristocracy and gentry on political life and to
concede electoral corruption, judicial bias, parliamentary obstruc-
tionism and Magyar-style *trasformismo*. But with regard to national
minorities János stresses the freedom given to immigrants, and he is
especially eloquent on the support and protection officially afforded
to the Jews. When he comes to those minorities—Slovaks, Rumanians,
members of the organized working class—who, unlike the Jews, would
not, or could not, be accommodated within the System, he is frankly
dismissive of the anti-Magyar charges:

> 'According to the careful documentation of Robert Seton-Watson
> in one critical decade (1898–1908) 503 Slovaks were indicted on
> charges ranging from incitement to riot to abusing the Hungarian
> flag, and in 81 trials drew a total of 79 years and 6 months. During
> the same period 216 Rumanians were sentenced to 38 years and 9
> months. These aggregate figures were impressive but a division of
> years by sentences yields averages of 1.6 and 2.2 months ... The
> records of the Socialist movement, as published by one of its leading
> members, show 916 indictments in the pre-war period resulting in
> an aggregate sentence of 24 years and 11 months or an approximate
> average of 12 days.'[38]

János almost certainly underestimates the harm done to the minorities by policies of Magyarization in his concern to demonstrate the
benefits available through assimilation. The thought of two to six
months in prison for employing one's own language doesn't seem to
worry him. On the other hand, although pointing out that the working
class comprised only 10% of the population, he is prepared to concede
the harshness of the official reaction to social democracy by the end
of the century:

> 'workers associations were harassed, their leaders arrested and
> hauled into courts, and their members placed under police surveil-
> lance. Riots were put down by gendarmes and soldiers firing into

[37] The article appears in *Revolution in Perspective. Essays on the Hungarian Soviet Republic*,
ed. A. C. Janos and W. B. Stottman (Berkeley, 1971), pp. 1–60.
[38] *Ibid.*, pp. 18–19.

crowds or charging them with fixed bayonets. Repression reached its peak under Banffy's premiership (1895-1899) when a recently published source claims 51 workers were killed and 114 wounded in pitched battles with law-enforcement authorities.'[39]

All in all, János' article must make us stop and think. Yet at the end of that process, it is difficult to accept his arguments. Hungary in the nineteenth century was, and considered itself to be, a western-type constitutional state. The social and economic problems encountered by it were not unknown in either Germany, France or Italy. Its peculiarity lay essentially in its racial composition, and had the Magyars represented 90 or 100% of the population, rather than merely 50%, it is indisputable that Hungary would have progressed extremely rapidly along the path of modern constitutional development.

The final strand in the counter-factual trend is that which suggests that the Habsburg Empire was merely unlucky, that potential saviours were available but that unfortunately, for one reason or another, they were unable to put their reform plans into practice. Before 1914 some observers—including Seton-Watson—believed that such a person was the Archduke Franz Ferdinand. Some historians also have favoured this view. However, it has long been clear that the heir to the throne was cast in an improbable role. A. J. P. Taylor's description of him as 'reactionary clerical, brutal ... overbearing [and] often insane' is probably nearer the mark.[40] Certainly, Vladimir Dedijer's investigations into Franz Ferdinand's 'reform plans' leave little room for doubt that the Archduke's support for 'Trialism' was merely a temporary aberration.[41] His real policy was one of clericalism, Germanism and centralism. As he himself once put it:

'If we want peace and quiet in the Austrian Monarchy, if we want the chance to conduct a stronger foreign policy beneficial to all nations, in association with our Allies, there is only one way and one necessity, and that is to smash the preponderance of the Magyars. Otherwise we shall with absolute certainty become a Slav Empire and trialism, which would be a misfortune, will be achieved.'[42]

His accession to the throne might well have sparked off the final catastrophe in any case. Tisza, the Hungarian premier, expected him to move against the Magyars and was quite prepared to resist. Franz

[39] Ibid., p. 43.
[40] A. J. P. Taylor, The Habsburg Monarchy (London, 1964), p. 242.
[41] V. Dedijer, The Road to Sarajevo (London, 1967).
[42] Ibid., p. 137.

Ferdinand, on the other hand, was reportedly ready to dismiss Tisza within twenty-four hours of acceding to the throne. Such an act by itself might well have ushered in the fall of the House of Habsburg.

In the 1950s and 1960s, curiously enough, Metternich was widely regarded by cold-war historians as the man who could have saved the Empire. They not only saw him as a sort of John Foster Dulles stemming the tide of red revolution in Europe; he was also portrayed as a federalist who, at heart, was almost liberal. Peter Viereck wrote in 1951[43] that Metternich in 1817 had 'urged freer institutions for the rest of the empire, with an embryonic parliament, which once started, would inevitably have assumed an ever greater governing power'. This view was given powerful backing in 1963 by Arthur G. Haas,[44] according to whom Metternich had tried to 'form the so badly-shaken Monarchy into an inwardly balanced and stable union of constituent states with equal rights', a policy of 'statesmanlike foresight and intelligence'[45] which, unfortunately, the Emperor Francis refused to adopt. As I have attempted to show in two articles,[46] however, Metternich was not interested in federalist reform. His plans of 1817 (and of 1847/8 as well for that matter) were aimed at centralizing the Monarchy. For, as he himself put it, 'only by centralizing the various branches of authority is it possible to establish its unity and hence its force. Power distributed is no longer power.'[47]

The latest thwarted saviour in the literature is Ernst von Koerber, prime minister of Austria between 1900 and 1904. Alexander Gerschenkron credited Koerber with a 'great plan' to save the Monarchy.[48] This involved a 'spurt' of industrialization which would have caused Czech and German workers to place their common economic interests before their national differences. For Koerber, according to Gerschenkron, believed in 'the primacy of the economic factor' and his success in 1902, when two investment bills were passed by the Reichsrat, enabled the Harvard professor to discern a 'lesson of history' at work, the validity of which transcended 'the spatial and temporal limits dealt with' in his book.[49] Perhaps so. But to a more.

---

[43] P. Viereck, 'New Views on Metternich', *Review of Politics*, xiii (1951), 225.

[44] A. G. Haas, *Metternich, Reorganisation and Nationality, 1813–1818* (Wiesbaden, 1963).

[45] A. G. Haas, 'Kaiser Franz, Metternich und die Stellung Illyriens', *Mitteilungen des Österreichischen Staatsarchivs*, 11 (1958), 397.

[46] A. Sked, 'Metternich and the Federalist Myth', *Crisis and Controversy. Essays in Honour of A. J. P. Taylor*, ed. A. Sked and C. Cook (London, 1976), pp. 1–22; 'The Metternich System', *Europe's Balance of Power, 1815–1848*, ed. A. Sked (London, 1979), pp. 98–121.

[47] Sked, 'The Metternich System', p. 111.

[48] Gerschenkron, *An Economic Spurt That Failed*.

[49] *Ibid.*, pp. 156–7.

cynical mind it might simply appear that all Gerschenkron did was to
chronicle the premier's failure to build a couple of canals. For Koerber's plans were sabotaged by his finance minister, the eminent econ-
omist Boehm-Bawerk. Koerber's considerable reputation must therefore rest on his undoubted successes in the political field: his conciliation conferences between Czech and German deputies; his treatment
of the press and his respect for civil rights in Austria; his support for
old-age pensions; and his renegotiation of the economic 'Ausgleich'
with Hungary. What might have happened had he succeeded in
building his canals is hardly one of the greatest unsolved mysteries of
modern times.

So much, then, for what I have called the counter-factual tradition.
The more it is examined, the more convinced I become that it ap-
proaches the problem of the Habsburg Monarchy from the wrong
direction. That is to say as an historical phenomenon it cannot be
understood from the bottom up, only from the top down. For time
and again it is clear that the fate of the nationalities and of reform
plans rested entirely with the dynasty, and that the dynasty had no
interest in reform. I shall explain why later; for the moment it may be
said that this was so despite the fact that the Habsburgs shared the
feeling, common in Central Europe in the late nineteenth century, of
impending doom. For if William Johnson, in his study of *The Austrian
Mind*,[50] can entitle various chapters 'Death as a Bulwark against
Change', 'Death as Ephemerality' and 'Death as Refuge: Suicide by
Austrian Intellectuals', Professor Wandruszka has shown that this
pessimistic outlook was not limited to Carl Schorske's favourite figures.[51] The Habsburgs themselves shared the mood. Franz Joseph,
for example, wrote to his mother in August 1866: 'One just has to
resist as long as possible, do one's duty to the last, and finally perish
with honour.' In his will he made arrangements in case 'the crown
should no longer remain with our House'. In it his daughter, Gisela,
was advised to claim her fortune on his death, for 'it would be safer in
Germany than in Vienna'. Likewise, the Crown Prince Rudolf, before
committing suicide at Mayerling, wrote to his sister, Maria Valerie,
advising her to leave Austria 'when Papa passes away' since, as he put
it, 'only I know what will happen then'.[52]

How consciously the Habsburgs feared the future, it is difficult to
say. Until the worst happened, however, they searched desperately
for an excuse to stay. Their excuses took several forms and were all
included in the so-called 'Austrian mission' or 'österreichischen Staat-

[50] W. Johnson, *The Austrian Mind: an Intellectual and Social History, 1848–1938* (Berkeley, 1972).
[51] Wandruszka, 'Finis Austriae?'
[52] *Ibid.*, p. 119.

sidee'. According to the latter, the Monarchy fulfilled various roles. There was the geographical role according to which the Empire was a natural geographical unit—the so-called 'Danubian Monarchy'; a related version made it an 'economic necessity' for Central Europe. Another role was the 'historical' one—protecting Europe from the Russians, now, rather than from the Turks—and this in turn was linked to the 'cultural' one of 'civilizing' the benighted Balkan Slavs. All these roles or missions were clearly spurious, but they allowed the dynasty to justify its existence in that peculiar way in which declining powers feel forced to do. There was one role which to the end, however, still carried some conviction. That was that the Habsburg Monarchy was a vital component in the European balance of power.

Here, in the last part of my paper, I should like to examine the British contribution to the historical literature and to contrast it briefly with the Austro-American one. This should not take too long for few British historians have written on the Habsburgs.

The British tradition, unlike the American one, has not been dependent on scholarship in exile. Nor has it viewed the history of the Monarchy in the same counter-factual way. True, distinguished contributions have been made to the literature by immigrant scholars such as Z. A. B. Zeman,[53] Harry Hanak[54] and Wilfried Fest.[55] But Fest and Hanak were more concerned with British policy towards the Monarchy than with the Monarchy itself, so that we are left with Zeman alone, whose study must, as a result, be left in a historiographical class of its own. His more recent work on the diplomacy of the First World War, on the other hand, like that of our greatest immigrant-scholar, Sir Lewis Namier—I'm thinking now of his essay on 'The Downfall of the Habsburg Monarchy'[56]—brings him (and Hanak and Fest, too, for that matter) nearer to what one may call the truly British tradition of Habsburg scholarship. This is not that of C. A. Macartney—whose works are all in the Austro-American tradition—but that of the Seton-Watsons,[57] H. Wickham Steed,[58] Roy

[53] See his *The Break-up of the Habsburg Empire, 1914-1918. A Study in National and Social Revolution* (London, 1961).

[54] See his *Great Britain and Austria-Hungary during the First World War. A Study in the Formation of Public Opinion* (London, 1962).

[55] See his *Peace or Partition. The Habsburg Monarchy and British Policy, 1914-1918* (London, 1978).

[56] L. B. Namier, *Vanished Supremacies. Essays on European History, 1812-1918* (London, 1958), ch. 10.

[57] I refer not only to R. W. Seton-Watson's well-known works, but also to at least one essay by his son, Hugh, 'Übernationale Monarchie und Nationalstaat', *Die Auflösung des Habsburgerreiches*, ed. Plaschka and Mack, pp. 366-76.

[58] See his *The Hapsburg Monarchy* (4th edn., London, 1919).

Bridge,[59] Norman Stone[60] and A. J. P. Taylor.[61] If I were not the modest man I am, I might even include myself.[62]

The British tradition of Habsburg scholarship distinguishes itself by looking at the Monarchy primarily from its position as a great power. Our interest in it arose from its place in the balance of power, so that Namier, Wickham Steed, and perhaps even Robert Seton-Watson were more concerned with the Habsburg dynasty's relations with the powers than with its relations with the nationalities. It is well known, of course, that these relationships themselves were inter-connecting ones but, none the less, the difference in emphasis of the British tradition is unmistakable. Indeed in Roy Bridge's recent work on Austrian foreign policy the stress on the primacy of that policy might even be regarded as an over-emphasis. For Bridge is at pains to point out that in July 1914 the Monarchy went to war exclusively for reasons of prestige. The 'view that the Dual Monarchy was by 1914 in a critical state bordering on dissolution, which rendered some foreign action imperative as a diversion or as a solution', he concedes, 'is not without a certain plausibility'. Yet it was Austria-Hungary's position as a great power which was at stake and 'in this situation, the domestic economic and military situation in the Monarchy could hardly have any really determining effect on the government's decision either way'.[63] This is perhaps an extreme position to take, but it is full-square in the British tradition. Austrian and American historians, like those of the Fischer School in Germany, would, I suspect, lay much greater emphasis on the 'Primat der Innenpolitik'.

The masterpiece of the British tradition is of course A. J. P. Taylor's *The Habsburg Monarchy*, not just a work of scholarship, but a work of genius. It is perhaps Taylor's best book and, although no longer up-to-date on many details, it remains, none the less, the best work on the subject in print. Much of the modern monographic literature merely establishes or reinforces the points which Taylor has already made, and since these are made with his accustomed wit and acerbity, the book is, characteristically, a delight to read. This cannot be said of every—or even many—works on Habsburg history.

Taylor's thesis—which is also to be found in his aforementioned

---

[59] See his *From Sadowa to Sarajevo: the Foreign Policy of Austria-Hungary, 1866-1914* (London, 1972); and *Great Britain and Austria-Hungary, 1906-14: A Diplomatic History* (London, 1972).

[60] See his many articles on civil-military relations in the Habsburg Empire, as well as *The Eastern Front 1914-17* (London, 1975).

[61] See, in particular, *The Habsburg Monarchy*.

[62] I refer to A. Sked, *The Survival of the Habsburg Empire: Radetzky, the Imperial Army and the Class War, 1848* (London, 1979).

[63] Bridge, *From Sadowa to Sarajevo*, p. 370.

review of Kann[64]—is as follows. The Habsburg Monarchy was fundamentally a machine for conducting foreign policy. Essentially the Monarchy was the territorial power-base, which the Habsburgs used in pursuit of their foreign-political aims. Their interest in the peoples of the Monarchy was, therefore, merely a proprietorial one, and meant that there could be no Kremsier-type reforms since these could only have served to deprive the Habsburgs of their power. Only reforms which left the Habsburgs in control—mainly those concerning local government—could, therefore, be adopted. This was why the dynasty was so fond of finding its doom in a 'Piedmont'. A Piedmont or a Serbia challenged the very basis of Habsburg power. As rival states they simply had no plans to preserve the Habsburg dynasty. Ironically, the nationalities inside the Monarchy were themselves prepared to tolerate this situation in order to be protected by Habsburg power. Or, in Taylor's words,

> 'in the last resort, the Habsburg Monarchy was not a device for enabling a number of nationalities to live together. It was an attempt to find a "third way" in Central Europe which should be neither German nor Russian.'

He adds:

> 'once the Habsburgs became Germany's satellites in war, they had failed in their mission. Their doom was of their own making.' [65]

Like Seton-Watson and Wickham Steed, Taylor—who elsewhere also stresses the weak internal condition of the monarchy—sees the German connection as fatal to Habsburg fortunes.

The British and Austro-American traditions have, therefore, been rather different ones. This is not to say, however, that representatives of the latter brand have not dealt with the role of the Habsburg Monarchy in international affairs. Distinguished contributions have, for example, been forthcoming from the Austro-American, Paul Schroeder.[66] Yet it is almost an irony of historiography that, according to Schroeder, the collapse of the Dual Monarchy can be primarily attributed to Britain. For Britain, according to Schroeder, refused the Habsburgs vital support and, blinded by short-term self-interest, failed to retain the Monarchy as an essential part of the balance of power. Once again, therefore, the two historiographical traditions divide. In Schroeder's words:

[64] Taylor, 'The Failure of the Habsburg Monarchy'.

[65] *Ibid.*, p. 132.

[66] See, in particular, *Austria, Great Britain and the Crimean War. The Destruction of the European Concert* (Ithaca and London, 1972); *Metternich's Diplomacy at its Zenith, 1820–1823* (Austin, 1962).

'Of course there was no great anti-Austrian plot. The British did not think of Austria as their enemy; they tried not to think of her at all. They did not plan to isolate and destroy her; they simply did not concern themselves (as they never had earlier in the nineteenth century) with the question of whether the concessions and defeats forced upon Austria before the war, and the territorial sacrifices to be imposed on her during and after it, would leave her viable. Britain undermined Austria's position before the war—indeed, throughout the nineteenth century—and assisted in her destruction during it, in a fit of absence of mind, a state from which many British historians on this subject have not yet emerged.'[67]

Despite all this, however, one can end on a note of optimism. There are many issues in fact on which British, Austrian and American scholars are now agreed. For example, there is little dispute that the Empire was not dismembered by the powers in 1918, but crumbled first of all from within. Most historians would also primarily blame the Habsburgs themselves for this. The fatal roles of the German connection and of the Russian Revolution are also recognized. More important still, recent scholarship has sought to investigate the connections between dynastic power, economic strength and nationalist development and unrest. This is true of scholarship in Britain, Europe and North America. One thinks of the recent work of István Deák[68] and Gunther Rothenberg[69] in America, of Herbert Mathis[70] in Vienna and (in the absence of practically anyone else) myself in this country.[71] The historiographical trends, indeed, are at last beginning to merge. Many useful international conferences on the Monarchy have recently been held and one anticipates even greater international co-operation in the future. With luck, this may encourage a revival of interest here.

[67] W. Schroeder, 'World War I as Galloping Gertie: a Reply to Joachim Remak', *Journal of Modern History*, 44 (1972), 341-2. On the other hand Barbara Jellavich (*The Habsburg Empire in European Affairs, 1814-1918* (New York, 1975), p. 175) merely accepts that Britain and Austria had different interests in the Near East and Balkans.

[68] See his *The Lawful Revolution. Louis Kossuth and the Hungarians, 1848-1849* (New York, 1979).

[69] See his *The Army of Francis Joseph* (West Lafayette, 1976).

[70] See, *inter alia*, his article 'Nationalitätenfrage und Wirtschaft in der Habsburgermonarchie', *Der Donauraum*, 15 (1970), 171-202.

[71] Sked, *The Survival of the Habsburg Empire*.

PRESIDENTIAL ADDRESS

By Sir John Habakkuk, M.A., F.B.A.

THE RISE AND FALL OF ENGLISH LANDED FAMILIES, 1600–1800: III. DID THE GENTRY RISE?

READ 21 NOVEMBER 1980

I want first to consider some of the statistical evidence that there was an increase in activity in the land market during the sixteenth century and the first half of the seventeenth. It has long been known that there was a substantial increase in fines levied during this period, i.e. in the fictitious suits which were, in substance, conveyances of land. Mr. Meeking observed in his introduction to the Surrey Feet of Fines for the period 1509–1558 that 'the average number of Fines levies each Term rose so steeply that the number of Surrey Fines levied in the years 4 & 5 Ph & M (1557–8) is more than five times as great as those levied during an average year of the period 1509–1530'.[1] Professor Stone's calculations based upon the fines for three counties suggest that the number more than doubled between 1560 and 1620.[2] A rough count for the country as a whole shows as one would expect a more moderate but still considerable increase; the annual number in the 1580s was under 3,000; in the 1590s it was over 3,000; and by the early seventeenth century it has risen to over 4,000. Besides the evidence of the fines, some information can be derived, though for a shorter period, from the returns of the income received by the Receiver-General of the Alienation Fines; this consisted of the fees payable on the writs which initiated the fictitious suit and also on licences and pardons connected with the alienation of property held *in capite*.[3] This income bore a relation to the value of the property; though the value

---

[1] *Abstracts of Surrey Feet of Fines, 1509–1558*, ed. C. A. F. Meekings, Surrey Rec. Soc., xix, 1946.

[2] L. Stone, *The Crisis of the Aristocracy, 1558–1641* (Oxford, 1965), p. 37.

[3] The termly accounts of the Receiver-General of the Alienation Fines for the seventeenth century are in P.R.O., E 101. The income is specified under three heads: the fees paid on writs of covenant, the writ most commonly used to initiate the fictitious legal suit; fees paid on writs of entry for lands not held in chief; income from licences to alienate (and pardons for alienation without licence) and writs of entry for lands held in chief. The receipts are total receipts, i.e. before the payment to the Hanaper of the rents reserved under the leases to the Lord Treasurer from 1590 onwards.

for this purpose was not the true value, the income gives some clue to the fluctuations in the aggregate value of transactions, and not merely in their number.

The use of fines, of course, was not limited to occasions when land was bought and sold, i.e. they were not employed only to assure a title obtained by an actual sale. They were used in family settlements, when trusts were created, when gifts were made, and sometimes when land was mortgaged.[4] We do not know which was their most common employment. We cannot be sure whether the rise in their number was due to a genuine increase in the total number of conveyances or to an extension in the use of fines as a result of changing conveyancing practices; nor, in so far as it represents an increase in conveyances, can we say how far these were sales and how far the creation or breaking of settlements.[5]

About a rapid short-run increase in fines it is possible to make a reasonable guess. Such an increase is more likely to be due to an increase in sales; neither the pattern of family settlement nor conveyancing practices were subject to abrupt changes. The interpretation of the long-term increase in fines is, however, much more uncertain. Early Tudor legislation promoted the use of fines, but there is no reason to suppose that later in the century there was an increase in their use, as distinct from an increase in transactions of the kind in which they were commonly used.[6] The real question is whether there was an increase in conveyances for purposes other than sale, particularly conveyances in connection with family settlements. Mr. Meeking found that the fines on properties covering several counties included a much higher proportion of the form (form D) which was used to create entails, and it is significant that these 'Divers Counties Fines' which include Surrey show no upward trend between 1510 and 1558, a period during which the fines confined to Surrey alone showed a remarkable increase. One might surmise that there was no great change in this period in habits of settlement among the families wealthy enough to own land in several counties. Later in the century

---

[4] For examples of their use, see *Calendar of Antrobus Deeds before 1625*, ed. R. B. Pugh (Wiltshire Archaeological Soc., iii, 1947), pp. xlvii–xlviii; Stone, *Crisis*, pp. 36–67. See also the exchange between Conrad Russell and Lawrence Stone on feet of fines and licences to alienate in *Econ. Hist. Rev.*, 2nd ser., xxv (1972), 117–23.

[5] I have attempted to ascertain which of the fines for the period 1571–1602 (listed in *A Calendar of the Feet of Fines relating to the County of Huntingdon*, ed. G. J. Turner (Cambridge Antiquarian Soc., xxxvii, 1913)) were used in tracing the manorial descents in the *V.C.H.* for Huntingdonshire, and the interpretation placed on each of them. The great majority of these fines relate to small properties but of the forty-seven which were relevant to manorial descents, twenty-one appear to relate to sales and twenty-six to settlements and other transactions.

[6] The popularity of fines was enhanced by the two Statutes of Fines, 4 Henry VII (1488–9), c. 24, and 32 Henry VIII (1540), c. 36, which provided certain safeguards.

the fines relating to several counties do show an increase, though the timing of the increase is not identical with that for all fines. There may also have been an extension of the habit of family settlement among landowners lower in the hierarchy. Possibly some of the increase in fines should be ascribed to changes of this nature. But it is difficult to believe that these can explain the major part of the increase. Nor is there anything in the chronology of the increase to suggest that a large part of it was due to an increase from enfeoffments to uses designed to avoid the forfeitures for recusancy introduced under the Acts of 1581 and 1606, though some increase on this account remains a possibility.

Even if it is assumed that the increase primarily reflects activity in the land market, the most difficult problems of interpretation remain. The fines record the number of conveyances, not the total amount of property conveyed, and the number of conveyances is in part determined by the total number of properties in existence. It has been argued by some historians that sale led to a division more often than to a consolidation of existing holdings. If this was the case, the increase in the number of units of ownership would itself lead to an increase in the number of sales. It would also, as a by-product, lead to an increase in the number of settlements and trusts and to an increase in the number of fines on this account. For these reasons an increase in fines, though the result of a genuine increase in sales, would exaggerate both the amount of land sold and the number of sales.

Moreover, even if the increase in fines was primarily a reflection of an increase in sales, many of the sales are unlikely to have had a significant effect on the distribution of property belonging to gentry and magnates. Most of the fines related to properties too small to have made much difference; to the assignment of beneficial leases, an activity becoming more common in the later sixteenth century; and some arose from the sale and purchase of urban property. In so far as the fines relate not only to small properties but to transactions between small proprietors, the statistics may give very little guidance as to volume of and motives for the sales by the gentry and magnates. To what extent the market in estates was linked to that in peasant properties is one of the unresolved problems of this period, but it is a reasonable conjecture that the small proprietors were particularly sensitive to short-term changes in fortune from which estate owners would be in some measure insulated.

Then again, some of the fines relate to properties which were resold several times; there is no way of telling, without a detailed examination of each fine, whether a rise in the number of fines was due to more properties being sold or to the more frequent sale of the same properties, though one makes much more difference than the other; a property which passes through several hands clocks up several sales but represents only one long-term transfer of land. The disposal of the former monastic lands let loose a good many small properties, likely to be sold and resold and well suited to be held as investments. Of Devon monastic property, slightly less than sixty per cent by value consisted of manors, and a number of these consisted predominantly of free and customary rents, agglomerations of small tenements which had assumed a manorial title, though they were scattered over several parishes. Many of such properties passed through several hands before settling down in the hands of those who intended to hold them for good. Some passed through several middlemen. Some certainly were bought and sold as a speculation. Some pieces were bought by small men who did not have the means to retain them. Some were resold because the first purchaser did not wish to hold scattered properties which he had been compelled by the methods of sale to take as a job lot. Some were resold because the purchaser had over-extended his resources and needed cash to pay the instalments due to Augmentation. There was a good deal of rationalization, consolidation and exchange of holdings after the main disposals of monastic lands had taken place. Some of the very rapid rise in fines in the 1540s and the two following decades was probably due to transactions of these kinds; and to this extent the figures exaggerate the rise in those transfers of land which affected the long-term distribution of property, though, by the same token, it conceals the true rate of increase later in the century.[7]

No firm conclusions can be reached without detailed studies of conveyancing practices. But my own inclination is to believe that the fines are evidence of an increase in the activity in the land market in the century or so before 1640, though not if its magnitude. One is more disposed to interpret the statistical evidence in this sense because there is qualitative evidence of the growth of the market. First, there is the evidence provided by the sale of monastic lands about the state of the land market in the years immediately before they were disposed of. Secondly, there is the evidence provided for the state of the land market in the early seventeenth century by the reaction of land sales and land prices in the crisis of the 1610s and 1620s. Thirdly, there is evidence from the development of regional differences in the price of land.

[7] *Devon Monastic Lands: Calendar of Particulars for Grants, 1536–1558*, ed. Joyce Youings (Devon and Cornwall Rec. Soc., new ser., i, 1955), p. x; Youings, 'Landlords in England: the Church', *The Agrarian History of England and Wales*, IV, ed. H. P. R. Finberg (Cambridge, 1967); G. W. O. Woodward, 'A Speculation in Monastic Lands', *Eng. Hist. Rev.*, lxxix (1964), 778–83; A. J. Slavin, *Politics and Profit; a Study of Sir Ralph Sadler, 1507–1547* (Cambridge, 1966), p. 201. The king could not be a cognizor of a fine, and therefore the sales by the Crown of the former monastic lands did not involve a fine, whereas a resale might and probably would do so.

When the Crown came first to dispose of the monastic lands, it set a standard rate which was to apply throughout the country: the demesne lands were to sell at twenty years' purchase, i.e. the price was to be calculated at twenty times the annual rent.[8] It is not clear why the Crown proceeded in this way, by adopting a flat, uniform rate, instead of trying to exact the highest possible price for each property, e.g. by asking for tenders, by putting the properties up for auction or by inducing, in some other way, competitive offers from interested parties. It may be that the flat rate was dictated simply by administrative convenience and the need to sell a large amount of property in a short time. Alternatively, it may be that there was nothing in the experience of the Crown's administrators to enable them to conceive of competitive bidding for land. Or, perhaps, they knew that there was unlikely to be much competition for particular properties. But in any case the adoption of a flat rate does suggest that the land market was very constricted.

We do not know for certain what determined the particular choice of twenty years. It is probable that this was the going rate in the sales of private land in the decades immediately before the monasteries were dispossessed and was simply adopted by the Crown for this reason. Thorold Rogers believed that land was normally valued at twenty years' purchase in the fifteenth century and McFarlane concluded that 'it was generally *assumed* that land would fetch about twenty times its annual *net* revenue'.[9] If twenty years' purchase was already standard in private transactions, this in itself suggests a restricted land market. It is possible, however, that current practice did not give such unambiguous guidance and that there was some element of arbitrariness in the choice. If so, it is significant that the lands were in fact sold at twenty years' purchase; for the Crown could only have enforced its view on a very inert land market. There is another point. The fact that the rate actually chosen, whether or not it was arbitrary, gave a yield about half the rate on loans suggests that land was bought and sold predominantly between men who did not compare relative yields because they had no experience of other assets, i.e. between existing landowners.

So much can be deduced from the Government's methods of proceeding in the matter. About the sales themselves there are four features which suggest that the land market was inactive on the eve of the sales. First, this large amount of property does not seem to have

[8] H. J. Habakkuk, 'The Market for Monastic Property, 1539-1603', *Econ. Hist. Rev.*, 2nd ser., x (1958), 362-80.

[9] J. E. Thorold Rogers, *History of Agriculture and Prices* (7 vols., Oxford, 1866-1902), IV, p. 100; *Six Centuries of Work and Wages* (London, 1884), pp. 287-8; K. B. McFarlane, *The Nobility of Later Medieval England* (Oxford, 1973), p. 57.

depressed the price. Whatever the reasons for choosing the rate, lands at twenty years' purchase were not cheap in the 1540s. Secondly, the rate was the same throughout the country—the same in Wales and Lancashire as in the Home Counties. Even in the early sixteenth century, land in some parts of the country must have been preferable, but, if so, the preference did not influence the price. Thirdly, there is no evidence of price competition for particular properties, i.e. of a purchaser acquiring a property he particularly desired by offering a higher rate. Where the rate exceeded twenty years it was normally because it was known to both seller and buyer that the annual rent was unusually below the true annual value, not because of multiple bidding. Royal favour, rather than price competition, settled the fate of any particularly desirable property. Fourthly, something may be deduced from the way in which this very large amount of property was paid for. Some of it was paid for in instalments and probably out of income. This is the way Sir Ralph Sadler paid for his purchases.[10] Some was paid for out of the proceeds of the purchasers' other estates. Dr. Virgoe has described how, from the 1520s, the fourth Duke of Norfolk 'began to sell off much of his outlying estates in the Midlands and elsewhere in order to purchase a very large share of the East Anglian lands of monastic houses dissolved by Wolsey in the 1520s and by Cromwell in the following decade'.[11] But this only pushes the problem of the source of funds a stage further back. Some purchasers must have borrowed. But there is no evidence of heavy borrowing, though the possibility is worth exploring that the Act of 1547 which legalized the taking of usury was designed to facilitate the raising of money. One is driven to the conclusion that the local families who, in the event, were the major beneficiaries of the transaction financed much of their purchase out of savings, either their own or their friends and relations. If this conjecture is correct there was, on the eve of the monastic confiscations, a substantial demand for land frustrated by the absence of land for sale and activated by the availability of monastic lands.

I have talked about an inactive land market, but these facts—both the way in which the Crown prepared to sell the monastic lands and the sales themselves—strongly suggest that in the early sixteenth century there was no market in the proper sense. They suggest, that is, that there were too few transactions to establish a market price by the competition of buyers and sellers, and that the price therefore was established by reference to a standard convention or by Government fiat.

[10] Slavin, *Politics and Profit*, p. 200.
[11] R. Virgoe, 'The Recovery of the Howards in East Anglia, 1485 to 1529', *Wealth and Power in Tudor England. Essays presented to S. T. Bindoff*, ed. E. W. Ives, R. J. Knecht and J. J. Scarisbrick (London, 1978), p. 20.

This view of the matter certainly accords with McFarlane's account of the land market in later medieval England. Writing of the two and a half centuries after 1290, McFarlane concluded: 'The question should be rather how *small* was the fraction of England that then changed hands by sale.' Almost always when substantial sales were made it was by men who were childless or at least had no male issue. 'The great mass of lay estates descended by inheritance or by will without ever coming into the market at all. If a man had money and wanted to buy he had to wait his chance.' [12] That is radically different from the land market in the sixteenth century, at least after 1540.

By the early seventeenth century the land market had changed profoundly, and one can see this from the reaction to the depression of the second and third decades. It is not my concern to examine the causes of this depression. But it is evident that there were strong deflationary influences at work and a contraction of demand both domestic and export. The depression in prices led to a check in the rise in rents and in many cases to falling rents, arrears, and inability to let farms. The depression also led to a fall in the price of land. There were several contemporary complaints to this effect. John Chamberlain complained in November 1620 of a general want of money so that 'land falls everywhere, and if you have money you may buy good land at thirteen or fourteen years purchase'. [13] In 1621, according to Sir Simon D'Ewes, the price of land fell from twenty years' purchase to sixteen or seventeen. The complaint was echoed in the debates on the Usury Bill of that year. This Bill was an attempt to rescue landowners by reducing the legal maximum rate of interest from ten per cent to eight per cent; and it was argued in the preamble that, because of the fall in rental income and the abatement in the value of land, landowners who had borrowed at ten per cent were unable to service their loans and were forced to sell their lands at very low rates. [14]

The income of the Receiver-General of the Alienation Fines fluctuated in these years in a way which may be significant. The annual average between 1602 and 1606 was £5,611. Between 1608 and 1611 it was £7,242. Between 1617 and 1623 it was £8,372, and in two years 1617 and 1619 it was over £9,000. In 1624 the income was £6,224 and in 1625 it was only £4,141. The figure for 1626 was £6,111 and the level remained low until the end of the decade. The low figure for

[12] McFarlane, *Nobility*, p. 55.

[13] *The Letters of John Chamberlain*, ed. N. E. McClure (2 vols., Philadelphia, 1939), II, 328, quoted by Menna Prestwich, *Cranfield: Politics and Profit under the Early Stuarts* (Oxford, 1966), p. 384.

[14] *The Autobiography of Sir Simon D'Ewes*, ed. J. O. Halliwell (2 vols., London, 1845), I, p. 180; *Commons Debates, 1621*, ed. W. Notestein, F. H. Relf and H. Simpson (7 vols., New Haven, 1935), IV, pp. 314-15, VII, p. 209; J. T. Cliffe, *The Yorkshire Gentry from the Reformation to the Civil War* (London, 1969), pp. 47, 146.

1625 may reflect the succession—the income for 1603 was also unusually low—and it is possible that some of the variation was due to
changes in administrative efficiency.[15] But it is difficult to see how this
can explain the marked rise and fall in so short a period. This chronology is not exactly what the complaints about sales would imply,
since the two highest years were 1617 and 1619; but the figures suggest
that conveyances were unusually high for about six years.

The chronology of the sales needs further investigation, but there
is no reason to doubt the contemporary complaints of many sales at
low prices. This is the first occasion known to me when buyers and
sellers departed from the convention of valuing land at twenty years'
purchase not merely in individual instances but generally.[16] These
years were significant in other ways. It was in the first two decades of
the seventeenth century that the problems were resolved of calculating
the true capital value of land let on long leases. The problem arose as
soon as the annual rent of land fell behind its full annual value, as it
did from the 1550s onwards, but until the early seventeenth century
only very rough and ready methods were available of taking the
difference into account. It is to these years of depression that belong
the first tables of interest specifically designed to make separate valuations of income in possession and income in reversion; Thomas
Clay's *Briefe Easie and Necessary Tables, of Interest and Rents forborne: as
also for the valuation of leases, annuities and purchases*, which first appeared
in 1618, enjoyed a second edition in 1622 and a much enlarged third
edition in 1624. And the third (1618) edition of John Norden's *The
Surveyor's Dialogue*, which in its first two editions (in 1607 and 1608)
contained nothing about calculating the capital value of land, included an additional book which dealt with the relative return on the
purchase of leases and of land in fee simple. The increased sophisti-
cation of valuation was not only a sign of greater need to value land;
in its turn it facilitated the development of a land market.

The depression also stimulated a consideration of the relation between the price of land (i.e. the rate at which the annual value of land
was capitalized) and the rate of interest. I know of no case in the
sixteenth century in which this relationship was recognized; indeed,
the fact that land was valued at twenty years' purchase to yield five
per cent at a time when the rate of interest was ten per cent suggests

[15] The fluctuations were more marked in the income from alienations than in that
from writs of covenant, but they were considerable in both. The combined total did not
exceed the 1619 level until 1633, and it was exceptionally high in 1637 (£10,202).

[16] The attempt to sell a large amount of Crown land in 1599 and in 1601 gradually
depressed the price of this property, and further investigation may show that these
sales also affected the private land market (R. B. Outhwaite, 'The Price of Crown
Land at the Turn of the Sixteenth Century', *Econ. Hist. Rev.*, 2nd ser., xx (1967),
229-40).

that land was generally valued in the sixteenth century without reference to the rate of interest. That there was a relationship was first suggested by Francis Bacon during a debate on a bill introduced in May 1606 to 'enlarge the statutes in force against Usury'. He repeated the point in more detail in his Essay on Usury of 1612. But even in 1612 Bacon wrote as if he were making an original and personal observation. It was during the controversies precipitated by the de-pression about the lowering of the legal maximum that the view was clearly expressed that the rate of interest regulated the price of land. Sir Thomas Culpepper expounded this view in a pamphlet published in 1621, and Bacon returned to the point in his paper on usury written in 1623.[17] The view rapidly became widely adopted. By 1649-51, when another trade depression brought a demand for a further reduction in the statutory maximum, one of the arguments used was that lowering the rate of interest would improve the market for the confiscated properties which the Commonwealth was attempting to sell. And, by the 1660s, the view that the price of land was determined by the rate of interest had become so much common doctrine that it led Sir Josiah Child, among others, to misinterpret the whole history of land prices in England.[18] The emergence of this recognition of the relation is additional evidence that the capitalization of landed income had become more sophisticated; it also suggests that there were now assets which could be compared with land and that, in deciding whether or not to purchase, men were influenced by the relative yield on these assets. This accords with what is known of the character of the purchasers. Referring to the purchasers of the former monastic properties in Lancashire, Dr. Haigh writes that the bulk of them were local gentlemen: 'with one or two exceptions, they were of established county families'. And the pattern of acquisition seems to have been very similar in Devon, Leicestershire and Wales.[19] By contrast, the purchasers of lands in the early seventeenth century included a high proportion of newcomers.[20]

[17] *The Parliamentary Diary of Robert Bowyer*, ed. D. H. Wilson (Minneapolis, 1931), p. 151; *The Works of Francis Bacon*, ed. J. Spedding, R. L. Ellis and D. D. Heath (14 vols., London, 1857-74), VI, pp. 473-7; *Letters and Life of Bacon*, ed. J. Spedding, VII, p. 417; Sir Thomas Culpepper the Elder, *Tract against the High Rate of Usurie* (1621).

[18] H. J. Habakkuk, 'The Long-term Rate of Interest and the Price of Land in the Seventeenth Century', *Econ. Hist. Rev.*, 2nd ser., v (1952), 26-45.

[19] C. Haigh, *The Last Days of the Lancashire Monasteries and the Pilgrimage of Grace* (Chetham Society, 3rd ser., xvii, 1969), p. 138; Glanmor Williams, 'The Dissolution of the Monasteries in Glamorgan', *Welsh History Review*, iii (1966), 23-43; P. Williams, 'The political and Administrative History of Glamorgan, 1536-1642', *Glamorgan County History*, IV, ed. G. Williams (Cardiff, 1974), p. 656, n. 132; T. Jones Pierce, 'Landlords in Wales', *Agrarian History*, IV, ed. Finberg, p. 386; J. Youings, 'The Terms of the Disposal of the Devon Monastic Lands, 1536-58', *Eng. Hist. Rev.*, lxix (1954), 31.

[20] Cliffe, *Yorkshire Gentry*, p. 95; H.M.C., *Buccleuch*, iii, p. 182.

The seventeenth century also saw the erosion of geographical uniformity in the rating of land. I have not been able to detect in the ratings of the Crown lands sold in the 1590s any tendency for the valuations to vary by regions; the variations in ratings arise from differences in type of property and the standard rate for rented agricultural land appears to have been forty years' purchase of the annual rent irrespective of region.[21] When the State sold confiscated properties in the 1640s and 1650s, the minimum rates it fixed applied uniformly to the whole country. The actual rates in the sales of these properties varied widely from one transaction to another, but purchases by tenants were rated uniformly at fifteen years' purchase, irrespective of region. These sales during the Interregnum were so closely involved with the discharge of Government debt that they may not reflect behaviour in the market in ordinary property. There are some signs of regional differentials in the 1620s. But unequivocal evidence does not come until the 1660s, when it is clear that the price of land varied considerably between regions. When, in 1667, Stephen Primatt published the first edition of his *The City and Country Purchaser and Builder* he contrasted the twenty years' purchase in Middlesex, Hertfordshire, in most parts of Surrey, Kent, Essex and Sussex, Buckinghamshire, with the fifteen, sixteen or seventeen years' purchase in Yorkshire, Lincolnshire, Norfolk, Suffolk.[22] The emergence of these variations was no doubt due mainly to the disproportionate growth of London during the seventeenth century and its dominance as a source of demand for land; in general land was dearest near London. But it was also a result of the gradual dissolution of conventions about land valuation which accompanied the growth of a more active land market.

This impression of the growth of an active land market is sustained by the studies of particular landed families and also by the estimates which have been made of sales by particular groups of landowners: Professor Stone's estimates of the sales by the peerage between 1558 and 1642 and Dr. Cliffe's for sales among Yorkshire gentry for the same period both show a very high level of activity.[23] Taking all these factors into account there can be no reasonable doubt that there was a considerable rise in activity in the land market in the century—possibly the century and a half—before 1640, and that the rise con-

[21] The Particulars for Grants for the later years of Elizabeth are in P.R.O., LR 2/70 seq.
[22] S(tephen) P(rimatt), *The City and Country Purchaser and Builder* (2nd edn., 1680). The first edition was in 1667. See also H. J. Habakkuk, 'The Price of Land in England, 1500–1700', *Wirtschaft, Geschichte und Wirtschaftsgeschichte. Festschrift zum 65. Geburtstag von Friedrich Lütz*, ed. W. Abel, K. Borchardt, H. Kellenbenz and W. Zorn (Stuttgart, 1966).
[23] Cliffe, *Yorkshire Gentry*, pp. 93 seq., 145, 161–2; Stone, *Crisis*, pp. 156–64.

cerned substantial properties sold by private landowners and not merely lightly held land, or peasant land. It is clear, if only from the marked regional differences in the stability of landed families, that all parts of the country were not equally affected, but the rise extended beyond the Home Counties.[24]

What is the explanation of the increase in activity? In my view, in the sixteenth, as in the eighteenth century, most landowners who sold did so in order to repay debt; the accidents of succession, inheritance by co-heirs or by a remote colateral, for example, might make an owner readier to sell, but even in such cases debt was usually one of the causes of sale. Families ran into debt for a great variety of reasons, and the combination of reasons in the case of any particular family often seems unique. But the general circumstances of some periods make it more difficult for families to keep out of debt. Tawney believed that landowners in the period before 1640 were likely to run into debt primarily because their incomes rose less than their expenses, and this, in turn, occurred in so far as it was difficult for them to tap the increasing annual values of their land. It was perhaps never very plausible to suppose that landed incomes suffered during an inflation marked mainly by a disproportionate rise in agricultural prices. The detailed studies made since Tawney wrote make it clear that though some landowners suffered in the way he suggested, the majority did not.[25]

To some extent the increase in activity in the land market must be attributed to general economic growth, to an increase in economic transactions of every kind. But there were some considerations which specifically affected land. The sales of land by the Crown stimulated rather than curbed the private land market. In the later sixteenth century it became easier to borrow, particularly for those who could offer land as security. The changes in the laws relating to usury, especially the Act of 1571, are no doubt a sign of increasing pressure to borrow, but they also facilitated borrowing. Moreover, with mere passage of time, contacts developed between borrowers and lenders, especially London lenders. Therefore landed families borrowed money for purposes which earlier in the century they would have met from income or have refrained from pursuing. Probably, too, there were changes in social habits, and a spread of tastes for luxuries, quite independently of any greater ease of borrowing.

Not only did debt increase, but debt was followed fairly rapidly by

[24] B. G. Blackwood, *The Lancashire Gentry and the Great Rebellion* (Chetham Soc., 3rd ser., xxv, 1978), p. 23.

[25] R. H. Tawney, 'The Rise of the Gentry, 1558–1640', *Econ. Hist. Rev.*, xi (1941); G. Batho, 'Landlords in England', *Agrarian History*, IV, ed. Finberg, pp. 291–7; Cliffe, *Yorkshire Gentry*, p. 48.

sale. In the fist place, the instruments of debt available until the early seventeenth century were essentially short-term; they could, of course, be renewed but they were not technically well adapted for this purpose. Even if the instruments of debt had been less deficient, it would not be surprising at this early stage in the development of the money market if moneyed men, while willing to lend, were not anxious to lend for long periods and might have difficulty, when they needed cash, in assigning their loans. The lawsuits of the period contain many examples of men who were compelled to sell estates because, although probably solvent in the sense that their assets were greater than their debts, they were illiquid, i.e. could not raise funds with sufficient promptness to repay importunate creditors.[26] There are other reasons why debt should have led to sale. The high level of interest rates meant that interest, if it fell into arrears, accumulated very rapidly; debt very easily got out of hand. Moreover, the fact that the return on land purchase was only half the rate of interest meant that sale and debt repayment substantially increased the landowner's net income—to a very much greater extent than it did in the later seventeenth century when the two yields had narrowed. In part, therefore, we can explain both the level of debt and the speed with which debt was followed by sale of assets as the result of the characteristics of the money market as it had evolved by the later sixteenth and early seventeenth centuries.[27]

From the 1590s onwards there was a further consideration. The Crown's need to borrow increased enormously, and its demands were 'sufficient to affect sensibly the terms on which private borrowers might raise money'.[28] The pressures on the money market were particularly great between 1624 and 1628 and again between 1638 and 1642, when they curtailed the funds available to landowners, whose competitive position was probably also weakened by the reduction of the statutory rate of interest in 1624. Finally, in the century before 1640, family settlements imposed few constraints on sale; this is evident from the fact that large sales were made without recourse to Parliament to break settlements. Thus an intelligible account can be given of the reasons for greater activity in the land market, though they are reasons which apply with more evident force to gentry and magnates than to peasant proprietors.

One evident result of this increased activity in the land market was an increase in the mobility of landed families; there were more families newly established by purchase in 1640 than there had been a century

---

[26] See, for example, the case of Robert Taylor (L. Stone, *An Elizabethan: Sir Horatio Palavicino* (Oxford, 1956), pp. 271–2).

[27] Stone, *Crisis*, pp. 522, 539–40.

[28] R. Ashton, *The Crown and the Money Market* (Oxford, 1960), p. 185.

earlier. Tawney believed that between 1560 and 1640 there was also an increase in the number of gentry as opposed to magnate families, or, more precisely, an increase in the proportion of land owned in the form of small or medium sized as opposed to very large estates. He believed, that is, that there was a change not only in the age-composition of landed families but also in the size-composition of their estates.[29] The calculations he adduced in support of this view cannot bear the weight he wished to place upon them, and the criticisms of them revealed so many difficulties that it is unlikely that anyone else will again wish to tackle the problem in this way. But the reasons he gave for supposing there was a shift from large to small estates still provide a convenient way into the problem.

Tawney's explanation of this change in the size-distribution of estates was subtle and complex, but essentially he thought that large estates were less viable and less able to respond to the problems of inflation than were middling and small estates. Large estates were, therefore, more likely to be eroded by sale. But Tawney's statistics do not in fact bear on this point. There is nothing in them to show whether or not the magnates of 1560 sold more of their estates in the following eighty years than did the gentry. It may be that vulnerability of estates had nothing to do with their size, and that the increase in the relative importance of middling estates was due to the fact that newcomers to the ranks of landownership predominantly bought properties of that size. A change in the size-distribution of estates (as a result of sales and purchases) may be the result of a bias either among sellers or among buyers.

Was there a bias among the sellers? It is difficult not to rise from a reading of Professor Stone's work with the feeling that magnates were particularly prone to sell. Stone was interested specifically in the peerage, not in large landowners *per se* (and there is some disagreement about how far the two groups coincided), but they provide some guide to the fortunes of the larger landowners. His calculations certainly show a marked decrease by sale in the manors owned by the families who in 1559 were peers. The older peerage, who on average owned fifty-four manors each in 1559, owned only thirty-four each in 1641. Reasons can also be suggested why the larger landowners should have been particularly prone to incur debts which were heavy in relation to their assets. They were more likely to overspend on conspicuous consumption and probably also more tempted to provide for their children on a lavish scale, particularly if they were involved in service to the Crown (which, under Elizabeth, did not yield commensurate rewards). They could also borrow more easily; wherever their estates lay, they had better contacts in London and could more easily

[29] Tawney, 'Rise of the Gentry', 33, n. 3.

command loans. Families with more modest estates, particularly those whóse homes were outside the Home Counties, were likely to wish and less able to indulge propensities to extravagance.[30]

It may therefore be that large landowners were more prone to sell. Until we have a parallel study of the fortunes of a cohort of more modestly endowed landowners over the same period we shall not know. There are, however, indications that the shedding of property was characteristic of landed families in general in this period. About one-third of Dr. Cliffe's gentry families in the period 1558–1642 sold at least a considerable part of their property. The final concords relate to all kinds of sellers; and among those who sold to the new men, gentry of every kind are as common as magnates. Moreover, other things being equal, a family was more likely to survive economically if it was well endowed. Of Yorkshire families, Dr. Cliffe writes that 'several of the families which went under in this period had at one time been leading gentry, with landed incomes of £1000 a year and upwards. If, however, the upper gentry were not invulnerable they were undoubtedly in a much better position to weather a financial crisis than the middling or lesser gentry.'[31] The well-endowed families could, of course, sell a great deal of property and survive. Still, the disappearance of many middling and lesser families shows that these groups, too, were under considerable pressure to sell. Perhaps the most reasonable conclusion is that in this period there were strong pressures on landed families irrespective of the size of their estates.

If this is so, any change in the size-composition of landed families depends on the characteristics of those who bought. How much of the property was bought by existing landed families, the transaction representing only a transfer within the landed interest? How much was bought by men who had not made their fortunes by owning land and wished to establish new landed families?

To this question it is not yet possible to give a quantitative answer. One can, however, point to one relevant distinction. In the late sixteenth and early seventeenth centuries, the market in substantial estates, properties capable of forming the basis of a landed family, was dominated by new men, i.e. by men who had not made their fortunes by owning land. The market in smaller properties—the manor, with a negligible demesne, the individual farm, the occasional field—was the interest of men who already had a substantial property in the locality, whether they were old established or had only recently acquired it. Of course, there was no hard and fast line. Purchasers varied in their notions of the size of the property which would enable them to set up as landed gentlemen; what would be adequate in one part

[30] Stone, *Crisis*, pp. 152, 156, 159, 197.
[31] Cliffe, *Yorkshire Gentry*, p. 158.

of the country might be derisory in another. And some new men built up a suitable estate by the accumulation of small properties. Of course, too, there are problems about defining new and established landed families. But in most cases the distinction is perfectly recognizable.

The predominance of new men among the purchasers of estates does not necessarily mean that existing landed families were too impoverished to save and to buy land. There are several examples of established landed families who improved their position within the social hierarchy by adding to their estates by purchase; e.g. the families studied by Miss Mousley (the Gorings of Burton, the Palmers of Angmering, the Pelhams of Laughton) or the upper and middling gentry of Yorkshire where Dr. Cliffe concludes that 'a substantial amount of land buying was being financed from the rents and profits of country estates'.[32] What the predominance of new men means is not only that their savings were in general larger but that a substantial landed estate was likely to be worth more to a new man who wished to acquire it in order to found a landed family, than it was to a family already established whose savings were normally devoted to purchases in their own immediate neighbourhood of properties which formed a natural extension of their main territorial base.

It is doubtful whether, in the century or so before 1640, the transactions between established landed families, though they affected the standing of particular families, had any systematic tendency to change the average size of property. A few established families had access to sources of income other than rents, and from this source were able to finance substantial purchases. But for the most part the sales and purchases between established families probably tended to cancel out. Depending on the accidents of family history—the incidence of minorities, of long widowhoods, of prudent owners and fortunate marriages—some established families gained in the long run and some lost. The transactions between existing landed families and the newcomers probably did more to influence the size-distribution of estates than sales and purchases between existing families.

About the size-distribution of new fortunes we can only speculate. One can, however, point to certain distinguishing features of the demand of moneyed men for land in this period. The principal consideration arises from the special role of land as an investment in this period. It was not merely the case that land was the most secure investment; there was no effective alternative to it, at least not on any significant scale. The moneyed man who wished to hold his assets in a form which yielded an income, gave security and held its value— the passive investor—bought land, an asset moreover which, though

[32] J. E. Mousley, 'The Fortunes of Some Gentry Families of Elizabethan Sussex', *Econ. Hist. Rev.*, 2nd ser., xi (1959), 477; Cliffe, *Yorkshire Gentry*, pp. 96, 117.

certainly not without its problems, required less skill and astuteness to manage than the other forms of asset available.

These facts are obvious enough. But their consequences for land-ownership have not been sufficiently emphasized. A higher proportion of savings were laid out in land than was the case a century or so later. This was true of large fortunes as well as of the modest competences of the small merchant or attorney in some provincial town. But it is most easily illustrated in the case of the large fortunes. Wealthy men bought land in advance of any decision about where they wished to establish a landed family; they bought widely scattered properties far removed from their main base; and they bought properties which, in the aggregate, were much greater than was needed simply to establish a landed family.

The purchases of Robert Brudenell, Chief Justice of the Common Pleas from 1521 to his death ten years later, touched seven counties. Between 1500 and 1514 he bought or leased fifteen manors besides individual parcels of land in the counties of Rutland, Leicester, North-ampton, Buckingham and Lincoln. The estate he so acquired was very scattered, but 'there was nothing unusual about this in the sixteenth century'. The great medieval estates consisted of estates distributed over several counties and those built up in the sixteenth and early seventeenth centuries were on the same pattern.[33] Sir William Fitzwilliam, who, out of the profits of trade and government services, built up an estate in the first three decades of the sixteenth century, concentrated on Essex and Northampton; but he also bought many estates distant from his two main seats, estates which must have been primarily for investment.[34] Sir Ralph Sadler's purchases were more concentrated in time (in 1539-40, 1544 and 1546-7) and more of them were of monastic property, but they have a comparable geographical spread—Essex, Kent, Middlesex, Yorkshire, Hertford-shire, Gloucestershire, Warwickshire and Worcestershire, etc. 'Apart from the two major complexes [in the Home Counties centred in Hertfordshire and Middlesex, and the great mass of lands in the Avon-Bristol region] Sadler held woodlands, messuages, manors and other parcels in twenty-five English and Welsh shires.'[35] So far as monastic properties are concerned, the geographical spread of Sadler's purchases was partly due to the fact that properties of a monastery were often, and especially in the 1540s, put up for sale, as they had been managed, as a bloc even if they were widely scattered geograph-ically. But a similar spread is also evident in estates not built up from non-monastic lands.

---

[33] Joan Wake, *The Brudenells of Deene* (London, 1953), pp. 27-8.
[34] M. E. Finch, *The Wealth of Five Northamptonshire Families, 1540-1640* (Northants Rec. Soc., xix, 1956), ch. iv.   [35] Slavin, *Politics and Profit*, pp. 193-4, 200.

Sir Thomas Egerton, who became Lord Chancellor of Ellesmere, or his executors acquired estates by purchase in Hertfordshire, Buckinghamshire, Shropshire, Cheshire and Middlesex.[36] Between 1540 and 1578, Sir Nicholas Bacon, in every year except two, acquired landed assets and these were in seven counties and in London. Several of his purchases were from their nature purely for investment: several others were of substantial properties in which motives were probably mixed; and on two of these, Redgrave and Gorhambury, he built a mansion, while on another—Stiffkey—he financed the building of a mansion by his son.[37] In the late sixteenth and early seventeenth centuries another great lawyer purchased in much the same pattern. In 1576, when he was twenty-four, Edward Coke paid £5 for a messuage and ten acres in the parish next to his ancestral home, and between that date and 1618 he made ninety-eight separate purchases of manors, lands, tenements and advowsons. He is said altogether to have spent over £100,000, and his major purchases extended to seven counties: Norfolk, Suffolk, Dorset, Staffordshire, Somerset, Cambridge and Oxford.[38] Sir William Craven and his son acquired land in Berkshire, Gloucester, Middlesex, Shropshire, Warwick, Northampton and Sussex.[39] The same pattern can be found in the purchases of Alderman Cockayne, another Lord Mayor of London, who died 'possessed of great estates of many counties', including major holdings in Leicestershire, Northamptonshire, Berkshire, Derbyshire, York and London.[40] Cranfield bought estates in Hertfordshire, Essex, Yorkshire, the Isle of Wight, Gloucestershire, Sussex, Ireland and (though this was for sentimental reasons) in Bedfordshire.[41] Long before he built up a family estate in Yorkshire, Sir Arthur Ingram bought as investments a large assortment of properties widely scattered over England. In the first two decades of the seventeenth century he acquired manors in Shropshire, Somerset, Essex, Warwickshire,

[36] G. Ormerod, *History of Cheshire*, ii, p. 456; *V.C.H., Herts.*, ii, pp. 145, 212, 451; *V.C.H., Bucks.*, iii, p. 407; B. Falk, *The Bridgewater Millions* (London, 1942), pp. 33, 39, 49.

[37] A. Simpson, *The Wealth of the Gentry, 1540–1660* (Cambridge, 1961), pp. 26, 46–50.

[38] C. W. James, *Chief Justice Coke, his Family and Descendants at Holkham* (London, 1929), pp. 143, 305–6.

[39] For the main Craven purchases, see *V.C.H., Berks.*, iv, pp. 105, 312; R. Bigland, *Historical ... Collections relative to the County of Gloucester* (2 vols., London, 1791–2), i, pp. 71, 221 and supplement, p. 320; *The History and Antiquities of Northamptonshire. Compiled from the Manuscript Collections of John Bridges* (2 vols., 1791), i, pp. 544, 604; *V.C.H., Warwicks.*, vi, p. 74; *V.C.H., Sussex*, vii, p. 224; *Trans. Shropshire Archaeological Soc.*, 2nd ser., viii (1896), 3.

[40] A. E. Cockayne, *Cockayne Memoranda* (2 vols., Congleton, 1869–73); P.R.O., SP 19/198, pp. 265–8, 269–71; 19/97, p. 32.

[41] R. H. Tawney, *Business and Politics under James I: Lionel Cranfield as Merchant and Minister* (Cambridge, 1958), p. 195.

Yorkshire, Suffolk and London. He owned lands in every part of England.[42]

This seems the main characteristic of the large purchasers before 1640: in the demand for land, social and investment considerations were very closely connected, and new fortunes were devoted to land on a larger scale than was prompted by social considerations alone.

How are we to interpret the high level of sales of land in the late sixteenth and early seventeenth centuries? Was this merely one of a number of periods of high activity, with some predecessors in the middle ages and some successors? Or does it mark the emergence for the first time of something which can be called, in the proper sense of the term, a market in land? If, as seems the most probable, it does represent a once-and-for-all development of this kind, did sales of land continue on an upward trend in the two centuries after 1640? Or did the early seventeenth century represent a peak, after which the trend was downward? Or did activity some time in the seventeenth century reach a plateau after which, though there were marked fluctuations, there was no perceptible trend? In particular, which view is true of the sales of properties which can be classified as landed estates?

In the light of recent work on the sale of land in the eighteenth century, these must now be regarded as open questions.[43] They are questions, too, which are not likely to be answered, as I once hoped they might be, by a study of the statistics of final concords, enrolled deeds of bargain and sale, and private acts for the sale of land to pay debts.[44] It is possible in the light of such evidence to identify short

---

[42] A. F. Upton, *Sir Arthur Ingram* (Oxford, 1961), pp. 44–5.

[43] Especially B. A. Holderness, 'The English Land Market in the Eighteenth Century: the Case of Lincolnshire', *Econ. Hist. Rev.*, 2nd ser., xxvii (1974), 557–76.

[44] The sustained fall in the number of fines did not occur until about the Restoration. It took place mainly in two stages, in the 1660s and in the 1710s. The annual average between 1654 and 1663 was 4,815; there was then a sharp fall, for between 1664 and 1673 the average was 3,738; between 1684 and 1693 (excluding 1688 for which the figures are defective) it was 3,489 p.a. In 1696 the number for the first time fell below 3,000 and (though the number in that year, viz. 2,363, was exceptionally low and in the four immediately following years the annual average was 3,311) in the eighteenth century it was almost invariably below 3,000, and no trend is apparent. This fall of forty per cent in forty years exaggerates the long-term change, since the figures were unusually high around 1660; but there clearly was some long-term change which requires explanation. It is, however, difficult to attribute the fall in the 1710s to diminished activity in the land market, because (a) it occurs at a time when the evidence of private acts suggests that, at least so far as estates are concerned, there was an increase of sales, and (b) it is not easily reconcilable with evidence for some geographical extension of the land market. In Lancashire, if the change in the composition of the gentry is a guide, the land market in the sixteenth century was inactive and became much livelier in the later seventeenth century; for between 1665 and 1695 more families entered and left the gentry than at any other time in the century (Blackwood, *Lancashire Gentry*, p. 161).

periods of high activity. Thus it seems clear that the 1650s were such a period, though many of the sales were of confiscated property and left no permanent mark on the distribution of landed property. I argued on a previous occasion that there were years of high sales during and immediately after the wars against Louis XIV. A very large amount of land, also, came on to the market in the years following the end of the War of American Independence.[45] But the general series do not enable one to judge whether more land was sold in, say, the 1720s than in the 1620s, or to compare the level of sales in the eighteenth century as a whole with the level in the century before 1640. For though the statistics cover the period from the sixteenth to the early nineteenth century, they change their significance in the course of the three centuries. The question of the level of sales is therefore a matter of debate. But something can be said about one contrast between the eighteenth century and the earlier period in the way in which new landed families were founded.

The fact that in the eighteenth century there were long-term investments which were in some measure substitutes for land altered the pattern of demand for land. Land, of course, retained very strong attractions simply as an investment, as it still does. For investors of a certain disposition, land remained pre-eminently the most favoured asset. 'I live on Bread and Butter and milk porridge,' said Peter Walter, 'and it must be land that contains the cows for this, whereas none of the stock companies have a single cow.' Walter laid out an enormous fortune principally in land.[46] So did Sampson Gideon, another great new fortune. There were also periods of crisis when the balance of advantage turned sharply against paper securities, and wealthy men sought eagerly for land, as they did during and immediately after the South Sea Bubble. Then again, some new fortunes were in the eighteenth century so large that the diverse portfolio dictated by prudence included a very large number of landed properties; the Marlborough fortune is a conspicuous instance. Where there was a wide range of options, the choice in any individual case would depend on a variety of personal circumstances. But if one compares fortunes of comparable magnitude, a much smaller part of them was laid out in land in the eighteenth century than in the sixteenth; and it was less likely to be spent on properties scattered over

[45] Between 1783 and 1787 (the year in which the post-war fall in interest rates finally occurred) the income of the Receiver-General of the Alienations rose from £4,501 6s. 8d. to £6,239, the highest figure for any year between the years investigated, 1731 to 1793 (P.R.O., E 105/2). See also the figures of receipts from auction duties cited in F. M. L. Thompson, 'The Land Market in the Nineteenth Century', *Oxford Economic Papers*, 9 (3) (1957), p. 288.

[46] H. Erskine-Hill, *The Social Milieu of Alexander Pope: Lives, Example and the Poetic Response* (Yale, 1975), p. 109.

several counties, as opposed to a single estate or a group of estates concentrated in a single region. A man of new wealth bought an estate primarily as a social base for a landed family; he was not indifferent to the return on his money but that was not his primary concern. Once he had acquired property adequate for this purpose, he had no need to acquire additional land far from his main estate, nor, in order to find a safe home for his fortune, to spend it all on land.

I have already quoted on another occasion Lord Mansfield, who left a vast fortune almost entirely in mortgages.[47] The distribution of his assets may have been influenced by the absence of a son. But take the case of another unusually successful eighteenth-century lawyer, Philip Yorke, later Lord Chancellor Hardwicke. Yorke, in the 1720s, bought land in the neighbourhood of Dover, where he had inherited property, but these were small farms and could not be developed as an estate. He failed in several attempts to buy a landed estate in this neighbourhood. As a country house, but not an estate, he bought a house near Croydon. In 1725 he bought an estate of £1,000 per annum in Hardwicke in Gloucester, 'probably', says his biographer, 'as an investment'. He did not finally acquire a proper landed basis for his family until 1740, when, aged fifty, as Lord Chancellor Hardwicke, he bought Wimpole in Cambridgeshire, where he later purchased adjoining lands. The value of his estates in Cambridgeshire and Gloucester was said in 1756 to be below £6,000 per annum, and can have been only a small part of his total assets.[48] At any period the form of demand for land is shaped in some degree by the size-distribution of the properties for sale; a wealthy newcomer cannot buy a large estate in a region entirely owned by peasant proprietors. In the sixteenth century wealthy newcomers bought properties without much regard to size and only limited regard to location. In the eighteenth century they were more discriminating as to both size and location.

When the change in pattern first began to show it is difficult to say. But it is significant that the two great fortunes of the late seventeenth century which have been studied in depth both show a degree of regional concentration. Sir John Banks acquired, between 1657 and 1682, estates which, except for a London town house, were all in Kent. 'He was seemingly quite uninterested in acquiring land outside the boundaries of the county to which he and his forbears belonged.' Sir Stephen Fox concentrated most of his purchases of estates in a single decade, the 1670s, and within a single region—East Somerset, where he built up a compact estate, and Wiltshire, where his purchases were

[47] C. H. S. Fifoot, *Lord Mansfield* (Oxford, 1936), p. 50.
[48] P. C. Yorke, *The Life and Correspondence of Philip Yorke, Earl of Hardwicke* (Cambridge, 1913), i, pp. 107-8; ii, p. 307.

scattered but in the same general area. When the main phase of his estate-building was over, he still had assets—a large part in mortgages—more than double the value of his landed property. Special circumstances brought his estate building to an end, in particular the growing likelihood that he would have no male heir. But the distribution of his wealth in this fashion would not have been feasible a century earlier.[49]

Did the gentry rise? In attempting an approach to an answer I should like to revert to a distinction made on an earlier occasion. Changes in the size-distribution of estates were determined by two different sets of influences, and by their interaction. In the first place, they were influenced by marriage, particularly with heiresses, and the provision for the offspring, particularly younger sons. In the second place, they were influenced by sales and purchases of land.

So far as marriages to heiresses are concerned, I have argued that such marriages tended to increase the size of landed estates and particularly to increase disproportionately the size of the estates which were already large. Though properties acquired through heiresses might after a time be lost by sale or gift, they generally represented a net long-term addition to the estate. I believe this to have been their general tendency in the century before 1640. But the effect of marriage in increasing the size of estates was to some extent offset by the provision for younger sons; before 1640 it was more common than it later became to provide for them by grants of land, a method of endowment which among many of the larger landowners was encouraged by the geographical dispersion of their estates, and which had the effect of multiplying gentry families.

So far as buying and selling were concerned, some of the newcomers did buy very substantial estates, but few even of these rivalled in extent the estates of established magnate families. This was simply because few lawyers, government servants or merchants could in a single lifetime save enough to acquire properties as large as the larger existing estates which represented an accumulation of estates by marriage over a number of generations. Many of the newcomers, too, bought medium-sized or small estates. The influx of newcomers before 1640, therefore, tended to reduce the amount of land held in the form of private estates of the largest size, irrespective of any bias among sellers. It would be a reasonable guess that as a net result of marriage, inheritance and sales, less land was owned in the form of large estates in 1600 than in 1500.

Now turn to the eighteenth century. It has been argued that from the later seventeenth century marriage among the magnate families

[49] D. C. Coleman, *Sir John Banks* (Oxford, 1963), ch. 3; C. Clay, *Public Finance and Private Wealth: the Career of Sir Stephen Fox* (Oxford, 1978), pp. 171-2.

was more clearly subordinated to the purposes of territorial aggrandizement than it was in the preceding century. Whether this was the case or not, many of the larger landowners of the sixteenth century had, by the eighteenth century, extended their estates by marriage in the intervening generations. Provision for younger sons, moreover, took a form less likely, at least in the short run, to erode the main family holding. Marriage and inheritance were therefore more favourable to the large estate than was generally the case before 1640.

The effect of activity in the land market is much more complex. There were clearly more fortunes made outside agriculture, from the professions, trade and industry, in the eighteenth century than in the century before 1640. This is true even of the first sixty years or so of the century when there appears to have been no marked change in the relative importance of agriculture; it is a reasonable guess that there were more merchants, lawyers and other professional men in 1740 than in 1640. But the number must have increased considerably in the last three decades of the eighteenth century when the relative importance of agriculture fell. There were thus, in the eighteenth century, more potential purchasers of land.

How was the increase in demand accommodated, and with what effect on the structure of landownership? One possibility is that there were changes in the supply of, and demand for, land independently of any changes in the price of land. Such an increase in the supply of land might occur as a result of increasing indebtedness among landowners, or of increasing severity of economic fluctuations, or of structural changes such as enclosure. Any one of these influences might increase not only the total acreage for sale, but also the total number of holdings. A fall in the demand for land, independent of price, might arise from the greater availability of investments which were close alternatives for land. Or there might be a shift in the geographical location of demand as a result of economic development in the provinces.

The second possibility is that there were changes in supply and demand brought about by an increase in the price of land which stimulated the former and depressed the latter. So far as sales are concerned, my own view has been that, though their timing was sensitive to changes in price, the volume of sales in the long run was determined independently of price and primarily by the level of landed indebtedness. But this may be too simple a view; even if most sales were made in order to repay debt, it may still be true that the landowners' view of the acceptable burden of debt was shaped by long-term changes in the price of land relative to the cost of debt. Even if there were constraints on the supply of estates, the enclosure movement increased the number of smaller properties. Mr. Turner has shown that, in Buckinghamshire, enclosures were accompanied by an increase in the turnover of properties; if the same is true of other counties, the total effect in the last three decades or so of the eighteenth century must have been considerable.[50] So far as purchases of land are in question, an increase in the price of land tended to shift some potential demand to alternative investments; this was one of the ways in which the return on land was kept broadly in line with the rate of interest. The increase also diverted some demand for land to areas of the country where land prices had lagged behind. Possibly, too, some demand was diverted to types of property which were undervalued or cheaper or simply more readily available; the absentee owners who appear in the land tax returns may in part reflect a diversion of this kind from estates to peasant land.

In some combination of these ways the increase in the number of potential purchasers was accommodated to the supply of available land. Even when information is abundant, it is difficult to disentangle changes in supply from those in demand, or to distinguish between the effects of changing preferences and those of price changes. The exercise is unusually difficult in the case of such a peculiar commodity as land. Any assessment of the relative force of these various possibilities must be largely conjectural. My own inclination is to believe that the accommodation was not made by an increase in the supply of estates for sale. In the eighteenth century the purchase of small estates by their larger neighbours was commoner than the creation of new small estates by the subdivision of large estates or by the conversion of peasant into gentry land, so that the total number of estates in existence was probably lower. For reasons given elsewhere, I think that in the three or four decades after the 1720s there was a decline in the number of estates for sale. Whether in the same period the supply of peasant properties was also lower is less clear, and it may be that in some parts of the country, in the neighbourhood of major provincial towns, an active market in peasant properties provided greater opportunities than before for the rich lawyers and merchants of the major towns of the neighbourhood to satisfy their need for land. But I think the major adjustments are likely to have taken place on the side of demand. The *nouveaux riches* of the eighteenth century established themselves on a more modest scale than had their counterparts before 1640. In this sense more of the newcomers established gentry-sized estates in the eighteenth century than before 1640.

[50] M. E. Turner, 'Parliamentary Enclosure and Landownership Change in Buckinghamshire', *Econ. Hist. Rev.*, 2nd ser., xxviii (1975), 574.

THE ROYAL HISTORICAL SOCIETY

REPORT OF COUNCIL, SESSION 1978-79

THE Council of the Royal Historical Society has the honour to present the following report to the Anniversary Meeting.

A conference on 'Regions and their Culture' was held at the University of East Anglia from 14 to 16 September 1978. The papers read were:

'Country, County and Town: Patterns of Regional Evolution in England', by Professor A. M. Everitt.

'Regional Art and Architecture', by Professor P. E. Lasko.

'The forms and uses of literacy in Venice and Florence in the Thirteenth and Fourteenth Centuries', by Dr. J. K. Hyde.

'The Cartographic Image of "the Country" in Early Modern England', by Mr V. F. C. Morgan.

'The Dutch Case: a National or a Regional Culture?', by Professor E. H. Kossmann. (The Prothero Lecture.)

Sixty-seven members of the Society and twenty-five guests attended. The Lord Mayor of Norwich held a reception for them on 15 September. It was decided to hold the tenth annual conference at University College, Cardiff from 13 to 15 September 1979, on the topic 'Bureaucracy'.

An evening party was held for members and guests at University College London on 5 July 1978 for which 140 acceptances were received.

The representation of the Society upon various bodies was as follows: Professor F. M. L. Thompson and Mr. A. T. Milne on the Joint Anglo-American Committee exercising a general supervision over the production of the *Bibliographies of British History*; Professor G. W. S. Barrow, Mr. T. A. M. Bishop, Dr. P. Chaplais and Professor P. H. Sawyer on the Joint Committee of the Society and the British Academy established to prepare an edition of Anglo-Saxon charters; Professor E. B. Fryde on a committee to regulate British co-operation in the preparation of a new repertory of medieval sources to replace Potthast's *Bibliotheca Historica Medii Aevi*; Professor P. Grierson on a committee to promote the publication of photographic records of the more significant collections of British coins; Professor H. G. Koenigsberger on the Advisory Council on the Export of Works of Art; the President and Mr. K. V. Thomas on the British National Committee of the International Historical Congress; Professor G. H. Martin on the Council of the British Records Association; Professor A. M. Everitt on the Standing Conference for Local History; Mr. M. R. D. Foot on the Committee to advise the publishers of *The Annual Register*; and Miss K. Major on the Lincoln Archaeological Trust. Council received reports from these representatives.

Professor W. N. Medlicott represents the Society on the Court of the University of Exeter and Professor J. A. S. Grenville on the Court of the University of Birmingham.

The Honorary Secretary and the Honorary Treasurer represented the Society at a one-day Conference on the administration of learned societies held at the Royal Society on 27 October 1978, and the Honorary Treasurer read a paper on 'Financial Administration—the External Aspects'.

The Society made a submission to the Public Records Committee appointed under the chairmanship of Sir Duncan Wilson to conduct an enquiry into the working of certain provisions of the Public Records Acts 1958 and 1967, after circularising selected scholars who from the nature of their historical interests were particularly concerned with the operation of the Acts.

The Vice-Presidents retiring under By-law XVI were Professor J. C. Holt and Professor J. Hurstfield. Professor J. H. Burns and Dr. R. F. Hunnisett were elected to replace them. The members of Council retiring under By-law XIX were Professor J. H. Burns, Mr. K. V. Thomas, Professor W. L. Warren and Professor Joyce Youings. Professor J. D. Hargreaves, Professor G. H. Martin, Professor J. J. Scarisbrick and Professor P. Smith were elected to fill the vacancies. Messrs. Beeby, Harmar and Co. were appointed auditors for the year 1978–79 under By-law XXXVIII.

Publications and Papers Read

The following works were published during the session: *Transactions, Fifth Series*, volume 29; *Camden Miscellany XXVII* (Camden, Fourth Series, volume 22) and *The Letters of the Third Viscount Palmerston to Laurence and Elizabeth Sulivan, 1804–63* (Camden, Fourth Series, volume 23); *The Annual Bibliography of British and Irish History* (1977 publications); and six volumes in the STUDIES IN HISTORY series *Church and State in Independent Mexico: a Study of the Patronage Debate, 1821–1857*, by M. P. Costeloe (volume 8), *An Early Welsh Microcosm: Studies in the Llandaff Charters*, by Wendy Davies (volume 9), *The British in Palestine: The Mandatory Government and the Arab-Jewish Conflict, 1917–1929*, by Bernard Wasserstein (volume 10), *Order and Equipoise: the Peerage and the House of Lords, 1783–1806*, by Michael McCahill (volume 11), *Preachers, Peasants and Politics in Southeast Africa 1835–1880. African Christian Communities in Natal, Pondoland and Zulu-*

land, by Norman Etherington (volume 12), and *Linlithgow and India: a Study of British Policy and the Political Impasse in India, 1936–1943*, by S. A. G. Rizvi (volume 13).

At the ordinary meetings of the Society the following papers were read:

'The Republic and the Iron Chancellor: the pattern of Franco-German relations, 1871–1890', by Professor W. R. Fryer. (13 October 1978.)
'Books of Orders: the Making of English Social Policy, 1577–1631', by Dr. P. A. Slack. (2 February 1979.)
'The Political Beliefs of Winston Churchill', by Dr. P. Addison. (2 March 1979.)
'Family, Community and Cult on the eve of the Gregorian Reform', by Mr. R. I. Moore. (11 May 1979.)

At the Anniversary Meeting on 17 November 1978, the President, Sir John Habakkuk, delivered an address on 'The Rise and Fall of English Landed Families, 1600–1800'.

The Alexander Prize was awarded to Dr. Peter Dewey, B.A., for his essay 'Food Production and Policy in the United Kingdom, 1914–1918', which was read on 8 June 1979.

The Whitfield Prize was awarded to Dr. Marie Axton for her volume *The Queen's Two Bodies: Drama and the Elizabethan Succession*.

Membership

Council records with regret the death of 21 Fellows and 3 Associates since June 1978. Among these Council would mention especially M. A. Cárcano, a Corresponding Fellow, and Professor W. Rees, a former Vice-President. The resignation of 9 Fellows, 8 Associates and 11 Subscribing Libraries was received. Professor J. F. Ade Ajayi and Professor Masao Maruyama were elected Corresponding Fellows. 64 Fellows and 11 Associates were elected and 10 Libraries were admitted. The membership of the Society on 30 June 1979 comprised 1358 Fellows (including 95 Life Fellows and 80 Retired Fellows), 35 Corresponding Fellows, 167 Associates and 765 Subscribing Libraries (1323, 34, 167 and 766 respectively on 30 June 1978). The Society exchanged publications with 13 Societies, British and foreign.

Finance

Council has taken advantage of a year of financial stability to make a provision of £8,600 towards the publication expenses of two new *Guides and Handbooks* which are in an advanced stage of preparation. Taking this into account the deficit on the year of £680 compares favourably with last year's surplus of £7,163. Over the year income increased by £1,303, whereas net expenditure, if provision for the above-mentioned volumes is excluded, increased by only £546. It is

particularly noteworthy that secretarial and administrative expenses
rose by only £36. Income from the sale of the Society's publications
increased by £214, continuing the trend set last year.

Despite the small deficit on the year's Income and Expenditure
Account, the Accumulated Funds of the Society continue to grow,
the year's increase being £10,938.

ROYAL HISTORICAL SOCIETY
Balance Sheet as at 30 June 1979

30.6.78 £			£	£
	ACCUMULATED FUNDS			
	General Fund			
58,791	As at 1 July 1978	67,635		
1,681	*Add* Surplus on sale of Investments. . .	—		
7,163*	*Less* Excess of Expenditure and Provisions over Income for the year	680		
67,635				66,955
	Sir George Prothero Bequest			
14,867	As at 1 July 1978	15,835		
968	*Add* Surplus on sale of Investment . . .	—		
15,835				15,835
	Reddaway Fund			
5,000	As at 1 July 1978			5,000
	Andrew Browning Fund			
74,778	As at 1 July 1978	76,134		
1,356	*Add* Surplus on sale of Investment . . .	6,931		
76,134				83,065
164,604				170,855
	Miss E. M. Robinson Bequest			
21,120	As at 1 July 1978	23,675		
762	Balance of Estate received	—		
1,710	Interest, Dividends and Tax recoverable . .	2,287		
83	*Add* Surplus on sale of Investment . . .	—		
23,675				25,962
	A. S. Whitfield Prize Fund			
9,330	As at 1 July 1978	9,513		
583	Interest, Dividends and Tax recoverable . .	554		
9,913		10,067		
400	*Less* Prize awarded	400		
9,513				9,667
	Studies in History Account			
7,086	As at 1 July 1978	9,205		
2,958	Contributions received in year	1,895		
415	Interest received	1,028		
367	Royalties	898		
10,826		13,026		
1,621	*Less* Expenditure	1,575		
9,205				11,451
£206,997				£217,935
	REPRESENTED BY:			
	Investments			
159,478	Quoted Securities—at cost	156,076		
	Market Values £214,242 (1978: £217,215)			
5,424	Local Authority Bond	5,424		
27,500	Money on 7-day Deposit	48,000		
—	Due from Stockbrokers	241		
192,402				209,741
	Current Assets			
	Balances at Bank:			
3,098	Current Accounts	5,450		
27,535	Deposit Accounts	23,332		
54	Cash in Hand	67		
2,759	Income Tax Repayment due	37		
282	Payments in advance	488		
910	Stock of paper in hand	3,082		
34,638		32,456		
	Less Current Liabilities			
9,050	Subscriptions received in advance . 2,963			
539	Conference Fees received in advance 489			
44	Sundry Creditors 110			
10,410	Provision for publications in hand . 20,700			
20,043		24,262		
14,595				8,194
£206,997				£217,935

Note : The cost of the Society's Library, Furniture and Office Equipment and the Stock of its publications has been written off to the Income and Expenditure Account as and when required.

*Surplus.

ROYAL HISTORICAL SOCIETY

Income & Expenditure Account for the Year Ended 30 June 1979

30.6.78 £				£
	INCOME			
580	Subscriptions for 1978/79: Associates .		623	
8,774	Libraries		8,275	
11,003	Fellows		11,355	
20,357				20,25:
	(The Society also had 95 Life Fellows at 30 June 1979)			
959	Tax recovered on covenanted Subscriptions .			1,05€
2,067	Arrears of Subscriptions received in the year .			1,49(
11,928	Interest and Dividends received and Income Tax re-covered			14,60!
421	Royalties and Reproduction Fees . . .			26:
720	Donations and Sundry Receipts			7:
£36,452				£37.75
	EXPENDITURE			
	Secretarial & Administrative Expenses			
6,662	Salaries, Pension contributions and National Insurance.		7,480	
996	General Printing and Stationery . . .		1,112	
1,498	Postage, Telephone and Sundries . . .		971	
691	Accountancy and Audit		810	
302	Office Equipment		57	
38	Insurance.		63	
370	Meetings and Conference Expenses (Net cost) .		600	
500	Computer Program for Direct Debits . .		—	
11,057				11,0(
	Publications			
430	Directors' Expenses		472	
	Publishing costs in year:			
	Transactions, Fifth Series, Vol. 28 (total cost)	5,534		
	Camden, Fourth Series, Vol. 21 (total cost)	5,921		
	Camden, Fourth Series, Vol. 22 (total cost)	5,529		
		16,984		
	Less Provision made 30 June 1978 .	10,410		
6,276			6,574	
	Reprinting: *Handbook of Dates* . .	690		
	Reprinting: *Texts and Calendars* . .	—		
	Advance payment Handbook No. 10 Vol. 1	51		
2,155			741	
	Provision for Publications in Progress:			
	Transactions, Fifth Series Vol. 29 .	5,800		
	Camden, Fourth Series Vol. 23 . .	6,300		
	Guides and Handbooks Suppl. No. 2 .	4,300		
	Guides and Handbooks No. 10 Vol. 1 .	4,300		
10,410			20,700	
	Preparation expenses *Annual Bibliography*	865		
	Less Royalties received . . .	268		
210			597	
176	Storage of Stock		136	
19,657			29,220	
2,186	*Less* Sales of Publications		2,400	
17,471				26,8
£28,528	*Carried forward*			£37.

£ 28,528		EXPENDITURE (contd.)		£ 37,913
		Brought forward		37,913
		LIBRARY AND ARCHIVES		
	377	Purchase of Books and Publications	454	
	260	Library Assistance and Equipment .	—	
637	—			454
		OTHER CHARGES		
	34	Alexander Prize and Expenses.	18	
	25	Subscriptions to other bodies .	25	
	25	Prothero Lecture Fee	25	
	40	Cost of Jubilee Loyal Address .	—	
124	—			68
29,289		TOTAL EXPENDITURE .		38,435
36,452		INCOME AS ABOVE		37,755
£7,163*		EXCESS OF EXPENDITURE AND PROVISIONS OVER INCOME FOR THE YEAR		£680

*Surplus

SIR JOHN HABAKKUK, *President.*
M. ROPER, *Treasurer.*

We have examined the foregoing Balance Sheet and Income and Expenditure Account with the books and vouchers of the Society. We have verified the Investments and Bank Balances appearing in the Balance Sheet. In our opinion the foregoing Balance Sheet and Income and Expenditure Account are properly drawn up so as to exhibit a true and fair view of the state of affairs of the Society according to the best of our information and the explanations given to us and as shown by the books of the Society.

BEEBY, HARMAR & CO.,
Chartered Accountants.

9, LEONARD STREET,
LONDON, EC2A 4QS
1st August 1979

THE DAVID BERRY TRUST
Receipts & Payments Account for the Year Ended 30 June 1979

30.6.78 £	*Receipts*		£
	BALANCE IN HAND 1 July 1978:		
	Cash at Bank:		
3	Current Account .	3	
230	Deposit Account .	178	
530	483.63 Shares Charities Official Investment Fund .	530	
763			71
100	DIVIDEND ON INVESTMENT per Charity Commissioners		1C
7	INTEREST RECEIVED ON DEPOSIT ACCOUNT		2
£870			£8:

	Payments		
103	THE DAVID BERRY MEDAL .		
11	ADVERTISEMENT—CHANGE IN SCHEME		
45	ADVERTISEMENT AND LEAFLET FOR ENTRIES		
	BALANCES IN HAND 30 June 1979:		
	Cash at Bank:		
3	Current Account .	3	
178	Deposit Account .	305	
530	483.63 Shares Charities Official Investment Fund (Market Value 30.6.79 £677)	530	
711			8
£870			£8

We have examined the above account with the books and vouchers of the Trust and find it to
in accordance therewith.

BEEBY, HARMAR & C
Chartered Accountar

79, LEONARD STREET,
LONDON, EC2A 4QS
31st August 1979

The late David Berry, by his will dated 23rd day of April 1926, left £1,000 to provide in every th
years a gold medal and prize money for the best essay on the Earl of Bothwell or, at the discretior
the Trustees, on Scottish History of the James Stuarts I to VI in memory of his father, the late R
David Berry.

The Trust is regulated by a scheme sanctioned by the Chancery Division of the High Court of Jus
dated 23rd day of January 1930, and made in an action 1927 A.1233 David Anderson Berry deceas
Hunter and another v. Robertson and another and since modified by an order of the Charity Comr
sioners made on 11th January 1978, removing the necessity to provide a medal.

The Royal Historical Society is now the Trustee. The Investment held on Capital Account cons
of 634 Charities Official Investment Fund Shares (Market Values £882).

The Trustee will in every second year of the three-year period advertise inviting essays.

THE ROYAL HISTORICAL SOCIETY

REPORT OF COUNCIL, SESSION 1980-1981

THE Council of the Royal Historical Society has the honour to present the following report to the Anniversary Meeting.

A conference on 'Minorities' was held at the University of Leicester from 11 to 13 September 1980. The papers read were:

'From Strangers to Minorities in West Africa', by Professor J. D. Hargreaves.

'Religious Belief and Social Conformity: the *Converso* Problem in Late Medieval Córdoba', by Dr. J. H. Edwards.

'From Monopoly to Minority: Catholicism in Tudor England', by Dr. C. A. Haigh.

'The Irish in Nineteenth-century Britain: Problems of Integration', by Mr. M. A. G. Ó Tuathaigh.

'Historians, the Nationality Question and the Downfall of the Habsburg Empire', by Dr. A. Sked.

Twenty-four members of the Society and ten guests attended. The University of Leicester held a reception for them on 12 September. It was decided to hold the twelfth annual conference at the University of Southampton from 10 to 12 September 1981, on the topic 'Treason and Loyalty'.

An evening party was held for members and guests at University College London on 2 July 1980 for which 144 acceptances were received.

The representation of the Society upon various bodies was as follows: Professor F. M. L. Thompson and Mr. A. T. Milne on the Joint Anglo-American Committee exercising a general supervision over the production of the *Bibliographies of British History*; Professor G. W. S. Barrow, Mr. T. A. M. Bishop, Dr. P. Chaplais and Professor P. H. Sawyer on the Joint Committee of the Society and the British Academy established to prepare an edition of Anglo-Saxon charters; Professor E. B. Fryde on a committee to regulate British co-operation in the preparation of a new repertory of medieval sources to replace Potthast's *Bibliotheca Historica Medii Aevi*; Professor H. G. Koenigsberger on the Advisory Council on the Export of Works of Art; Professor G. H. Martin on the Council of the British Records Association; Professor A. M. Everitt on the Standing Conference for Local History; Mr. M. R. D. Foot on the Committee to advise the publishers of *The Annual Register*; Dr. C. R. J. Currie on the British Standards Institution Sub-Committee for drafting a new British standard for citing unpublished documents by bibliographical references. During the year Professor H. R. Loyn replaced Professor P. Grierson as the Society's representative on a committee to promote the publication of photographic records of the more significant collections of British coins; the

President and Professor J. J. Scarisbrick replaced Sir John Habakkuk and Mr. K. V. Thomas on the British National Committee of the International Historical Congress, and Professor K. Cameron replaced Miss K. Major on the Lincoln Archaeological Trust. Council received reports from its representatives.

Professor W. N. Medlicott represents the Society on the Court of the University of Exeter, Professor J. A. S. Grenville on the Court of the University of Birmingham, Professor Glanmor Williams on the Court of the University College of Swansea, and Professor C. N. L. Brooke on the British Sub-Commission of the Commission Internationale d'Histoire Ecclésiastique Comparée.

Sir John Habakkuk retired from the Presidency of the Society at the end of 1980. Council wishes to record its gratitude to him for his discerning and urbane conduct of the work of the Society. During the year Mr. E. L. C. Mullins and Mr. M. Roper resigned as Honorary Librarian and Honorary Treasurer after respectively 10 and 7 years in office. Council wishes to record its appreciation of the long and excellent service given by both. Dr. C. J. Kitching and Dr. A. G. Watson accepted Council's invitation to become Honorary Treasurer and Honorary Librarian respectively. Also during the year, Mr. J. S. Roper, the Society's Honorary Solicitor, died. Council wishes to record its appreciation of the helpful and valued service he gave to the Society. Professor R. M. Goode has accepted Council's invitation to fill the vacancy.

The Honorary Secretary represented the Society at the second one-day Conference on the administration of learned societies held at the Royal Society on 9 July 1980, on the topic 'Conservation Problems facing Learned Societies'.

During the year Council authorized the sending of a letter to the Chief Executive of the North Yorkshire County Council expressing its concern at the introduction of admission fees at the North Yorkshire Record Offices at Northallerton and York for consultation of information in the search rooms. Council has continued to maintain a close watch on the fate of the Public Record Office in Chancery Lane. The statement by the Lord Chancellor last December that a study group had been established to consider the feasibility of concentrating all public records on a single site at Kew has led to the establishment of a small working party consisting of the President, the Director of the Institute of Historical Research, the President of the Historical Association and the President of the Economic History Society to co-ordinate a response to the proposals of the Lord Chancellor's Public Record Office Feasibility Study Group.

At the Anniversary Meeting on 21 November 1980 at which the President, Sir John Habakkuk, retired under By-law XV, Professor J. C. Holt was elected to replace him. The Vice-Presidents retiring

under By-law XVI were Professor P. Grierson and Professor P. Ma-
thias. Professor P. H. Sawyer, Professor R. L. Storey and Mr. K. V.
Thomas were elected to replace them and to fill the vacancy left by
the elevation of Professor Holt to the presidency. The members of
Council retiring under By-law XIX were Professor R. Ashton, Profes-
sor D. C. Coleman, Professor B. Pullan and Dr. Joan Thirsk. Mr.
Peter Burke, Professor R. B. Dobson, Professor G. S. Holmes and
Professor D. E. Luscombe were elected to fill the vacancies. Sir John
Habakkuk was elected an Honorary Vice-President. Messrs. Beeby,
Harmar and Co. were appointed auditors for the year 1980-81 under
By-law XXXVIII.

Publications and Papers Read

Transactions, Fifth Series, volume 31, and *Guide to the Reports of the U.S.
Strategic Bombing Survey* (Guides and Handbooks, Suppl. Series No. 2)
went to press during the session and are due to be published in
November 1981 and September 1981, respectively. The following
works were published during the session: *Guide to the Local Administrative
Units of England*, volume 1 (Guides and Handbooks, No. 10), and *A
Guide to Bishops' Registers to 1646* (Guides and Handbooks, No. 11):
these were issued in place of a modern Camden and medieval Camden
respectively; the *Annual Bibliography of British and Irish History* (1979
publications); and five volumes in the STUDIES IN HISTORY series: *The
Purchase System in the British Army, 1660–1871*, by A. P. C. Bruce (volume
20); *The Manning of the British Navy during the Seven Years' War*, by
Stephen Gradish (volume 21); *Law-making and Law-makers in British
History*, by Alan Harding (ed.) (volume 22); *John Russell: First Earl of
Bedford*, by D. Willen (volume 23); *The Political Career of Sir Robert
Naunton*, by Roy Schreiber (volume 24).

The Library Association awarded the McColvin Prize to Professor
F. A. Youngs for his *Guide to the Local Administrative Units of England*,
volume 1.

At the ordinary meetings of the Society the following papers were
read:

'Charles II and his Parliaments', by Dr. J. L. Miller. (6 February 1981.)
'The Resettlement of England after the Barons' War, 1264–67', by Dr.
    C. H. Knowles. (20 March 1981.)
'Boethius in the Carolingian Schools', by Dr. Margaret T. Gibson. (24
    April 1981.)
'A Defence of World History', by Professor W. H. McNeill. (1 July 1981.)
    (The Prothero Lecture.)

The Alexander Prize was awarded to Mr. Christopher Tyerman
for his essay 'Marino Sanudo Torsello and the Lost Crusade: Lobbying in the Fourteenth Century', which was read on 29 May 1981. Mr.
Stephen Pierce was nominated *proxime accessit*.

The Whitfield Prize was awarded to Mr. D. L. Rydz for his *The Parliamentary Agents: A History*. Council authorized an increase in the award from £400 to £600, starting with the 1982 Prize.

Membership

Council records with regret the deaths of Dr. Ingvar Andersson, Professor W. P. Coolhaas, and Professor F. L. Ganshof, Corresponding Fellows, and of 21 Fellows and 2 Associates. Among these Council would mention especially Dame Lucy Sutherland, an Hon. Vice-President; Professor S. T. Bindoff and Professor J. Hurstfield, former Vice-Presidents; Professor May McKisack, Professor A. R. Myers, Professor G. R. Potter, former members of Council, and Mr. J. S. Roper, the Honorary Solicitor. The resignations of 5 Associates and 9 Subscribing Libraries were received. Professor Walther Hubatsch, Professor F. S. L. Lyons and Professor W. H. McNeill were elected Corresponding Fellows. 59 Fellows and 8 Associates were elected and 6 Libraries were admitted. The membership of the Society on 30 June 1981 comprised 1,417 Fellows (including 87 Life Fellows and 88 Retired Fellows), 38 Corresponding Fellows, 172 Associates and 756 Subscribing Libraries (1,379, 38, 171 and 759 respectively on 30 June 1980). The Society exchanged publications with 12 Societies, British and foreign.

Finance

The appearance of an overall deficit of £1,195 in the income and expenditure account is actually an indication of the generally success-ful outcome of the financial year, since Council had budgeted for a substantially greater deficit in order to promote an unusually ambi-tious publications programme. Expenditure rose by over 10%, domi-nated by *Guide to the Local Administrative Units of England*, volume I (Guides and Handbooks No. 10), easily the most expensive publica-tion ever undertaken by the Society and which proved so successful that a reprint was ordered within the year. Members will wish to note that publications of this magnitude within the existing level of subscriptions would be inconceivable were it not for the Andrew Browning Fund.

In November, Council, with the advice of Cazenoves, undertook a thorough review of investments, reducing the Society's holdings in low-yielding equities in an endeavour to maximize income. All the items sold had made healthy gains, as indicated in the Balance Sheet. Falling interest rates and continued uncertainty in the markets meant that investment income rose by only 4%, whilst overall income fell by a similar amount. No increase in members' subscriptions is thought necessary at present.

ROYAL HISTORICAL SOCIETY

BALANCE SHEET AS AT 30 JUNE 1981

30.6.80

£	£	ACCUMULATED FUNDS			£
	66,955	GENERAL FUNDS			
	592	As at 1 July 1980		73,748	
	6,201	*Add* Surplus on sale of Investments . . .		23,682	
		Add Excess of Income over Expenditure . . .		—	
	73,748			97,430	
		Less Excess of Expenditure and Provisions			
	—	over Income for the year		1,195	
73,748					96,235
		SIR GEORGE PROTHERO BEQUEST			
		As at 1 July 1980		15,835	
15,835		*Add* Surplus on sale of Investment . . .		208	
					16,043
5,000		REDDAWAY FUND			
		As at 1 July 1980			5,000
		ANDREW BROWNING FUND			
	83,065	As at 1 July 1980		82,001	
	(−1,064)	*Add* Surplus on sale of investments . . .		3,944	
82,001					85,945
176,584					£203,223
	25,962	MISS E. M. ROBINSON BEQUEST			
	3,068	As at 1 July 1980		29,030	
29,030		Interest, Dividends and Tax recoverable . . .		3,395	
					32,425
	9,667	A. S. WHITFIELD PRIZE FUND			
	1,092	As at 1 July 1980		10,359	
		Interest, Dividends and Tax recoverable . . .		1,121	
	10,759			11,480	
	400	*Less* Prize awarded 400			
		Less Loss on sale of Investment . . . 60		460	
10,359					11,020
	11,451	STUDIES IN HISTORY ACCOUNT			
	400	As at 1 July 1980		13,447	
	1,673	Contributions received in year		—	
	2,458	Interest received		1,814	
		Royalties received		1,192	
	15,982			16,453	
13,447	2,535	*Less* Expenditure		2,522	13,931
229,420					£260,599
		REPRESENTED BY:			
		INVESTMENTS			
	186,942	Quoted securities—at cost		193,727	
		Market Values £279,958			
		(1980: £240,386)			
	5,424	Local Authority Bond		5,424	
	16,500	Money at Call		23,000	
209,267	401	Due from Stockbrokers		35	
					222,186
		CURRENT ASSETS			
		Balances at Bank:			
	5,380	Current Accounts		5,259	
	41,137	Deposit Accounts		60,650	
	36	Cash in Hand		48	
	821	Income Tax Repayable		4,177	
	427	Payments in advance		799	
	8,110	Stock of paper in hand		4,046	
	55,911			74,979	
		Less CURRENT LIABILITIES			
	3,434	Subscriptions received in advance .	3,199		
	275	Conference Fees received in advance	586		
	20	Sundry Creditors	2,738		
	32,029	Provision for Publications in hand .	30,043		
	35,758			36,566	
20,153					38,413
229,420					£260,599

NOTE: The cost of the Society's Library, Furniture and Office Equipment and the Stock of its publications has been written off to the Income and Expenditure Account as and when acquired.

ROYAL HISTORICAL SOCIETY

Income and Expenditure Account for the Year Ended 30 June 1981

30.6.80

INCOME

£	£		£	£
	625	Subscriptions for 1980/81: Associates	601	
	10,416	Libraries	10,651	
	11,827	Fellows	11,336	
22,868				22,588
		(The Society also had 87 Life Fellows at 30 June 1981)		
1,004		Tax recovered on Covenanted Subscriptions . . .		1,010
1,453		Arrears of Subscriptions received in the year . . .		793
		Interest and Dividends received and Income Tax		
22,875		recovered		23,851
2,702		Royalties and Reproduction Fees		543
522		Donations and Sundry Receipts		580
51,424				£49,365

EXPENDITURE

SECRETARIAL AND ADMINISTRATIVE EXPENSES

£		£	£
	Salaries, Pension Contributions and National		
9,135	Insurance	11,755	
1,034	General Printing and Stationery	1,418	
1,229	Postage, Telephone and Sundries	1,723	
943	Accountancy and Audit	886	
10	Office Equipment	—	
110	Insurance	250	
793	Meetings and Conference Expenses (net cost) . .	977	
13,254			17,009

PUBLICATIONS

£		£	£	£
483	Directors' Expenses		537	
	Publishing costs in year:			
	Transactions, Fifth Series, Vol.			
	30 (total cost) . . .	7,582		
	Camden Fourth Series, Vol. 25			
	(total cost) . . .	7,337		
	Guides and Handbooks, No. 10,			
	Vol. 1	17,325		
	Guides and Handbooks, No. 11 . .	9,541		
		41,785		
	Less Provision made 30th June			
	1980 . . .	32,029		
493			9,756	
	Provisions for Publications in progress:			
	Transactions, Fifth Series,			
	Vol. 31	8,500		
	Guides and Handbooks, Supplement			
	No. 2	5,543		
	Guides and Handbooks, No. 10,			
32,029	Vol. 2	16,000	30,043	
	Preparation Expenses *Annual*			
	Bibliography	1,002		
(−345)	*Less* Royalties received . . .	611		
			391	
100	Storage and Insurance of Stock		118	
32,760			40,845	
2,247	Less Sales of Publications . . .	2,915		
	Sales of back numbers of			
	Transactions . . .	5,387	8,302	
30,513				32,54
43,767	*Carried forward*			49,55

30.6.30				£	£
£	£	*Brought forward*			49,552
43,767					
		LIBRARY AND ARCHIVES			
	1,307	Purchase of Books and Publications	649		
	—	Library Assistance	178		
1,307	——			——	827
		OTHER CHARGES			
	95	Alexander Prize and Expenses	74		
	25	Subscriptions to other bodies	32		
	29	Prothero Lecture Fee	75		
149	—			——	181
45,223		TOTAL EXPENDITURE			50,560
51,424		INCOME AS ABOVE			49,365
(Surplus) 6,201		EXCESS OF EXPENDITURE AND PROVISIONS OVER INCOME FOR THE YEAR			£1,195

J. C. HOLT, *President.*
C. J. KITCHING, *Treasurer.*

   We have examined the foregoing Balance Sheet and Income and Expenditure Account which have been prepared under the Historical Cost Convention with the books and vouchers of the Society. We have verified the Investments and Bank Balances appearing in the Balance Sheet. In our opinion the foregoing Balance Sheet and Income and Expenditure Account are properly drawn up so as to exhibit a true and fair view of the state of affairs of the Society according to the best of our information and the explanations given to us and as shown by the books of the Society.

BEEBY, HARMAR & CO.,
Chartered Accountants

79, LEONARD STREET,
LONDON, EC2A 4QS,
6th August 1981

THE DAVID BERRY TRUST

Receipts and Payments Account for the Year Ended 30 June 1981

30.6.80				
£	£	*Receipts*	£	£
		BALANCES IN HAND 1 July 1980:		
		Cash at Bank:		
	3	Current Account	3	
	305	Deposit Account	493	
		483.63 Shares Charities Official ·		
838	530	Investment Fund	530	
				1,026
		DIVIDEND ON INVESTMENT per Charity		
135		Commissioners		134
53		INTEREST RECEIVED ON DEPOSIT ACCOUNT . .		66
1,026				£1,226

		Payments		
—		Advertisement in *The Times*		54
		BALANCES IN HAND 30 June 1981:		
		Cash at Bank:		
	3	Current Account	3	
	493	Deposit Account	639	
		483.63 Shares Charities Official Investment		
1,026	530	Fund at cost (Market Value 30.6.81—£790) . .	530	1,172
1,026				£1,226

We have examined the above account with the books and vouchers of the Trust and find it to be in accordance therewith.

BEEBY, HARMAR & CO.,
Chartered Accountants

79, LEONARD STREET,
LONDON, EC2A 4QS.
6th August 1981

The late David Berry, by his will dated 23rd day of April 1926, left £1,000 to provide in every three years a gold medal and prize money for the best essay on the Earl of Bothwell or, at the discretion of the Trustees, on Scottish History of the James Stuarts I to VI, in memory of his father, the late Rev. David Berry.

The Trust is regulated by a scheme sanctioned by the Chancery Division of the High Court of Justice dated 23rd day of January 1930, and made in an action 1927 A1233 David Anderson Berry deceased, Hunter and another *v.* Robertson and another and since modified by an order of the Charity Commissioners made on 11th January 1978, removing the necessity to provide a medal.

The Royal Historical Society is now the Trustee. The Investment held on Capital Account consists of 634 Charities Official Investment Fund Shares (Market Value £1,035).

The Trustee will in every second year of the three-year period advertise, inviting essays.

ALEXANDER PRIZE

The Alexander Prize was established in 1897 by L. C. Alexander, F.R.Hist.S. It consists of a silver medal awarded annually for an essay upon some historical subject. Candidates may select their own subject provided such subject has been previously submitted to and approved by the Literary Director. The essay must be a genuine work of original research, not hitherto published, and one which has not been awarded any other prize. It must not exceed 6,000 words in length and must be sent in on or before 1 November of any year. The detailed regulations should be obtained in advance from the Secretary.

LIST OF ALEXANDER PRIZE ESSAYISTS (1898–1981)[1]

1898. F. Hermia Durham ('The relations of the Crown to trade under James I').

1899. W. F. Lord, BA ('The development of political parties during the reign of Queen Anne').

1901. Laura M. Roberts ('The Peace of Lunéville').

1902. V. B. Redstone ('The social condition of England during the Wars of the Roses').

1903. Rose Graham ('The intellectual influence of English monasticism between the tenth and the twelfth centuries').

1904. Enid W. G. Routh ('The balance of power in the seventeenth century').

1905. W. A. P. Mason, MA ('The beginnings of the Cistercian Order').

1906. Rachel R. Reid, MA ('The Rebellion of the Earls, 1569').

1908. Kate Hotblack ('The Peace of Paris, 1763').

1909. Nellie Nield, MA ('The social and economic condition of the unfree classes in England in the twelfth and thirteenth centuries').

1912. H. G. Richardson ('The parish clergy of the thirteenth and fourteenth centuries').

1917. Isobel D. Thornely, BA ('The treason legislation of 1531–1534').

1918. T. F. T. Plucknett, BA ('The place of the Council in the fifteenth century').

1919. Edna F. White, MA ('The jurisdiction of the Privy Council under the Tudors').

1920. J. E. Neale, MA ('The Commons Journals of the Tudor Period').

1922. Eveline C. Martin ('The English establishments on the Gold Coast in the second half of the eighteenth century').

1923. E. W. Hensman, MA ('The Civil War of 1648 in the east midlands').

1924. Grace Stretton, BA ('Some aspects of mediæval travel').

1925. F. A. Mace, MA ('Devonshire ports in the fourteenth and fifteenth centuries').

1926. Marian J. Tooley, MA ('The authorship of the *Defensor Pacis*').

[1] No award was made in 1900, 1907, 1910, 1911, 1913, 1914, 1921, 1946, 1948, 1956, 1969, 1975, and 1977. The Prize Essays for 1909 and 1919 were not published in the *Transactions*. No Essays were submitted in 1915, 1916 and 1943.

1927. W. A. Pantin, BA ('Chapters of the English Black Monks, 1215–1540').
1928. Gladys A. Thornton, BA, PhD ('A study in the history of Clare, Suffolk, with special reference to its development as a borough').
1929. F. S. Rodkey, AM, PhD ('Lord Palmerston's policy for the rejuvenation of Turkey, 1839–47').
1930. A. A. Ettinger, DPhil ('The proposed Anglo-Franco-American Treaty of 1852 to guarantee Cuba to Spain').
1931. Kathleen A. Walpole, MA ('The humanitarian movement of the early nineteenth century to remedy abuses on emigrant vessels to America').
1932. Dorothy M. Brodie, BA ('Edmund Dudley, minister of Henry VII').
1933. R. W. Southern, BA ('Ranulf Flambard and early Anglo-Norman administration').
1934. S. B. Chrimes, MA, PhD ('Sir John Fortescue and his theory of dominion').
1935. S. T. Bindoff, MA ('The unreformed diplomatic service, 1812–60').
1936. Rosamund J. Mitchell, MA, BLitt ('English students at Padua, 1460–1475').
1937. C. H. Philips, BA ('The East India Company "Interest", and the English Government, 1783–4').
1938. H. E. I. Phillips, BA ('The last years of the Court of Star Chamber, 1630–41').
1939. Hilda P. Grieve, BA ('The deprived married clergy in Essex, 1553–61').
1940. R. Somerville, MA ('The Duchy of Lancaster Council and Court of Duchy Chamber').
1941. R. A. L. Smith, MA, PhD ('The *Regimen Scaccarii* in English monasteries').
1942. F. L. Carsten, DPhil ('Medieval democracy in the Brandenburg towns and its defeat in the fifteenth century').
1944. Rev. E. W. Kemp, BD ('Pope Alexander III and the canonization of saints').
1945. Helen Suggett, BLitt ('The use of French in England in the later middle ages').
1947. June Milne, BA ('The diplomacy of John Robinson at the court of Charles XII of Sweden, 1697–1709').
1949. Ethel Drus, MA ('The attitude of the Colonial Office to the annexation of Fiji').
1950. Doreen J. Milne, MA, PhD ('The results of the Rye House Plot, and their influence upon the Revolution of 1688').
1951. K. G. Davies, BA ('The origins of the commission system in the West India trade').
1952. G. W. S. Barrow, BLitt ('Scottish rulers and the religious orders, 1070–1153').
1953. W. E. Minchinton, BSc (Econ) ('Bristol—metropolis of the west in the eighteenth century').
1954. Rev. L. Boyle, OP ('The *Oculus Sacerdotis* and some other works of William of Pagula').
1955. G. F. E. Rudé, MA, PhD ('The Gordon riots: a study of the rioters and their victims').
1957. R. F. Hunnisett, MA, DPhil ('The origins of the office of Coroner').
1958. Thomas G. Barnes, AB, DPhil ('County politics and a puritan *cause célèbre*: Somerset churchales, 1633').

1959. Alan Harding, BLitt ('The origins and early history of the Keeper of the Peace').
1960. Gwyn A. Williams, MA, PhD ('London and Edward I').
1961. M. H. Keen, BA ('Treason trials under the law of arms').
1962. G. W. Monger, MA, PhD ('The end of isolation: Britain, Germany and Japan, 1900–1902).
1963. J. S. Moore, BA ('The Domesday teamland: a reconsideration').
1964. M. Kelly, PhD ('The submission of the clergy').
1965. J. J. N. Palmer, BLitt ('Anglo-French negotiations, 1390–1396').
1966. M. T. Clanchy, MA, PhD ('The Franchise of Return of Writs').
1967. R. Lovatt, MA., DPhil, PhD ('The *Imitation of Christ* in late medieval England').
1968. M. G. A. Vale, MA, DPhil ('The last years of English Gascony, 1451–1453').
1970. Mrs Margaret Bowker, MA, BLitt ('The Commons Supplication against the Ordinaries in the light of some Archidiaconal Acta').
1971. C. Thompson, MA ('The origins of the politics of the Parliamentary middle groups, 1625–1629').
1972. I. d'Alton, BA ('Southern Irish Unionism: A study of Cork City and County Unionists, 1884–1914').
1973. C. J. Kitching, BA, PhD ('The quest for concealed lands in the reign of Elizabeth I').
1974. H. Tomlinson, BA ('Place and Profit: an Examination of the Ordnance Office, 1660–1714').
1976. B. Bradshaw, MA, BD ('Cromwellian reform and the origins of the Kildare rebellion, 1533–34').
1978. C. J. Ford, BA ('Piracy or Policy: The Crisis in the Channel, 1400–1403').
1979. P. Dewey, BA, PhD ('Food Production and Policy in the United Kingdom, 1914–1918').
1980. Ann L. Hughes, MA, PhD ('Militancy and Localism: Warwickshire Politics and Westminster Politics, 1643–1647').
1981. C. J. Tyerman, MA ('Marino Sanudo Torsello and the Lost Crusade: Lobbying in the Fourteenth Century').

DAVID BERRY PRIZE

The David Berry Prize was established in 1929 by David Anderson-Berry in memory of his father, the Reverend David Berry. It consists of a money prize awarded every three years for Scottish history. Candidates may select any subject dealing with Scottish history within the reigns of James I to James VI inclusive, provided such subject has been previously submitted to and approved by the Council of the Royal Historical Society. The essay must be a genuine work of original research not hitherto published, and one which has not been awarded any other prize. The essay should be between 6,000 and 10,000 words, excluding footnotes and appendices. It must be sent in on or before 31 October 1982.

LIST OF DAVID BERRY PRIZE ESSAYISTS (1937–76)[1]

1937. G. Donaldson, MA ('The polity of the Scottish Reformed Church *c.* 1460–1580, and the rise of the Presbyterian movement').

1943. Rev. Prof. A. F. Scott Pearson, DTh, DLitt ('Anglo-Scottish religious relations, 1400–1600').

1949. T. Bedford Franklin, MA, FRSE ('Monastic agriculture in Scotland, 1440–1600').

1955. W. A. McNeill, MA ('"Estaytt" of the king's rents and pensions, 1621').

1958. Prof. Maurice Lee, PhD ('Maitland of Thirlestane and the foundation of the Stewart despotism in Scotland').

1964. M. H. Merriman ('Scottish collaborators with England during the Anglo-Scottish war, 1543–1550').

1967. Miss M. H. B. Sanderson ('Catholic recusancy in Scotland in the sixteenth century').

1970. Athol Murray, MA, LLB, PhD ('The Comptroller, 1425–1610').

1973. J. Kirk, MA, PhD ('Who were the Melvillians: A study in the Personnel and Background of the Presbyterian Movement in late Sixteenth-century Scotland').

1976. A. Grant, BA, DPhil ('The Development of the Scottish Peerage').

[1]No Essays were submitted in 1940 and 1979. No award was made in 1946, 1952 and 1961.

WHITFIELD PRIZE

The Whitfield Prize was established by Council in 1976 as a money prize of £400 out of the bequest of the late Professor Archibald Stenton Whitfield, and is awarded annually to the author of the best work on an historical subject connected with England or Wales published or accepted for publication in the Society's STUDIES IN HISTORY series. The Award is made by Council in March of each year, upon the recommendation of the Editorial Board of STUDIES IN HISTORY, in respect of works published or accepted for publication in that series during the preceding calendar year. The Society reserves the right to withhold the award for any year in which no qualified work of a sufficiently high standard offers itself to the Editorial Board.

LIST OF WHITFIELD PRIZE WINNERS (1977–1980)

1977. K. D. Brown, MA, PhD (*John Burns*).
1978. Marie Axton, MA, PhD (*The Queen's Two Bodies: Drama and the Elizabethan Succession*).
1979. Patricia Crawford, MA, PhD (*Denzil Holles, 1598–1680: A study of his Political Career*).
1980. D. L. Rydz (*The Parliamentary Agents: A History*).

THE ROYAL HISTORICAL SOCIETY

(INCORPORATED BY ROYAL CHARTER)

OFFICERS AND COUNCIL— 1980

Patron
HER MAJESTY THE QUEEN

President
SIR JOHN HABAKKUK, MA, FBA.

Honorary Vice-Presidents
PROFESSOR C. R. CHENEY, MA, DLitt, LittD, FBA.
PROFESSOR A. G. DICKENS, CMG, MA, DLit, DLitt, LittD, FBA, FSA.
PROFESSOR G. R. ELTON, MA, PhD, LittD, FBA.
PROFESSOR SIR KEITH HANCOCK, KBE, MA, DLitt, FBA.
PROFESSOR R. A. HUMPHREYS, OBE, MA, PhD, DLitt, LittD, DLitt, DUniv.
THE HON SIR STEVEN RUNCIMAN, MA, DPhil, LLD, LittD, DLitt, LitD, DD,
      DHL, FBA, FSA.
SIR RICHARD SOUTHERN, MA, DLitt, LittD, DLitt, FBA.

Vice-Presidents
PROFESSOR P. GRIERSON, MA, LittD, FBA, FSA.
PROFESSOR P. MATHIAS, MA, FBA.
PROFESSOR J. MCMANNERS, MA, FBA.
PROFESSOR F. M. L. THOMPSON, MA, DPhil, FBA.
PROFESSOR J. H. BURNS, MA, PhD.
R. F. HUNNISETT, MA, DPhil.
PROFESSOR J. C. HOLT, MA, DPhil, FBA, FSA.
PROFESSOR GLANMOR WILLIAMS, MA, DLitt.

242

STANDING COMMITTEES—1980

Finance Committee
PROFESSOR T. C. BARKER, MA, PhD.
PROFESSOR J. H. BURNS.
PROFESSOR D. C. COLEMAN.
P. J. C. FIRTH.
PROFESSOR G. H. MARTIN.
And the Officers.

Publications Committee
DR P. F. CLARKE.
PROFESSOR RAGNHILD HATTON.
PROFESSOR H. R. LOYN.
PROFESSOR G. H. MARTIN.
PROFESSOR VALERIE PEARL, MA, DPhil, FSA.
PROFESSOR J. R. POLE, MA, PhD.
PROFESSOR J. J. SCARISBRICK.
PROFESSOR F. M. L. THOMPSON.
And the Officers.

Library Committee
PROFESSOR J. H. BURNS.
PROFESSOR P. COLLINSON.
PROFESSOR J. C. HOLT, MA, DPhil, FBA, FSA.
MRS I. J. THIRSK.
And the Officers.

LIST OF FELLOWS OF THE
ROYAL HISTORICAL SOCIETY

Names of Officers and Honorary Vice-Presidents are printed in capitals.
Those marked* have compounded for their annual subscriptions.

Abbott, A. W., CMG, CBE, Frithys Orchard, West Clandon, Surrey.
Abramsky, Professor Chimen A., MA, Dept of Hebrew and Jewish Studies,
   University College London, Gower Street, London WC1E 6BT.
Adair, Professor J. E., MA, PhD, Newlands Cottage, 41 Pewley Hill, Guild-
   ford, Surrey.
Adam, Professor R. J., MA, Easter Wayside, Hepburn Gardens, St Andrews
   KY16 9LP.
Adamthwaite, Professor A. P., BA, PhD, Dept of History, The University,
   Loughborough LE11 3TU.
Addison, P., MA, DPhil, Dept of History, The University, William Robertson
   Building, George Square, Edinburgh EH8 9JY.
*Addleshaw, The Very Rev. G. W. O., Flat 3, New Manor Home, 37 Station
   Road, Thames Ditton, Surrey.
Ainsworth, Sir John, Bt, MA, c/o National Library, Dublin 2, Ireland.
Akrigg, Professor G. P. V., BA, PhD, FRSC, 4633 West 8th Avenue, Van-
   couver, B.C., V6R 2A6, Canada.
Alcock, Professor L., MA, FSA, 29 Hamilton Drive, Glasgow G12 8DN.
Alder, G. J., BA, PhD, Dept of History, The University, Whiteknights,
   Reading RH6 2AA.
Alderman, G., MA, DPhil, 172 Colindeep Lane, London NW9 6EA.
Allan, D. G. C., MSc(Econ), PhD, 18c Franconia Road, London SW4 9EQ.
Allen, D. F., BA, PhD, School of History, The University, P.O. Box 363,
   Birmingham B15 2TT.
Allen, D. H., BA, PhD, 105 Tuddenham Avenue, Ipswich, Suffolk IP4 2HG.
ALLMAND, C. T., MA, DPhil, FSA, (*Literary Director*), 111 Menlove
   Avenue, Liverpool L18 3HP.
Altholz, Professor J., PhD, Dept of History, University of Minnesota, 614
   Social Sciences Building, Minneapolis, Minn. 55455, U.S.A.
Altschul, Professor M., PhD, Case Western Reserve University, Cleveland,
   Ohio 44106, U.S.A.
Anderson, Professor M. S., MA, PhD, London School of Economics, Hough-
   ton Street, London WC2A 2AE.
Anderson, Mrs O. R., MA, BLitt, Westfield College, London NW3 7ST.
Anderson, Miss S. P., MA, BLitt, 17-19 Chilworth Street, London W2
   3QU.
Andrew, C. M., MA, PhD, Corpus Christi College, Cambridge CB2 1RH.
Anglesey, The Most Hon., The Marquess of, FSA, FRSL, Plas-Newydd,
   Llanfairpwll, Anglesey LL61 6DZ.
Anglo, Professor S., BA, PhD, FSA, Dept of History of Ideas, University
   College, Swansea SA2 8PP.
Annan, Lord, OBE, MA, DLitt, DUniv, University of London, Senate
   House, Malet Street, London WC1E 7HU.
Annis, P. G. W., BA, 70 Northcote Road, Sidcup, Kent DA14 6PW.

Appleby, J. S., Little Pitchbury, Brick Kiln Lane, Great Horkesley, Colchester, Essex CO6 4EU.

Armstrong, Miss A. M., BA, 7 Vale Court, Mallord Street, London SW3.

Armstrong, C. A. J., MA, FSA, Gayhurst, Lincombe Lane, Boars Hill, Oxford OX1 5DZ.

Armstrong, Professor F. H., PhD, University of Western Ontario, London 72, Ontario, Canada.

Armstrong, W. A., BA, PhD, Eliot College, The University, Canterbury, Kent CT2 7NS.

Arnstein, Professor W. L., PhD, Dept of History, University of Illinois at Urbana–Champaign, 309 Gregory Hall, Urbana, Ill. 61801, U.S.A.

Artibise, Professor Alan F. J., PhD, 4431 Valmont Place, Victoria, B.C., V8N 5R7, Canada.

Ashton, Professor R., PhD, The Manor House, Brundall, near Norwich NOR 86Z.

Ashworth, Professor W., BSc(Econ), PhD, Dept of Econ. and Soc. History, The University, Bristol BS8 1RJ.

Aston, Mrs M. E., MA, DPhil, Castle House, Chipping Ongar, Essex.

Aston, T. H., MA, FSA, Corpus Christi College, Oxford OX1 4JF.

Auchmuty, Professor J. J., CBE, MA, PhD, DLitt, LLD, MRIA, FAHA, 9 Glynn Street, Hughes, ACT 2605, Australia.

Austin, M. R., BD, MA, PhD, The Glead, 2a Louvain Road, Derby DE3 6BZ.

Avery, D. J., MA, BLitt, 6 St James's Square, London SW1.

Axelson, Professor E. V., DLitt, Box 15, Constantia, 7848, S. Africa.

* Aydelotte, Professor W. O., PhD, State University of Iowa, Iowa City, Iowa, U.S.A.

Aylmer, G. E., MA, DPhil, FBA, St Peter's College, Oxford OX1 2DL.

Bahlman, Dudley W. R., PhD, Dept of History, Williams College, Williamstown, Mass. 01267, U.S.A.

Baillie, H. M. G., MBE, MA, FSA, 12b Stanford Road, London W8 3QJ.

Bailyn, Professor B., MA, PhD, LittD, LHD, Widener J., Harvard University, Cambridge, Mass. 02138, U.S.A.

Baker, D., BSc, PhD, Dept of History, Christ Church College, Canterbury, Kent CT1 1QU.

Baker, J. H., LLD, PhD, MA, St Catharine's College, Cambridge CB2 1RL.

Baker, L. G. D., MA, BLitt, Christ's Hospital, Horsham, West Sussex.

Baker, T. F. T., BA, Camden Lodge, 50 Hastings Road, Pembury, Kent.

Ballhatchet, Professor K. A., MA, PhD, 11 The Mead, Ealing, London W13.

Banks, Professor J. A., MA, Dept of Sociology, The University, Leicester LE1 7RH.

Barber, M. C., BA, PhD, Dept of History, The University, Whiteknights, Reading, Berks. RG6 2AA.

Barber, R. W., MA, FSA, Stangrove Hall, Alderton, near Woodbridge, Suffolk IP12 3BL.

Barker, E. E., MA, PhD, FSA, 60 Marina Road, Little Altcar, Formby, Merseyside L37 6BP.

Barker, Professor T. C., MA, PhD, Minsen Dane, Brogdale Road, Faversham, Kent.

Barkley, Professor the Rev. J. M., MA, DD, 2 College Park, Belfast, N. Ireland.

*Barlow, Professor F., MA, DPhil, FBA, Middle Court Hall, Kenton, Exeter.

Barnard, T. C., MA, DPhil, Hertford College, Oxford OX1 3BW.
Barnes, Miss P. M., PhD, Public Record Office, Chancery Lane, London WC2A 1LR.
Barnes, Professor T. G., AB, DPhil, University of California, Berkeley, Calif. 94720, U.S.A.
Barratt, Miss D. M., DPhil, The Corner House, Hampton Poyle, Kidlington, Oxford.
Barratt, Professor G. R. de V., PhD, 197 Belmont Avenue, Ottawa, Canada K1S OV7.
Barron, Mrs C. M., MA, PhD, 35 Rochester Road, London NW1.
Barrow, Professor G. W. S., MA, BLitt, DLitt, FBA, FRSE, The Old Manse, 19 Westfield Road, Cupar, Fife KY15 5AP.
Bartlett, C. J., PhD, 5 Strathspey Place, West Ferry, Dundee DD5 1QB.
Batho, Professor G. R., MA, Dept of Education, The University, 48 Old Elvet, Durham DH1 3JH.
Baugh, Professor Daniel A., PhD, Dept of History, McGraw Hall, Cornell University, Ithaca, N.Y. 14850, U.S.A.
Baxter, Professor S. B., PhD, 608 Morgan Creek Road, Chapel Hill, N.C. 27514, U.S.A.
Baylen, Professor J. O., MA, PhD, Georgia State University, 33 Gilmer Street S.E., Atlanta, Georgia 30303, U.S.A.
Beachey, Professor R. W., BA, PhD, 1 Rookwood, De La Warr Road, Milford-on-Sea, Hampshire.
Beales, D. E. D., MA, PhD, Sidney Sussex College, Cambridge CB2 3HU.
Beales, H. L., DLitt, 16 Denman Drive, London NW11.
Bealey, Professor F., BSc(Econ), Dept of Politics, The University, Taylor Building, Old Aberdeen AB9 2UB.
Bean, Professor J. M. W., MA, DPhil, 622 Fayerweather Hall, Columbia University, New York, N.Y. 10027, U.S.A.
Beardwood, Miss Alice, BA, BLitt, DPhil, 415 Miller's Lane, Wynnewood, Pa, U.S.A.
Beasley, Professor W. G., PhD, FBA, 172 Hampton Road, Twickenham, Middlesex TW2 5NJ.
Beattie, Professor J. M., PhD, Dept of History, University of Toronto, Toronto M5S 1A1, Canada.
Beaumont, H., MA, Silverdale, Severn Bank, Shrewsbury.
Beckerman, John S., PhD, 225 Washington Avenue, Hamden, Ct. 06518, U.S.A.
Beckett, Professor J. C., MA, 19 Wellington Park Terrace, Belfast 9, N. Ireland.
Beckingsale, B. W., MA, 8 Highbury, Newcastle upon Tyne NE2 3DX.
Bedarida, Professor F., CBE, 13 rue Jacob, 75006 Paris, France.
Beddard, R. A., MA, DPhil, Oriel College, Oxford OX1 4EW.
Beeler, Professor J. H., PhD, 1302 New Garden Road, Greensboro, N.C. 27410, U.S.A.
* Beer, E. S. de, CBE, MA, DLitt, FBA, FSA, 31 Brompton Square, London SW3 2AE.
Beer, Professor Samuel H., PhD, Faculty of Arts & Sciences, Harvard University, Littauer Center G-15, Cambridge, Mass. 02138, U.S.A.
Begley, W. W., 17 St Mary's Gardens, London SE11.
Behrens, Miss C. B. A., MA, Dales Barn, Barton, Cambridge.
Bell, P. M. H., BA, BLitt, School of History, The University, P.O. Box 147, Liverpool L69 3BX.

Beller, E. A., DPhil, Dept of History, Princeton University, N.J. 08540, U.S.A.

Beloff, Professor M., DLitt, FBA, St Antony's College, Oxford OX2 6JF.

Bennett, Capt. G. M., RN (ret.), DSC, Stage Coach Cottage, 57 Broad Street, Ludlow, Shropshire SY8 1NH.

Bennett, Rev. Canon G. V., MA, DPhil, FSA, New College, Oxford OX1 3BN.

Bennett, R. F., MA, Magdalene College, Cambridge CB3 0AG.

Bentley, M., BA, PhD, Dept of History, The University, Sheffield S10 2TN.

Best, Professor G. F. A., MA, PhD, School of European Studies. The University, Falmer, Brighton, Sussex BN1 9QN.

Biddiss, Professor M. D., MA, PhD, Dept of History, The University, White-knights, Reading RG6 2AA.

Biddle, M., MA, FSA, Winchester Research Unit, 13 Parchment Street, Winchester.

Bidwell, Brig. R. G. S., OBE, Royal United Services Institute, Whitehall, London SW1A 2ET.

Binney, J. E. D., DPhil, 6 Pageant Drive, Sherborne, Dorset.

Birch, A., MA, PhD, University of Hong Kong, Hong Kong.

Bishop, A. S., BA, PhD, Flat 8, William Court, 85 Highfield Hill, London SE19 3QF.

Bishop, T. A. M., MA, The Annexe, Manor House, Hemingford Grey, Hunts.

Black, Professor Eugene C., PhD, Dept of History, Brandeis University, Waltham, Mass. 02154, U.S.A.

Blair, P. Hunter, MA, LittD, Emmanuel College, Cambridge CB2 3AP.

Blake, E. O., MA, PhD, Roselands, Moorhill Road, Westend, Southampton SO3 3AW.

Blake, Professor J. W., CBE, MA, DLitt, 141 Seacoast Road, Limavady, Co Londonderry, N. Ireland.

Blake, Lord, MA, FBA, The Provost's Lodgings, The Queen's College, Oxford OX1 4AW.

Blakemore, H., PhD, 43 Fitzjohn Avenue, Barnet, Herts.

*Blakey, Professor R. G., PhD, c/o Mr Raymond Shove, Order Dept, Library, University of Minnesota, Minneapolis, Minn., U.S.A.

Blakiston, H. N., BA, 6 Markham Square, London SW3.

Blanning, T. W. C., MA, PhD, Sidney Sussex College, Cambridge CB2 3HU.

Blaxland, Major W. G., Lower Heppington, Street End, Canterbury, Kent CT4 7AN.

Blewett, Professor N., BA, DipEd, MA, DPhil, School of Social Sciences, Flinders University of S. Australia, Bedford Park, S. Australia 5042.

Blomfield, Mrs K., 8 Elmdene Court, Constitution Hill, Woking, Surrey GU22 7SA.

Blunt, C. E., OBE, FBA, FSA, Ramsbury Hill, Ramsbury, Marlborough, Wilts.

*Bolsover, G. H., OBE, MA, PhD, 7 Devonshire Road, Hatch End, Middle-sex HA5 4LY.

Bolton, Miss Brenda, BA, Dept of History, Westfield College, London NW3 7ST.

Bolton, Professor G. C., MA, DPhil, 6 Melvista Avenue, Claremont, Western Australia 6010.

Bolton, Professor W. F., AM, PhD, FSA, Douglass College, Rutgers University, New Brunswick, N.J. 08903, U.S.A.

Bond, B. J., BA, MA, Dept of War Studies, King's College, London WC2R 2LS.
Bond, M. F., CB, OBE, MA, FSA, 19 Bolton Crescent, Windsor, Berks.
Booker, J. M. L., BA, MLitt, White Hall, The Street, Wickham Bishops, Witham, Essex CM8 3NN.
Boon, G. C., BA, FSA, FRNS, National Museum of Wales, Cardiff CF1 3NP.
Borrie, M. A. F., BA, 142 Culford Road, London N1.
Bossy, Professor J. A., MA, PhD, Dept of History, University of York, Heslington, York YO1 5DD.
Bottigheimer, Professor Karl S., Dept of History, State University of New York at Stony Brook, Long Island, N.Y., U.S.A.
Bourne, Professor K., BA, PhD, London School of Economics, Houghton Street, London WC2A 2AE.
Bowker, Mrs M., MA, BLitt, The Cottage, Bailrigg Lane, Lancaster.
Bowyer, M. J. F., 32 Netherhall Way, Cambridge.
*Boxer, Professor C. R., DLitt, FBA, Ringshall End, Little Gaddesden, Berkhamsted, Herts.
Boyce, D. G., BA, PhD, Dept of Political Theory and Government, University College, Swansea SA2 8PP.
Boyle, Professor the Rev. L. E., DPhil, STL, Pontifical Institute of Mediaeval Studies, 59 Queen's Park, Toronto 181, Canada.
Boyle, T., Cert.Ed, BA, MPhil, Jersey Cottage, Mark Beech, Edenbridge, Kent TN8 5NS.
Boynton, L. O. J., MA, DPhil, FSA, Westfield College, London NW3 7ST.
Brading, D. A., MA, PhD, 28 Storey Way, Cambridge.
Bradshaw, B., MA, BD, PhD, Queens' College, Cambridge CB3 9ET.
Brand, P. A., MA, DPhil, Faculty of Law, University College Dublin, Belfield, Dublin 4, Ireland.
Brandon, P. F., BA, PhD, Greensleeves, 8 St Julian's Lane, Shoreham-by-Sea, Sussex BN4 6YS.
Breck, Professor A. D., MA, PhD, LHD, DLitt, University of Denver, Denver, Colorado 80210, U.S.A.
Brentano, Professor R., DPhil, University of California, Berkeley, Calif., U.S.A.
Brett, M., MA, DPhil, 7 Bardwell Road, Oxford OX2 6SU.
Bridge, F. R., PhD, The Poplars, Rodley Lane, Rodley, Leeds.
Bridges, R. C., BA, PhD, Dept of History, University of Aberdeen, King's College, Aberdeen AB9 2UB.
Briggs, Lord, BSc(Econ), MA, DLitt, Provost, Worcester College, Oxford OX1 2HB.
Briggs, J. H. Y., MA, Dept of History, University of Keele, Staffs. ST5 5BG.
Briggs, R., MA, All Souls College, Oxford OX1 4AL.
Brock, Professor M. G., MA, Nuffield College, Oxford OX1 1NF.
Brock, Professor W. R., MA, PhD, Dept of History, University of Glasgow, Glasgow G12 8QQ.
Brogan, D. H. V., MA, Dept of History, University of Essex, Colchester CO4 3SQ.
* Bromley, Professor J. S., MA, Merrow, Dene Close, Chilworth, Southampton SO1 7HL.
*Brooke, Professor C. N. L., MA, LittD, FBA, FSA, Faculty of History, West Road, Cambridge CB3 9EF.
Brooke, J., BA, 63 Hurst Avenue, Chingford, London E4 8DL.
Brooke, Mrs R. B., MA, PhD, c/o Faculty of History, West Road, Cambridge CB3 9EF.

Brooks, N. P., MA, DPhil, The University, St Andrews, Fife KY16 9AJ.
Brown, Professor A. L., MA, DPhil, Dept of History, The University, Glasgow G12 8QQ.
Brown, G. S., PhD, 1720 Hanover Road, Ann Arbor, Mich. 48103, U.S.A.
Brown, Judith M., MA, PhD, Dept of History, The University, Manchester M13 9PL.
Brown, K. D., BA, MA, PhD, Dept of Economic and Social History, The Queen's University, Belfast BT7 1NN, N. Ireland.
Brown, Miss L. M., MA, PhD, 93 Church Road, Hanwell, London W7.
Brown, Professor M. J., MA, PhD, 333 South Candler Street, Decatur, Georgia 30030, U.S.A.
Brown, P. R. Lamont, MA, FBA, Hillslope, Pullen's Lane, Oxford.
Brown, R. A., MA, DPhil, FSA, King's College, Strand, London WC2R 2LS.
Bruce, J. M., MA, 6 Albany Close, Bushey Heath, Herts. WD2 3SG.
Brundage, Professor J. A., Dept of History, University of Wisconsin at Milwaukee, Milwaukee, Wisconsin, U.S.A.
Bryant, Sir Arthur (W. M.), CH, CBE, LLD, Myles Place, 68 The Close, Salisbury, Wilts.
Bryson, Professor W. Hamilton, School of Law, University of Richmond, Richmond, Va. 23173, U.S.A.
Buchanan, R. A., MA, PhD, School of Humanities and Social Sciences, The University, Claverton Down, Bath BA2 7AY.
Buckland, P. J., MA, PhD, 6 Rosefield Road, Liverpool L25 8TF.
Bueno de Mesquita, D. M., MA, PhD, 283 Woodstock Road, Oxford OX2 7NY.
Buisseret, Professor D. J., MA, PhD, The Newberry Library, 60 West Walton Street, Chicago, Ill. 60610, U.S.A.
Bullock, Lord, MA, DLitt, FBA, St Catherine's College, Oxford OX1 3UJ.
Bullough, Professor D. A., MA, FSA, Dept of Mediaeval History, 71 South Street, St Andrews, Fife KY16 9AJ.
Burke, U. P., MA, Emmanuel College, Cambridge CB2 3AP.
Burleigh, The Rev. Professor J. H. S., BD, 21 Kingsmuir Drive, Peebles, EH45 9AA.
Burns, Professor J. H., MA, PhD, 39 Amherst Road, London W13.
Burroughs, P., PhD, Dalhousie University, Halifax, Nova Scotia, Canada.
Burrow, J. W., MA, PhD, Sussex University, Falmer, Brighton BN1 9QX.
Bury, J. P. T., MA, LittD, Corpus Christi College, Cambridge CB2 1RH.
Butler, Professor L. H., MA, DPhil, Royal Holloway College, Englefield Green, Surrey TW20 0EX.
Butler, R. D'O., CMG, MA, All Souls College, Oxford OX1 4AL.
Byerly, Professor B. F., BA, MA, PhD, Dept of History, University of Northern Colorado, Greeley, Colorado 80631, U.S.A.
Bythell, D., MA, DPhil, Dept of Economic History, University of Durham, 23-26 Old Elvet, Durham City DH1 3HY.

Cabaniss, Professor J. A., PhD, University of Mississippi, Box No. 253, University, Mississippi 38677, U.S.A.
Callahan, Professor Thomas, Jr., PhD, Dept of History, Rider College, Lawrenceville, N.J. 08648, U.S.A.
Calvert, Brig. J. M. (ret.), DSO, MA, 33a Mill Hill Close, Haywards Heath, Sussex.
Calvert, P. A. R., MA, PhD, AM, Dept of Politics, University of Southampton, Highfield, Southampton SO9 5NH.

Cameron, A., BA, 46 Dunster Road, West Bridgford, Nottingham.
Cameron, Professor J. K., MA, BD, PhD, St Mary's College, University of St Andrews, Fife KY16 9JU.
Cameron, Professor K., PhD, Dept of English, The University, Nottingham NG7 2RD.
Campbell, Professor A. E., MA, PhD, School of History, University of Birmingham, P.O. Box 363, Birmingham B15 2TT.
Campbell, J., MA, Worcester College, Oxford OX1 2HB.
* Campbell, Professor Mildred L., PhD, Vassar College, Poughkeepsie, N. Y., U.S.A.
Campbell, Professor R. H., MA, PhD, University of Stirling, Stirling FK9 4LA.
Canny, Professor N. P., MA, PhD, Dept of History, University College, Galway, Ireland.
Cant, R. G., MA, DLitt, 2 Kinburn Place, St Andrews, Fife KY16 9DT.
Cantor, Professor Norman F., PhD, University of Illinois at Chicago Circle, Box 4348, Chicago, Illinois 60680, U.S.A.
Capp, B. S., MA, DPhil, Dept of History, University of Warwick, Coventry, Warwickshire CV4 7AL.
*Carlson, Leland H., PhD, (address unknown).
Carlton, Professor Charles, Dept of History, North Carolina State University, Raleigh, N.C. 27607, U.S.A.
Carman, W. Y., FSA, 94 Mulgrave Road, Sutton, Surrey.
Carr, A. D., MA, PhD, Dept of Welsh History, University College of North Wales, Bangor, Gwynedd.
Carr, A. R. M., MA, FBA, St Antony's College, Oxford OX2 6JF.
Carr, W., PhD, 22 Southbourne Road, Sheffield S10 2QN.
Carrington, Miss Dorothy, 3 Rue Emmanuel Arene, 20 Ajaccio, Corsica.
Carter, Mrs A. C., MA, 12 Garbrand Walk, Ewell, Epsom, Surrey.
Carter, Jennifer J., BA, PhD, Johnston Hall, College Bounds, Old Aberdeen AB9 2TT.
Casey, J., BA, PhD, School of Modern Languages and European History, University of East Anglia, Norwich NR4 7TJ.
Catto, R. J. A. I., MA, Oriel College, Oxford OX1 4EW.
Chadwick, Professor W. O., DD, DLitt, FBA, Selwyn Lodge, Cambridge CB3 9DQ.
Challis, C. E., MA, PhD, 14 Ashwood Villas, Headingley, Leeds 6.
Chalmers, C. D., Public Record Office, Kew, Richmond, Surrey TW9 4DU.
Chambers, D. S., MA, DPhil, Warburg Institute, Woburn Square, London WC1H 0AB.
Chandaman, Professor C. D., BA, PhD, 23 Bellamy Close, Ickenham, Uxbridge UB10 8SJ.
Chandler, D. G., MA, Hindford, Monteagle Lane, Yately, Camberley, Surrey.
Chaplais, P., PhD, FBA, FSA, Lew Lodge, Mount Owen Road, Bampton, Oxford.
Charles-Edwards, T. M., DPhil, Corpus Christi College, Oxford OX1 4JF.
*CHENEY, Professor C. R., MA, DLitt, LittD, FBA, 236 Hills Road, Cambridge CB2 2QE.
Chibnall, Mrs Marjorie, MA, DPhil, FBA, 6 Millington Road, Cambridge CB3 9HP.
Child, C. J., OBE, MA, PhM, 94 Westhall Road, Warlingham, Surrey CR3 9HB.
Childs, J. C. R., BA, PhD, School of History, The University, Leeds LS2 9JT.

Childs, Wendy R., MA, PhD, School of History, The University, Leeds LS2
9JT.

Chrimes, Professor S. B., MA, PhD, LittD, 24 Cwrt-y-Vil Road, Penarth,
South Glam. CF6 2HP.

Christianson, Assoc. Professor P. K., PhD, Dept of History, Queen's University, Kingston, Ontario K7L 3N6, Canada.

Christie, Professor I. R., MA, FBA, 10 Green Lane, Croxley Green, Herts.
WD3 3HR.

Church, Professor R. A., BA, PhD, School of Social Studies, University of
East Anglia, Norwich NOR 88C.

Cirket, A. F., 71 Curlew Crescent, Bedford.

Clanchy, M. T., MA, PhD, FSA, Medieval History Dept, The University,
Glasgow G12 8QQ.

Clark, A. E., MA, 32 Durham Avenue, Thornton Cleveleys, Blackpool FY5
2DP.

Clark, Professor Dora Mae, PhD, 134 Pennsylvania Ave., Chambersburg,
Pa. 17201, U.S.A.

Clark, P. A., MA, Dept of History, The University, Leicester LE1 7RH.

Clarke, P. F., MA, PhD, St John's College, Cambridge CB2 1TP.

Clementi, Miss D., MA, DPhil, Flat 7, 43 Rutland Gate, London SW7
1BP.

Clemoes, Professor P. A. M., BA, PhD, Emmanuel College, Cambridge CB2
3AP.

Cliffe, J. T., BA, PhD, 263 Staines Road, Twickenham, Middx. TW2 5AY.

Clive, Professor J. L., PhD, 38 Fernald Drive, Cambridge, Mass. 02138,
U.S.A.

Clough, C. H., MA, DPhil, FSA, School of History, The University, P.O.
Box 147, Liverpool L69 3BX.

Cobb, H. S., MA, FSA, 1 Child's Way, Hampstead Garden Suburb, London
NW11.

Cobban, A. B., MA, PhD, School of History, The University, P.O. Box 147,
Liverpool L69 3BX.

Cockburn, J. S., LLB, LLM, PhD, c/o Public Record Office, Chancery Lane,
London WC2A 1LR.

Cocks, E. J., MA, Middle Lodge, Ardingly, Haywards Heath, Sussex.

*Code, Rt. Rev. Monsignor Joseph B., MA, STD, FRHistD, Littd., The
Pierre Choteau, 4440 Lindell Blvd., St Louis, Missouri 63108, U.S.A.

Cohn, H. J., MA, DPhil, University of Warwick, Coventry CV4 7AL.

Cohn, Professor N., MA, DLitt, FBA, 61 New End, London NW3.

Coleman, B. I., MA, PhD, Dept of History, The University, Exeter EX4
4QH.

Coleman, Professor D. C., BSc(Econ), PhD, FBA, Over Hall, Cavendish,
Sudbury, Suffolk.

Coleman, Professor F. L., MA, PhD, Dept of Economics & Econ. History,
Rhodes University, P.O. Box 94, Grahamstown 6140, S. Africa.

Collier, W. O., MA, FSA, 34 Berwyn Road, Richmond, Surrey.

Collinge, J. M., BA, 36 Monks Road, Enfield, Middlesex EN2 8BH.

Collins, Mrs I., MA, BLitt, School of History, The University, P.O. Box 147,
Liverpool L69 3BX.

Collinson, Professor P., MA, PhD, Keynes College, The University, Canterbury, Kent CT2 7NS.

Colvin, H. M., CBE, MA, FBA, St John's College, Oxford OX1 3JP.

Conacher, Professor J. B., MA, PhD, 151 Welland Avenue, Toronto 290,
Ontario, Canada.

Congreve, A. L., MA, FSA, Orchard Cottage, Cranbrook, Kent TN17 3NW.
Connell-Smith, Professor G. E., PhD, 7 Braids Walk, Kirkella, Hull, Yorks. HU10 7PA.
Constable, G., PhD, Dumbarton Oaks, 1703 32nd Street, Washington, D.C. 20007, U.S.A.
Contamine, Professor P., DèsL., 12 Villa Croix-Nivert, 75015 Paris, France.
Conway, Professor A. A., MA, University of Canterbury, Christchurch 1, New Zealand.
Cook, A. E., MA, PhD, 20 Nicholas Road, Hunter's Ride, Henley-on-Thames, Oxon.
Cook, C. P., MA, DPhil, 182 Stoneleigh Park Road, Ewell, Epsom, Surrey.
Cooke, Professor J. J., PhD, Dept of History, College of Liberal Arts, University of Mississippi, University, Miss. 38677, U.S.A.
Coolidge, Professor R. T., MA, BLitt, History Dept, Loyola Campus, Concordia University, 7141 Sherbrooke Street West, Montreal, Quebec H4B 1R6, Canada.
Cope, Professor Esther S., PhD, Dept of History, Univ. of Nebraska, Lincoln, Neb. 68508, U.S.A.
Corfield, Penelope J., MA, PhD, 99 Salcott Road, London SW11 6DF.
Cornell, Professor Paul G., PhD, Dept of History, University of Waterloo, Waterloo, Ontario, Canada N2L 3G1.
Cornford, Professor J. P., MA, The Brick House, Wicken Bonhunt, Saffron Walden, Essex CB11 3UG.
Cornwall, J. C. K., MA, 1 Orchard Close, Copford Green, Colchester, Essex.
Corson, J. C., MA, PhD, Mossrig, Lilliesleaf, Melrose, Roxburghshire.
Coss, P. R., BA, PhD, 7 Alexandra Way, Hall Close Chase, Cramlington, Northumberland.
Costeloe, M. P., BA, PhD, Hispanic and Latin American Studies, The University, 83 Woodland Road, Bristol BS8 1RJ.
Cowan, I. B., MA, PhD, University of Glasgow, Glasgow G12 8QQ.
Coward, B., BA, PhD, Dept of History, Birkbeck College, Malet Street, London WC1E 7HX.
Cowdrey, Rev. H. E. J., MA, St Edmund Hall, Oxford OX1 4AR.
Cowie, Rev. L. W., MA, PhD, 38 Stratton Road, Merton Park, London SW19 3JG.
Cowley, F. G., PhD, 17 Brookvale Road, West Cross, Swansea, W. Glam.
Cox, D. C., BA, PhD, 9 Mount Way, Pontesbury, Shrewsbury, Shropshire SY5 0RB.
Craig, R. S., BSc(Econ), 27 Ridgmount Gardens, Bloomsbury, London WC1E 7AS.
Cramp, Professor Rosemary, MA, BLitt, FSA, Department of Archaeology, The Old Fulling Mill, The Banks, Durham.
Crampton, R. J., BA, PhD, Rutherford College, The University, Canterbury, Kent CT2 7NP.
Craton, Professor M. J., BA, MA, PhD, Dept of History, University of Waterloo, Waterloo, Ontario, Canada.
*Crawley, C. W., MA, 1 Madingley Road, Cambridge.
Cremona, His Hon. Chief Justice Professor J. J., KM, DLitt, PhD, LLD, DrJur, 5 Victoria Gardens, Sliema, Malta.
Crisp, Olga, BA, PhD, 'Zarya', 1 Millbrook, Esher, Surrey.
Croft, Pauline, MA, DPhil, Dept of History, Royal Holloway College, Egham, Surrey TW20 0EX.
Crombie, A. C., BSc, MA, PhD, Trinity College, Oxford OX1 3BH.

Cromwell, Miss V., MA, University of Sussex, Falmer, Brighton, Sussex BN1 9QX.

Crook, D., MA, PhD, Public Record Office, Chancery Lane, London WC2A 1LR.

Cross, Miss M. C., MA, PhD, Dept of History, University of York, York YO1 5DD.

Crowder, C. M. D., MA, DPhil, Queen's University, Kingston, Ontario, Canada K7L 3N6.

Crowder, M., MA, 5 Bentinck Street, London W1M 5RN.

Crowe, Miss S. E., MA, PhD, 112 Staunton Road, Headington, Oxford.

Cruickshank, C. G., MA, DPhil, 15 McKay Road, Wimbledon Common, London SW20.

Cruickshanks, Eveline G., PhD, Full Point, Off Clarendon Road, Sevenoaks, Kent.

Cumming, Professor A., MA, DipMA, PGCE, PhD, Centre for Education Studies, University of New England, Armidale, Australia 2351.

Cumming, I., MEd, PhD, 672A South Titirangi Road, Titirangi, Auckland, New Zealand.

Cummins, Professor J. S., PhD, University College London, Gower Street, London WC1E 6BT.

Cumpston, Miss I. M., MA, DPhil, Birkbeck College, Malet Street, London WC1E 7HX.

Cunliffe, Professor M. F., MA, BLitt, DHL, Dept of American Studies, University of Sussex, Falmer, Brighton BN1 9QN.

Cunningham, Professor A. B., MA, PhD, Simon Fraser University, Burnaby 2, B.C., Canada.

Currie, C. R. J., MA, DPhil, Institute of Historical Research, Senate House, Malet Street, London WC1E 7HU.

Curtis, Professor L. Perry, PhD, Dept of History, Brown University, Providence, R.I. 02912, U.S.A.

Curtis, Timothy C., PhD, 16 Sherburn Park Drive, Rowlands Gill, Tyne and Wear.

Cushner, Rev. N. P., SJ, MA, 168 West Humboldt, Buffalo, New York 14214, U.S.A.

*Cuttino, Professor G. P., DPhil, FSA, Department of History, Emory University, Atlanta, Ga., 30322, U.S.A.

Dacre, Lord, MA, FBA, Peterhouse, Cambridge CB2 1RD.

Dakin, Professor D., MA, PhD, 7 Langside Avenue, London SW15.

Daunton, M. J., BA, PhD, Dept of History, University College London, Gower Street, London WC1E 6BT.

Davenport, Professor T. R. H., MA, PhD, Dept of History, Rhodes University, P.O. Box 94, Grahamstown 6140, South Africa.

Davies, C. S. L., MA, DPhil, Wadham College, Oxford OX1 3PN.

Davies, Canon E. T., BA, MA, 11 Tŷ Brith Gardens, Usk, Gwent.

Davies, I. N. R., MA, DPhil, 22 Rowland Close, Wolvercote, Oxford.

Davies, P. N., MA, PhD, Cmar, Croft Drive, Caldy, Wirral, Merseyside.

Davies, R. G., MA, PhD, Dept of History, The University, Manchester M13 9PL.

Davies, Professor R. R., BA, DPhil, University College of Wales, Dept of History, 1 Laura Place, Aberystwyth SY23 2AU.

Davies, Wendy, BA, PhD, Dept of History, University College London, Gower Street, London WC1E 6BT.

* Davis, G. R. C., MA, DPhil, 214 Somerset Road, London SW19 5JE.

Davis, Professor R. H. C., MA, FBA, FSA, 56 Fitzroy Avenue, Harborne, Birmingham B17 8RJ.

Davis, Professor Richard W., Dept of History, Washington University, St Louis, Missouri 63130, U.S.A.

* Dawe, D. A., 46 Green Lane, Purley, Surrey.

Deane, Miss Phyllis M., MA, Newnham College, Cambridge CB3 9DF.

* Deeley, Miss A. P., MA, 41 Linden Road, Bicester, Oxford.

de la Mare, Miss A. C., MA, PhD, Bodleian Library, Oxford.

Denham, E. W., MA, 27 The Drive, Northwood, Middx., HA6 1HW.

Dennis, P. J., MA, PhD, Dept of History, Royal Military College, Duntroon, A.C.T. 2600, Australia.

Denton, J. H., BA, PhD, Dept of History, The University, Manchester M13 9PL.

Dewey, P. E., BA, PhD, Dept of History, Royal Holloway College, Englefield Green, Surrey TW20 0EX.

DICKENS, Professor A. G., CMG, MA, DLit, DLitt, LittD, FBA, FSA, Institute of Historical Research, University of London, Senate House, London WC1E 7HU.

Dickinson, H. T., MA, PhD, Dept of Modern History, The University, Edinburgh EH8 9YL.

Dickinson, Rev. J. C., MA, FSA, Yew Tree Cottage, Barngarth, Cartmel, South Cumbria.

Dickson, P. G. M., MA, DPhil, St Catherine's College, Oxford OX1 3UJ.

Diké, Professor K. O., MA, PhD, Dept of History, Harvard University, Cambridge, Mass. 02138, U.S.A.

Dilks, Professor D. N., BA, Dept of International History, The University, Leeds LS2 9JT.

Dilworth, Rev. G. M., OSB, MA, PhD, Columba House, 16 Drummond Place, Edinburgh EH3 6PL.

Dinwiddy, J. R., PhD, Dept of History, Royal Holloway College, Englefield Green, Surrey TW20 0EX.

Ditchfield, G. McC, BA, PhD, Eliot College, University of Kent, Canterbury, Kent CT2 7NP.

Dobson, Professor R. B., MA, DPhil, Dept of History, The University, Heslington, York YO1 5DD.

Dockrill, M. L., MA, BSc(Econ), PhD, King's College, Strand, London WC2R 2LS.

* Dodwell, Miss B., MA, The University, Reading RG6 2AH.

Dodwell, Professor C. R., MA, PhD, FSA, History of Art Department, The University, Manchester M13 9PL.

Dolley, Assoc. Professor R. H. M., BA, MRIA, FSA, Dept of History, University of New England, 2351 Armidale, N.S.W., Australia.

Don Peter, The Right Revd. Monsignor W. L. A., MA, PhD, Bethany, Bolawalana, Negombo, Sri Lanka.

*Donaldson, Professor G., MA, PhD, DLitt, FBA, 6 Pan Hay, Dysart, Fife KY1 2TL.

Donaldson, Professor P. S., MA, PhD, Dept of Humanities, 14n-422, Massachusetts Institute of Technology, Cambridge, Mass. 02139, U.S.A.

*Donaldson-Hudson, Miss R., BA, (address unknown).

Donoughue, B., MA, DPhil, 7 Brookfield Park, London NW5 1ES.

Dore, R. N., MA, Holmrook, 19 Chapel Lane, Hale Barns, Altrincham, Cheshire WA15 0AB.

Douglas, Professor D. C., MA, DLitt, FBA, 4 Henleaze Gardens, Bristol.

Downer, L. J., MA, LLB, Mediaeval Studies, Australian National University, Canberra, Australia.
Doyle, A. I., MA, PhD, University College, The Castle, Durham.
Doyle, W., MA, DPhil, Dept of History, The University, Heslington, York YO1 5DD.
Driver, J. T., MA, BLitt, 25 Abbot's Grange, Chester CH2 1AJ.
*Drus, Miss E., MA, The University, Southampton SO9 5NH.
Duckham, Professor B. F., MA, Dept of History, St David's University College, Lampeter, Dyfed SA48 7ED.
Duggan, C., PhD, King's College, Strand, London WC2R 2LS.
Dugmore, The Rev. Professor C. W., DD, Thame Cottage, The Street, Puttenham, Guildford, Surrey GU3 1AT.
Duke, A. C., MA, Dept of History, The University, Southampton SO9 5NH.
Duly, L. C., PhD, Bemidji State University, Bemidji, Minn. 56601, U.S.A.
Dumville, D. N., MA, PhD, Dept of Anglo-Saxon, Norse and Celtic, 9 West Road, Cambridge CB3 9DP.
Dunbabin, J. P. D., MA, St Edmund Hall, Oxford OX1 4AR.
Duncan, Professor A. A. M., MA, The University, 9 University Gardens, Glasgow G12 8QH.
Dunham, Professor W. H., PhD, 200 Everit Street, New Haven, Conn. 06511, U.S.A.
Dunn, Professor R. S., PhD, Dept of History, The College, University of Pennsylvania, Philadelphia, Pa. 19104, U.S.A.
Dunning, R. W., BA, PhD, FSA, Musgrove Manor East, Barton Close, Taunton TA1 4RU.
Durack, Mrs I. A., MA, PhD, University of Western Australia, Crawley, Western Australia.
Durie, A. J., MA, PhD, Dept of Economic History, Edward Wright Building, The University, Aberdeen AB9 2TY.
Dykes, D. W., MA, Cherry Grove, Welsh St Donats, nr Cowbridge, Glam. CF7 7SS.

Earle, P., BSc(Econ), PhD, Dept of Economic History, London School of Economics, Houghton Street, London WC2A 2AE.
Eastwood, Rev. C. C., PhD, Heathview, Monks Lane, Audlem, Cheshire.
Eckles, Professor R. B., PhD, Apt 2, 251 Brahan Blvd., San Antonio, Texas 78215, U.S.A.
Ede, J. R., CB, MA, Palfreys, East Street, Drayton, Langport, Somerset TA10 0JZ.
Edmonds, Professor E. L., MA, PhD, University of Prince Edward Island, Charlottetown, Prince Edward Island, Canada.
Edwards, F. O., SJ, BA, FSA, 114 Mount Street, London W1Y 6AH.
Edwards, Professor R. W. D., MA, PhD, DLitt, 21 Brendan Road, Donnybrook, Dublin 4, Ireland.
Ehrman, J. P. W., MA, FBA, FSA, The Mead Barns, Taynton, Nr Burford, Oxfordshire OX8 5UH.
Eisenstein, Professor Elizabeth L., PhD, 82 Kalorama Circle N.W., Washington D.C. 20008, U.S.A.
Eldridge, C. C., PhD, Dept of History, Saint David's University College, Lampeter, Dyfed SA48 7ED.
Elliott, Professor J. H., MA, PhD, FBA, King's College, Strand, London WC2R 2LS.
Ellis, R. H., MA, FSA, Cloth Hill, 6 The Mount, London NW3.

Ellis, S. G., BA, MA, PhD, Dept of History, University College, Galway, Ireland.

Ellul, M., BArch, DipArch, 'Pauline', 55 Old Railway Road, Birkirkara, Malta.

Elrington, C. R., MA, FSA, Institute of Historical Research, Senate House, London WC1E 7HU.

ELTON, Professor G. R., MA, PhD, LittD, FBA, 30 Millington Road, Cambridge CB3 9HP.

Elvin, L., FSA, FRSA, 10 Almond Avenue, Swanpool, Lincoln LN6 0HB.

*Emmison, F. G., MBE, PhD, DUniv, FSA, 8 Coppins Close, Chelmsford, Essex CM2 6AY.

d'Entrèves, Professor A. P., DPhil, Strada Ai Ronchi 48, Cavoretto 10133, Torino, Italy.

Erickson, Charlotte, J., PhD, London School of Economics, Houghton Street, London WC2A 2AE.

*Erith, E. J., Shurlock House, Shurlock Row, Berkshire.

Erskine, Mrs A. M., MA, BLitt, FSA, 44 Birchy Barton Hill, Exeter EX1 3EX.

Evans, Mrs A. K. B., PhD, FSA, White Lodge, 25 Knighton Grange Road, Leicester LE2 2LF.

Evans, Sir David (L.), OBE, BA, DLitt, 2 Bay Court, Doctors Commons Road, Berkhamsted, Herts.

Evans, E. J., MA, PhD, Dept of History, Furness College, University of Lancaster, Bailrigg, Lancaster LA1 4YG.

Evans, Gillian R., PhD, Sidney Sussex College, Cambridge CB2 3HU.

Evans, R. J., MA, DPhil, School of European Studies, University of East Anglia, Norwich NR4 7TJ.

Evans, R. J. W., MA, PhD, Brasenose College, Oxford OX1 4AJ.

Evans, The Very Rev. S. J. A., CBE, MA, FSA, The Old Manor, Fulbourne, Cambs.

Everitt, Professor A. M., MA, PhD, The University, Leicester LE1 7RH.

Eyck, Professor U. F. J., MA, BLitt, Dept of History, University of Calgary, Alberta T2N IN4, Canada.

Fage, Professor J. D., MA, PhD, Centre of West African Studies, The University, Birmingham B15 2TT.

Fagg, J. E., MA, 47 The Avenue, Durham DH1 4ED.

Fairs, G. L., MA, Thornton House, Bean Street, Hay-on-Wye, Hereford HR3 5AN.

Falkus, M. E., BSc (Econ), Dept of History, London School of Economics, Houghton Street, London WC2A 2AE.

Farmer, D. F. H., BLitt, FSA, The University, Reading RG6 2AH.

Farr, M. W., MA, FSA, 12 Emscote Road, Warwick.

Fearn, Rev. Prebendary H., MA, PhD, Holy Trinity Vicarage, 6 Wildwood, Northwood, Middlesex.

Fell, Miss C. E., MA, Dept of English, The University, Nottingham NG7 2RD.

Fenlon, D. B., BA, PhD, Pontifico Collegio Beda, Viale di S. Paolo 18, 00146 Rome.

Fenn, Rev. R. W. D., MA, BD, FSAScot, The Ditch, Bradnor View, Kington, Herefordshire.

Ferguson, Professor A. B., PhD, Dept of History, 6727 College Station, Duke University, Durham, N.C. 27708, U.S.A.

Feuchtwanger, E., MA, PhD, Highfield House, Dean Sparsholt, nr Winchester, Hants.
Fieldhouse, D. K., MA, Nuffield College, Oxford OX1 1NF.
Finer, Professor S. E., MA, All Souls College, Oxford OX1 4AL.
Fines, J., MA, PhD, 119 Parklands Road, Chichester.
Finlayson, G. B. A. M., MA, BLitt, 11 Burnhead Road, Glasgow G43 2SU.
Finley, Professor M. I., MA, PhD, DLitt, FBA, Darwin College, Cambridge CB3 9EU.
Fisher, D. J. V., MA, Jesus College, Cambridge CB3 9AD.
Fisher, Professor F. J., MA, London School of Economics, Houghton Street, London WC2A 2AE.
Fisher, F. N., Duckpool, Ashleyhay, Wirksworth, Derby DE4 4AJ.
Fisher, J. R., BA, MPhil, PhD, 6 Meadway, Upton, Wirral, Merseyside L49 6JG.
Fisher, R. M., MA, PhD, Dept of History, University of Queensland, St Lucia, Queensland, Australia 4067.
Fisher, Professor S. N., PhD, Box 162, Worthington, Ohio 43085, U.S.A.
Fitch, Dr M. F. B., FSA, 37 Avenue de Montoie, 1007 Lausanne, Switzerland.
Fletcher, A. J., MA, 16 Southbourne Road, Sheffield S10 2QN.
*Fletcher, The Rt Hon The Lord, PC, BA, LLD, FSA, The Barn, The Green, Sarratt, Rickmansworth, Herts. WD3 6BP.
Flint, Professor J. E., MA, PhD, Dalhousie University, Halifax, Nova Scotia B3H 3J5, Canada.
Flint, Valerie I. J., MA, DPhil, Dept of History, The University, Private Bag, Auckland, New Zealand.
Floud, Professor R. C., MA, DPhil, Dept of History, Birkbeck College, Malet Street, London WC1E 7HX.
Fogel, Professor Robert W., PhD, Littauer Center 209, Cambridge, Mass. 02138, U.S.A.
Foot, M. R. D., MA, BLitt, 88 Heath View, London N2 0QB.
Forbes, D., MA, 89 Gilbert Road, Cambridge.
Ford, W. K., 48 Harlands Road, Haywards Heath, West Sussex RH16 1LS.
Forster, G. C. F., BA, FSA, The University, Leeds LS2 9JT.
Foster, Professor Elizabeth R., AM, PhD, 205 Strafford Avenue, Wayne, Pa. 19087, U.S.A.
Foster, R. F., MA, PhD, Dept of History, Birkbeck College, Malet Street, London WC1E 7HX.
Fowler, Professor K. A., BA, PhD, 2 Nelson Street, Edinburgh 3.
Fox, L., OBE, DL, LHD, MA, FSA, FRSL, Silver Birches, 27 Welcombe Road, Stratford-upon-Avon.
Fox, R., MA, DPhil, The University, Bailrigg, Lancaster LA1 4YG.
Frame, R. F., MA, PhD, Dept of History, The University, 43 North Bailey, Durham DH1 3HP.
Francis, A. D., CBE, MVO, MA, 21 Cadogan Street, London SW3.
Franklin, R. M., BA, Baldwins End, Eton College, Windsor, Berks.
*Fraser, Miss C. M., PhD, 39 King Edward Road, Tynemouth, Tyne and Wear NE30 2RW.
Fraser, D., BA, MA, PhD, 12 Primley Park Avenue, Leeds LS17 7JA.
Fraser, Professor Peter, MA, PhD, Dept of History, Dalhousie University, Halifax 8, Nova Scotia, Canada.
Freeden, M. S., DPhil, Mansfield College, Oxford OX1 3TF.
Frend, Professor W. H. C., MA, DPhil, DD, FRSE, FSA, Marbrae, Balmaha, Stirlingshire.

Fritz, Professor Paul S., BA, MA, PhD, Dept of History, McMaster University, Hamilton, Ontario, Canada.
Fryde, Professor E. B., DPhil, Preswylfa, Trinity Road, Aberystwyth, Dyfed.
Fryde, Natalie M., BA, DrPhil, Preswylfa, Trinity Road, Aberystwyth, Dyfed.
*Fryer, Professor C. E., MA, PhD, (address unknown).
Fryer, Professor W. R., BLitt, MA, 68 Grove Avenue, Chilwell, Beeston, Notts. NG9 4DX.
Frykenberg, Professor R. E., MA, PhD, 1840 Chadbourne Avenue, Madison, Wis. 53705, U.S.A.
Fuidge, Miss N. M., 13 Havercourt, Haverstock Hill, London NW3.
*Furber, Professor H., MA, PhD, History Department, University of Pennsylvania, Philadelphia, Pa., U.S.A.
Fussell, G. E., DLitt, 55 York Road, Sudbury, Suffolk CO10 6NF.
Fyrth, H., BSc(Econ), Dept of Extra Mural Studies, University of London, 7 Ridgemount Street, London WC1.

Gabriel, Professor A. L., PhD, FMAA, CFIF, CFBA, P.O. Box 578, University of Notre Dame, Notre Dame, Indiana 46556, U.S.A.
* Galbraith, Professor J. S., BS, MA, PhD, University of California, Los Angeles, Calif. 90024, U.S.A.
Gale, Professor H. P. P., OBE, PhD, 6 Nassau Road, London SW13 9QE.
Gale, W. K. V., 19 Ednam Road, Goldthorn Park, Wolverhampton WV4 5BL.
Gann, L. H., MA, BLitt, DPhil, Hoover Institution, Stanford University, Stanford, Calif. 94305, U.S.A.
Gash, Professor N., MA, BLitt, FBA, Gowrie Cottage, 73 Hepburn Gardens, St Andrews, Fife.
Gee, E. A., MA, DPhil, FSA, 28 Trentholme Drive, The Mount, York YO2 2DG.
Genet, J.-Ph, Agrégé d'Histoire, 98 Boulevard Beaumarchais, Paris 75011.
Gentles, Professor I., BA, MA, PhD, Dept of History, Glendon College, University of York, Toronto, Canada.
Gerlach, Professor D. R., MA, PhD, University of Akron, Akron, Ohio 44325, U.S.A.
GIBBS, G. C., MA, (*Hon. Secretary*), Birkbeck College, Malet Street, London WC1E 7HX.
Gibbs, Professor N. H., MA, DPhil, All Souls College, Oxford OX1 4AL.
Gibson, Margaret T., MA, DPhil, School of History, The University, P.O. Box 147, Liverpool L69 3BX.
Gifford, Miss D. H., PhD, FSA, Public Record Office, Chancery Lane, London WC2A 1LR.
Gilbert, Professor Bentley B., PhD, Dept of History, University of Illinois at Chicago Circle, Box 4348, Chicago, Ill. 60680, U.S.A.
Gilley, S., BA, DPhil, Dept of Theology, University of Durham, Abbey House, Palace Green, Durham DH1 3RS.
Ginter, Professor D.E., AM, PhD, Dept of History, Sir George Williams University, Montreal 107, Canada.
Girtin, T., MA, Butter Field House, Church Street, Old Isleworth, Mddx.
Gleave, Group Capt. T. P., CBE, RAF (ret.), Willow Bank, River Gardens, Bray-on-Thames, Berks.
*Glover, Professor R. G., MA, PhD, Carleton University, Ottawa 1, Canada.
*Godber, Miss A. J., MA, FSA, Mill Lane Cottage, Willington, Bedford.

*Godfrey, Professor J. L., MA, PhD, 231 Hillcrest Circle, Chapel Hill, N.C., U.S.A.

Goldsmith, Professor M. M., PhD, Dept of Politics, University of Exeter, Exeter EX4 4RJ.

Goldthorp, L. M., MA, Wilcroft House, Pecket Well, Hebden Bridge, West Yorks. HX7 8QY.

Gollin, Professor A., DLitt, University of California, Dept of History, Santa Barbara, Calif. 93106, U.S.A.

Gooch, John, BA, PhD, Dept of History, The University, Bailrigg, Lancaster LA1 4YG.

Goodman, A. E., MA, BLitt, Dept of Medieval History, The University, Edinburgh EH8 9YL.

Goodspeed, Professor D. J., BA, 164 Victoria Street, Niagara-on-the-Lake, Ontario, Canada.

*Gopal, Professor S., MA, DPhil, 30 Edward Elliot Road, Mylapore, Madras, India.

Gordon-Brown, A., Velden, Alexandra Road, Wynberg, CP., South Africa.

Goring, J. J., MA, PhD, Little Iwood, Rushlake Green, Heathfield, East Sussex TN21 9QS.

Gorton, L. J., MA, 41 West Hill Avenue, Epsom, Surrey.

Gosden, P. H. J. H., MA, PhD, The University, School of Education, Leeds LS2 9JT.

Gough, Professor Barry M., PhD, History Dept, Wilfrid Laurier University, Waterloo, Ontario, Canada N2L 3C5.

Gowing, Professor Margaret, MA, DLitt, BSc(Econ), FBA, Linacre College, Oxford OX1 1SY.

*Graham, Professor G. S., MA, PhD, DLitt, LLD, Hobbs Cottage, Beckley, Rye, Sussex.

Gransden, Mrs A., MA, PhD, FSA, Dept of History, The University, Nottingham NG7 2RD.

Grattan-Kane, P., 12 St John's Close, Helston, Cornwall.

Graves, Professor Edgar B., PhD, LLD, LHD, 318 College Hill Road, Clinton, New York 13323, USA.

Gray, Professor J. R., MA, PhD, School of Oriental and African Studies, University of London, London WC1E 7HP.

Gray, J. W., MA, Dept of Modern History, The Queen's University of Belfast, Belfast BT7 1NN, N. Ireland.

Gray, Miss M., MA, BLitt, 10 Clod Lane, Haslingden, Rossendale, Lancs. BB4 6LR.

Greaves, Mrs R. L., PhD, 1920 Hillview Road, Lawrence, Kansas 66044, U.S.A.

Green, H., BA, 16 Brands Hill Avenue, High Wycombe, Bucks. HP13 5QA.

Green, Rev. V. H. H., MA, DD, Lincoln College, Oxford OX1 3DR.

Greene, Professor Jack P., Dept of History, Johns Hopkins University, Baltimore, Md. 21218, U.S.A.

Greenhill, B. J., CMG, DPh, FSA, National Maritime Museum, Greenwich, London SE10 9FN.

Greenleaf, Professor W. H., BSc(Econ), PhD, University College, Singleton Park, Swansea SA2 8PP.

Greenslade, M. W., JP, MA, FSA, 20 Garth Road, Stafford ST17 9JD.

Gregg, E., MA, PhD, Dept of History, University of South Carolina, Columbia, S.C. 29208, U.S.A.

Grenville, Professor J. A. S., PhD, University of Birmingham, P.O. Box 363, Birmingham B15 2TT.

Gresham, C. A., BA, DLitt, FSA, Bryn-y-deryn, Criccieth, Caerns. LL52 oHR.

Grierson, Professor P., MA, LittD, FBA, FSA, Gonville and Caius College, Cambridge CB2 1TA.

Grieve, Miss H. E. P., BA, 153 New London Road, Chelmsford, Essex.

Griffiths, R. A., PhD, University College, Singleton Park, Swansea SA2 8PP.

Grimble, I., PhD, 13 Saville Road, Twickenham, Middx.

Grimm, Professor H. J., PhD, Department of History, 216 North Oval Drive, The Ohio State University, Columbus 10, Ohio, U.S.A.

Grisbrooke, W. J., MA, St Marys, Oscott College, Chester Road, Sutton Coldfield, West Midlands B73 5AA.

*Griscom, Rev. Acton, MA, (address unknown).

Gruner, Professor Wolf D., Wilhelmshohenstrasse 6a, D-8130 Starnberg, West Germany.

Gum, Professor E. J., PhD, 2043 N.55th Street, Omaha, Nebraska 68104, U.S.A.

Guy, J. A., PhD, Dept of History, The University, Queens Road, Bristol BS8 1RJ.

HABAKKUK, Sir John (H.), MA, FBA, Jesus College, Oxford OX1 3DW.

Haber, Professor F. C., PhD, 3026 2R Street NW, Washington, D.C. 20007, U.S.A.

Hackett, Rev. M. B., OSA, BA, PhD, Austin Friars School, Carlisle CA3 9PB.

Haffenden, P. S., PhD, 36 The Parkway, Bassett, Southampton.

Haigh, C. A., MA, PhD, Christ Church, Oxford OX1 1DP.

Haight, Mrs M. Jackson, PhD, 3 Wolger Road, Mosman, N.S.W. 2088, Australia.

Haines, R. M., MA, MLitt, DPhil, FSA, 20 Luttrell Avenue, London SW15.

Hainsworth, D. R., MA, PhD, Dept of History, University of Adelaide, North Terrace, Adelaide, South Australia 5001.

Hair, Professor P. E. H., MA, DPhil, School of History, The University, P.O. Box 147, Liverpool L69 3BX.

Hale, Professor J. R., MA, FBA, FSA, University College London, Gower Street, London WC1E 6BT.

Haley, Professor K. H. D., MA, BLitt, 15 Haugh Lane, Sheffield 11.

Hall, Professor A. R., MA, PhD, DLitt, FBA, 14 Ball Lane, Tackley, Oxford OX5 3AG.

Hall, Professor B., MA, PhD, FSA, St John's College, Cambridge CB2 1TP.

Hallam, Elizabeth M., BA, PhD, Public Record Office, Chancery Lane, London WC2A 1LR.

Hallam, Professor H. E., MA, PhD, University of Western Australia, Nedlands 6009, Western Australia.

Hamer, Professor D., MA, DPhil, History Dept, Victoria University of Wellington, P.O. Box 196, Wellington, New Zealand.

Hamilton, B., BA, PhD, The University, Nottingham NG7 2RD.

Hammersley, G. F., BA, PhD, University of Edinburgh, William Robertson Building, George Square, Edinburgh EH8 9JY.

Hampson, Professor N., MA, Ddel'U, 305 Hull Road, York YO1 3LB.

Hand, Professor G. J., MA, DPhil, Faculty of Law, University of Birmingham, P.O. Box 363, Birmingham B15 2TT.

Hanham, H. J., MA, PhD, School of Humanities and Social Science, Massachusetts Institute of Technology, Cambridge, Mass. 02139, U.S.A.

Hannah, L., MA, DPhil, Business History Unit, Lionel Robbins Building, 10 Portugal Street, London WC2A 2HD.
Harding, Professor A., MA, BLitt, School of History, The University, P.O. Box 147, Liverpool L69 3BX.
Harding, H. W., BA, LLD, 39 Annunciation Street, Sliema, Malta.
Hargreaves, Professor J. D., MA, 'Balcluain', Raemoir Road, Banchory, Kincardineshire.
Harkness, Professor D. W., MA, PhD, Dept of Irish History, The Queen's University, Belfast BT7 1NN.
Harman, Rev. L. W., 72 Westmount Road, London SE9.
Harris, G., MA, 4 Lancaster Drive, London NW3.
Harris, Mrs J. F., BA, PhD, 30 Charlbury Road, Oxford OX1 3UJ.
Harris, Professor J. R., MA, PhD, The University, P.O. Box 363, Birmingham B15 2TT.
Harrison, B. H., MA, DPhil, Corpus Christi College, Oxford OX1 4JF.
Harrison, C. J., BA, PhD, The University, Keele, Staffs. ST5 5BG.
Harrison, Professor Royden, MA, DPhil, 4 Wilton Place, Sheffield S10 2BT.
Harriss, G. L., MA, DPhil, Magdalen College, Oxford OX1 4AU.
Hart, C. J. R., MA, MB, DLitt, Goldthorns, Stilton, Peterborough, Northants. PE7 3RH.
Hart, Mrs J. M., MA, St Anne's College, Oxford OX2 6HF.
Harte, N. B., BSc(Econ), Dept of History, University College London, Gower Street, London WC1E 6BT.
Hartwell, R. M., MA, DPhil, Nuffield College, Oxford OX1 1NF.
Harvey, Miss B. F., MA, BLitt, Somerville College, Oxford OX2 6HD.
Harvey, Margaret M., MA, DPhil, St Aidan's College, Durham DH1 3LJ.
Harvey, Professor P. D. A., MA, DPhil, FSA, Dept of History, The University, Durham DH1 3EX.
Harvey, Sally P. J., MA, PhD, St Hilda's College, Oxford OX4 1DY.
Haskell, Professor F. J., MA, FBA, Trinity College, Oxford OX1 3BH.
Haskins, Professor G. L., AB, LLB, JD, MA, University of Pennsylvania, The Law School, 3400 Chestnut Street, Philadelphia, Pa. 19104 U.S.A.
Haslam, E. B., MA, 1 Lakeside, Beckenham, Kent BR3 2LX.
Hassall, W. O., MA, DPhil, FSA, The Manor House, 26 High Street, Wheatley, Oxford OX9 1XX.
Hatcher, M. J., BSc(Econ), PhD, Corpus Christi College, Cambridge CB2 1RH.
Hatley, V.A., BA, ALA, 6 The Crescent, Northampton NN1 4SB.
Hatton, Professor Ragnhild M., PhD, London School of Economics, Houghton Street, London WC2A 2AE.
Havighurst, Professor A. F., MA, PhD, 11 Blake Field, Amherst, Mass. 01002, U.S.A.
Havinden, M. A., MA, BLitt, Dept of Economic History, Amory Building, The University, Exeter.
Havran, Professor M. J., MA, PhD, Corcoran Dept of History, Randall Hall, University of Virginia, Charlottesville, Va. 22903, U.S.A.
Hay, Professor D., MA, DLitt, FBA, Dept of History, The University, Edinburgh EH8 9JY.
Hayes, P. M., MA, DPhil, Keble College, Oxford OX1 3PG.
Hazlehurst, G. C. L., BA, DPhil, FRSL, Research School of Social Sciences, Institute of Advanced Studies, Australian National University, P.O. Box 4, A.C.T. 2600, Australia.
Headlam-Morley, Miss A., BLitt, MA, 29 St Mary's Road, Wimbledon, London SW19.

Hearder, Professor H., PhD, University College, Cathays Park, Cardiff CF1 1XL.

Helmholz, R. H., PhD, LLB, School of Law, Washington University, St Louis, Mo. 63130, U.S.A.

Hembry, Mrs P. M., PhD, Pleasant Cottage, Crockerton, Warminster, Wilts. BA12 8AJ.

Hemleben, S. J., MA, DPhil, (address unknown).

Hendy, M. F., MA, Dept of History, The University, Birmingham B15 2TT.

Henning, Professor B. D., PhD, History of Parliament, 34 Tavistock Square, London WC1H 9EZ.

Hennock, Professor E. P., MA, PhD, School of History, University of Liverpool, P.O. Box 147, Liverpool L69 3BX.

Hernon, Professor J. M., PhD, Dept of History, University of Massachusetts, Amherst, Mass. 01002, U.S.A.

Hexter, Professor J. H., PhD, Dept of History, 237 Hall of Graduate Studies, Yale University, New Haven, Conn. 06520, U.S.A.

Highfield, J. R. L., MA, DPhil, Merton College, Oxford OX1 4JD.

Hill, B. W., BA, PhD, School of English and American Studies, University of East Anglia, Norwich NR4 7TJ.

Hill, J. E. C., MA, DLitt, FBA, Woodway, Sibford Ferris, nr. Banbury, Oxfordshire OX15 5RA.

Hill, Professor L. M., AB, MA, PhD, 5066 Berean Lane, Irvine, Calif. 92664, U.S.A.

*Hill, Miss M. C., MA, Crab End, Brevel Terrace, Charlton Kings, Cheltenham, Glos.

*Hill, Professor Rosalind M. T., MA, BLitt, FSA, Westfield College, Kidderpore Avenue, London NW3 7ST.

Hilton, Professor R. H., DPhil, FBA, University of Birmingham, P.O. Box 363, Birmingham B15 2TT.

Himmelfarb, Professor Gertrude, PhD, The City University of New York, Graduate Center, 33 West 42 St, New York, N.Y. 10036, U.S.A.

Hind, R. J., BA, PhD, Dept of History, University of Sydney, Sydney, N.S.W. 2006, Australia.

*Hinsley, Professor F. H., MA, St John's College, Cambridge CB2 1TP.

Hirst, Professor D. M., PhD, Dept of History, Washington University, St Louis, Missouri, U.S.A.

Hockey, The Rev. S. F., BA, Quarr Abbey, Ryde, Isle of Wight PO33 4ES.

*Hodgett, G. A. J., MA, FSA, King's College, Strand, London WC2R 2LS.

Holdsworth, Professor C. J., MA, PhD, FSA, 5 Pennsylvania Park, Exeter EX4 6HD.

Hollaender, A. E. J., PhD, FSA, 119 Narbonne Avenue, South Side, Clapham Common, London SW4 9LQ.

*Hollingsworth, L. W., PhD, Flat 27, Mayfair, 74 Westcliff Road, Bournemouth BH4 8BG.

Hollis, Patricia, MA, DPhil, 30 Park Lane, Norwich NOR 47F.

Hollister, Professor C. Warren, MA, PhD, University of California, Santa Barbara, Calif. 93106, U.S.A.

Holmes, Professor Clive A., MA, PhD, Dept of History, McGraw Hall, Cornell University, N.Y. 14853, U.S.A.

Holmes, G. A., MA, PhD, 431 Banbury Road, Oxford.

Holmes, Professor G. S., MA, DLitt, Tatham House, Burton-in-Lonsdale, Carnforth, Lancs.

Holroyd, M. de C. F., 85 St Mark's Road, London W10.

HOLT, Professor J. C., MA, DPhil, FBA, FSA, (*President*), Faculty of History, West Road, Cambridge CB3 9EF.

Holt, Professor P. M., MA, DLitt, FBA, School of Oriental and African Studies, Malet Street, London WC1E 7HP.

Honey, Professor, J. R. de S., MA, DPhil, 5 Woods Close, Oadby, Leicester LE2 4FJ.

Hook, Mrs Judith, MA, PhD, Dept of History, Taylor Building, King's College, Old Aberdeen AB9 2UB.

Hope, R. S. H., 25 Hengistbury Road, Bournemouth, Dorset BH6 4DQ.

Hopkins, E., MA, PhD, 77 Stevens Road, Stourbridge, West Midlands DY9 0XW.

Hoppen, K. T., MA, PhD, Dept of History, The University, Hull HU6 7RX.

Horwitz, Professor H. G., BA, DPhil, Dept of History, University of Iowa, Iowa City, Iowa 52242, U.S.A.

Houlbrooke, R.A., MA, DPhil, Faculty of Letters and Social Sciences, The University, Reading RG6 2AA.

*Howard, C. H. D., MA, 15 Sunnydale Gardens, London NW7.

*Howard, Professor M. E., CBE, MC, DLitt, FBA, All Souls College, Oxford OX1 4AL.

Howarth, Mrs J. H., MA, St Hilda's College, Oxford OX4 1DY.

Howat, G. M. D., MA, MLitt, Old School House, North Moreton, Didcot, Oxfordshire OX11 9BA.

Howell, Miss M. E., MA, PhD, 3 Field Close, Compton Down, Winchester, Hants. SO21 2AE.

Howell, Professor R., MA, DPhil, Dept of History, Bowdoin College, Brunswick, Maine 04011, U.S.A.

Howells, B. E., MA, Whitehill, Cwm Ann, Lampeter, Dyfed.

Hudson, Miss A., MA, DPhil, Lady Margaret Hall, Oxford OX2 6QA.

Hufton, Professor Olwen H., PhD, 40 Shinfield Road, Reading, Berks.

Hughes, J. Q., BArch, PhD, 10a Fulwood Park, Liverpool L17 5AH.

Hull, F., BA, PhD, Roundwell Cottage, Bearsted, Maidstone, Kent ME14 4EU.

Hulton, P. H., BA, FSA, 46 St Paul's Road, London N1.

HUMPHREYS, Professor R. A., OBE, MA, PhD, DLitt, LittD, DLitt, DUniv, 13 St Paul's Place, Canonbury, London N1 2QE.

Hunnisett, R. F., MA, DPhil, 54 Longdon Wood, Keston, Kent BR2 6EW.

Hunt, Professor K. S., PhD, MA, Dept of History, Rhodes University, Grahamstown 6140, South Africa.

Hurst, M. C., MA, St John's College, Oxford OX1 3JP.

Hurt, J. S., BA, BSc(Econ), PhD, 66 Oxford Road, Moseley, Birmingham B13 9SQ.

*Hussey, Professor Joan M., MA, BLitt, PhD, FSA, Royal Holloway College, Englefield Green, Surrey TW20 0EX.

Hyams, P. R., MA, DPhil, Pembroke College, Oxford OX1 1DW.

*Hyde, H. Montgomery, MA, DLit, Westwell House, Tenterden, Kent.

Hyde, Professor J. K., MA, PhD, The University, Manchester M13 9PL.

Ingham, Professor K., OBE, MA, DPhil, The Woodlands, 94 West Town Lane, Bristol BS4 5DZ.

Ingram Ellis, Professor E. R., MA, PhD, Dept of History, Simon Fraser University, Burnaby, B.C., V5A 1S6, Canada.

Ives, E. W., PhD, 214 Myton Road, Warwick.

Jack, Professor R. I., MA, PhD, University of Sydney, Sydney, N.S.W., Australia.

Jack, Mrs. S. M., MA, BLitt, University of Sydney, Sydney, N.S.W., Australia.
Jackman, Professor S. W., PhD, FSA, 1065 Deal Street, Victoria, British Columbia, Canada.
Jackson, E. D. C., FSA, (address unknown).
Jagger, Rev. P. J., MA, MPhil, St Deiniol's Library, Hawarden, Deeside, Clwyd CH5 3DF.
James, Edward, MA, DPhil, Dept of History, The University, Heslington, York YO1 5DD.
James, M. E., MA, University of Durham, 43–45 North Bailey, Durham.
James, Professor Robert R., MA, FRSL, The Stone House, Great Gransden, nr Sandy, Beds.
Jasper, The Very Rev. R. C. D., DD, The Deanery, York YO1 2JD.
Jeffs, R. M., MA, DPhil, FSA, 6a Gladstone Road, Sheffield S10 3GT.
Jenkins, Professor D., MA, LLM, LittD, Adeilad Hugh Owen, Penglais, Aberystwyth SY23 3DY.
Jeremy, D. J., BA, MLitt, PhD, 16 Britannia Gardens, Westcliff-on-Sea, Essex SS0 8BN.
Jewell, Miss H. M., MA, PhD, 30 Heathfield, Adel, Leeds LS16 6AQ.
John, E., MA, The University, Manchester M13 9PL.
Johnson, D. J., BA, 41 Cranes Park Avenue, Surbiton, Surrey.
Johnson, Professor D. W. J., BA, BLitt, University College London, Gower Street, London WC1E 6BT.
*Johnson, J. H., MA, Whitehorns, Cedar Avenue, Chelmsford, Essex.
Johnston, Professor Edith M., MA, PhD, Dept of History, Macquarie Univ., North Ryde, N.S.W. 2113, Australia.
Johnston, Professor S. H. F., MA, Fronhyfryd, Llanbadarn Road, Aberystwyth, Dyfed.
Jones, D. J. V., BA, PhD, Dept of History, University College of Swansea, Singleton Park, Swansea SA2 8PP.
Jones, Dwyryd W., MA, DPhil, The University, Heslington, York YO1 5DD.
Jones, Revd. F., BA, PhD, 4a Castlemain Avenue, Southbourne, Bournemouth, Dorset.
Jones, G. A., MA, PhD, Dept of History, Faculty of Letters, University of Reading, Whiteknights, Reading, Berks. RG6 2AH.
Jones, G. E., MA, PhD, MEd, 130 Pennard Drive, Pennard, Gower, West Glamorgan.
Jones, Professor G. Hilton, PhD, Dept of History, Eastern Illinois University, Charleston, Ill. 61920, U.S.A.
Jones, G. J., MPhil, The Croft, Litchard Bungalows, Bridgend, Glam.
Jones, Professor G. W., BA, MA, DPhil, Dept of Government, London School of Economics, Houghton Street, London WC2A 2AE.
Jones, H. W., MA, PhD, 32 Leylands Terrace, Bradford BD9 5QR.
Jones, Professor I. G., MA, 12 Laura Place, Aberystwyth, Dyfed.
Jones, J. D., MA, PhD, Carisbrooke Castle Museum, Newport, Isle of Wight PO30 1XY.
Jones, Professor J. R., MA, PhD, School of English and American Studies, University Plain, Norwich NOR 30A.
Jones, Professor M. A., MA, DPhil, Dept of History, University College London, Gower Street, London WC1E 6BT.
Jones, Mrs Marian H., MA, Glwysgoed, Caradog Road, Aberystwyth, Dyfed.
Jones, M. C. E., MA, DPhil, FSA, The University, Nottingham NG7 2RD.

Jones, The Rev. Canon O. W., MA, The Vicarage, Builth Wells, Powys LD2 3BS.
Jones, P. J., DPhil, Brasenose College, Oxford OX1 4AJ.
Jones, Professor W. J., PhD, Dept of History, The University of Alberta, Edmonton T6G 2E1, Canada.
Jones-Parry, Sir Ernest, MA, PhD, 3 Sussex Mansions, Old Brompton Road, London SW7.
Jordan, Professor P. D., PhD, LLD, 26 Cascade Terrace, Burlington, Iowa 52601, U.S.A.
Judd, D., BA, PhD, Dept of History and Philosophy, Polytechnic of North London, Prince of Wales Road, London NW6.
Judson, Professor Margaret A., PhD, 8 Redcliffe Avenue, Highland Park, N.J. 08904, U.S.A.
Jukes, Rev. H. A. Ll., MA, STh, 1 St Mary's Court, Ely, Cambs. CB7 4HQ.

Kaeuper, Professor R. W., MA, PhD, 151 Village Lane, Rochester, New York 14610, USA.
Kamen, H. A. F., MA, DPhil, The University, Warwick, Coventry CV4 7AL.
Kanya-Forstner, A. S., PhD, Dept of History, York University, 4700 Keele Street, Downsview, Ontario M3J 1P3, Canada.
*Kay, J., MA, 44 Red Hall Way, Leeds LS14 1EF.
Keeler, Mrs Mary F., PhD, 302 West 12th Street, Frederick, Maryland 21701, U.S.A.
Keen, L. J., MPhil, Dip Archaeol, FSA, 7 Church Street, Dorchester, Dorset.
Keen, M. H., MA, Balliol College, Oxford OX1 3BJ.
Kellas, J. G., MA, PhD, Dept of Politics, Glasgow University, Adam Smith Building, Glasgow G12 8RT.
Kellaway, C. W., MA, FSA, 2 Grove Terrace, London NW5.
Kellett, J. R., MA, PhD, Dept of Economic History, University of Glasgow, Glasgow G12 8QQ.
Kelly, Professor T., MA, PhD, FLA, 9 Squirrel Green, Formby, Merseyside L37 1NZ.
Kemp, Miss B., MA, FSA, St Hugh's College, Oxford OX2 6LE.
Kemp, B. R., BA, PhD, 12 Redhatch Drive, Earley, Reading, Berks.
Kemp, The Right Rev. E. W., DD, The Lord Bishop of Chichester, The Palace, Chichester, Sussex PO19 1PY.
Kemp, Lt-Commander P. K., RN, Malcolm's, 51 Market Hill, Maldon, Essex.
Kennedy, J., MA, 14 Poolfield Avenue, Newcastle-under-Lyme, Staffs. ST5 2NL.
Kennedy, P. M., BA, DPhil, School of English and American Studies, University of East Anglia, Norwich NOR 88C.
Kent, Professor C. A., DPhil, Dept of History, University of Saskatchewan, Saskatoon, Sask. S7N 6WO, Canada.
Kent, Professor J. H. S., MA, PhD, Dept of Theology, University of Bristol, Senate House, Bristol BS8 1TH.
Kent, Miss M. R., PhD, BA, School of Social Sciences, Deakin University, Geelong, Victoria, Australia.
Kenyon, Professor J. P., PhD, Dept of History, The University, Hull HU6 7RX.
Ker, N. R., CBE, MA, DLitt, FBA, FSA, Slievemore, Foss, by Pitlochry, Perthshire.
Kerridge E. W. J., PhD, 6 Llys Tudur, Myddleton Park, Denbigh LL16 4AL.
Ketelbey, Miss C. D. M., MA, 18 Queen's Gardens, St Andrews, Fife.

Kettle, Miss A. J., MA, FSA, Dept of Mediaeval History, 71 South Street, St Andrews, Fife.
Khanna, Kahan Chand, MA, PhD, Ravensdale, Simla-2, India.
Kiernan, Professor V. G., MA, 27 Nelson Street, Edinburgh EH3 6LJ.
*Kimball, Miss E. G., BLitt, PhD, 200 Leeder Hill Drive, Apt 640, Hamden, Conn. 06517, U.S.A.
King, E. J., MA, PhD, Dept of History, The University, Sheffield S10 2TN.
King, P. D., BA, PhD, Lancaster View, Bailrigg, Lancaster.
Kinsley, Professor J., MA, PhD, DLitt, FBA, University of Nottingham, Nottingham NG7 2RD.
Kirby, D. P., MA, PhD, Manoraven, Llanon, Dyfed.
Kirby, J. L., MA, FSA, 209 Covington Way, Streatham, London SW16 3BY.
Kirk, J., MA, PhD, Dept of Scottish History, University of Glasgow, Glasgow G12 8QQ.
Kishlansky, Professor Mark, Dept of History, University of Chicago, 1126 East 59th Street, Chicago, Illinois 60637, U.S.A.
Kitchen, Professor Martin, BA, PhD, Dept of History, Simon Fraser University, Burnaby, B.C. V5A 1S6, Canada.
KITCHING, C. J., BA, PhD, (*Hon. Treasurer*) 11 Creighton Road, London NW6 6EE.
Klibansky, Professor R., MA, PhD, DPhil, FRSC, 608 Leacock Building, McGill University, P.O. Box 6070, Station A, Montreal H3C 3G1, Canada.
Knafla, Professor L. A., BA, MA, PhD, Dept of History, University of Calgary, Alberta, Canada.
Knecht, R. J., MA, 22 Warwick New Road, Leamington Spa, Warwickshire.
*Knight, L. Stanley, MA, Little Claregate, 1 The Drive, Malthouse Lane, Tettenhall, Wolverhampton.
Knowles, C. H., PhD, University College, Cathays Park, Cardiff CF1 1XL.
Koch, H. W., BA, Dept of History, University of York, Heslington, York YO1 5DD.
Kochan, L. E., MA, PhD, 237 Woodstock Road, Oxford OX2 7AD.
Koenigsberger, Dorothy M. M., BA, PhD, 41a Lancaster Avenue, London NW3.
Koenigsberger, Professor H. G., PhD, Dept of History, King's College, Strand, London WC2R 2LS.
Kohl, Professor Benjamin G., AB, MA, PhD, Dept of History, Vassar College, Poughkeepsie, New York 12601, U.S.A.
Korr, C. P., MA, PhD, 4466 West Pine Avenue, St Louis, Mo. 63108, U.S.A.
Koss, Professor S. E., Dept of History, Columbia University, New York, N.Y. 10027, U.S.A.
Kossmann, Professor E. H., DLitt, Rijksuniversiteit te Groningen, Groningen, The Netherlands.

Lambert, The Hon. Margaret, CMG, PhD, 39 Thornhill Road, Barnsbury Square, London N1 1JS.
Lamont, W. M., PhD, Manor House, Keighton Road, Denton, Newhaven, Sussex BN9 0AB.
Lancaster, Miss J. C., CBE, MA, FSA, 43 Craigmair Road, Tulse Hill, London SW2 2DQ.
Lander, J. R., MA, MLitt, Social Science Centre, University of Western Ontario, London, Ont. N6A 5C2, Canada.
Landes, Professor D. S., PhD, Widener U, Harvard University, Cambridge, Mass. 02138, U.S.A.

Landon, Professor M. de L., MA, PhD, Dept of History, The University, Mississippi 38677 U.S.A.

Langford, P., MA, DPhil, Lincoln College, Oxford OX1 3DR.

La Page, J., FSA, Craig Lea, 44 Bank Crest, Baildon, West Yorkshire.

Larkin, Professor the Rev J. F., CSV, PhD, 1212 East Euclid Street, Arlington Heights, Illinois 60004, U.S.A.

Larner, J. P., MA, The University, Glasgow G12 8QQ.

Lasko, Professor P. E., BA, FSA, Courtauld Institute of Art, 20 Portman Square, London W1H 0BE.

Latham, R. C., CBE, MA, Magdalene College, Cambridge CB3 0AG.

Lawrence, Professor C. H., MA, DPhil, Bedford College, Regent's Park, London NW1 4NS.

*Laws, Lieut-Colonel M. E. S., OBE, MC, Bank Top Cottage, Seal Chart, Sevenoaks, Kent.

Laws, Captain W. F., BA, MLitt, 9 The Glebe, Thorverton, Devon EX5 5LS.

Leddy, J. F., MA, BLitt, DPhil, University of Windsor, Windsor, Ontario, Canada.

Lee, J. M., MA, BLitt, Dept of Politics, Birkbeck College, 7–15 Gresse Street, London W1A 1PA.

Legge, Professor M. Dominica, MA, DLitt, FBA, 191a Woodstock Road, Oxford OX2 7AB.

Lehmann, Professor J. H., PhD, De Paul University, 25E Jackson Blvd., Chicago, Ill. 60604, U.S.A.

Lehmberg, Professor S. E., PhD, Dept of History, University of Minnesota, Minneapolis, Minn. 55455, U.S.A.

Lenman, B. P., MA, MLitt, FSA(Scot), 'Cromalt', 50 Lade Braes, St Andrews, Fife KY16 9DA.

Le Patourel, Professor J. H., MA, DPhil, Ddel'U, FBA, Westcote, Hebers Ghyll Drive, Ilkley, West Yorkshire LS29 9QH.

Leslie, Professor R. F., BA, PhD, Market House, Church Street, Charlbury, Oxford OX7 3PP.

Lester, Professor M., PhD, Dept of History, Davidson College, Davidson, N.C. 28036, U.S.A.

Levine, Professor Mortimer, PhD, 529 Woodhaven Drive, Morgantown, West Va. 26505, U.S.A.

Levy, Professor F. J., PhD, University of Washington, Seattle, Wash. 98195, U.S.A.

Lewin, G. R., BA, Camilla House, Forest Road, East Horsley, Surrey KT24 5BB.

Lewis, Professor A. R., MA, PhD, History Dept, University of Massachusetts, Amherst, Mass, 01003, U.S.A.

Lewis, Professor B., PhD, FBA, Near Eastern Studies Dept, Jones Hall, The University, Princeton, N.J. 08540, U.S.A.

Lewis, C. W., BA, FSA, University College, Cathays Park, Cardiff CF1 1XL.

Lewis, P. S., MA, All Souls College, Oxford OX1 4AL.

Lewis, R. A., PhD, University College of North Wales, Bangor, Gwynedd LL57 2DG.

Leyser, K., MA, Magdalen College, Oxford OX1 4AU.

*Lindsay, Mrs H., MA, PhD, (address unknown).

Linehan, P. A., MA, PhD, St John's College, Cambridge CB2 1TP.

Lipman, V. D., CVO, MA, DPhil, FSA, 9 Rotherwick Road, London NW11 9DG.

Livermore, Professor H. V., MA, Sandycombe Lodge, Sandycombe Road, St Margarets, Twickenham, Middx.
Lloyd, H. A., BA, DPhil, The University, Cottingham Road, Hull HU6 7RX.
Loach, Mrs J., MA, Dept of Modern History, Somerville College, Oxford OX2 6HD.
Loades, Professor D. M., MA, PhD, University College of North Wales, Bangor, Gwynedd LL57 2DG.
Lobel, Mrs M. D., BA, FSA, 16 Merton Street, Oxford.
Lockie, D. McN., MA, Chemin de la Panouche, Saint-Anne, 06130 Grasse, France.
Lockyer, R. W., MA, Dept of History, Royal Holloway College, Englefield Green, Surrey TW20 0EX.
Logan, F. D., MA, MSD, Emmanuel College, 400 The Fennway, Boston, Mass. 02115, U.S.A.
London, Miss Vera C. M., MA, 55 Churchill Road, Church Stretton, Shropshire SY6 6EP.
Longley, D. A., BA, King's College, The University, Old Aberdeen AB9 2UB.
Loomie, Rev. A. J., SJ, MA, PhD, Fordham University, New York, N.Y. 10458, U.S.A.
Lourie, Elena, MA, DPhil, Dept of History, University of The Negev, P.O. Box 4653, Beer Sheva, Israel.
Lovatt, R. W., MA, DPhil, Peterhouse, Cambridge CB2 1RD.
Lovell, J. C., BA, PhD, Eliot College, University of Kent, Canterbury CT2 7NS.
Lovett, A. W., MA, PhD, 26 Coney Hill Road, West Wickham, Kent BR4 9BX.
Lowe, P. C., BA, PhD, The University, Manchester M13 9PL.
Loyn, Professor H. R., MA, FBA, FSA, Westfield College, Kidderpore Avenue, London NW3 7ST.
Lucas, C. R., MA, DPhil, Balliol College, Oxford OX1 3BJ.
Lucas, P. J., MA, PhD, University College, Belfield, Dublin 4, Ireland.
Luft, Rev. Canon H. M., MA, MLitt, 44 St Michael's Road, Blundellsands, Highfurlong, Liverpool L23 7UN.
*Lumb, Miss S. V., MA, Torr-Colin House, 106 Ridgway, Wimbledon, London SW19.
Luscombe, Professor D. E., MA, PhD, 129 Prospect Road, Totley Rise, Sheffield S17 4HX.
Luttrell, A. T., MA, DPhil, Dept of History, The Royal University of Malta, Msida, Malta.
Lyman, Professor R. W., PhD, 350 East 57th Street, Apt 14-B, New York, N.Y. 10022, U.S.A.
Lynch, Professor J., MA, PhD, University College London, Gower Street, London WC1E 6BT.
Lyon, Professor Bryce D., PhD, Dept of History, Brown University, Providence, Rhode Island 02912, U.S.A.
Lyons, Professor F. S. L., MA, PhD, LittD, The Provost, Trinity College, Dublin, Ireland.
Lyttelton, The Hon. N. A. O., BA, St Antony's College, Oxford OX2 6JF.

Mabbs, A. W., Public Record Office, Chancery Lane, London WC2A 2LR.
Macaulay, J. H., MA, PhD, 44 Fonthill Road, Aberdeen AB1 2UJ.

LIST OF FELLOWS

McBriar, Professor A. M., BA, DPhil, FASSA, Dept of History, Monash University, Clayton, Victoria 3168, Australia.
MacCaffrey, Professor W. T., PhD, 745 Hollyoke Center, Harvard University, Cambridge, Mass. 02138, U.S.A.
McCaughan, Professor R. E. M., MA, BArch, Hon DSc, FSA, FRAnthI, RIBA, 'Rowan Bank', Kingsley Green, Fernhurst, West Sussex GU27 3LL.
McConica, Professor J. K., CSB, MA, DPhil, All Souls College, Oxford OX1 4AL.
McCord, Professor N., PhD, 7 Hatherton Avenue, Cullercoats, North Shields, Northumberland.
McCracken, Professor J. L., MA, PhD, 79 Ballaghmore Road, Bushmills, Co Antrim, N. Ireland.
MacCurtain, Margaret B., MA, PhD, Dept of History, University College, Belfield, Dublin 4, Ireland.
McCusker, J. J., MA, PhD, Dept of History, University of Maryland, College Park, Maryland 20742, U.S.A.
MacDonagh, Professor O., MA, PhD, Research School of Social Sciences, Institute of Advanced Studies, Australian National University, P.O. Box 4, A.C.T. 2600, Australia.
Macdonald, Professor D. F., MA, DPhil, 11 Arnhall Drive, Dundee.
McDonald, Professor T. H., MA, PhD, R. R. 1, Site 1A, Peachland, B.C., VOH 1XO, Canada.
McDowell, Professor R. B., PhD, LittD, Trinity College, Dublin, Ireland.
Macfarlane, A., MA, DPhil, PhD, King's College, Cambridge CB2 1ST.
Macfarlane, L. J., PhD, FSA, King's College, University of Aberdeen, Aberdeen AB9 1FX.
McGrath, P. V., MA, University of Bristol, Bristol BS8 1RJ.
MacGregor, D. R., MA, ARIBA, FSA, 99 Lonsdale Road, London SW13 9DA.
McGurk, J. J. N., BA, MPhil, Conway House, Stanley Avenue, Birkdale, Southport, Merseyside.
McGurk, P. M., PhD, Birkbeck College, Malet Street, London WC1E 7HX.
Machin, G. I. T., MA, DPhil, Dept of Modern History, University of Dundee, Dundee DD1 4HN.
MacIntyre, A. D., MA, DPhil, Magdalen College, Oxford OX1 4AU.
McKendrick, N., MA, Gonville and Caius College, Cambridge CB2 1TA.
McKenna, Professor J. W., MA, PhD, 1444 Old Gulph Road, Villanova, Pa. 19085, U.S.A.
Mackesy, P. G., MA, DPhil, DLitt, Pembroke College, Oxford OX1 1DW.
McKibbin, R. I., MA, DPhil, St John's College, Oxford OX1 3JP.
*Mackie, Professor J. D., CBE, MC, MA, LLD, FSAScot, 67 Downanside Road, Glasgow W2.
McKinley, R. A., MA, 42 Boyers Walk, Leicester Forest East, Leicester.
McKitterick, Rosamond D., MA, PhD, Newnham College, Cambridge CB3 9DF.
Maclagan, M., MA, FSA, Trinity College, Oxford OX1 3BH.
MacLeod, Professor R. M., AB, PhD, Dept of Science Education, Institute of Education, Bedford Way, London WC1H 0AL.
*McManners, Professor J., MA, DLitt, FBA, Christ Church, Oxford OX1 1DP.
MacMichael, N. H., FSA, 2B Little Cloister, Westminster Abbey, London SW1.
MacNiocaill, Professor G., PhD, DLitt, Dept of History, University College, Galway, Ireland.

McNulty, Miss P. A., BA, 84B Eastern Avenue, Reading RG1 5SF.
Macpherson, Professor C. B., BA, MSc(Econ), DSc(Econ), DLitt, LLD, FRSC, University of Toronto, Toronto, M5S 1A1, Canada.
Madariaga, Miss Isabel de, PhD, 25 Southwood Lawn Road, London N6.
Madden, A. F. McC., DPhil, Nuffield College, Oxford OX1 1NF.
Maddicott, J. R., MA, DPhil, Exeter College, Oxford OX1 3DP.
Maehl, Professor W. H., PhD, College of Liberal Studies, Office of the Dean, 1700 Asp Avenue, Suite 226, Norman, Oklahoma 73037, U.S.A.
Maffei, Professor Domenico, MLL, DrJur, Via delle Certhia 19, 53100 Siena, Italy.
Magnus-Allcroft, Sir Phillip, Bt., CBE, FRSL, Stokesay Court, Craven Arms, Shropshire SY7 9BD.
Maguire, W. A., MA, PhD, 18 Harberton Park, Belfast, N. Ireland BT9 6TS.
Mahoney, Professor T. H. D., AM, PhD, MPA, Massachusetts Institute of Technology, Cambridge, Mass. 02138, U.S.A.
*Major, Miss K., MA, BLitt, LittD, FBA, FSA, 21 Queensway, Lincoln.
Mallett, Professor M. E., MA, DPhil, University of Warwick, Coventry CV4 7AL.
Malone, Professor J. J., PhD, 110–4th Street N.E., Washington, D.C. 20002, U.S.A.
Mann, Miss J. de L., MA, The Cottage, Bowerhill, Melksham, Wilts.
Manning, Professor A. F., Bosweg 27, Berg en Dal, The Netherlands.
Manning, B. S., MA, DPhil, The University, Oxford Road, Manchester M13 9PL.
Manning, Professor R. B., PhD, 2848 Coleridge Road, Cleveland Heights, Ohio 44118, U.S.A.
Mansergh, Professor P. N. S., OBE, MA, DPhil, DLitt, LittD, FBA, The Master's Lodge, St John's College, Cambridge.
Marchant, The Rev Canon R. A., PhD, BD, Laxfield Vicarage, Woodbridge, Suffolk IP13 8DT.
Marett, W. P., BSc(Econ), BCom, MA, PhD, 20 Barrington Road, Stoney-gate, Leicester LE2 2RA.
Margetts, J., MA, DipEd, DrPhil, 5 Glenluce Road, Liverpool L19 9BX.
Markus, Professor R. A., MA, PhD, The University, Nottingham NG7 2RD.
Marriner, Sheila, MA, PhD, Dept of Economic History, Eleanor Rathbone Building, Myrtle Street, P.O. Box 147, Liverpool L69 3BX.
Marsh, Professor Peter T., PhD, Dept of History, Syracuse University, Syracuse, New York 13210, U.S.A.
Marshall, J. D., PhD, Brynthwaite, Charney Road, Grange-over-Sands, Cumbria LA11 6BP.
Marshall, P. J., MA, DPhil, King's College, Strand, London WC2R 2LS.
Martin, E. W., Crossways, 41 West Avenue, Exeter EX4 4SD.
Martin, Professor G. H., MA, DPhil, 21 Central Avenue, Leicester LE2 1TB.
Martin, Professor Miguel, Universidad de Panamá, Estafeta Universitaria, Panama City.
Martindale, Jane M., MA, DPhil, School of English and American Studies, University of East Anglia, Norwich NR4 7TJ.
Marwick, Professor A. J. B., MA, BLitt, Dept of History, The Open University, Walton Hall, Walton, Bletchley, Bucks.
Mason, E. Emma, BA, PhD, Dept of History, Birkbeck College, Malet Street, London WC1E 7HX.
Mason, F. K., Beechwood, Watton, Norfolk IP25 6AB.
Mason, J. F. A., MA, DPhil, FSA, Christ Church, Oxford OX1. 1DP.

Mason, T. W., MA, DPhil, St Peter's College, Oxford OX1 2DL.

Mather, F. C., MA, 69 Ethelburt Avenue, Swaythling, Southampton.

Mathias, Professor P., MA, FBA, All Souls College, Oxford OX1 4AL.

*Mathur-Sherry, Tikait Narain, BA, LLB, 3/193 4 Prem-Nagar, Dayal-bagh, Agra-282005 (U.P.), India.

Matthew, Professor D. J. A., MA, DPhil, The University, Reading RG6 2AA.

Matthew, H. C. G., MA, DPhil, Christ Church, Oxford OX1 1DP.

Mattingly, Professor H. B., MA, Dept of Ancient History, The University, Leeds LS2 9JT.

Mayr-Harting, H. M. R. E., MA, DPhil, St Peter's College, Oxford OX1 2DL.

Mbaeyi, P. M., BA, DPhil, c/o Holy Rosary School, Umuhu-Okabia, P. A., Orlu, Imo State, Nigeria.

Medlicott, Professor W. N., MA, DLit, DLitt, 2 Cartref, Ellesmere Road, Weybridge, Surrey.

Meek, Christine E., MA, DPhil, 3145 Arts Building, Trinity College, Dublin 2, Ireland.

Meek, D. E., MA, BA, Dept of Celtic, University of Edinburgh, George Square, Edinburgh EH8 9JX.

Meller, Miss Helen E., BA, PhD, 2 Copenhagen Court, Denmark Grove, Alexandra Park, Nottingham NG3 4LF.

Merson, A. L., MA, The University, Southampton SO9 5NH.

Mews, Stuart, PhD, Dept of Religious Studies, Cartmel College, Bailrigg, Lancaster.

Micklewright, F. H. A., MA, PhD, 228 South Norwood Hill, London SE25.

Midgley, Miss L. M., MA, 84 Wolverhampton Road, Stafford ST17 4AW.

Miller, Professor A., BA, MA, PhD, Dept of History, University of Texas, Houston, Texas, U.S.A.

Miller, E., MA, LittD, 36 Almoners Avenue, Cambridge CB1 4PA.

Miller, Miss H., MA, Univerity College of North Wales, Bangor, Gwynedd.

Miller, J., MA, PhD, Dept of History, Queen Mary College, Mile End Road, London E1 4NS.

Milne, A. T., MA, 9 Frank Dixon Close, London SE21 7BD.

Milne, Miss D. J., MA, PhD, King's College, Aberdeen.

Milsom, Professor S. F. C., MA, FBA, 23 Bentley Road, Cambridge CB2 2AW.

Minchinton, Professor W. E., BSc(Econ), The University, Exeter EX4 4PU.

Mingay, Professor G. E., PhD, Mill Field House, Selling Court, Selling, nr Faversham, Kent.

Mitchell, C., MA, BLitt, LittD, Woodhouse Farmhouse, Fyfield, Abingdon, Berks.

Mitchell, L. G., MA, DPhil, University College, Oxford OX1 4BH.

Mitchison, Mrs R. M., MA, Great Yew, Ormiston, East Lothian EH35 5NJ.

Momigliano, Professor A. D., DLitt, FBA, University College London, Gower Street, London WC1E 6BT.

Mommsen, Professor Dr W. J., German Historical Institute, 42 Russell Square, London WC1B 5DA.

Mondey, D. C., 175 Raeburn Avenue, Surbiton, Surrey KT5 9DE.

Moody, Professor T. W., MA, PhD, Trinity College, Dublin, Ireland.

Moore, B. J. S., BA, University of Bristol, 67 Woodland Road, Bristol BS8 1UL.

Moore, Professor Cresap, University of California, Los Angeles, California 90024, U.S.A.

Moore, R. I., MA, The University, Sheffield S10 2TN.
*Moorman, Mrs M., MA, 22 Springwell Road, Durham DH1 4LR.
Morey, Rev. Dom R. Adrian, OSB, MA, DPhil, LittD, Benet House, Mount Pleasant, Cambridge CB3 0BL.
Morgan, B. G., BArch, PhD, Tan-y-Fron, 43 Church Walks, Llandudno, Gwynedd.
Morgan, David R., MA, PhD, Dept of Politics, Roxby Building, The University, P.O. Box 147, Liverpool L69 3BX.
Morgan, K. O., MA, DPhil, The Queen's College, Oxford OX1 4BH.
Morgan, Miss P. E., 1A The Cloisters, Hereford HR1 2NG.
Morgan, Victor, BA, School of English and American Studies, University of East Anglia, Norwich NR4 7TJ.
*Morrell, Professor W. P., CBE, MA, DPhil, 20 Bedford Street, St Clair, Dunedin SW1, NewZealand.
Morrill, J. S., MA, DPhil, Selwyn College, Cambridge CB3 9DQ.
Morris, The Rev. Professor C., MA, 53 Cobbett Road, Bitterne Park, Southampton SO2 4HJ.
Morris, G. C., MA, King's College, Cambridge CB2 1ST.
Morris, Professor R. B., PhD, 151 Ridgeway Street, Mount Vernon, New York 10552, U.S.A.
Morton, Miss C. E., MA, FSA, The Studio, Chaldon Herring, nr Dorchester, Dorset DT2 8DN.
Morton, Professor W. L., MA, BLitt, LLD, DLitt, 10A 300 Roslyn Road, Winnipeg, Manitoba R3L 0H4, Canada.
Mosse, Professor W. E. E., MA, PhD, Dawn Cottage, Ashwellthorpe, Norwich, Norfolk.
Mullins, E. L. C., OBE, MA, Instiute of Historical Research, University of London, Senate House, London WC1E 7HU.
Muntz, Miss I. Hope, FSA, The Studio, Chaldon Herring, nr Dorchester, Dorset DT2 8DN.
Murdoch, D. H., MA, School of History, The University, Leeds LS2 9JT.
Murray, A., MA, BA, BPhil, University College, Oxford OX1 4BH.
Murray, Athol L., MA, LLB, PhD, 33 Inverleith Gardens, Edinburgh EH3 5PR.
Myres, J. N. L., CBE, MA, LLD, DLitt, DLit, FBA, FSA, The Manor House, Kennington, Oxford OX1 5PH.

Naidis, Professor M., PhD, 10847 Canby Avenue, Northridge, California 91324, U.S.A.
Nath, Dwarka, MBE, 13 Harrington Road, South Norwood, London SE25 4LU.
Nef, Professor J. U., PhD, 2726 N Street NW, Washington, D.C. 20007, U.S.A.
Nelson, Janet L., BA, PhD, Dept of History, King's College, Strand, London WC2R 2LS.
New, Professor J. F. H., Dept of History, Waterloo University, Waterloo, Ontario, Canada.
Newitt, M. D. D., BA, PhD, Queen's Building, University of Exeter, EX4 4QH.
Newman, A. N., MA, DPhil, 33 Stanley Road, Leicester.
Newsome, D. H., MA, LittD, Master's Lodge, Wellington College, Crowthorne, Berks. RG11 7PU.
Nicholas, Professor David, PhD, Dept of History, University of Nebraska, Lincoln, Nebraska 68588, U.S.A.
Nicholas, Professor H. G., MA, FBA, New College, Oxford OX1 3BN.

Nicol, Mrs A., MA, BLitt, Public Record Office, Chancery Lane, London WC2A 1LR.
Nicol, Professor D. M., MA, PhD, King's College, London WC2R 2LS.
Noakes, J. D., MA, DPhil, Queen's Bldg., The University, Exeter EX4 4QH.
Norman, E. R., MA, PhD, Peterhouse, Cambridge CB2 1RD.

Obolensky, Professor Dimitri, MA, PhD, DLitt, FBA, FSA, Christ Church, Oxford OX1 1DP.
O'Day, A., MA, PhD, Polytechnic of North London, Prince of Wales Road, London NW5.
O'Day, Mrs M. R., BA, PhD, 77A St Clements Street, Oxford OX4 1AW.
*Offler, Professor H. S., MA, 28 Old Elvet, Durham DH1 3HN.
O'Gorman, F., BA, PhD, The University, Manchester M13 9PL.
O'Higgins, The Rev J., SJ, MA, DPhil, Campion Hall, Oxford.
Olney, R. J., MA, DPhil, Historical Manuscripts Commission, Quality Court, Chancery Lane, London WC2.
Orde, Miss A., MA, PhD, 8 Wearside Drive, Durham DH1 1LE.
Orme, N. I., MA, DPhil, The University, Exeter EX4 4QH.
*Orr, J. E., MA, ThD, DPhil, 11451 Berwick Street, Los Angeles, Calif. 90049, U.S.A.
Ó Tuathaigh, M. A. G., MA, Dept of History, University College, Galway, Ireland.
Otway-Ruthven, Professor A. J., MA, PhD, 7 Trinity College, Dublin, Ireland.
Outhwaite, R. B., MA, PhD, Gonville and Caius College, Cambridge CB2 1TA.
Ovendale, R., MA, DPhil, Dept of International Politics, University College of Wales, Aberystwyth SY23 3DB.
Owen, A. E. B., MA, 35 Whitwell Way, Coton, Cambridge CB3 7PW.
Owen, Mrs D. M., MA, FSA, 35 Whitwell Way, Coton, Cambridge CB3 7PW.
Owen, G. D., MA, PhD, 4 St Aubyn's Mansions, Kings Esplanade, Hove, Sussex.
Owen, J. B., BSc, MA, DPhil, Lincoln College, Oxford OX1 3DR.

Pagden, A. R. D., BA, Girton College, Cambridge CB3 0JG.
Palliser, D. M., MA, DPhil, 14 Verstone Croft, Birmingham B31 2QE.
Pallister, Miss Anne, BA, PhD, The University, Reading RG6 2AA.
Palmer, J. J. N., BA, BLitt, PhD, 59 Marlborough Avenue, Hull.
Parish, Professor P. J., BA, Dept of Modern History, The University, Dundee DD1 4HN.
Parker, N. G., MA, PhD, Dept of Modern History, St Salvator's College, The University, St Andrew's, Fife KY16 9AJ.
Parker, R. A. C., MA, DPhil, The Queen's College, Oxford OX1 4BH.
Parker, The Rev. Dr T. M., MA, DD, FSA, 36 Chalfont Road, Oxford OX2 6TH.
Parkes, M. B., BLitt, MA, FSA, Keble College, Oxford OX1 3PG.
*Parkinson, Professor C. N., MA, PhD, Les Caches House, St Martins, Guernsey, C.I.
Parris, H. W., MA, PhD, 15 Murdoch Road, Wokingham, Berks. RG11 2DG.
Parry, Professor J. H., MA, PhD, Pinnacle Road, Harvard, Mass. 01451, U.S.A.
Parsloe, C. G., MA, 1 Leopold Avenue, London SW19 7ET.

Patrick, Rev J. G., MA, PhD, DLitt, 7920 Teasdale Court, University City, St. Louis, Missouri 63130, U.S.A.

Patterson, Professor A. T., MA, 14 Cresta Court, Eastern Parade, Southsea TO4 9RB.

Pavlowitch, Steven K., MA, LesL, Dept of History, The University, Southampton SO9 5NH.

Payne, Professor Peter L., BA, PhD, 14 The Chanonry, Old Aberdeen AB2 1RP.

Peake, Rev. F. A., DD, DSLitt, Dept of History, Laurentian University, Sudbury, Ontario P3E 2C6, Canada.

Pearl, Professor Valerie, MA, DPhil, FSA, 11 Church Row, Hampstead, London NW3 6UT.

Pearn, B. R., OBE, MA, The White House, Beechwood Avenue, Aylmerton, Norfolk NOR 25Y.

Peek, Miss H. E., MA, FSA, FSAScot, Taintona, Moretonhampstead, Newton Abbot, Devon TQ13 8LG.

Peele, Miss Gillian R., BA, BPhil, Lady Margaret Hall, Oxford OX2 6QA.

Pelham, R. A., MA, PhD, Orchard End, Church Road, West Lavington, Midhurst, West Sussex GU29 0EH.

Pennington, D. H., MA, Balliol College, Oxford OX1 3BJ.

Perkin, Professor H. J., MA, Borwicks, Caton, Lancaster.

Peters, Professor E. M., PhD, Dept of History, University of Pennsylvania, Philadelphia 19174, U.S.A.

Petti, Professor A. G. R., MA, DLit, FSA, Dept of English, University of Calgary, Alberta T2N 1N4, Canada.

Philips, Professor Sir Cyril (H.), MA, PhD, DLitt, 3 Winterstoke Gardens, London NW7.

Phillips, Sir Henry (E. I.), CMG, MBE, MA, 34 Ross Court, Putney Hill, London SW15.

Phillips, J. R. S., BA, PhD, FSA, Dept of Medieval History, University College, Dublin 4, Ireland.

Phythian-Adams, C. V., MA, Dept of English Local History, The University, Leicester LE1 7RH.

Pierce, Professor G. O., MA, Dept of History, University College, P.O. Box 95, Cardiff CF1 1XA.

Pitt, H. G., MA, Worcester College, Oxford OX1 2HB.

Platt, C. P. S., MA, PhD, FSA, 24 Oakmount Avenue, Highfield, Southampton.

Platt, Professor D. C. St M., MA, DPhil, St Antony's College, Oxford OX2 6JF.

Plumb, Professor J. H., PhD, LittD, FBA, FSA, Christ's College, Cambridge CB2 3BU.

Pocock, Professor J. G. A., PhD, Johns Hopkins University, Baltimore, Md. 21218, U.S.A.

Pole, Professor J. R., MA, PhD, St Catherine's College, Oxford OX1 3UJ.

Pollard, A. J., BA, PhD, 22 The Green, Hurworth-on-Tees, Darlington, Co Durham DL2 2AA.

Pollard, Professor S., BSc(Econ), PhD, Dept of Economic History, The University, Sheffield S10 2TN.

Polonsky, A. B., BA, DPhil, Dept of International History, London School of Economics, Houghton Street, London WC2A 2AE.

Port, M. H., MA, BLitt, Queen Mary College, Mile End Road, London E1 4NS.

Porter, A. N., MA, PhD, Dept of History, King's College, Strand, London WC2R 2LS.

Porter, B. E., BSc(Econ), PhD, Dept of International Politics, University College of Wales, Aberystwyth, Dyfed SY23 3DB.

Porter, H. C., MA, PhD, Faculty of History, West Road, Cambridge CB3 9EF.

Postan, Professor Sir Michael, MA, FBA, Peterhouse, Cambridge CB2 1RD.

*Potter, Professor G. R., MA, PhD, FSA, Herongate, Derwent Lane, Hathersage, Sheffield S30 1AS.

Potter, J., BA, MA(Econ), London School of Economics, Houghton Street, London WC2A 2AE.

Powell, W. R., BLitt, MA, FSA, 2 Glanmead, Shenfield Road, Brentwood, Essex.

Powicke, Professor M. R., MA, University of Toronto, Toronto M5S 1AI, Canada.

Prall, Professor Stuart E., MA, PhD, Dept of History, Queen's College, C.U.N.Y., Flushing, N.Y. 11367, U.S.A.

Prest, W. R., MA, DPhil, Dept of History, University of Adelaide, North Terrace, Adelaide 5001, S. Australia.

Preston, Professor A. W., PhD, Dept of History, Royal Military College of Canada, Kingston, Ontario K7L 2W3, Canada.

*Preston, Professor R. A., MA, PhD, Duke University, Durham, N.C., U.S.A.

Prestwich, J. O., MA, The Queen's College, Oxford OX1 4AW.

Prestwich, Mrs M., MA, St Hilda's College, Oxford OX4 1DY.

Prestwich, M. C., MA, DPhil, Dept of History, 43/46 North Bailey, Durham DH1 3EX.

Price, A. W., 19 Bayley Close, Uppingham, Leicestershire LE15 9TG.

Price, Rev. D. T. W., MA, St David's University College, Lampeter, Dyfed SA48 7ED.

Price, F. D., MA, BLitt, FSA, Keble College, Oxford OX1 3PG.

Price, Professor Jacob M., AM, PhD, University of Michigan, Ann Arbor, Michigan 48104, U.S.A.

Pritchard, Professor D. G., PhD, 11 Coedmor, Sketty, Swansea, W. Glam. SA2 8BQ.

Pronay, N., BA, School of History, The University, Leeds LS2 9JT.

Prothero, I. J., BA, PhD, The University, Manchester M13 9PL.

*Pugh, Professor R. B., MA, DLit, FSA, 67 Southwood Park, London N6.

Pugh, T. B., MA, BLitt, 28 Bassett Wood Drive, Southampton SO2 3PS.

Pullan, Professor B. S., MA, PhD, Dept of History, The University, Manchester M13 9PL.

Pulman, M. B., MA, PhD, University of Denver, Colorado 80210, U.S.A.

Pulzer, P. G. J., MA, PhD, Christ Church, Oxford OX1 1DP.

Quinn, Professor D. B., MA, PhD, DLit, DLitt, LLD, DHL, 9 Knowsley Road, Liverpool L19 0PF.

Rabb, Professor T. K., MA, PhD, Princeton University, Princeton, N.J. 08540, U.S.A.

Radford, C. A. Ralegh, MA, DLitt, FBA, FSA, Culmcott, Uffculme, Cullompton, Devon EX15 3AT.

*Ramm, Miss A., MA, DLitt, Somerville College, Oxford OX2 6HD.

*Ramsay, G. D., MA, DPhil, 15 Charlbury Road, Oxford OX2 6UT.

Ramsey, Professor P. H., MA, DPhil, Taylor Building, King's College, Old Aberdeen AB9 1FX.

Ranft, Professor B. McL., MA, DPhil, 16 Eliot Vale, London SE3.

Ranger, Professor T., MA, DPhil, The University, Manchester M13 9PL.

Ransome, D. R., MA, PhD, Rill Cottage, Great Bealings, Woodbridge, Suffolk.

Rawcliffe, Carole, BA, PhD, 24 Villiers Road, London NW2.

Rawley, Professor J. A., PhD, University of Nebraska, Lincoln, Nebraska 68508, U.S.A.

Ray, Professor R. D., BA, BD, PhD, University of Toledo, 2801 W. Bancroft Street, Toledo, Ohio 43606, U.S.A.

Read, Professor D., BLitt, MA, PhD, Darwin College, University of Kent at Canterbury, Kent CT2 7NY.

Reader, W. J., BA, PhD, 67 Wood Vale, London N10 3DL.

Reeves, Professor A. C., MA, PhD, Dept of History, Ohio University, Athens, Ohio 45701, U.S.A.

Reeves, Miss M. E., MA, PhD, 38 Norham Road, Oxford OX2 65Q.

Reid, Professor L. D., MA, PhD, 200 E. Brandon Road, Columbia, Mo. 65201, U.S.A.

Reid, Professor W. S., MA, PhD, University of Guelph, Guelph, Ontario, Canada.

Renold, Miss P., MA, 5 Connaught Road, New Malden, Surrey KT3 3PZ.

Reuter, T. A., MA, DPhil, 89 Redhills, Exeter, Devon EX4 1SH.

Reynolds, Miss S. M. G., MA, 26 Lennox Gardens, London SW1.

Richards, J. M., MA, Dept of History, The University, Bailrigg, Lancaster LA1 4YG.

Richards, Rev. J. M., MA, BLitt, STL, Heythrop College, 11–13 Cavendish Square, London W1M 0AN.

Richardson, K. E., MA, PhD, Lanchester Polytechnic, Priory Street, Coventry.

Richardson R. C., BA, PhD, King Alfred's College, Winchester.

Richardson, Professor W. C., MA, PhD, Louisiana State University, Baton Rouge, Louisiana, U.S.A.

Richmond, C. F., DPhil, 59 The Covert, The University, Keele, Staffs. ST5 5BG.

Richter, M., DrPhil, Dept of Medieval History, University College, Dublin 4, Ireland.

Rigold, S. E., MA, FSA, 2 Royal Crescent, London W11.

Riley, P. W. J., BA, PhD, The University, Manchester M13 9PL.

Riley-Smith, Professor J. S. C., MA, PhD, Tandem House, North Street, Winkfield, Windsor, Berks. SL4 4TB.

Rimmer, Professor W. G., MA, PhD, University of N.S.W., P.O. Box 1, Kensington, N.S.W. 2033, Australia.

Ritcheson, Professor C. R., DPhil, Dept of History, University of Southern California, Los Angeles 90007, U.S.A.

Roach, Professor J. P. C., MA, PhD, 1 Park Crescent, Sheffield S10 2DY.

Robbins, Professor Caroline, PhD, 815 The Chetwynd, Rosemont, Pa. 19010, U.S.A.

Robbins, Professor K. G., MA, DPhil, Dept of History, The University, Glasgow G12 8QQ.

Roberts, Professor J. M., MA, DPhil, The University, Southampton SO9 5NH.

Roberts, Professor M., MA, DPhil, DLit, FilDr, FBA, 38 Somerset Street, Grahamstown 6140, C.P., South Africa.

Roberts, P. R., MA, PhD, FSA, Keynes College, The University of Kent at Canterbury, Kent CT2 7NP.

Roberts, Professor R. C., PhD, 284 Blenheim Road, Columbus, Ohio 43214, U.S.A.

Roberts, Professor R. S., PhD, University of Zimbabwe, Salisbury, P.B. 167H, Zimbabwe.

Robinson, K. E., CBE, MA, DLitt, LLD, The Old Rectory, Church Westcote, Kingham, Oxford OX7 6SF.

Robinson, R. A. H., BA, PhD, School of History, The University, Birmingham B15 2TT.

Robinton, Professor Madeline R., MA, PhD, 210 Columbia Heights, Brooklyn, New York, U.S.A.

Rodger, N. A. M., MA, DPhil, 97 Speldhurst Road, London W4.

*Rodkey, F. S., AM, PhD, 152 Bradley Drive, Santa Cruz, Calif., U.S.A.

Rodney, Professor W., MA, PhD, 14 Royal Roads Military College, Victoria, B.C., Canada.

Roe, F. Gordon, FSA, 19 Vallance Road, London N22 4UD.

Roebuck, Peter, BA, PhD, Dept of History, New University of Ulster, Coleraine, N. Ireland BT48 7JL.

Rogers, Professor A., MA, PhD, FSA, New University of Ulster, Coleraine, N. Ireland BT52 1SA.

Rogister, J. M. J., BA, DPhil, 4 The Peth, Durham DH1 4PZ.

Rolo, Professor P. J. V., MA, The University, Keele, Staffordshire ST5 5BG.

Roorda, Professor D. J., University of Leiden, Leiden 2, The Netherlands.

Roots, Professor I. A., MA, FSA, Dept of History, University of Exeter, Exeter EX4 4QH.

Roper, M., MA, Public Record Office, Ruskin Avenue. Kew, Richmond, Surrey TW9 4DU.

Rose, P. L., MA, D.enHist (Sorbonne), Dept of History, James Cook University, Douglas, Queensland 4811, Australia.

Rosenthal, Professor Joel T., PhD, State University, Stony Brook, New York 11794, U.S.A.

Roseveare, H. G., PhD, King's College, Strand, London WC2R 2LS.

Roskell, Professor J. S., MA, DPhil, FBA, The University, Manchester M13 9PL.

Roskill, Captain S. W., CBE, DSC, RN (ret.), Frostlake Cottage, Malting Lane, Cambridge CB3 9HF.

Ross, Professor C. D., MA, DPhil, Wills Memorial Building, Queen's Road, Bristol BS8 1RJ.

Rothney, Professor G. O., PhD, Dept of History, University of Manitoba, Winnipeg R3T 2N2, Canada.

Rothrock, Professor G. A., MA, PhD, Dept of History, University of Alberta, Edmonton, Alberta T6G 2H4, Canada.

Rouse. Professor R. H., MA, PhD, Dept of History, University of California, Los Angeles, California 90024, U.S.A.

Rousseau, P. H., MA, DPhil, 44 Bellevue Avenue, Northcote, Auckland 9, New Zealand.

*Rowe, Miss B. J. H., MA, BLitt, St Anne's Cottage, Winkton, Christchurch, Hants.

Rowe, W. J., DPhil, 4 Roslin Road, Irby, Wirral, Merseyside L61 3UH.

Rowse, A. L., MA, DLitt, DCL, FBA, All Souls College, Oxford OX1 4AL.

ROY, I., MA, DPhil, (*Assistant Literary Director*), Dept of History, King's College, Strand, London WC2R 2LS.

Roy, Professor R. H., MA, PhD, 2841 Tudor Avenue, Victoria, B.C., Canada.

Royle, E., MA, PhD, Dept of History, The University, Heslington, York YO1 5DD.

Rubens, A., FRICS, FSA, 16 Grosvenor Place, London SW1.

Rubini, D. A., DPhil, Temple University, Philadelphia 19122, Penn., U.S.A.

Rubinstein, Professor N., PhD, Westfield College, Hampstead, London NW3 7ST.

Ruddock, Miss A. A., PhD, FSA, Wren Cottage, Heatherwood, Midhurst, W. Sussex GU29 9LH.

Rudé, Professor G. F. E., MA, PhD, The Oast House, Hope Farm, Beckley, nr Rye, E. Sussex.

Rule, Professor John C., MA, PhD, Ohio State University, 230 West 17th Avenue, Columbus, Ohio 43210, U.S.A.

*RUNCIMAN, The Hon. Sir Steven, MA, DPhil, LLD, LittD, DLitt, LitD, DD, DHL, FBA, FSA, Elshieshields, Lockerbie, Dumfriesshire.

Runyan, Professor Timothy J., Cleveland State University, Cleveland, Ohio 44115, U.S.A.

Rupp, Professor the Rev. E. G., MA, DD, FBA, 42 Malcolm Place, King Street, Cambridge CB1 1LS.

Russell, Professor C. S. R., MA, Yale University, New Haven, Conn. 06520, U.S.A.

Russell, Mrs J. G., MA, DPhil, St Hugh's College, Oxford OX2 6LE.

Russell, Professor P. E., MA, FBA, 23 Belsyre Court, Woodstock Road, Oxford OX2 6HU.

Ryan, A. N., MA, School of History, University of Liverpool, P.O. Box 147, Liverpool L69 3BX.

Rycraft, P., BA, Dept of History, The University, Heslington, York YO1 5DD.

Ryder, A. F. C., MA, D.Phil, Dept of History, Wills Memorial Building, Queen's Road, Bristol BS8 1RJ.

Sachse, Professor W. L., PhD, 4066 Whitney Avenue, Mt. Carmel, Conn. 06518, U.S.A.

Sainty, J. C., MA, 22 Kelso Place, London W8.

*Salmon, Professor E. T., MA, PhD, 36 Auchmar Road, Hamilton, Ontario LPC 1C5, Canada.

Salmon, Professor J. H. M., MA, MLitt, DLit, Bryn Mawr College, Bryn Mawr, Pa. 19101, U.S.A.

*Saltman, Professor A., MA, PhD, Bar Ilan University, Ramat Gan, Israel.

Samaha, Professor Joel, PhD, Dept of Criminal Justice Studies, University of Minnesota, Minneapolis, U.S.A.

Sammut, E., KM, MA, LLD, 4 Don Rua Street, Sliema, Malta.

Samuel, E. R., BA, MPhil, 8 Steynings Way, London N12 7LN.

Sanderson, Professor G. N., MA, PhD, Dept of Modern History, Royal Holloway College, Englefield Green, Surrey TW20 0EX.

Sar Desai, Professor Damodar R., MA, PhD, Dept of History, University of California, Los Angeles, Calif. 90024, U.S.A.

Saville, Professor J., BSc(Econ), Dept of Economic and Social History, The University, Hull HU6 7RX.

Sawyer, Professor P. H., MA, The University, Leeds LS2 9JT.

Sayers, Miss J. E., MA, BLitt, FSA, 17 Sheffield Terrace, Campden Hill, London W8.

Scammell, G. V., MA, Pembroke College, Cambridge CB2 1RF.
Scammell, Mrs Jean, MA, Clare Hall, Cambridge.
Scarisbrick, Professor J. J., MA, PhD, 35 Kenilworth Road, Leamington Spa, Warwickshire.
Schoeck, Professor R. J., PhD, Dept of English, University of Colorado, Boulder 80309, U.S.A.
Schofield, A. N. E. D., PhD, 15 Westergate, Corfton Road, London W5.
Schofield, R. S., MA, PhD, 27 Trumpington Street, Cambridge CB2 1QA.
Schwoerer, Professor Lois G., PhD, 7213 Rollingwood Drive, Chevy Chase, Maryland 20015, U.S.A.
Scott, H. M., MA, PhD, Dept of Modern History, The University, St. Salvator's College, St Andrews, Fife.
Scouloudi, Miss I., MSc(Econ), FSA, 67 Victoria Road, London W8 5RH.
Seaborne, M. V. J., MA, Chester College, Cheyney Road, Chester CH1 4BJ.
Searle, G. R., MA, PhD, School of English and American Studies, University of East Anglia, University Plain, Norwich NR4 7TJ.
Seary, Professor E. R., MA, PhD, LittD, DLitt, FSA, South River, Newfoundland AoA 3WO, Canada.
Seaver, Professor Paul S., MA, PhD, Dept of History, Stanford University, Stanford, Calif. 94305, U.S.A.
Sell, Rev. A. P. F., BA, BD, MA, PhD, 40 Hobart Drive, Walsall WS5 3NL.
Semmel, Professor Bernard, PhD, Dept of History, State University of New York at Stony Brook, Stony Brook, N.Y. 11790, U.S.A.
Serjeant, W. R., BA, 51 Derwent Road, Ipswich IP3 0QR.
Seton-Watson, C. I. W., MC, MA, Oriel College, Oxford OX1 4EW.
Seton-Watson, Professor G. H. N., MA, FBA, Dept of Russian History, School of Slavonic Studies, London WC1E 7HU.
Shackleton, R., MA, DLitt, LittD, FBA, FSA, FRSL, All Souls College, Oxford OX1 4AL.
Shannon, Professor R. T., MA, PhD, Dept of History, University College, Swansea SA2 8PP.
Sharp, Mrs M., MA, PhD, 59 Southway, London NW11 6SB.
Sharpe, K. M., MA, DPhil, Dept of History, University of Southampton, Southampton SO9 5NH.
Shaw, I. P., MA, 3 Oaks Lane, Shirley, Croydon, Surrey CR0 5HP.
Shead, N. F., MA, BLitt, 8 Whittliemuir Avenue, Muirend, Glasgow G44 3HU.
Sheils, W. J., PhD, 186 Stockton Lane, York YO3 0EY.
Shennan, Professor J. H., PhD, Dept of History, University of Lancaster, Bailrigg, Lancaster LA1 4YG.
Sheppard, F. H. W., MA, PhD, FSA, 55 New Street, Henley-on-Thames, Oxon RG9 2BP.
Sherborne, J. W., MA, 26 Hanbury Road, Bristol BS8 2EP.
Sherwood, R. E., Sandy Hill Cottage, Sandy Hill Lane, Weybourne, Holt, Norfolk NR25 7HW.
Simmons, Professor J., MA, (address unknown.)
Simpson, G. G., MA, PhD, FSA, Taylor Building, King's College, Old Aberdeen AB9 2UB.
Sinar, Miss J. C., MA, 60 Wellington Street, Matlock, Derbyshire DE4 3GS.
Siney, Professor Marion C., MA, PhD, 2676 Mayfield Road, Cleveland Heights, Ohio 44106, U.S.A.
Singhal, Professor D. P., MA, PhD, University of Queensland, St Lucia, Brisbane, Queensland 4067, Australia.

Skidelsky, Professor R. J. A., BA, PhD, 32 Gt Percy Street, London WC1.
Skinner, Professor Q. R. D., MA, Christ's College, Cambridge CB2 3BU.
Slack, P. A., MA, DPhil, Exeter College, Oxford OX1 3DP.
Slade, C. F., PhD, FSA, 28 Holmes Road, Reading, Berks.
Slater, A. W., MSc(Econ), 146 Castelnau, London SW13 9ET.
Slatter, Miss M. D., MA, Rose Cottage, Old Road, Studley, Calne, Wilts.
Slavin, Professor A. J., PhD, College of Arts & Letters, University of Louis-
    ville, Louisville, Kentucky 40268, U.S.A.
Smail, R. C., MBE, MA, PhD, FSA, Sidney Sussex College, Cambridge CB2
    3HU.
*Smalley, Miss B., MA, PhD, FBA, 5c Rawlinson Road, Oxford OX2 6UE.
Smith, A. G. R., MA, PhD, 5 Cargil Avenue, Kilmacolm, Renfrewshire.
Smith, A. Hassell, BA, PhD, School of English and American Studies, Uni-
    versity of East Anglia, Norwich NR4 7TJ.
Smith, B. S., MA, FSA, Historical Manuscripts Commission, Quality Court,
    Chancery Lane, London WC2A 1HP.
Smith, Charles Daniel, PhD, 114 Sims, Syracuse University, Syracuse, N.Y.
    13210, U.S.A.
Smith, D. M., MA, PhD, FSA, Borthwick Institute of Historical Research,
    St Anthony's Hall, York YO1 2PW.
Smith, E. A., MA, Dept of History, Faculty of Letters, The University,
    Whiteknights, Reading RG6 2AA.
Smith, F. B., MA, PhD, Research School of Social Sciences, Institute of
    Advanced Studies, Australian National University, A.C.T. 2600,
    Australia.
Smith, Professor Goldwin A., MA, PhD, DLitt, Wayne State University,
    Detroit, Michigan 48202, U.S.A.
Smith, J. Beverley, MA, University College, Aberystwyth SY23 2AX.
Smith, Joseph, BA, PhD, Dept of History, The University, Exeter EX4 4QH.
Smith, Professor L. Baldwin, PhD, Northwestern University, Evanston, Ill.
    60201, U.S.A.
Smith, Professor P., MA, DPhil, Dept of History, The University, Southamp-
    ton S09 5NH.
Smith, S., BA, PhD, Les Haies, 40 Oatlands Road, Shinfield, Reading, Berks.
Smith, W. H. C., BA, PhD, Flat A, 110 Blackheath Hill, London SE10 8AG.
Smith, W. J., MA, 5 Gravel Hill, Emmer Green, Reading, Berks. RG4
    8QN.
*Smyth, Rev. Canon C. H. E., MA, 12 Manor Court, Pinehurst, Cambridge.
Snell, L. S., MA, FSA, FRSA, 27 Weoley Hill, Selly Oak, Birmingham B29
    4AA.
Snow, Professor V. F., MA, PhD, Dept of History, Syracuse University, 311
    Maxwell Hall, Syracuse, New York 13210, U.S.A.
Snyder, Professor H. L., MA, PhD, 4646 Woodside Drive, Baton Rouge, La.
    70808, U.S.A.
Soden, G. I., MA, DD, Buck Brigg, Hanworth, Norfolk.
Somers, Rev. H. J., JCB, MA, PhD, St Francis Xavier University, Antigon-
    ish, Nova Scotia, Canada.
Somerville, Sir Robert, KCVO, MA, FSA, 15 Foxes Dale, Blackheath, Lon-
    don SE3 9BD.
SOUTHERN, Sir Richard (W.), MA, DLitt, LittD, DLitt, FBA, The Presi-
    dent's Lodgings, St John's College, Oxford OX1 3JP.
Southgate, D. G., BA, DPhil, 40 Camphill Road, Broughty Ferry, Dundee,
    Scotland.
Spalding, Miss R., MA, 34 Reynards Road, Welwyn, Herts.

Speck, W. A., MA, DPhil, The University, Newcastle upon Tyne NE1 7RU.
Spencer, B. W., BA, FSA, 6 Carpenters Wood Drive, Chorleywood, Herts.
Spiers, E. D., MA, PhD, 487 Street Lane, Leeds, West Yorkshire LS17 6LA.
Spooner, Professor F. C., MA, PhD, The University, 23 Old Elvet, Durham DH1 3HY.
Spring, Professor D., PhD, Dept of History, Johns Hopkins University, Baltimore, Md. 21218, U.S.A.
Spufford, Mrs H. M., MA, PhD, Walnut Tree House, 36 High Street, Haddenham, Cambs. CB6 3XB.
Spufford, P., MA, PhD, Queens' College, Cambridge CB3 9ET.
Squibb, G. D., QC, FSA, The Old House, Cerne Abbas, Dorset DT2 7JQ.
Stanley, Professor G. F. G., MA, BLitt, DPhil, Library, Mount Allison University, Sackville, New Brunswick, Canada.
Stansky, Professor Peter, PhD, Dept of History, Stanford University, Stanford, Calif. 94305, U.S.A.
Steefel, Lawrence D., MA, PhD, 3420 Heritage Drive, Apt. 117, Edina, Mn. 55435, U.S.A.
Steele, E. D., MA, PhD, The University, Leeds LS2 9JT.
Steinberg, J., MA, PhD, Trinity Hall, Cambridge CB2 1TJ.
Steiner, Mrs Zara S., MA, PhD, New Hall, Cambridge CB3 0DF.
Stephens, W. B., MA, PhD, FSA, 37 Batcliffe Drive, Leeds 6.
Steven, Miss M. J. E., PhD, 3 Bonwick Place, Garran, A.C.T. 2605, Australia.
Stevenson, D., BA, PhD, Dept of History, Taylor Building, King's College, Old Aberdeen AB1 0EE.
Stevenson, Miss J. H., BA, c/o Institute of Historical Research, Senate House, Malet Street, London WC1E 7HU.
Stewart, A. T. Q., MA, PhD, Dept of Modern History, The Queen's University, Belfast BT7 1NN.
Stitt, F. B., BA, BLitt, William Salt Library, Stafford.
Stockwell, A. J., MA, PhD, Dept of History, Royal Holloway College, Egham, Surrey TW20 0EX.
Stone, E., MA, DPhil, FSA, Keble College, Oxford OX1 3PG.
Stone, Professor L., MA, Princeton University, Princeton, N.J., 08540, U.S.A.
*Stones, Professor E. L. G., PhD, FSA, 34 Alexandra Road, Parkstone, Poole, Dorset BH14 9EN.
Storey, Professor R. L., MA, PhD, 19 Elm Avenue, Beeston, Nottingham NG9 1BU.
Storry, J. G., Farrington's Copse, Fittleworth, Nr Pulborough, Sussex.
Story, Professor G. M., BA, DPhil, 335 Southside Road, St John's, Newfoundland, Canada.
*Stoye, J. W., MA, DPhil, Magdalen College, Oxford OX1 4AU.
Street, J., MA, PhD, 6 Thulborn Close, Teversham, Cambridge.
Strong, Mrs F., MA, South Cloister, Eton College, Windsor SL4 6DB.
Strong, R., BA, PhD, FSA, Victoria & Albert Museum, London SW7.
Stuart, C. H., MA, Christ Church, Oxford OX1 1DP.
Studd, J. R., PhD, Dept of History, The University, Keele, Staffs. ST5 5BG.
Sturdy, D. J., BA, PhD, Dept of History, New University of Ulster, Coleraine, N. Ireland BT52 1SA.
Supple, B. E., BSc (Econ), PhD, MA, Nuffield College, Oxford OX1 1NF.
Surman, Rev. C. E., MA, 352 Myton Road, Leamington Spa CV31 3NY.
Sutherland, Professor D. W., DPhil, State University of Iowa, Iowa City, Iowa 52240, U.S.A.

Sutherland, N. M., MA, PhD, St John's Hall, Bedford College, London NW1 4NS.

Swanson, R. N., MA, PhD, School of History, The University, P.O. Box 363, Birmingham B15 2TT.

Swanton, M. J., BA, PhD, FSA, Queen's Building, The University, Exeter EX4 4QH.

Swart, Professor K. W., PhD, LittD, University College London, Gower Street, London WC1E 6BT.

Sweet, D. W., MA, PhD, Dept of History, The University, 43 North Bailey, Durham.

Swinfen, D. B., MA, DPhil, 14 Cedar Road, Broughty Ferry, Dundee.

Sydenham, M. J., PhD, Carleton University, Ottawa 1, Canada.

Syrett, Professor D., PhD, 46 Hawthorne Terrace, Leonia, N.J. 07605, U.S.A.

Taft, Barbara, PhD, 3101 35th Street, Washington, D.C. 20016, U.S.A.

Talbot, C. H., PhD, BD, FSA, 47 Hazlewell Road, London SW15.

Tamse, Coenraad Arnold, DLitt, De Krom, 12 Potgieterlaan, 9752Ex Haren (Groningen), The Netherlands.

Tanner, J. I., CBE, MA, PhD, Flat One, 57 Drayton Gardens, London SW10 9RU.

Tarling, Professor P. N., MA, PhD, LittD, University of Auckland, Private Bag, Auckland, New Zealand.

Tarn, Professor J. N., B.Arch, PhD, FRIBA, Dept of Architecture, The University, P. O. Box 147, Liverpool L69 3BX.

Taylor, Arnold J., CBE, MA, DLitt, FBA, FSA, Rose Cottage, Lincoln's Hill, Chiddingfold, Surrey GU8 4UN.

Taylor, Professor Arthur J., MA, The University, Leeds LS2 9JT.

Taylor, H. W., BA, MA, Dept of Economic and Social History, The University, Nottingham NG7 2RD.

Taylor, J., MA, The University, Leeds LS2 9JT.

Taylor, J. W. R., 36 Alexandra Drive, Surbiton, Surrey KT5 9AF.

Taylor, R. T., MA, PhD, Dept of Political Theory and Government, University College of Swansea, Swansea SA2 8PP.

Taylor, W., MA, PhD, FSAScot, 25 Bingham Terrace, Dundee.

Teichova, Professor Alice, BA, PhD, University of East Anglia, University Plain, Norwich NR4 7TJ.

Temperley, H., BA, MA, PhD, School of English and American Studies, University of East Anglia, Norwich NR4 7TJ.

Temple, Nora C., BA, PhD, University College, Cardiff CF1 1XL.

Templeman, G., CBE, MA, DCL, DL, FSA, Barton Corner, 2A St Augustine's Road, Canterbury, Kent.

Thirsk, Mrs. I. Joan, PhD, FBA, St Hilda's College, Oxford OX4 1DY.

Thistlethwaite, Professor F., CBE, DCL, LHD, University of East Anglia, Norwich NR4 7TJ.

Thomas, Professor H. S., MA, University of Reading, Reading RG6 2AH.

Thomas, Rev. J. A., MA, PhD, 164 Northfield Lane, Brixham, Devon TQ5 8RH.

Thomas, K. V., MA, FBA, St John's College, Oxford OX1 3JP.

Thomas, P. D. G., MA, PhD, University College, Aberystwyth SY23 2AU.

Thomas, W. E. S., MA, Christ Church, Oxford OX1 1DP.

Thomis, Professor M. I., MA, PhD, University of Queensland, St Lucia, Brisbane 4067, Australia.

Thompson, A. F., MA, Wadham College, Oxford OX1 3PN.

Thompson, Mrs D. K. G., MA, School of History, The University, P.O. Box 363, Birmingham B15 2TT.
Thompson, D. M., MA, PhD, Fitzwilliam College, Cambridge CB3 0DG.
Thompson, E. P., MA, Wick Episcopi, Upper Wick, Worcester.
Thompson, Professor F. M. L., MA, DPhil, FBA, Institute of Historical Research, Senate House, London WC1E 7HU.
Thomson, J. A. F., MA, DPhil, The University, Glasgow G12 8QQ.
Thomson, R. M., MA, PhD, Dept of History, University of Tasmania, Box 252C, GPO, Hobart, Tasmania 7001, Australia.
*Thomson, T. R. F., MA, MD, FSA, Cricklade, Wilts.
Thorne, C., BA, School of European Studies, University of Sussex, Brighton BN1 9QX.
Thornton, Professor A. P., MA, DPhil, 6 Glen Edyth Drive, Toronto M4V 2W2, Canada.
*Thrupp, Professor S. L., MA, PhD, University of Michigan, Ann Arbor, Mich. 48104, U.S.A.
Thurlow, The Very Rev. A. G. G., MA, FSA, The Deanery, Gloucester.
Tibbutt, H. G., FSA, 12 Birchdale Avenue, Kempston, Bedford.
Tomkeieff, Mrs O. G., MA, LLB, 88 Moorside North, Newcastle upon Tyne NE4 9DU.
Tomlinson, H. C., BA, 10 Connaught Close, Wellington College, Crowthorne, Berkshire RG11 7PU.
Townshend, C. J. N., MA, DPhil, The Hawthorns, Keele, Staffordshire.
Toynbee, Miss M. R., MA, PhD, FSA, 22 Park Town, Oxford OX2 6SH.
Trebilcock, R. C., MA, Pembroke College, Cambridge CB2 1RF.
*Trevor-Roper, Professor H. R., (see under Lord Dacre).
Trickett, Professor A. Stanley, MA, PhD, 236 South Lake Drive, Lehigh Acres, Florida 33936, U.S.A.
Tsitsonis, S. E., PhD, 6 Foskolou Street, Halandri, Athens, Greece.
Tyacke, N. R. N., MA, DPhil, 1A Spencer Rise, London NW5.
Tyler, P., BLitt, MA, DPhil, University of Western Australia, Nedlands, Western Australia 6009.

Ugawa, Professor K., BA, MA, PhD, 1008 Ikebukuro, 2 Chome, Toshima-ku, Tokyo 171, Japan.
Ullmann, Professor W., MA, LittD, FBA, Trinity College, Cambridge CB2 1TQ.
Underdown, Professor David, MA, BLitt, Dept of History, Brown University, Providence, Rhode Island 02912, U.S.A.
Underhill, C. H., The Lodge, Needwood, Burton-upon-Trent, Staffs. DE13 9PQ.
Upton, A. F., MA, 5 West Acres, St Andrews, Fife.

Vaisey, D. G., MA, FSA, 12 Hernes Road, Oxford.
Vale, M. G. A., MA, DPhil, St John's College, Oxford OX1 3JP.
Van Caenegem, Professor R. C., LLD, PhD, Veurestraat 18, 9821 Afsnee, Belgium.
Van Roon, Professor Ger, Dept of Contemporary History, Vrije Universiteit, Amsterdam, Koningslaan 31–33, The Netherlands.
Vann, Professor Richard T., PhD, Dept of History, Wesleyan University, Middletown, Conn. 06457, U.S.A.
*Varley, Mrs J., MA, FSA, 164 Nettleham Road, Lincoln.
Vaughan, Sir (G.) Edgar, KBE, MA, 27 Birch Grove, West Acton, London W3 9SP.

Veale, Elspeth M., BA, PhD, 31 St Mary's Road, Wimbledon, London SW19 7BP.

Véliz, Professor C., BSc, PhD, Dept. of Sociology, La Trobe University, Melbourne, Victoria 3083, Australia.

Vessey, D. W. T. C., MA, PhD, 10 Uphill Grove, Mill Hill, London NW7.

Villiers, Lady de, MA, BLitt, 4 Church Street, Beckley, Oxford.

Virgoe, R., BA, PhD, University of East Anglia, School of English and American Studies, Norwich NR4 7TJ.

Waddell, Professor D. A. G., MA, DPhil, University of Stirling, Stirling FK9 4LA.

*Wagner, Sir Anthony (R.), KCVO, MA, DLitt, FSA, College of Arms, Queen Victoria Street, London EC4.

Waites, B. F., MA, FRGS, 6 Chater Road, Oakham, Rutland LE15 6RY.

Walcott, R., MA, PhD, 14 Whig Street, Dennis, Mass. 02638, U.S.A.

Waley, D. P., MA, PhD, Dept of Manuscripts, British Library, London WC1B 3DG.

Walford, A. J., MA, PhD, FLA, 45 Parkside Drive, Watford, Herts.

Walker, Rev. Canon D. G., DPhil, FSA, University College, Swansea SA2 8PP.

Wallace, Professor W. V., MA, Institute of Soviet and East European Studies, University of Glasgow, Glasgow G12 8LQ.

Wallace-Hadrill, Professor J. M., MA, DLitt, FBA, All Souls College, Oxford OX1 4AL.

Wallis, Miss H. M., MA, DPhil, FSA, 96 Lord's View, St John's Wood Road, London NW8 7HG.

Wallis, P. J., MA, 27 Westfield Drive, Newcastle upon Tyne NE3 4XY.

Walne, P., MA, FSA, County Record Office, County Hall, Hertford.

Walsh, T. J., MA, PhD, MB, BCh, 5 Lower George Street, Wexford, Ireland.

Walvin, J., BA, MA, DPhil, Dept of History, The University, Heslington, York YO1 5DD.

Wangermann, E., MA, DPhil, The University, Leeds LS2 9JT.

*Ward, Mrs G. A., PhD, FSA, Unsted, 51 Hartswood Road, Brentwood, Essex.

Ward, Professor J. T., MA, PhD, Dept of Economic History, McCance Bldg., 16 Richmond Street, Glasgow G1 1XQ.

Ward, Professor W. R., DPhil, University of Durham, 43 North Bailey, Durham.

*Warmington, Professor E. H., MA, 48 Flower Lane, London NW7.

Warner, Professor G., MA, Dept of History, The University, Leicester LE1 7RH.

Warren, Professor W. L., MA, DPhil, FRSL, Dept of Modern History, The Queen's University, Belfast, N. Ireland BT7 1NN.

Wasserstein, B. M. J., MA, DPhil, Dept of Modern History, The University, Sheffield S10 2TN.

*Waterhouse, Professor E. K., CBE, MA, AM, FBA, Overshot, Badger Lane, Hinksey Hill, Oxford.

*Waters, Lt-Commander D. W., RN, FSA, Jolyons, Bury, nr Pulborough, West Sussex.

Watkin, Rev. Dom Aelred, OSB, MA, FSA, St Benet's, Beccles, Suffolk NR34 9NR.

WATSON, A. G., MA, DLitt, FSA, (*Hon. Librarian*), University College London, Gower Street, London WC1E 6BT.

Watson, D. R., MA, BPhil, Dept of Modern History, The University, Dundee DD1 4HN.

Watson, J. S., MA, The University, College Gate, North Street, St Andrews, Fife, Scotland.

Watt, Professor D. C., MA, London School of Economics, Houghton Street, London WC2A 2AE.

Watt, Professor D. E. R., MA, DPhil, Dept of Mediaeval History, St Salvator's College, St Andrews, Fife KY16 9AL.

Watt, Professor J. A., BA, PhD, Dept of History, The University, Newcastle upon Tyne NE1 7RU.

Watts, M. R., BA, DPhil, Dept of History, The University, Nottingham NG7 2RD.

Webb, Professor Colin de B., BA, MA, Dept of History, University of Cape Town, Rondebosch 7700, South Africa.

Webb, J. G., MA, 11 Blount Road, Pembroke Park, Old Portsmouth, Hampshire PO1 2TD.

Webb, Professor R. K., PhD, 3307 Highland Place NW., Washington DC 20008, U.S.A.

Webster (A.) Bruce, MA, FSA, 5 The Terrace, St Stephens, Canterbury.

Webster, C., MA, DSc, Corpus Christi College, Oxford OX1 4JF.

Wedgwood, Dame (C.) Veronica, OM, DBE, MA, LittD, DLitt, LLD, Whitegate, Alciston, nr Polegate, Sussex.

Weinbaum, Professor M., PhD, 133–33 Sanford Avenue, Flushing, N.Y. 11355, U.S.A.

Weinstock, Miss M. B., MA, 26 Wey View Crescent, Broadway, Weymouth, Dorset.

Wells, R. A. E., BA, DPhil, Dept of Humanities, Brighton Polytechnic, Falmer, Brighton, Sussex.

Wendt, Professor Bernd-Jurgen, DrPhil, Beim Andreasbrunnen 8, 2 Hamburg 20, West Germany.

Wernham, Professor R. B., MA, Marine Cottage, 63 Hill Head Road, Hill Head, Fareham, Hants.

*Weske, Mrs Dorothy B., AM, PhD, Oakwood, Sandy Spring, Maryland 20860, U.S.A.

West, Professor F. J., PhD, Deakin University Interim Council, Cnr. Fenwick and Little Ryrie Streets, Geelong, Victoria 3220, Australia.

Weston, Professor Corinne C., PhD, 200 Central Park South, New York, N.Y. 10019, U.S.A.

*Whatmore, Rev. L. E., MA, St Wilfred's, South Road, Hailsham, Sussex.

Wheatley, R. R. A., MA, BLitt, Library and Records Dept, Foreign and Commonwealth Office, Cornwall House, Stamford Street, London SE1.

Whelan, The Rt. Rev. Abbot C. B., OSB, MA, Belmont Abbey, Hereford HR2 9RZ.

White, Professor B. M. I., MA, DLit, FSA, 3 Upper Duke's Drive, Eastbourne, Sussex BN20 7XT.

White, Rev. B. R., MA, DPhil, 55 St Giles', Regent's Park College, Oxford.

*Whitelock, Professor D., CBE, MA, LittD, FBA, FSA, 30 Thornton Close, Cambridge.

Whiteman, Miss E. A. O., MA, DPhil, FSA, Lady Margaret Hall, Oxford OX2 6QA.

Whiting, J. R. S., MA, DLitt, 15 Lansdown Parade, Cheltenham, Glos.

Whittam, J. R., MA, BPhil, PhD, Dept of History, University of Bristol, Senate House, Bristol BS8 1TH.

Wiener, Professor J. H., BA, PhD, City College of New York, Convent Avenue at 138th Street, N.Y. 10031, U.S.A.
Wilkie, Rev. W., MA, PhD, Dept of History, Loras College, Dubuque, Iowa 52001, U.S.A.
Wilks, Professor M. J., MA, PhD, Dept of History, Birkbeck College, Malet Street, London WC1E 7HX.
*Willan, Professor T. S., MA, DPhil, 3 Raynham Avenue, Didsbury, Manchester M20 0BW.
Williams, D., MA, PhD, DPhil, University of Calgary, Calgary, Alberta T2N 1N4, Canada.
Williams, Sir Edgar (T.), CB, CBE, DSO, MA, 94 Lonsdale Road, Oxford OX2 7ER.
Williams, Professor Glanmor, MA, DLitt, University College, Swansea SA2 8PP.
Williams, Professor Glyndwr, BA, PhD, Queen Mary College, Mile End Road, London E1 4NS.
Williams, Professor G. A., MA, PhD, University College, Cardiff CF1 1XL.
Williams, J. A., BSc(Econ), MA, 44 Pearson Park, Hull, E. Yorks. HU5 2TG.
Williams, P. H., MA, DPhil, New College, Oxford OX1 3BN.
Williams, T. I., MA, DPhil, 20 Blenheim Drive, Oxford OX2 8DG.
Wilson, Professor C. H., MA, FBA, Jesus College, Cambridge CB5 8BL.
Wilson, Dr D. M., MA, FSA, The British Museum, London WC1B 3DG.
Wilson, H. S., BA, BLitt, Dept of History, The University, York YO1 5DD.
Wilson, K. M., MA, DPhil, 8 Woodland Park Road, Headingley, Leeds 6.
Wilson, R. G., BA, PhD, University of East Anglia, School of Social Studies, University Plain, Norwich NR4 7TJ.
Wilson, Professor T., MA, DPhil, Dept of History, University of Adelaide, Adelaide, South Australia.
Winks, Professor R. W. E., MA, PhD, 648 Berkeley College, Yale University, New Haven, Conn. 06520, U.S.A.
Winter, J. M., BA, PhD, Pembroke College, Cambridge CB2 1RF.
Wiswall, Frank L., Jr., BA, JuD, PhD, Meadow Farm, Castine, Maine 04421, U.S.A.
Withrington, D. J., MA, MEd, Centre for Scottish Studies, University of Aberdeen, King's College, Old Aberdeen AB9 2UB.
Wolffe, B. P., MA, BLitt, DPhil, Highview, 19 Rosebarn Avenue, Exeter EX4 6DY.
Wong, John Yue-Wo, BA, DPhil, Dept of History, University of Sydney, N.S.W., Australia 2006.
*Wood, Rev. A. Skevington, PhD, Cliff House, Calver, Sheffield S30 1XG.
Wood, Mrs S. M., MA, BLitt, St Hugh's College, Oxford OX2 6LE.
Woodfill, Professor W. L., PhD, University of California, Davis, Calif. 95616, U.S.A.
Wood-Legh, Miss K. L., BLitt, PhD, DLitt, 49 Owlstone Road, Cambridge.
Woods, J. A., MA, PhD, The University, Leeds LS2 9JT.
Woolf, Professor S. J., MA, DPhil, University of Essex, Wivenhoe Park, Colchester CO4 3SQ.
Woolrych, Professor A. H., BLitt, MA, Patchetts, Caton, nr Lancaster.
Worden, A. B., MA, DPhil, St Edmund Hall, Oxford OX1 4AR.
Wormald, B. H. G., MA, Peterhouse, Cambridge CB2 1RD.
Wormald, Jennifer M., MA, PhD, Dept of Scottish History, The University, Glasgow G12 8QQ.
Wortley, The Rev. J. T., MA, PhD, History Dept, University of Manitoba, Winnipeg, Manitoba R3T 2N2, Canada.

Wright, A. D., MA, DPhil, School of History, The University, Leeds LS2 9JT.
Wright, Professor E., MA, Institute of United States Studies, 31 Tavistock Square, London WC1H 9EZ.
Wright, Rev. Professor J. Robert, DPhil, General Theological Seminary, 175 Ninth Avenue, New York N.Y. 10011, U.S.A.
Wright, L. B., PhD, 3702 Leland Street, Chevy Chase, Md. 20015, U.S.A.
Wright, Maurice, BA, DPhil, Dept of Government, Dover Street, Manchester M13 9PL.
Wroughton, J. P., MA, 6 Ormonde House, Sion Hill, Bath BA1 2UN.

Yates, W. N., MA, Kent Archives Office, County Hall, Maidstone, Kent ME14 1XH.
Yost, Professor John K., MA, STB, PhD, Dept of History, University of Nebraska, Lincoln, Neb. 68508, U.S.A.
Youings, Professor Joyce A., BA, PhD, Dept of History, The University, Exeter EX4 4QH.
Youngs, Professor F. A., Jr. Dept of History, Louisiana State University, Baton Rouge, Louisiana, 70803, U.S.A.

Zagorin, Professor P., PhD, Dept of History, College of Arts and Sciences, University of Rochester, River Campus Station, Rochester, N.Y. 14627, U.S.A.
Zeldin, T., MA, DPhil, St Antony's College, Oxford OX2 6JF.
Ziegler, P. S., FRSL, 22 Cottesmore Gardens, London W8.

ASSOCIATES OF THE
ROYAL HISTORICAL SOCIETY

Adams, S. L., BA, MA, DPhil, 4 North East Circus Place, Edinburgh EH3 6SP.
Addy, J., MA, PhD, 66 Long Lane, Clayton West, Huddersfield HD8 9PR.
Ash, Marinell, BA, MA, PhD, 42 Woodburn Terrace, Edinburgh EH10 4ST.
Ashton, Ellis, MBE, FRSA, 1 King Henry Street, London N16.

Baird, Rev. E. S., BD, (address unknown).
Baker, Miss A. M., The Wolds, 109 Spetchley Road, Worcester WR5 2LS.
Begley, M. R., 119 Tennyson Avenue, King's Lynn, Norfolk.
Bernard, G. W., MA, DPhil, Randall Lines House, The Polytechnic, Wolverhampton.
Bird, E. A., 29 King Edward Avenue, Rainham, Essex RN13 9RH.
Blackwood, B., FRIBA, FRTPI, FSAScot, Ebony House, Whitney Drive, Stevenage SG1 4BL.
Boyes, J. H., 129 Endlebury Road, Chingford, London E4 6PX.
Brake, Rev. G. Thompson, 19 Bethell Avenue, Ilford, Essex.
Bratt, C., 65 Moreton Road, Upton, Merseyside L49 4NR.
Bridge, A. E., 115 Ralph Road, Saltley, Birmingham B8 1NA.
Brocklesby, R., BA, The Elms, North Eastern Road, Thorne, Doncaster, S. Yorks. DN8 4AS.
Bryant, W. N., MA, PhD, College of S. Mark and S. John, Derriford Road, Plymouth, Devon.
Burton, Commander R. C., RN(ret.), Great Streele Oasthouse, Framfield, Sussex.
Butler, Mrs M. C., MA, 4 Castle Street, Warkworth, Morpeth, Northumberland NE65 0UW.

Cable, J. A., MA, MEd, ALCM, 21 Malvern Avenue, York YO2 5SF.
Cairns, Mrs W. N., MA, Alderton House, New Ross, Co. Wexford, Ireland.
Carter, F. E. L., CBE, MA, 8 The Leys, London N2 0HE.
Cary, Sir Roger, Bt., BA, 23 Bath Road, London W4.
Chandra, Shri Suresh, MA, MPhil, B1/2 Havelock Road Colony, Lucknow 226001, India.
Chappell, Rev. M. P., MA, 4 Greymouth Close, Hartburn, Stockton-on-Tees, Cleveland TS18 5LF.
Cobban, A. D., 11 Pennyfields, Warley, Brentwood, Essex CM14 5JP.
Condon, Miss M. M., BA, 56 Bernard Shaw House, Knatchbull Road, London NW10.
Cooksley, P. G., 14 Wallington Court, Wallington, Surrey SM6 0HG.
Cooper, Miss J. M., MA, PhD, 1 William Street, New Marston, Oxford OX3 0ES.
Cox, A. H., Winsley, 11A Bagley Close, West Drayton, Middlesex.
Cox, Benjamin, 147 Cheltenham Road, Evesham, Worcester.
Creighton-Williamson, Lt.-Col. D., 2 Church Avenue, Farnborough, Hants.

d'Alton, Ian, BA, PhD, Dept of Economic Planning and Development, Upper Merrion Street, Dublin 2, Ireland.

Daniels, C. W., MEd., FRSA, 'Brookfield', St John's Royal Latin School, Buckingham MK18 1AX.
Davies, G. J., BA, 3 Oakbury Drive, Preston, Weymouth, Dorset DT3 6JB.
Davies, P. H., BA, 64 Hill Top, Hampstead Garden Suburb, London NW11.
Dawson, Mrs S. L., 41 Richards Way, West Harnham, Salisbury, Wilts. SP2 8NT.
Dowse, Rev. I. R., The Vicarage, Main Street, Hollym, Withernsea, N. Humberside HU19 2RS.
Draffen of Newington, George, MBE, KLJ, MA, Meadowside, Balmullo, Leuchars, Fife KY16 0AW.
Drew, J. H., MA, FRSA, 19 Forge Road, Kenilworth, Warwickshire.
Dunster, E. R., BA, LCP, 5 Brittania Road, Southsea, Hampshire.

Edbury, P. W., MA, PhD, Dept of History, University College, Cardiff CF1 1XL.
Elliott Rev. W., BA, The Vicarage, Far Forest, nr Kidderminster, Worcs. DY14 9TT.
Emberton, W. J., Firs Lodge, 13 Park Lane, Old Basing, Basingstoke, Hants.
Emsden, N., Strathspey, Lansdown, Bourton-on-the-Water, Cheltenham, Glos. GL54 2AR.

Fawcett, Rev. T. J., BD, PhD, The Vicarage, 63 Michaelson Avenue, Torrisholme, Morecambe.
Franco de Baux, Don Victor, KCHS, KCN, 8 Hippodrome Mews, London W11 4NN.
Freeman, Miss J., 11 St Georges Avenue, London N7.
Fryer, J., BA, Greenfields, Whitemore, nr. Congleton, Cheshire.

Goodman, K. W. G., MA, PhD, Coreley, Cynlas Street, Rhos, Wrexham, Clwyd LL14 1PU.
Graham, Mrs J. M., MA, PhD, Dept of History, University of Waikato, Private Bag, Hamilton, New Zealand.
Granger, E. R., Bluefield, Blofield, Norfolk.
Grant, A., BA, DPhil, Dept of Modern History, The Queen's University, Belfast BT7 1NN.
Greatrex, Professor Joan G., MA, The Highlands, Great Donard, Symonds Yat, Herefordshire HR9 6DX.
Green, P. L., MA, 9 Faulkner Street, Gate Pa, Tauranga, New Zealand.
Gurney, Mrs. S. J., 'Albemarle', 13 Osborne Street, Wolverton, Milton Keynes MK12 5HH.
Guy, Rev. J. R., BA, Selden End, Ash, nr Martock, Somerset TA12 6NS.

Hall, P. T., Accrington College of Further Education, Sandy Lane, Accrington, Lancs.
Hanawalt, Mrs. B. A., MA, PhD, Indiana University, Bloomington, Indiana 47401, U.S.A.
Hardy, P. E., 'Higher Langaton', 47 Park Lane, Pinhoe, Exeter, Devon EX4 9HP.
Harfield, Major A. G., Little Beechwood, Childe Okeford, Dorset DT11 8EH.
Harmar, A. P., FCA, Pear Tree Cottage, Dene Street, Dorking, Surrey RH4 2BZ.

Hawkes, G. I., BA, MA, PhD, Linden House, St Helens Road, Ormskirk, Lancs.

Hawtin, Miss G., BA, PhD, FSAScot, FRSAI, Honey Cottage, 5 Clifton Road, London SW19 4QX.

Heal, Mrs F., PhD, 22 Houndean Rise, Lewes, Sussex BN7 1EO.

Heath, P., MA, Dept of History, The University, Hull HU6 7RX.

Henderson-Howat, Mrs A. M. D., 7 Lansdown Crescent, Edinburgh EH12 5EQ.

Hillman, L. B., BA, 18 Creswick Walk, Hampstead Garden Suburb, London NW11.

Hoare, E. T., 70 Addison Road, Enfield, Middx.

Hodge, Mrs G., 85 Hadlow Road, Tonbridge, Kent.

Hope, R. B., MA, MEd, PhD, 5 Partis Way, Newbridge Hill, Bath, Avon BA1 3QG.

Hopewell, S., MA, Headmaster's House, Royal Russell School, Addington, Croydon, Surrey CR9 5BX.

Hughes, R. G., 'Hafod', 92 Main Road, Smalley, Derby DE7 6DS.

Jackson, A., BA, 14 Latimer Lane, Guisborough, Cleveland.

James, T. M., BA, MA, PhD, 26 St Michael's Close, Crich, Matlock, Derbyshire DE4 5DN.

Jarvis, L. D., Middlesex Cottage, 86 Mill Road, Stock, Ingatestone, Essex.

Jarvis, S. M., 7 Sherwood Drive, Chelmsford, Essex.

Jermy, K. E., MA, Cert. Archaeol, FRSA, 8 Thelwall New Road, Thelwall, Warrington, Cheshire WA4 2JF.

Jerram-Burrows, Mrs L. E., Parkanaur House, 88 Sutton Road, Rochford, Essex.

Johnston, F. R., MA, 20 Russell Street, Eccles, Manchester.

Johnstone, H. F. V., 96 Wimborne Road, Poole, Dorset BH15 2DA.

Jones, Dr N. L., Dept of History & Geography, Utah State University, UMC 07, Logan, Utah 84322, U.S.A.

Joy, E. T., MA, BSc(Econ), Cheveley Cottage, 10 High Street, Stetchworth, Newmarket, Suffolk CB8 9JJ.

Keefe, T. K., BA, PhD, Dept of History, Appalachian State University, Boone, North Carolina 28608, U.S.A.

Keir, Mrs G. I., BA, BLitt, 17 Old Harpenden Road, St Albans AL3 6AX.

Kennedy, M. J., BA, Dept of Medieval History, The University, Glasgow G12 8QQ.

Knight, G. A., BA, 36 Trinder Way, Wickford, Essex SS12 0HQ.

Knowlson, Rev. G. C. V., 21 Wilton Crescent, Alderley Edge, Cheshire SK9 7RE.

Lea, R. S., MA, 29 Crestway, London SW15.

Lead, P., BA, 3 Montrose Court, Holmes Chapel, Cheshire CW4 7JJ.

Leckey, Joseph J., MSc(Econ), LCP, FRSAI, Dept of Continuing Education, New University of Ulster, Londonderry, N. Ireland BT48 7JL.

Lee, Professor M. du P., PhD, Douglass College, Rutgers University, NB, NJ 08903, U.S.A.

Lewin, Mrs J., MA, 3 Sunnydale Gardens, Mill Hill, London NW7.

Lewis, J. B., MA, CertEd, FRSA, 16 Rushfield Road, Westminster Park, Chester CH4 7RE.

Lewis, Professor N. B., MA, PhD, 78 Old Dover Road, Canterbury, Kent CT1 3DB.

McIntyre, Miss S. C., BA, DPhil, West Midland College of Higher Education, Walsall, West Midlands.

McKenna, Rev. T. J., P.O. Box 1444, Canberra City, A.C.T. 2601, Australia.

McLeod, D. H., BA, PhD, Dept of Theology, The University, P.O. Box 363, Birmingham B15 2TT.

Meatyard, E., BA, DipEd, Guston, Burial Lane, Church Lane, Llantwit Major, S. Glam.

Metcalf, D. M., MA, DPhil, 40 St Margaret's Road, Oxford OX2 6LD.

Mills, H. J., BSc, MA, 71 High Street, Billingshurst, West Sussex.

Morgan, D. A. L., MA, Dept of History, University College London, Gower Street, London WC1E 6BT.

Munson, K. G., 'Briar Wood', 4 Kings Ride, Seaford, Sussex BN25 2LN.

Nagel, L. C. J., BA, 61 West Kensington Court, London W14.

Newman, L. T., LRIC, CEng, MIGasE, AMInstF, 27 Mallow Park, Pinkneys Green, Maidenhead, Berks.

Noonan, J. A., BA, MEd, HDE, St Patrick's Comprehensive School, Shannon, Co. Clare, Ireland.

Obelkevich, J., MA, (address unknown).

Oggins, R. S., PhD, c/o Dept of History, State University of New York, Binghamton, N.Y. 13901, U.S.A.

Oldham, C. R., MA, Te Whare, Walkhampton, Yelverton, Devon PL20 6PD.

Pam, D. O., 44 Chase Green Avenue, Enfield, Middlesex EN2 8EB.

Parsons, Mrs M. A., MA, (address unknown).

Partridge, Miss F. L., BA, 17 Spencer Gardens, London SW14 7AH.

Pasmore, H. S., MB, BS, South Cottage, Ham Gate Avenue, Ham Common, Richmond, Surrey TW10 5HB.

Paton, L. R., 49 Lillian Road, Barnes, London SW13.

Paulson, E., BSc(Econ), 11 Darley Avenue, Darley Dale, Matlock, Derbys. DE4 2GB.

Perry, E., FSAScot, 28 Forest Street, Hathershaw, Oldham OL8 3ER.

Perry, K., MA, 14 Highland View Close, Colehill, Wimborne, Dorset.

Pitt, B. W. E., Merryfield House, Ilton, Ilminster, TA19 9EX.

Porter, S., BA, MLitt, Dept of History, King's College, London WC2R 2LS.

Priestley, E. J., MA, MPhil, 33 Grange Road, Shrewsbury, Shropshire SY3 9DG.

Raban, Mrs S. G., MA, PhD, Dept of History, Homerton College, Cambridge.

Raspin, Miss A., London School of Economics, Houghton Street, London WC2A 2AE.

Rendall, Miss J., BA, PhD, Dept of History, University of York, Heslington, York YO1 5DD.

Richards, N. F., PhD, 376 Maple Avenue, St Lambert, Prov. of Quebec, Canada J4P 2S2.

Roberts, S. G., MA, DPhil, 23 Beech Avenue, Radlett, Herts. WD7 7DD.

Rosenfield, M. C., AB, AM, PhD, Box 395, Mattapoisett, Mass. 02739, U.S.A.

Russell, Mrs E., BA, c/o Dept of History, Yale University, New Haven, Conn. 06520, U.S.A.

Sabben-Clare, E. E., MA, The Shambles, Yarnton Road, Cassington, Oxford OX8 1DY.
Sainsbury, F., 16 Crownfield Avenue, Newbury Park, Ilford, Essex.
Saksena, D. N., D-105 Curzon Road Apts., New Delhi, 11–00 01, India.
Scannura, C. G., 1/11 St Dominic Street, Valletta, Malta.
Schweizer, Karl W., MA, PhD, 4 Harrold Drive, Bishop's University, Lennoxville, Quebec, Canada.
Scott, The Rev. A. R., MA, BD, PhD, Ahorey Manse, Portadown, Co. Armagh, N. Ireland.
Scott, J. B., MA, DPhil, 3, 8th Avenue, Summerstrand, Port Elizabeth 6001, South Africa.
Seddon, P. R., BA, PhD, The University, Nottingham NG7 2RD.
Sellers, J. M., MA, 9 Vere Road, Pietermaritzburg, Natal, S. Africa.
Shores, C. F., ARICS, 40 St Mary's Crescent, Hendon, London NW4 4LH.
Sibley, Major R. J., 8 Ways End, Beech Avenue, Camberley, Surrey.
Sloan, K., BEd, MPhil, 6 Netherwood Close, Fixby, Huddersfield, Yorks.
Sorensen, Mrs M. O., MA, 8 Layer Gardens, London W3 9PR.
Sparkes, I. G., FLA, 124 Green Hill, High Wycombe, Bucks.
Stafford, D. S., BA, 10 Highfield Close, Wokingham, Berks. RG11 1DG.

Thewlis, J. C., BA, PhD, The University, Hull HU6 7RX.
Thomas, D. L., BA, Public Record Office, Chancery Lane, London WC2A 1LR.
Thomas, Miss E. J. M., BA, 8 Ravenscroft Road, Northfield End, Henley-on-Thames, Oxon.
Thomas, J. H., BA, PhD, Dept of Historical and Literary Studies, Portsmouth Polytechnic, Southsea, Portsmouth PO5 3AT.
Thompson, C. L. F., MA, Orchard House, Stanford Road, Orsett, nr Grays, Essex RM16 3BX.
Thompson, L. F., Orchard House, Stanford Road, Orsett, nr Grays, Essex RM16 3BX.
Tracy, J. N., BA, MPhil, PhD, c/o P. Huth Esq, 6 Chaucer Court, 28 New Dover Road, Canterbury, Kent.
Tristram, B., DipEd, (address unknown).
Tudor, Victoria M., BA, PhD, 122 Anderton Park Road, Moseley, Birmingham B13 9DQ.

Waldman, T. G., MA, 1530 Locust Street, Philadelphia, Pa. 19102, U.S.A.
Walker, J. A., 1 Sylvanus, Roman Wood, Bracknell, Berkshire RG12 4XX.
Wall, Rev. J., BD, MA, PhD, Ashfield, 45 Middleton Lane, Middleton St George, nr Darlington, Co Durham.
Wallis, K. W., BA (address unknown).
Warrillow, E. J. D., MBE, FSA, Hill-Cote, Lancaster Road, Newcastle, Staffs.
Weise, Selene H. C., PhD, 22 Hurd Street, Mine Hill, New Jersey 07801, U.S.A.
Wilkinson, F. J., 40 Great James Street, Holborn, London WC1N 3HB.
Williams, A. R., BA, MA, 5 Swanswell Drive, Granley Fields, Cheltenham, Glos.
Williams, C. L. Sinclair, ISO, The Old Vicarage, The Green, Puddletown, nr Dorchester, Dorset.
Williams, G., ALA, 32 St John's Road, Manselton, Swansea SA5 8PP.
Williams, H. (address unknown).

Williams, P. T., FSAScot, FRSA, FFAS, Bryn Bueno, Whitford Street, Holywell, Clwyd.
Windeatt, M. C., Whitestones, Hillyfields, Winscombe, Somerset.
Windrow, M. C., 40 Zodiac Court, 165 London Road, Croydon, Surrey.
Wood, A. W., 11 Blessington Close, London SE13.
Wood, J. O., BA, MEd, Fountains, Monument Gardens, St Peter Port, Guernsey, C.I.
Woodall, R. D., BA, Bethel, 7 Wynthorpe Road, Horbury, nr Wakefield, Yorks. WF4 5BB.
Woodfield, R., BD, MTh, 43 Playfield Crescent, London SE22.
Worsley, Miss A. V., BA, 3D St George's Cottages, Glasshill Street, London SE1.
Wright, J. B., BA, White Shutters, Braunston, Leicester LE15 8QT.

Zerafa, Rev. M. J., St Dominic's Priory, Valletta, Malta.

CORRESPONDING FELLOWS

Ajayi, Professor J. F. Ade, University of Ibadan, Ibadan, Nigeria, West Africa.

Berend, Professor T. Ivan, Hungarian Academy of Sciences, 1361 Budapest V, Roosevelt-tèr 9, Hungary.
Bischoff, Professor B., DLitt, 8033 Planegg C. München, Ruffini-Allee 27, West Germany.
Boorstin, Daniel J., MA, LLD, 3541 Ordway Street, N.W., Washington, DC 20016, U.S.A.
Braudel, Professor F., Commission des Archives Diplomatiques, Ministère des Affaires Étrangères, 37 Quai d'Orsay, 75007 Paris, France.

Cipolla, Professor Carlo M., University of California, Berkeley Campus, Berkeley, Calif. 94720, U.S.A.
Coolhaas, Professor W. P., Gezichtslaan 71, Bilthoven, The Netherlands.
Crouzet, Professor F. M. J., 6 rue Benjamin Godard, 75016 Paris, France.

Donoso, R., Presidente de la Sociedad Chilena de Historia y Geografia, Casilla 1386, Santiago, Chile.
Duby, Professor G., Collège de France, 11 Place Marcelin-Berthelot, 75005 Paris, France.

Garin, Professor Eugenio, via Giulio Cesare Vanini 28, 50129 Florence, Italy.
Gieysztor, Professor Aleksander, Polska Akademia Nauk, Wydzial I Nauk, Rynek Starego Miasta 29/31, 00-272 Warszawa, Poland.
Giusti, Rt Rev. Mgr M., JCD, Archivio Segreto Vaticano, Vatican City, Italy.
Glamann, Professor K., DrPhil, Frederiksberg, Bredegade 13A, 2000 Copenhagen, Denmark.
Gopal, Professor S., MA, DPhil, Centre for Historical Studies, Jawaharlal Nehru University, New Mehrauli Road, New Delhi-110067, India.
Gwynn, Professor the Rev. A., SJ, MA, DLitt, Milltown Park, Dublin 6, Ireland.

Hancock, Professor Sir Keith, KBE, MA, DLitt, FBA, Australian National University, Box 4, P.O., Canberra, ACT, Australia.
Hanke, Professor L. U., PhD, University of Massachusetts, Amherst, Mass. 01002, U.S.A.
Heimpel, Professor Dr H., DrJur, Dr Phil, former Direktor des Max Planck-Instituts für Geschichte, Gottingen, Dahlmannstr. 14, Germany.

Inalcik, Professor Halil, PhD, The University of Ankara, Ankara, Turkey.

Kossmann, Professor E. H., DLitt, Rijksuniversiteit te Groningen, Groningen, The Netherlands.
Kuttner, Professor S., MA, JUD, SJD, LLD, Institute of Medieval Canon Law, University of California, Berkeley, Calif. 94720, U.S.A.

Ladurie, Professor E. B. LeRoy, Collège de France, 11 Place Marcelin-Berthelot, 75005 Paris, France.

Maruyama, Professor Masao, 2-44-5 Higashimachi, Kichijoji, Musashino-shi, Tokyo 180, Japan.
Michel, Henri, 32 rue Leningrad, Paris 75008, France.

Peña y Cámara, J. M. de la, Avenida Reina, Mercedes 65, piso 7-B, Seville 12, Spain.

Rodrigues, Professor José Honório, Rua Paul Redfern 23, ap. C.O.1, Rio de Janeiro, Gb. ZC-37, Brazil.

Sapori, Professor A., Università Commerciale Luigi Bocconi, Via Sabbatini 8, Milan, Italy.
Slicher van Bath, Professor B. H., Gen. Fouldesweg 113, Wageningen, The Netherlands.

Thapar, Professor Romila, Dept of Historical Studies, Jawaharlal Nehru University, New Mehrauli Road, New Delhi-110067, India.

Thorne, Professor S. E., MA, LLB, LittD, LLD, FSA, Law School of Harvard University, Cambridge, Mass. 02138, U.S.A.

Van Houtte, Professor J. A., PhD, FBA, Termunkveld, Groeneweg 51, Egenhoven, Heverlee, Belgium.
Verlinden, Professor C., PhD, 3 Avenue du Derby, 1050 Brussels, Belgium.

Wolff, Professor Philippe, 3 rue Espinasse, 31000 Toulouse, France.
Woodward, Professor C. Vann, PhD, Yale University, 104 Hall of Graduate Studies, New Haven, Conn. 06520, U.S.A.

Zavala, S., LLD, Montes Urales 310, Mexico 10, D.F., Mexico.

TRANSACTIONS AND PUBLICATIONS

OF THE

ROYAL HISTORICAL SOCIETY

The publications of the Society issued under subscription to Fellows and Sub-
scribing Libraries include the *Transactions*, supplemented in 1897 by the
Camden Series (formerly the Camden Society, 1838–97); since 1937 by a series
of *Guides and Handbooks* and, from time to time, by miscellaneous publications.
Additional copies of these publications may be purchased by Fellows and
Subscribing Libraries at a reduction of 25 per cent of the listed price. Corresponding Fellows, Retired Fellows and Associates receive only *Transactions*
(Corresponding Fellows do so free of expense) but may purchase at a reduction of 25 per cent one copy of each of the other publications. The Society
also began in 1937 an annual bibliography of *Writings on British History*, for
the continuation of which the Institute of Historical Research accepted
responsibility in 1965; it publishes, in conjunction with the American Historical Association, a series of *Bibliographies of British History*.

TRANSACTIONS

Copies of *Transactions, Fifth Series*, Vol. 20 onwards may be purchased from
Boydell and Brewer Ltd., P.O. Box 9, Woodbridge, Suffolk IP12 3DF. £8.50.
(Special price to members £6.38.)

Volumes out of print in *Transactions*, Old, New, Third, Fourth and Vols. 1–
19 in the *Fifth Series* may be obtained from Kraus-Thomson Organization
Ltd.

Old series, 1872–82. Vols. I to X.
New series, 1884–1906. Vols. I to XX.
Third series, 1907–17. Vols. I to XI.
Fourth series, 1918–50. Vols. I to XXXII.
Fifth series, 1951–   . Vols. I to XXX.

MISCELLANEOUS PUBLICATIONS

Copies of the following, which are still in print, may be ordered from Boydell
and Brewer Ltd.

Domesday Studies, 2 vols, Edited by P. E. Dove, 1886. £3.50. (Vol. I out
of print.)
The *Domesday Monachorum* of Christ Church, Canterbury. 1944. £15.
The Royal Historical Society, 1868–1968. By R. A. Humphreys. 1969. £1.25.

BIBLIOGRAPHIES ISSUED IN CONJUNCTION WITH THE
AMERICAN HISTORICAL ASSOCIATION

Copies of the following cannot be supplied by the Society, but may be ordered
through a bookseller. If members have difficulty in obtaining volumes at the
special price, reference should be made to the Society.

Bibliography of English History to 1485. Based on the Sources and Literature of English History from earliest times by Charles Gross. Revised and expanded by Edgar B. Graves. 1975. Oxford Univ. Press. £20. (Special price, £15.)

Bibliography of British History: Tudor Period, 1485–1603. Edited by Conyers Read. 1st edn. 1933; 2nd edn. 1959; 3rd edn. 1978. Harvester Press. £25.00.

Bibliography of British History: Stuart period, 1603–1714. 2nd edn. Edited by Mary F. Keeler, 1970. Oxford Univ. Press. £17.50 (Special price, £13.13.)

Bibliography of British History: The Eighteenth Century, 1714–1789. Edited by S. Pargellis and D. J. Medley. 1st edn. 1951; 2nd edn. 1977. Harvester Press. £25.00.

Supplement to Bibliography of British History: 1714–89. Edited by S. M. Pargellis and D. J. Medley. Edited by A. T. Milne and A. N. Newman, *in preparation.*

Bibliography of British History: 1789–1851. Edited by Lucy M. Brown and Ian R. Christie, 1977. Oxford Univ. Press. £17.50. (Special price £13.13.)

Bibliography of British History: 1851–1914. Edited by H. J. Hanham, 1976. Oxford Univ. Press. £20.00. (Special price, £15.00.)

WRITINGS ON BRITISH HISTORY

Copies of the following may be obtained from the Institute of Historical Research, University of London, Senate House, Malet Street, WC1E 7HU.

Writings on British History, 1946–1948. Compiled by D. J. Munro. 1973. £15.00.

Writings on British History, 1949–1951. Compiled by D. J. Munro. 1975. £15.00.

Writings on British History, 1952–1954. Compiled by J. M. Sims. 1975. £15.00.

Writings on British History, 1955–1957. Compiled by J. M. Sims and P. M. Jacob. 1977. £15.00.

Writings on British History, 1958–1959. Compiled by H. J. Creaton. 1977. £15.00.

Writings on British History, 1960–1961. Compiled by C. H. E. Philpin and H. J. Creaton. 1978. £15·00.

Writings on British History, 1962–1964. Compiled by H. J. Creaton. 1979. £17.00.

Writings on British History, 1965–1966. Compiled by H. J. Creaton. 1981. £18.00.

Reprints of volumes before 1946 are obtainable from Dawson Book Service, Cannon Street, Folkestone, Kent.

GUIDES AND HANDBOOKS

Copies of the following may be obtained from Boydell and Brewer Ltd. P.O. Box 9, Woodbridge, Suffolk IP12 3DF.

Main series

1. Guide to English commercial statistics, 1696–1782. By G. N. Clark, with a catalogue of materials by Barbara M. Franks. 1938. (Out of print.)
2. Handbook of British chronology. Edited by F. M. Powicke and E. B. Fryde, 1st edn. 1939; 2nd edn. 1961. £8.00.

3. Medieval libraries of Great Britain, a list of surviving books. Edited by N. R. Ker, 1st edn. 1941; 2nd edn. 1964. £8.00.
4. Handbook of dates for students of English history. By C. R. Cheney. 1978. £3.50.
5. Guide to the national and provincial directories of England and Wales, excluding London, published before 1856. By Jane E. Norton. 1950. (Out of print.)
6. Handbook of Oriental history. Edited by C. H. Philips. 1963. £3.50.
7. Texts and calendars: an analytical guide to serial publications. Edited by E. L. C. Mullins. 1st edn. 1958; 2nd edn. 1978. £8.00.
8. Anglo-Saxon charters. An annotated list and bibliography. Edited by P. H. Sawyer. 1968. £8.00.
9. A Centenary Guide to the Publications of the Royal Historical Society, 1868–1968. Edited by A. T. Milne. 1968. £3.50.
10. A Guide to the Local Administrative Units of England. Vol. I. Edited by F. A. Youngs, Jr. 1980; 2nd edn. 1981. £25.00.
11. A Guide to Bishops' Registers to 1646. Edited by D. M. Smith. 1981. £15.00.

Supplementary series.

1. A Guide to the Papers of British Cabinet Ministers, 1900–1951. Edited by Cameron Hazlehurst and Christine Woodland. 1974. £4.50.
2. A Guide to the Reports of the U.S. Strategic Bombing Survey. Edited by Gordon Daniels. 1981. £12.00.

Provisionally accepted for future publication:

A Handbook of British Currency. Edited by P. Grierson and C. E. Blunt.
Texts and calendars: an analytical guide to serial publications. Supplement, 1957–77. By E. L. C. Mullins.
A Guide to the Records and Archives of Mass Communications. Edited by Nicholas Pronay.
A Guide to the Maps of the British Isles. Edited by Helen Wallis.

THE CAMDEN SERIES

Camden Series volumes published before the *Fourth Series* are listed in A. T. Milne's *A Centenary Guide to the Publications of the Royal Historical Society.*
    Copies of volumes in the *Camden Fourth Series* may be purchased from Boydell and Brewer Ltd. £10.00. (Special price to members £7.50.)
    Volumes out of print in the *Camden Old* and *New Series* may be obtained from Johnson Reprint Co. Ltd., and volumes out of print in the *Camden Third Series* may be obtained from Boydell and Brewer Ltd.

FOURTH SERIES

1. Camden Miscellany, Vol. XXII: 1. Charters of the Earldom of Hereford, 1095–1201. Edited by David Walker. 2. Indentures of Retinue with John of Gaunt, Duke of Lancaster, enrolled in Chancery, 1367–99. Edited by N. B. Lewis. 3. Autobiographical memoir of Joseph Jewell, 1763–1846. Edited by A. W. Slater. 1964.

2. Documents illustrating the rule of Walter de Wenlock, Abbot of Westminster, 1283–1307. Edited by Barbara Harvey. 1965.
3. The early correspondence of Richard Wood, 1831–41. Edited by A. B. Cunningham. 1966. (Out of print.)
4. Letters from the English abbots to the chapter at Cîteaux, 1442–1521. Edited by C. H. Talbot. 1967.
5. Select writings of George Wyatt. Edited by D. M. Loades. 1968.
6. Records of the trial of Walter Langeton, Bishop of Lichfield and Coventry (1307–1312). Edited by Miss A. Beardwood. 1969.
7. Camden Miscellany, Vol. XXIII: 1. The Account Book of John Balsall of Bristol for a trading voyage to Spain, 1480. Edited by T. F. Reddaway and A. A. Ruddock. 2. A Parliamentary diary of Queen Anne's reign. Edited by W. A. Speck. 3. Leicester House politics, 1750–60, from the papers of John second Earl of Egmont. Edited by A. N. Newman. 4. The Parliamentary diary of Nathaniel Ryder, 1764–67. Edited by P. D. G. Thomas. 1969.
8. Documents illustrating the British Conquest of Manila, 1762–63. Edited by Nicholas P. Cushner. 1971.
9. Camden Miscellany, Vol. XXIV: 1. Documents relating to the Breton succession dispute of 1341. Edited by M. Jones. 2. Documents relating to the Anglo-French negotiations, 1439. Edited by C. T. Allmand. 3. John Benet's Chronicle for the years 1400 to 1462. Edited by G. L. Harriss. 1972.
10. Herefordshire Militia Assessments of 1663. Edited by M. A. Faraday. 1972.
11. The early correspondence of Jabez Bunting, 1820–29. Edited by W. R. Ward. 1972.
12. Wentworth Papers, 1597–1628. Edited by J. P. Cooper. 1973.
13. Camden Miscellany, Vol. XXV: 1. The Letters of William, Lord Paget. Edited by Barrett L. Beer and Sybil Jack. 2. The Parliamentary Diary of John Clementson, 1770–1802. Edited by P. D. G. Thomas. 3. J. B. Pentland's Report on Bolivia, 1827. Edited by J. V. Fifer. 1974.
14. Camden Miscellany, Vol. XXVI: 1. Duchy of Lancaster Ordinances, 1483. Edited by Sir Robert Somerville. 2. A Breviat of the Effectes devised for Wales. Edited by P. R. Roberts. 3. Gervase Markham, The Muster-Master. Edited by Charles L. Hamilton. 4. Lawrence Squibb, A Book of all the Several Offices of the Court of the Exchequer (1642). Edited by W. H. Bryson. 5. Letters of Henry St. John to Charles, Earl of Orrery, 1709–11. Edited by H. T. Dickinson. 1975.
15. Sidney Ironworks Accounts, 1541–73. Edited by D. W. Crossley. 1975.
16. The Account-Book of Beaulieu Abbey. Edited by S. F. Hockey. 1975.
17. A calendar of Western Circuit Assize Orders, 1629–48. Edited by J. S. Cockburn. 1976.
18. Four English Political Tracts of the later Middle Ages. Edited by J.-Ph. Genet. 1977.
19. Proceedings of the Short Parliament of 1640. Edited by Esther S. Cope in collaboration with Willson H. Coates. 1977.
20. Heresy Trials in the Diocese of Norwich, 1428–31. Edited by N. P. Tanner. 1977.
21. Edmund Ludlow: A Voyce from the Watch Tower (Part Five: 1660–1662). Edited by A. B. Worden. 1978.
22. Camden Miscellany, Vol. XXVII: 1. The Disputed Regency of the Kingdom of Jerusalem, 1264/6 and 1268. Edited by P. W. Edbury. 2.

George Rainsford's *Ritratto d'Ingliterra* (1556). Edited by P. S. Donaldson. 3. The Letter-Book of Thomas Bentham, Bishop of Coventry and Lichfield, 1560–1561. Edited by Rosemary O'Day and Joel Berlatsky. 1979.

23. The Letters of the Third Viscount Palmerston to Laurence and Elizabeth Sulivan, 1804–63. Edited by Kenneth Bourne. 1979.
24. Documents illustrating the crisis of 1297–98 in England. Edited by M. Prestwich. 1980.
25. The Diary of Edward Goschen, 1900–1914. Edited by C. H. D. Howard. 1980.

Provisionally accepted for future publication:

The *Acta* of Archbishop Hugh of Rouen (1130–64). Edited by T. Waldman.
Cartularies of Reading Abbey. Edited by B. R. Kemp.
Correspondence of William Camden. Edited by Richard DeMolen.
Early Paget Correspondence. Edited by C. J. Harrison and A. C. Jones.
R. R. Angerstein's English Diary, 1753–55. Edited by Torsten Berg.
English Suits before the Parlement of Paris, 1420–36. Edited by C. A. J. Armstrong and C. T. Allmand.
Documents on the origin of the British Association for the Advancement of Science 1828–31. Edited by A. W. Thackray and J. B. Morrell.
The Devonshire Diary, 1757–62. Edited by K. W. Schweizer and P. D. Brown.
The Letters of the Barrington Family, 1628–32. Edited by A. Searle.
Vita Mariae Reginae Anglie. Edited by D. MacCulloch.
The Account of the Great Household of Humphrey, first Duke of Buckingham, for the year 1452–3. Edited by Mrs. M. Harris.
Letters of J. A. Blackwell concerning events in Hungary, 1848–9. Edited by A. Sked.
Supplementary Documents of the English Lands of the Abbey of Bec. Edited by Marjorie Chibnall.

STUDIES IN HISTORY

Studies in History is a series of historical monographs, preferably of no more than about 90,000 words, intended to help solve the increasing difficulties encountered by historians in getting their books accepted for publication, especially young scholars seeking first publication. Those interested in submitting works for consideration by the Editorial Board should write to the Editorial Assistant, c/o The Royal Historical Society, University College London, Gower Street, WC1E 6BT from whom further details can be obtained. No typescripts should be sent until asked for.

Orders for volumes should be sent, with remittance, to Swift Printers Ltd, 1–7 Albion Place, Britton St, London EC1M 5RE.

1. F. F. Foster: *The Politics of Stability: A Portrait of the Rulers in Elizabethan London.* 1977. £11·40.
2. Rosamond McKitterick, *The Frankish Church and the Carolingian Reforms 789–895.* 1977. £13·40.
3. K. D. Brown, *John Burns.* 1977. £9·40.
4. D. Stevenson, *Revolution and Counter-Revolution in Scotland, 1644–1651.* 1977. £12·30.
5. Marie Axton, *The Queen's Two Bodies: Drama and the Elizabethan Succession.* 1978. £11·40.

6. Anne Orde: *Great Britain and International Security, 1920–1926*. 1978. £11·80.
7. J. H. Baker (ed), *Legal Records and the Historian* (Papers read to the 2nd Conference on Legal History, held at Cambridge in 1975). 1978. £11·40.
8. M. P. Costeloe, *Church and State in Independent Mexico: a Study of the Patronage Debate, 1821–1857*. 1978. £12·70.
9. Wendy Davies, *An Early Welsh Microcosm: Studies in the Llandaff Charters*. 1978. £11·00.
10. Bernard Wasserstein: *The British in Palestine: The Mandatory Government and the Arab-Jewish Conflict, 1917–1929*. 1978. £13·60.
11. Michael McCahill: *Order and Equipoise: the Peerage and the House of Lords, 1783–1806*. 1979. £15·00.
12. Norman Etherington. *Preachers, Peasants and Politics in Southeast Africa 1835–1880. African Christian Communities in Natal, Pondoland and Zululand*. 1979. £14·00
13. S. A. G. Rizvi: *Linlithgow and India: A Study of British Policy and the Political Impasse in India, 1936–1943*. 1979. £15·00.
14. David McLean: *Britain and her Buffer-state: The Collapse of the Persian Empire, 1890–1914*. 1979. £11·20.
15. Howard Tomlinson: *Guns and Government: The Ordnance Office under the later Stuarts*. 1979. £17·00.
16. Patricia Crawford: *Denzil Holles, 1598–1680: A study of his Political Career*. 1979. £15·60.
17. D. L. Rydz: *The Parliamentary Agents: A History*. 1979. £15·30.
18. Uri Bialer: *The Shadow of the Bomber: The Fear of Air Attack and British Politics 1932–1939*. 1980. £14·00.
19. David Parker: *La Rochelle and the French Monarchy: Conflict and Order in Seventeenth-Century France*. 1980. £16.50.
20. A.P.C. Bruce: *The Purchase System in the British Army, 1660–1871*. 1980. £13.00.
21. Stephen Gradish: *The Manning of the British Navy during the Seven Years War*. 1980. £15.25.
22. Alan Harding (ed.) *Lawmaking and Lawmakers in British History* (Papers presented to the Edinburgh Legal History Conference 1977). 1980. £15.25.
23. Diane Willen: *John Russell First Earl of Bedford*. 1981. £13.00.

Members of the Society may obtain volumes in the series at a special price.

ANNUAL BIBLIOGRAPHY OF BRITISH AND IRISH HISTORY

Editor: G. R. Elton

1. *Publications of 1975* (1976)
2. *Publications of 1976* (1977)
3. *Publications of 1977* (1978)
4. *Publications of 1978* (1979)
5. *Publications of 1979* (1980)

Orders for volumes to the Harvester Press Ltd., 17 Ship Street, Brighton, Sussex, England, from whom prices may be obtained.